MERGERS AND ACQUISITIONS
IN BANKING AND FINANCE

MERGERS AND ACQUISITIONS IN BANKING AND FINANCE
What Works, What Fails, and Why

Ingo Walter

UNIVERSITY PRESS
2004

OXFORD

UNIVERSITY PRESS

Oxford   New York
Auckland   Bangkok   Buenos Aires   Cape Town   Chennai
Dar es Salaam   Delhi   Hong Kong   Istanbul   Karachi   Kolkata
Kuala Lumpur   Madrid   Melbourne   Mexico City   Mumbai   Nairobi
São Paulo   Shanghai   Taipei   Tokyo   Toronto

Copyright © 2004 by Oxford University Press, Inc.

Published by Oxford University Press, Inc.
198 Madison Avenue, New York, New York 10016

www.oup.com

Oxford is a registered trademark of Oxford University Press

Library of Congress Cataloging-in-Publication Data
Walter, Ingo.
Mergers and acquisitions in banking and finance : what works, what
fails, and why / by Ingo Walter.
p.   cm.
ISBN 0-19-515900-4
1. Bank mergers. 2. Financial institutions—Mergers. I. Title.
HG1722.W35   2004
332.1'068'1—dc22   2003015483

9 8 7 6 5 4 3 2 1

Printed in the United States of America
on acid-free paper

Preface

On April 6, 1998, the creation of Citigroup through the combination of Citicorp and Travelers Inc. was announced to the general applause of analysts and financial pundits. The "merger of equals" created the world's largest financial services firm—largest in market value, product range, and geographic scope. Management claimed that strict attention to the use of capital and rigorous control of costs (a Travelers specialty) could be combined with Citicorp's uniquely global footprint and retail banking franchise to produce uncommonly good revenue and cost synergies. In the four years that followed, through the postmerger *Sturm und Drang* and a succession of further acquisitions, Citigroup seemed to outperform its rivals in both market share and shareholder value by a healthy margin. Like its home base, New York City, it seemed to show that the unmanageable could indeed be effectively managed through what proved to be a rather turbulent financial environment.

On September 13, 2000, another New York megamerger was announced. Chase Manhattan's acquisition of J.P. Morgan & Co. took effect at the end of the year. Commentators suggested that Morgan, once the most respected bank in the United States, had at last realized that it was not possible to go it alone. In an era of apparent ascendancy of "universal banking" and financial conglomerates, where greater size and scope would be critical, the firm sold out at 3.7 shares of the new J.P. Morgan Chase for each legacy Morgan share. Management of both banks claimed significant cost synergies and revenue gains attributable to complementary strengths in the two firms' respective capabilities and client bases. Within two years the new stock had lost some 44% of its value (compared to no value-loss for Citigroup over the same period), many important J.P. Morgan bankers had left, and the new firm had run into an unusual number of business setbacks, even as the board awarded top management some $40 million in 2002 for "getting the deal done."

Even acknowledging that the jury remains out in terms of the long-term results, how is it that two major deals launched by people at the top of their professions, approved by boards presumably representing shareholder interests, could show such different interim outcomes? Is it in the structure of the deals themselves? The strategic profile of the competitive platform that resulted? The details of how the integration was accomplished? The people involved and their ability to organize and motivate the troops? Or, in the light of both banks landing right in the middle of some of the worst corporate and financial market scandals in history, will the two deals end up looking much the same? These are some of the critical issues we attempt to address in this book.

The financial services sector is about halfway through one of the most dramatic periods of restructuring ever undergone by a major industry—a reconfiguration whose impact has carried well beyond shareholders of the firms involved into the domain of regulation and public policy as well as global competitive performance and economic growth. Financial services have therefore been a center of gravity of global mergers and acquisitions activity. The industry comprises a surprisingly large share of the value of merger activity worldwide.

In this book I have attempted to lay out, in a clear and intuitive but also comprehensive way, what we know—or think we know—about reconfiguration of the financial services sector through mergers and acquisitions (M&A). This presumed understanding includes the underlying drivers of the mergers and acquisitions process itself, factual evidence as to whether the basic economic concepts and strategic precepts used to justify M&A deals are correct, and the efficacy of merger implementation—notably the merger integration dynamic.

Chapter 1 describes the activity-space occupied by the financial services industry, with a discussion of the four principal businesses comprising the financial services sector—commercial banking, investment banking, insurance, and asset management. This description includes profiles of subsectors such as retail brokerage, insurance brokerage, private banking, and wholesale banking, and how they are linked in terms of the functions performed. The objective of this introductory chapter is to provide a "helicopter" overview of the financial services businesses engaged in restructuring through mergers. The chapter provides some background for readers not fully familiar with the industry or (as it often the case) familiar only with a relatively narrow segment of the industry.

Chapter 2 positions financial services M&A deal-flow within the overall context of global mergers and acquisitions activity, assessing the structure of M&A volume in terms of in-market and cross-market dimensions (both functionally and geographically). It considers North American, European, and selected Asian financial services transactions in order to provide a context for discussing the underlying causes of structural changes in the industry, often under very different economic and regulatory conditions.

Chapter 3 provides a comprehensive review of the economic drivers of mergers and acquisitions in the financial services sector. Where does shareholder-value creation and destruction come from? How important are economies of scale, economies of scope, market power, conflicts of interest and managerial complexity, too-big-to-fail support by taxpayers, conglomerate discounts, and other factors—and how likely are they to influence market share and stock price performance of financial services firms engaged in M&A activity? It also suggests a framework for thinking about financial services M&A deals that integrates the economic and financial motivations raised in the preceding chapter into a consistent valuation framework. From a shareholder perspective, mergers are supposed to be accretive—they are supposed to add value in terms of total returns to investors. They almost always do that for the sellers. Often they do not succeed for the buyers, who sometimes find that the combined firm is actually worth less than the value of the acquiring firm before the merger. This chapter uses a "building block" approach to identify the possible sources of shareholder value gains and losses in merger situations.

Chapter 4 is the first of two that deal with merger integration. The underlying economics of an M&A transaction in the end determine whether the acquirer is "doing the right thing." The managerial and behavioral dimensions of the integration process determine whether the acquirer is "doing the thing right." That is, failures and successes can involve either *strategic targeting* or *strategic implementation*. Best for firms and their shareholders is obviously "doing the right thing right." Not so good is "doing the wrong thing" and "doing the right thing poorly." The financial sector has probably had far more than its share of mergers and acquisitions that have failed or performed far below potential because of mistakes in integration. This chapter focuses on the key managerial issues, including the level of integration required and the historic development of integration capabilities on the part of the acquiring firm, disruptions in human resources and firm leadership, cultural issues, timeliness of decision making, and interface management.

Chapter 5 continues the discussion on integration with specific regard to information and transactions-processing technology. It has often been argued that information is at the core of the financial services industry—information about products, markets, clients, economic sectors, and geographies. At the same time, it is also one of the most transactions-intensive industries in the world. It stands at the heart of the payments system of economies and engages in all kinds of transactions, ranging from individual monetary transfers and stock brokerage to institutional securities sales and trading. Transactions must be timely, accurate, and inexpensive in order for financial services firms to remain competitive, so the industry invests billions in information technology (IT) systems annually. Whether things go right or wrong in mergers of acquisitions depends heavily on how the firms handle technology.

Chapter 6 takes a look at the facts—what we know about whether financial sector mergers have "worked" or not. It considers all the evidence, attempting to do so in a careful and dispassionate way by avoiding the kinds of unsupported assertions that often accompany M&A deals in the financial services sector. The chapter considers the evidence based on well over 50 studies undertaken by central banks, financial regulators, management consultancies, and academics worldwide. Inevitably, there is disagreement on some of the findings—especially because meaningful international empirical work is extraordinarily difficult in this industry. But the basic conclusions seem clear and compelling. Whether mergers and acquisitions in the financial services sector have been successful tends to be difficult to assess in terms of shareholder value creation in the early 2000s. There is a need to separate between the company-related implications and the effects of the market at large, as reflected by the evolution of the post-bubble stock market decline. In addition, one needs to be cognizant of the fact that unfavorable business conditions and other adverse circumstances can cast an economic shadow over even the best-conceived deals.

Chapter 7 puts financial services M&A activity in the context of national and global financial architecture. Restructuring in this industry matters a great deal to the shareholders, managers, and employees of the firms involved. But it also matters from the perspective of the safety and soundness, efficiency and creativity of the financial system. The industry is "special" in many ways. It deals with other people's money. Its performance affects every other economic sector and the fate of whole economies. Problems it encounters can easily become systemic and can trigger crises that are hard to contain and whose impact ranges far beyond the industry itself. Chapter 7 considers what kinds of financial structures seem to be emerging as a result of reconfiguration through M&A deals and what the financial structures mean in the broader economic and political context.

This book is based on two decades of observing and teaching about the evolution of the financial services industry in a rapidly evolving global economic, regulatory, and technological environment. I have tried to take a dispassionate approach to an issue unusually replete with both scorn and hype. In this respect, a certain distance from the financial firms doing the restructuring has helped, as have discussions with academic colleagues, senior executives, and regulators. So has a growing body of literature about what works and what doesn't.

A number of people assisted with various parts of this book. Gayle De Long was extremely helpful in compiling the evidence on financial sector M&A available so far in the literature—I join her in paying tribute to her father, George A. DeLong (1922–2002), a hero in every sense of the word.

Shantanu Chakraboty and David L. Remmers helped with several of the case studies and issues related to merger integration, while Ralph Welpe was instrumental in surveying the evidence on IT integration contained in Chapter 5. Harvey Poniachek provided helpful comments and corrections on the final manuscript. Particularly helpful in developing the ideas and assembling facts behind this book over the years were Allen Berger, Arnoud Boot, Lawrence Goldberg, Richard Herring, Christine Hirsczowicz, Ernst Kilgus, Richard Levich, David Rogers, Anthony Santomero, Anthony Saunders, Roy Smith, Gregory Udell, and Maurizio Zollo. All are owed a debt of gratitude, although none can be held responsible for errors of fact or interpretation.

Contents

MERGERS AND ACQUISITIONS
IN BANKING AND FINANCE

1

Global Financial Services Reconfiguration

Few industries have encountered as much strategic turbulence in recent years as has the financial services sector. In response to far-reaching regulatory and technological change, together with important shifts in client behavior and the *de facto* globalization of specific financial functions and markets, the organizational structure of the industry has been profoundly displaced. A great deal of uncertainly remains about the nature of any future equilibrium in the industry's contours. At the same time, a major part of the industry has been effectively globalized, linking borrowers and lenders, issuers and investors, risks and risk takers around the world. This chapter presents a coherent analytical framework for thinking about financial firms worldwide, and spells out some of the key consequences for their strategic positioning and strategy implementation by management.

The discussion begins with the generic processes and linkages that comprise financial intermediation—the basic financial "hydraulics" that ultimately drive efficiency and innovation in the financial system. It then describes the specific financial activities that form the playing field of financial sector reconfiguration—commercial banking, securities and investment banking, insurance, and asset management. Virtually all M&A activity in the financial services sector takes place within and between these four areas of activity.

A STYLIZED PROCESS OF FINANCIAL INTERMEDIATION

The central component of any structural overview of a modern banking and financial system is the nature of the conduits through which the financial assets of the ultimate savers flow to the liabilities of the ultimate users of finance. These conduits involve alternative and competing modes of financial intermediation, or "contracting," between counterparties in financial transactions both within and between national financial systems.

A guide to thinking about financial contracting and the role of financial institutions and markets is summarized in Figure 1-1. The diagram depicts the financial process (flow of funds) among the different sectors of the economy in terms of underlying environmental and regulatory determinants or drivers, as well as the generic advantages needed to profit from three primary linkages:

1. *Fully intermediated financial flows.* Savings (the ultimate sources of funds in financial systems) may be held in the form of deposits or alternative types of claims issued by commercial banks, savings organizations, insurance companies, or other types of financial institutions that finance themselves by placing their liabilities directly with the general public. Financial institutions ultimately use these funds to purchase assets issued by nonfinancial entities such as households, firms, and governments.

2. *Securitized intermediation.* Savings may be allocated directly or indirectly via fiduciaries and collective investment vehicles to the purchase of securities publicly issued and sold by various public and private sector organizations in the domestic and international financial markets.

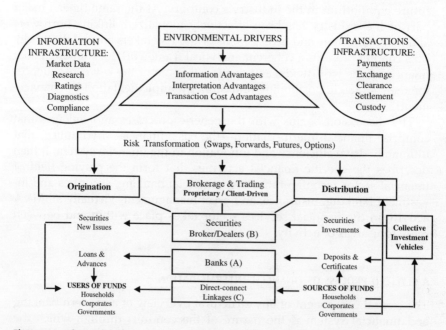

Figure 1-1. Alternative Financial Intermediation Flows. Source: Roy C. Smith and Ingo Walter, *Global Banking*, Second Edition (New York: Oxford University Press, 2003).

3. *Direct-connect mechanisms between ultimate borrowers and lenders.* Savings surpluses may be allocated to borrowers through various kinds of direct-sale mechanisms, such as private placements, usually involving fiduciaries as intermediaries.

Ultimate *users* of funds comprise the same three segments of the economy as the ultimate sources of funds, namely the household or consumer sector, the business sector, and the government sector.

1. *Households* may finance purchases by means of personal loans from banks or by loans secured by purchased assets (hire-purchase or installment loans). These may appear on the asset side of the balance sheets of credit institutions for the duration of the respective loan contracts or on a revolving basis, or they may be sold off into the financial market in the form various kinds of securities backed by mortgages, consumer credits, or other kinds of receivables.
2. *Businesses* may borrow from banks in the form of unsecured or asset-backed straight or revolving credit facilities or they may sell debt obligations (for example commercial paper, receivables financing, fixed-income securities of various types) or equities directly into the financial market.
3. *Governments* may likewise borrow from credit institutions (sovereign borrowing) or issue securities directly in the domestic capital market or in various bond markets abroad (sovereign issues).

Borrowers such as corporations and governments also have the possibility of privately issuing and placing their obligations with institutional investors, thereby circumventing both credit institutions and the public debt and equity markets. As noted, household debt can also be repackaged as asset-backed securities and sold privately to institutional investors.

In the first mode of financial contracting in Figure 1-1, depositors buy the "secondary" financial claims or liabilities issued by credit institutions and benefit from liquidity, convenience, and safety through the ability of financial institutions to diversify risk and improve credit quality by means of professional management and monitoring of their holdings of primary financial claims (both debt and equity). Savers can choose from among a set of standardized contracts and receive payments, services, and interest.

In the second mode of financial intermediation in Figure 1-1, investors can select their own portfolios of financial assets directly from among the publicly issued debt and equity instruments on offer. This method of supplying funds may provide a broader range of options than standardized bank contracts, and permit the larger investors to tailor portfolios more closely to their own objectives while still achieving acceptable liquidity through rapid and cheap execution of trades. Banks and other financial institutions that are part of the domestic payments mechanism assist savers who choose this route. Investors may also choose to have their portfolios professionally managed, for a fee, through various types of mutual funds and pension funds (fiduciary asset pools)—designated in Figure 1-1 as collective investment vehicles.

In the third mode of financial intermediation, institutional investors can buy large blocks of privately issued securities. In doing so, they may face a liquidity penalty—due to the absence or limited availability of a liquid secondary market—for which they are rewarded by a higher yield. However, directly placed securities can be specifically tailored to more closely match issuer and investor requirements than can publicly issued securities.

Value to ultimate savers and investors, inherent in the alternative financial processes described here, comes in the form of a combination of yield, safety, and liquidity. Value to ultimate users of funds accrues in the form of a combination of financing cost, transactions cost, flexibility, and liquidity. This value can be enhanced through credit backstops, guarantees, and derivative instruments such as forward rate agreements, caps, collars, futures, and options. The various markets can be linked functionally and geographically, both domestically and internationally. Functional linkages permit bank receivables, for example, to be repackaged and sold to nonbank investors. Privately placed securities, once they have been seasoned, may be sold in public markets. Geographic linkages make it possible for savers and issuers to gain additional benefits in foreign and offshore markets, thereby enhancing liquidity and yield, reducing portfolio risk, or lowering transaction costs. Within a national financial system such as the United States, flow of funds accounts such as Table 1-1 attempt to capture the structure of net borrowing and lending.

A variety of types of financial services firms carry out the functions described in Figure 1-1. Commercial banks, savings banks, and other thrift institutions tend to dominate the deposit-taking and credit business identified at the beginning of the chapter as the fully intermediated mode of financial linkages. Investment banks and securities firms (broker-dealers) tend to carry out the underwriting, trading, and distribution functions bracketed in the second, capital markets-based form of financial intermediation, along with advisory services and various other client-related or proprietary activities. Asset managers are active in the allocation of fiduciary asset pools on the right side of Figure 1-1, focusing on an array of clients that runs from wealthy individuals to pension funds. And insurance companies' basic business of risk management is complemented by their role as financial intermediaries (investing insurance reserves and the savings component of life insurance) and as pure asset managers (called *third-party* business in the insurance world).

These four types of institutions may be combined in various ways. Commercial and investment banking may be undertaken by the same firm, so may commercial banking and insurance (known as *bancassurance*

Table 1-1 Total Net U.S. Borrowing and Lending in Credit Markets (Excludes corporate equities and mutual fund shares)

	2001	2002		2001	2002
1. **Total Net Borrowing**	2047.1	2308.6	27. **Total Net Lending**	2047.1	2308.6
2. Domestic Nonfinancial Sectors	1125.9	1363.7	28. Domestic Nonfederal nonfinancial sectors	−24.1	84.6
3. Federal Government	−5.6	257.5	29. Household Sector	−52.7	55.7
4. Nonfederal Sectors	1131.5	1106.2	30. Nonfinancial Corporate Business	−11.5	2.2
5. Household Sectors	611.8	756.9	31. Nonfarm noncorporate Business	2.0	0.9
6. Nonfinancial Corporate Business	253.3	62.1	32. State and Local Governments	38.1	25.8
7. Nonfarm Noncorporate Business	156.8	131.8	33. Federal Government	6.0	7.7
8. Farm Business	7.5	8.0	34. Rest of the World	320.6	416.9
9. State and Local Governments	102.2	147.4	35. Financial Sectors	1744.6	1799.5
10. Rest of the World	−37.4	22.5	36. Monetary Authority	39.9	77.7
11. Financial Sectors	958.5	922.4	37. Commercial Banking	205.2	410.0
12. Commercial Banking	52.9	48.3	38. U.S. Chartered Commercial Banks	191.6	393.7
13. U.S. Chartered Commercial Banks	30.2	30.3	39. Foreign Banking Offers in U.S.	−0.6	6.6
14. Foreign Banking Offices in U.S.	−0.9	−0.2	40. Banking Holding Companies	4.2	3.1
15. Banking Holding Companies	23.6	18.2	41. Banks in U.S. Affiliated Areas	10.0	6.6
16. Savings Institutions	7.4	−13.8	42. Savings Institutions	42.8	35.5
17. Credit Unions	1.5	2.0	43. Credit Unions	41.5	44.1
18. Life Insurance Companies	0.6	2.0	44. Bank Personal Trusts and Estates	−28.1	0.9
19. Government-Sponsored Enterprises	290.8	232.4	45. Life Insurance Companies	130.9	214.9
20. Federally related mortgage pools	338.5	328.1	46. Other Insurance Companies	9.0	30.5
21. ABS Issuers	317.6	263.9	47. Private Pension Funds	20.3	31.0
22. Finance Companies	−0.2	43.7	48. State and Local Govt. Retirement Funds	−17.7	3.8
23. Mortgage Companies	0.7	0.7	49. Money Makers Mutual Funds	246.0	−25.3

(*continued*)

Table 1-1 (*continued*)

	2001	2002
24. REITs	2.5	18.6
25. Brokers and Dealers	1.4	−1.8
26. Funding Corporations	−55.2	−1.9

	2001	2002
50. Mutual Funds	126.0	144.2
51. Closed-end Funds	7.1	4.0
52. Exchange Traded Funds	0.0	3.7
53. Government-Sponsored Enterprises	309.0	222.4
54. Federally Related Mortgage Pools	338.5	328.1
55. ABS Issuers	291.4	241.2
56. Finance Companies	−5.7	17.5
57. Mortgage Companies	1.4	1.5
58. REITs	6.7	23.5
59. Brokers and Dealers	92.4	30.6
60. Funding Corporations	−112.2	−40.3

Source: Federal Reserve Flow of Funds Accounts.

or *Allfinanz* in parts of Europe). A number of insurance companies have been active in the investment banking business. And virtually all types of firms have targeted asset management as a promising field of activity. It is when the economic dynamics of the financial intermediation process is subjected to stress—whether from regulatory reforms or technological change, or simply from changes in client behavior or strategic rethinking of market opportunities—that restructuring pressure is felt among the various players and corporate actions such as M&A deals usually follow.

SEARCHING FOR FINANCIAL EFFICIENCY

End users of the financial system can usually be counted on to constantly search for the best deals. Households seek the highest rates of return and best investment opportunities, as well as the easiest access to credit on the most favorable terms; corporations seek a lower cost of capital; public sector agencies look for lower borrowing costs; and all end users look for good ideas that will help them maximize their financial welfare. Obtaining the best price usually involves what economists call *static efficiency*. Obtaining innovative products and services and harvesting productivity gains within the financial intermediation process usually involve what economists call *dynamic efficiency*. Both of these concepts will be discussed in greater detail in Chapter 7.

Against a background of continuous pressure for static and dynamic efficiency, financial markets and institutions have evolved and converged. Table 1-2 gives some indication of recent technological changes in financial intermediation, particularly leveraging the properties of the Internet. Although not all of these initiatives have been successful or will survive, some have clearly enhanced financial intermediation efficiencies. Internet applications have already dramatically cut information and transaction costs for both retail and wholesale end users of the financial system, as well as for the financial intermediaries themselves. The examples of on-line banking, insurance, and retail brokerage given in Table 1-1 are well known and continue to evolve and change the nature of the process, sometimes turning prevailing business models on their heads. For example, financial intermediaries have traditionally charged for transactions and provided advice almost for free, but increasingly are forced to provide transactions services almost for free and to charge for advice. The new models are often far more challenging for market participants than the older ones were.

At the same time, on-line distribution of financial instruments such as commercial paper, equities, and bonds in primary capital markets not only cuts the cost of market access but also improves and deepens the distribution process—including providing issuers with information on the investor-base. Figure 1-1 suggests that on-line distribution is only one further step to cutting out the intermediary altogether by putting the issuer and the investor or fiduciary into direct electronic contact with each other. The same is true in secondary markets, as shown in Table 1-2, with an array of competitive bidding utilities in foreign exchange and other financial instruments, as well as inter-dealer brokerage, cross-matching, and electronic communications networks (ECNs). When all is said and done, Internet-based technology overlay is likely to have turbocharged the cross-penetration story depicted in Figure 1-1, placing greater competitive pressure on many of the participating financial institutions.

Table 1-2 E-Applications in Financial Services 2002

Retail banking
On-line banking (CS Group, Bank-24, E*loan, ING Direct, Egg)

Insurance
ECoverage (P&C) (defunct 2002)
EPrudential term and variable life

Retail brokerage
E-brokerage (Merrill Lynch, Morgan Stanley, Fidelity, Schwab, E*trade, CSFB Direct)

Primary capital markets
E-based CP & bond distribution (UBS Warburg, Goldman Sachs)

E-based direct issuance
Governments (TreasuryDirect, World Bank)
Municipals (Bloomberg Municipal, MuniAuction, Parity)
Corporates (CapitaLink [defunct], Intervest)
IPOs (W.R. Hambrecht, Wit Soundview, Schwab, E*Trade)

Secondary Financial Markets
Forex (Atriax [defunct 2002], Currenex, FXall, FX Connect)
Governments (Bloomberg Bond Trader, QV Trading Systems, TradeWeb EuroMTS)
Municipals (QV Trading Systems, Variable Rate Trading System)
Corporates (QV Trading Systems)
Government debt cross-matching (Automated Bond System, Bond Connect, Bondnet)
Municipal debt cross-matching (Automated Bond System)
Corporate debt cross-matching (Automated Bond System, Bond Connect, Bondlink,
    Bondnet Limitrader, BondBook [defunct 2001])
Debt interdealer brokerage (Brokertec, Primex)
Equities—ECNs (Instinet, Island, Redi-Book, B-Trade, Brut, Archipelago, Strike,
    Eclipse)
Equities-cross-matching (Barclays Global Investors, Optimark)
Research (Themarkets.com)

End-user Platforms
Corporate finance end-user platforms
(CFOWeb.com [defunct])
Institutional investor utilities
Household finance utilities (Quicken 2002, Yodlee.com)

A further development consists of attempts at automated end-user platforms. Both CFOWeb.com (now defunct) for corporate treasury operations and Quicken 2003 for households provided real-time downloads of financial positions, risk profiles, market information, research, and so on. By allowing end users to cross-buy financial services from best-in-class vendors, such utilities could eventually upset conventional thinking that focuses on cross-selling, notably at the retail end of the end-user spectrum. If this is correct, financial firms that are multifunctional strategies may end up trapped in the wrong business model, as open-architecture approaches facilitating easy access to best-in-class suppliers begin to gain market share.

Both static and dynamic efficiency in financial intermediation are of great importance from the standpoint of national and global resource allocation. That is, since financial services can be viewed as inputs to real economic processes, the level of national output and income—as well as its rate of economic growth—are directly or indirectly affected. A retarded financial services sector can be a major impediment to a nation's overall economic performance. Financial system retardation represents a burden on the final consumers of financial services and potentially reduces the level of private and social welfare. It also represents a burden on producers by raising their cost of capital and eroding their competitive performance in domestic and global markets. These inefficiencies ultimately distort the allocation of labor as well as capital.

THE FACTS—SHIFTS IN INTERMEDIARY MARKET SHARES

Developments over the past several decades in intermediation processes and institutional design both across time and geography are striking. In the United States commercial banks—institutions that accept deposits from the pubic and make commercial loans—have seen their market share of domestic financial flows between end-users of the financial system decline from about 75% in the 1950s to under 25% today. The change in Europe has been much less dramatic, and the share of financial flows running though the balance sheets of banks continues to be well over 60% but declining nonetheless. And in Japan banks continue to control in excess of 70% of financial intermediation flows. Most emerging-market countries cluster at the highly intermediated end of the spectrum, but in some of these economies there is also factual evidence of incipient declines in market shares of traditional banking intermediaries as local financial markets develop. Classic banking functionality, in short, has been in long-term decline more or less worldwide.

Where has all the money gone? Although reversals occur in times of financial turbulence, disintermediation as well as financial innovation and expanding global linkages have redirected financial flows through the securities markets. Figure 1-2 shows developments in the United States

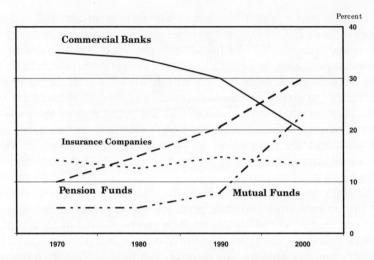

Figure 1-2. U.S. Financial Assets, 1970–2000. Source: Board of Governors of
the Federal Reserve System.

from 1970 to 2000, highlighting the extent of commercial bank market
share losses and institutional investor gains. While the United States may
be an extreme case, even in highly intermediated financial systems like
Germany (Figure 1-3) direct equity holdings and managed funds increased from 9.6 to 22.7% in just the 1990–2000 period.

Ultimate savers increasingly use the fixed-income and equity markets
directly and through fiduciaries. Vastly improved technology enables such
markets to provide substantially the same functionality as classic banking
relationships—immediate access to liquidity, transparency, safety, and so
on—at a higher rate of return. The one thing they cannot guarantee is
settlement at par, which in the case of transaction balances (for example
money market mutual funds) is mitigated by portfolio constraints that
require high-quality, short-maturity financial instruments. Ultimate users
of funds have benefited from enhanced access to financial markets across
a broad spectrum of maturity and credit quality by using conventional
and structured financial instruments. Although market access and financing cost normally depend on the current state of the market, credit and
liquidity backstops can be easily provided.

At the same time, a broad spectrum of derivatives overlays the markets,
making it possible to tailor financial products to the needs of end users
with increasing granularity, further expanding the availability and reducing the cost of financing on the one hand and promoting portfolio optimization on the other. The end users have themselves been forced to become
more performance oriented in the presence of much greater transparency
and competitive pressures, since justifying departures from highly disci-

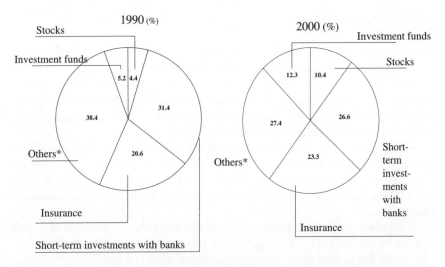

Figure 1-3. Private Asset Allocation in German Households (*includes fixed interest deposits, long-term investments with banks, and building society deposits). Data: Organization for Economic Cooperation and Development.

plined financial behavior on the part of corporations, public authorities, and institutional investors has become increasingly difficult.

In the process, three important and related differences are encountered in this generic financial-flow transformation. First, by moving from banking to securities markets, intermediation has shifted from book-value to market-value accounting. Second, intermediation has shifted from more intensively regulated to less intensively regulated firms that generally require less oversight and less capital. Third, the regulatory focus in this context has migrated from institutions to markets. All three of these shifts have clear implications for the efficiency properties of financial systems and for their transparency, safety, and soundness. All three were severely tested by the revelations of U.S. corporate scandals in the early 2000s, which called into question just about every facet of the market-driven system of corporate governance—the role of management, boards of directors, audit committee, and compensation committees within corporations and the role of auditors, lawyers, analysts, rating agencies, regulators, and institutional investors in the external environment of corporations.

The following sections of this chapter will outline the key attributes of each of the four pillars of the financial services industry (commercial banking, insurance, securities, and asset management) in order to indicate the source of restructuring pressure and M&A deal flow. The four pillars are depicted in a taxonomy of M&A transactions in Figure 2-1 in the following chapter.

COMMERCIAL BANKING

Commercial banking encompasses a variety of different businesses involving products and markets that have highly differentiated structural and competitive characteristics. Some are quite homogeneous and, unless distorted by government policies, have many of the attributes of efficient markets—intense competition, ease of entry and exit, low transaction and information costs, rapid adjustment to change, and very thin profit margins. Others involve substantial monopoly elements, with high degree of product differentiation, natural or artificial barriers to entry, and substantial competitive power on the part of individual firms. There are at least four broad product categories that define the domain of commercial banking.

First, there is deposit taking in domestic markets, markets abroad, and off-shore markets. This asset gathering involves demand and time deposits of residents and nonresidents, including those of individuals, corporations, governments, and other banks (redeposits). Competition for deposits is often intense, with funding costs dependent in part on the perceived safety and soundness of the institution, its sophistication, the efficiency of its retail deposit-gathering capabilities, and the range of customer services it offers. On the other side of the commercial bank balance sheet, lending remains a mainstay of the banking industry. Commercial lending includes secured and unsecured loans to individuals, small business, corporations, other banks, governments, trade and project finance, and so forth.

Competition in domestic markets for commercial banking services varies from exceedingly intense to essentially monopolistic in some of the more concentrated financial systems. Returns tend to vary with the degree of competition prevailing in the local environment, the complexity and riskiness of deals, and the creditworthiness borrowers. Specific commercial banking functions include initiation and maintenance of contact with borrowers or other customers and the quality of credit risk assessment and management.

Second, loan syndication is a key wholesale commercial banking activity. It involves the structuring of short-term loans and "bridge" financing, credit backstops and enhancements, longer-term project financing, and standby borrowing facilities for corporate, governmental, and institutional clients. The loan syndicate manager often "sells down" participations to other banks and institutional investors. The loans may also be repackaged through special purpose vehicles into securities that are sold to capital market investors. Syndicated credit facilities are put together by lead managers who earn origination fees and—jointly with other major syndicating banks—earn underwriting fees for fully committed facilities. These fees usually differ according to the complexity of the transaction and the credit quality of the borrower, and there are additional commitment, legal, and agency fees involved as well.

Global lending volume increased rapidly in the 1990s and the early 2000s. The business has been very competitive, with loan spreads often squeezed to little more than 10 to 20 basis points. Wholesale loans tend to be funded in the interbank market. In recent years, some investment banks moved into lending that was once almost exclusively the domain of commercial banks, and many commercial banks backed away from lending to focus on structuring deals and trying to leverage their lending activity into fee-based services. The firms coming in found it important to be able to finance client requirements with senior bank loans (as least temporarily), as well as securities issues, especially in cases of mergers and acquisitions on which they were advising. Those departing the business were concerned about the high costs of doing business and the low returns, although as commercial banks pressed into investment banking they seemed to find their lending and loan-structuring capabilities to be a strategic asset, especially in tough economic times. (The problem of lending-related cross-subsidies and conflicts of interest will be discussed in later chapters.)

Third are treasury activities, comprising trading and dealing in deposits to help fund the bank, foreign exchange contracts, financial futures and options, and so forth. These operations are functionally linked to position the institution to profit from shifts in markets within acceptable limits of exposure to risk. A key element is the management of sources and uses of funds, namely, mismatching the maturity structure of commercial banking assets and liabilities in the light of the shape of the yield curve, expectations about future interest rate movements, and anticipated liquidity needs. The bank must anticipate market developments more correctly and consistently than the competition, and it must move faster if it is to earn more than a normal return on its capital. Those it trades with must have different (less correct) expectations or be slower and less sophisticated if it is to excel in this activity. All of this must be accomplished in an environment in which all major players have simultaneous access to more or less the same information. It is a fiercely competitive business.

Fourth, a traditional commercial banking product line comprises transactions financing and cash management. These functions involve financial transfers, collections, letters of credit, and acceptances. Many of them have a somewhat routine character, with relatively little scope for product differentiation and incremental returns. Still, there have been a number of innovations, particularly in the areas of process technology, systems, and data transmission, so that commercial payments have sometimes proven to be quite attractive for banks.

Commercial banking activities have several characteristics that make them a particular focus for M&A transactions. These include (1) high-cost distribution and transactions infrastructures such as branch networks and IT platforms that lend themselves to rationalization; (2) overcapacity brought on by traditions of protection and distortion of commercial banking competition, and sometimes by the presence of public-sector or mutual thrift institutions and commercial banks (such overcapacity presents an opportune target for restructuring, in the process eliminating redundant capital and human personnel); (3) slow-growing markets that rarely outpace the overall rate of economic growth and usually lag it due to encroaching financial disintermediation, exacerbating the overcapacity problem; and (4) mature products that make innovation difficult in the *production* of financial services, combined with sometimes dramatic innovation on the *distribution* side, notably Internet-based commercial banking.

INSURANCE

The principal activities of the insurance industry are non-life insurance, life insurance, and fiduciary asset management (so-called "third-party" business), which is discussed separately below. Non-life insurance includes property, casualty, and health-related operations. Reinsurance adds a global activity that provides liability coverage for insurers themselves. Life insurance comprises whole-life and term-life policies and, increasingly, savings and pension products that are annuity-based.

The two traditional sources of insurance company income are earnings on policies—known as technical profits and losses—and earnings on invested premiums from policyholders. Technical profits and losses refer to the difference between policy premiums earned and claims and/or benefits paid. In some countries, insurers are required to invest the majority of their premiums in government bonds, but most countries allow investment in a range of high-quality, conservative assets, together with establishing a *technical reserve* liability on their balance sheet. The technical reserve reflects the estimated cost of claims and benefit payments that the insurer could ultimately be required to pay.

The insurance industry has long had to contend with a rapidly changing and more difficult market environment. Non-life business weakened in the 1990s due to falling premiums and stagnant demand growth, while both non-life and life segments were adversely affected by lower interest rates, resulting in reduced investment income. However, there were profit-sharing agreements on most of the fixed income life business, while new production was heavily unit-linked, which limited the damage to the companies. Active asset and liability management also at times limited damage to individual insurers.

Non-life Insurance

Across most geographic markets, non-life insurance premiums have declined since the mid-1990s. A general slack in demand and excess capacity drove prices down. Until the World Trade Center terrorist attack in September 2001, premium levels had come down in the United States by 17%, even though the value of new policies increased significantly. Some risks underwritten in the London market only commanded half the premiums of a few years earlier. In most industrialized countries, the market growth for personal non-life insurance has been sluggish as well, having grown since the mid-1990s at a slower rate than GDP. Commercial lines of insurance hardly fared better. Multinational companies, which had been large buyers of insurance in the past, were buying less coverage and in some cases managed their global risks internally through self-insurance. A growing number of companies felt that insurance was no longer an absolute necessity. Some discovered that premiums significantly exceeded their actual losses over time.

Some non-life insurers were buoyed by the strong equity markets of the late 1990s, which swelled the value of their investments and resulted in the industry's highest net-asset values ever. Such firms suffered commensurately from subsequent equity market declines. Since capital determines underwriting capacity, the surplus capital generated during the equity market boom created overcapacity in the industry. Excess capacity led to intensified underwriting activity both in Europe and the United States, triggering price wars, which made it difficult for weaker companies to survive. Declining investment returns due to lower interest rates compounded the problem of falling premium revenues and profitability. Non-life insurance liabilities were backed largely by government bonds. The losses incurred by a large number of insurers as a result of the events of September 11, 2001, abruptly caused premiums to rise, eliminated overcapacity, and tended to raise equity values among non-life insurers and insurance brokers, at least temporarily.

Life Insurance

Prospects in life insurance were more attractive for a time due to the strong market growth since the early 1990s in retirement savings and pensions. In industrialized countries, the pensions business benefited from an aging population and threatened cutbacks in government social security benefits. However, life insurance was also affected by a "yield pinch." Historically, the investments for life policyholders in many countries were allocated to fixed-income securities, mostly government bonds. With these traditional life products, insurers guaranteed their clients a fixed rate of return that was usually set by regulators. However, the spread between the insurer's investment yield and its guarantee to policyholders was dramatically narrowed due to declining interest rates.

This situation seriously damaged the profitability of both old and new business. The life of outstanding liabilities to policyholders often exceeded that of the underlying bond assets, which periodically matured and had to be rolled over at successively lower yields. For new policies, insurers could only invest new premiums at rates that were either close to or below those guaranteed to policyholders. By the early 2000s, some insurers had started to reduce their guarantees to better match lower interest rates.

Life insurers fared better by promoting unit-linked products with variable returns for new life policies. Unit-linked products, also known as "separate asset account" policies, were usually tied to the performance of equity investments. Unlike traditional life products bearing a guaranteed return, the investment risk under a unit-linked product was borne by the policyholder. Under this business model, income was earned from asset management fees rather than from participating in investment returns. The unit-linked product provided another important benefit by requiring lower capital reserves than traditional policies—sometimes as much as 25% of traditional products' capital requirements—since clients were assuming the risks directly.

By the early 2000s, life insurance was thus in the process of reinventing itself into what became increasingly an asset management-based business. Indeed, some of the larger insurers had adopted a strategy of asset management as a core business by leveraging their investment expertise. These companies offered separate asset management products to satisfy demand from both retail and institutional clients and to compete with banks that had made inroads into life insurance with annuity-linked products. Nonetheless, the life insurance industry as a whole fell on hard times in the early 2000s.

Demutualization and Consolidation

Many insurers—notably in the life sector—traditionally operated as mutuals, in which ownership was vested in policyholders, not shareholders. Without shareholder pressure, mutual insurance companies are often less efficient than their shareholder-owned competitors. The mutual form of ownership also hindered consolidation through mergers and acquisitions, because a mutual is first required to demutualize to become a stock company—after obtaining consent from its policyholders—in order to use its shares as acquisition currency. By the early 2000s, the trend toward demutualization had been under way for some time industrywide, especially in the United States and Japan. Some of the largest U.S. life insurance companies, including Metropolitan Life, John Hancock, and Prudential, proceeded down the demutualization track. In Europe there were significant insurance demutualizations, as well as Old Mutual, the dominant South African insurer, which issued shares in London.

The insurance industry has become increasingly consolidated both across and within national markets, and this trend is not likely to fade anytime soon. Because of lower margins from intense competition, insurers felt increasingly pressured to diversify outside of their home markets to spread risks and gain access to new business. Greater size has been perceived to provide economies of scale and tighter control of expenses through improved technology. Cost cutting has seemed clearly more advantageous at the national level between domestic insurance rivals than between companies based in different countries or expansion into other segments of the financial services industry with few overlapping operations.

Consolidation has also been viewed by many as a way to reduce industry overcapacity, especially in the non-life business. However, others found such benefits to be somewhat illusory, since size has not seemed to provide greater market power and control over prices. The late 1990s and early 2000s were notable for some of the largest mergers within the industry. In addition, there were external shocks such as the creation of the euro-zone, where national legislation usually required that insurers back their liabilities largely with assets denominated in the same currency. With the introduction of the euro, this restriction was effectively removed for insurers operating in the euro-zone's participating countries. The disappearance of currency risks also encouraged the growth in equity investments by insurers, with a shift away from a country-based investment approach to a pan-European sector-based approach. Finally, a single currency provided much greater access to the European bond market through its larger size and greater diversity of financial instruments. This allowed insurers to achieve a better matching of assets and liabilities by buying longer-term bonds across borders. For example, a Spanish insurer could add German government bonds of a longer maturity than were available locally to its portfolio.

Both life insurance and non-life insurance were overdue for restructuring, but for different reasons. In non-life, the issue was overcapacity and a boom-bust cycle that was exacerbated by the losses associated with the 2001 World Trade Center terrorist attack in New York. In life insurance, underwriting problems due to falling interest rates, continued demutualization, as well as efforts to focus on asset-gathering forms of life insurance, provided motivation for continued consolidation. Added to this was the fact that the national markets of some of the major insurers were close to saturation, so that growth would have to come from expansion into other markets, and the result was bound to be a spate of M&A activity within the insurance sector.

SECURITIES SERVICES

Securities services are among the financial-sector activities that have had important catalytic effects on the global economy. Investment banks have been key players. They help reduce information and transaction costs, help raise capital, bring buyers and sellers together, improve liquidity, and generally make a major contribution to both the static (resource-allocation) and dynamic (growth-related) dimensions of economic efficiency.

Figure 1-4 is a convenient way to represent the scope and breadth of the global securities markets. At the core of the market structure are foreign exchange and money market instruments. There is virtually complete transparency in these markets, high liquidity, large numbers of buy-

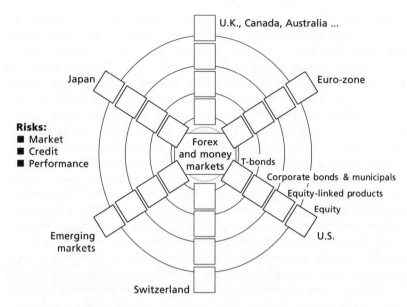

Figure 1-4. Stylized Structure of Global Financial Markets.

ers and sellers—probably as close to the economists' definition of perfect competition that one gets in global financial markets.

Moving out from the center of the diagram, the next most perfect market comprises sovereign debt instruments in their respective national markets, which carry no credit risk (only market risk) for residents, and are usually broadly and continuously traded. Sovereign debt instruments purchased by foreign investors, of course, also carry foreign exchange risk and the (arguably minor) risk of repudiation of sovereign obligations to foreign investors. If these sovereign debt instruments are denominated in foreign currencies, they carry both currency risk and country risk (the risk of inability or unwillingness to service foreign currency debt). Sovereign debt instruments run the gamut from AAA-rated obligations that may be traded in broad and deep markets all the way to noninvestment grade, highly speculative "country junk."

Next come state, local, and corporate bonds, which range across the quality spectrum from AAA-rated corporate and municipal securities that trade in liquid markets fractionally above sovereigns all the way to high-yield noninvestment grade and nonrated bonds. Also included in this category are asset-backed securities and syndicated bank loans, which may be repackaged and resold as bonds, such as collateralized loan obligations (CLOs).

Then there are common stocks of corporations that trade in secondary markets and constitute the core of the brokerage business. Equity securities are underwritten and distributed by investment banks. Between corporate bonds and equities lie hybrid financial instruments such as convertible bonds and preferred stocks and warrants to buy securities at some time in the future, which in turn can sometimes be "stripped" and sold in the covered warrant market. Well out on the periphery of Figure 1-4 are venture capital and private equity, investments that tend to be speculative and have little or no liquidity until an exit vehicle is found through sale to another company or an initial public offering.

As one moves from the center of Figure 1-4 to the periphery in any given financial market environment, the tendencies are for information and transactions costs to rise, liquidity to fall, and risks (market risk, credit risk, and/or performance risk) to rise. Along the way, there are a host of structured financial products and derivatives that blend various characteristics of the underlying securities in order to better fit into investors' portfolio requirements and/or issuer or borrower objectives. There are also index-linked securities and derivatives, which provide opportunities to invest in various kinds of asset baskets.

Finally, each geographic context is different in terms of market size, composition, liquidity, infrastructure, market participants, and related factors. Some have larger and more liquid government bond markets than others. Some have traditions of bank financing of business and industry, while others rely more heavily on public and private debt markets. Some have broad and deep equity markets, while others rely on permanent institutional or "control group" shareholdings. Some are far more innovative and performance-oriented than others. In addition to structural differences, some—such as the euro-zone since its creation in 1999—may be subject to substantial and rapid shift. Such discontinuities can be highly favorable to the operations of wholesale and investment banking firms and can provide rich opportunities for arbitrage. But they can also involve considerable risk.

Securities firms that perform well tend to have strong comparative advantages in the *least perfect* segments of the global financial market. Banks with large positions in traditional markets that are not easily accessed by others are examples of this. Sometimes, financial intermediaries specialize in particular sectors, types of clients, regions, or products. Some have strong businesses in the major wholesale markets and as a result are able to selectively leverage their operating platforms to access markets that are less efficient and more rewarding. They may also be able to cross-link on a selective basis both the major and peripheral markets as interest rates, exchange rates, market conditions, and borrower or investor preferences change. For example, a savvy intermediary could finance the floating-rate debt needs of a highly-rated American corporation by issuing fixed rate Australian dollar bonds at an especially good rate, and then swap the proceeds into floating rate U.S. dollars. These kinds of cross-links—permitting the intermediary to creatively marry opportunistic users of finance to opportunistic investors under ever-changing market conditions—often separate the winners from the losers in global capital markets.

The securities industry thus involves a range of businesses that service the financial and strategic needs of corporate and institutional clients, trading counterparties, and institutional investors. The principal functions of the securities industry are the following.

Market Access

The securities market new-issue activity usually involves an underwriting function that is performed by investment banks. Corporations or government agencies issue the securities. Sovereign governments tend to issue bonds to the markets directly, without underwriting. The U.S. securities market accommodates the greatest volume of new issues, and the international securities markets based in Europe comprise most of the rest.

Underwriting of *debt* securities is usually carried out through domestic and international syndicates of securities firms with access to local investors, investors in various important foreign markets such as Japan and Switzerland, and investors in offshore markets (for example, Eurobonds) by using one of several distribution techniques. In some markets *private placements* occur when securities are directed not at public investors but only at selected institutional investors. Access to various foreign markets is facilitated by means of interest-rate and currency swaps (swap-driven issues). Some widely distributed, multimarket issues have become known as *global issues.* In some markets, intense competition and deregulation have narrowed spreads to the point that the number of firms in underwriting syndicates has declined over time. In some cases, a single participating firm handles an entire issue in a so-called "bought deal."

Commercial paper and medium-term note (MTN) programs maintained by corporations, under which they can issue short-term and medium-term debt instruments on their own credit standing and more or less uniform legal documentation, have become good substitutes for bank credits. Financial institutions provide services in designing these programs, obtaining credit ratings, and dealing the securities into the market when issued. In recent years, MTN programs have become one of the most efficient ways for corporate borrowers to tap the major capital markets.

Underwriting of *equity* securities is usually heavily concentrated in the home country of the issuing firm. Normally, the investor base and the secondary market trading and liquidity are found in the home country. Corporations periodically issue new shares for business capital. Another important source of new supplies of stocks to the market has come from government privatization programs. New issues of stocks may also involve companies issuing shares to the public for the first time (initial public offerings) or later as secondary issues, or existing shareholders of large ownership positions selling their holdings and companies selling additional shares to existing shareholders (rights issues).

Trading

Once issued, bonds, notes, and shares become trading instruments in the financial markets, and underwriters usually remain active as market-makers and as proprietary investors for their own accounts. Secondary market trading is also conducted in other instruments, including foreign exchange (a market traditionally dominated by commercial banks but increasingly penetrated by insurance companies and investment banking firms as well), derivative securities of various types, and commodities and precious metals. Trading activities include market-making (executing client orders, including block trades), proprietary trading (speculation for the firm's own account), program trading (computer-driven arbitrage between different markets), and risk arbitrage (usually involving speculative purchases of stock on the basis of public information relating to pending mergers and acquisitions).

Brokerage

So-called "agency business" is an important and traditional part of the securities and investment banking industry. Its key area is brokerage, involving executing buy or sell orders for customers without actually taking possession of the security or derivative contract, sometimes including complex instructions based on various contingencies in the market. Brokerage can be oriented to retail or wholesale (institutional) business. Many of the financial market utilities discussed earlier are aimed at providing more efficient vehicles for classic brokerage functions as they affect both individual and institutional investors.

Investment Research

Research into factors affecting the various financial markets, individual securities and derivatives, specific industries, and macroeconomic conditions have become an important requirement for competitive performance in investment banking. Research is made available to clients by more or less independent analysts within the firm. Research analysts' reputation and compensation depend on the quality of their insights, which are usually focused on specific industries or sectors in the case of equity research. The value of research provided to clients depends critically on its quality and timeliness, and is often compensated by business channeled through the firm, such as brokerage commissions and underwriting or advisory mandates. Closely allied are other research activities—often highly technical modeling exercises—involving innovative financial instruments that link market developments to value-added products for issuer-clients, investor-clients, or both. Over the years, research carried out by investment banks (called *sell-side* research) became more important in soliciting and retaining investment banking clients, a condition that increasingly placed their objectivity in question. This eventually developed to the point of absurdity, as analysts were shown to have sold out to the investment banking side of their firms, thus becoming little more than glorified salespeople. Investigations and prosecution eventually led to charges of fraudulent and misleading research and a $1.4 billion settlement with leading securities firms—and the likelihood of major class action litigation to come.

Hedging and Risk Management

Hedging and risk management mainly involves the use of derivative instruments to reduce exposure to market and credit risk associated with individual securities transactions or markets affecting corporate, institutional, or individual clients. These include forward rate agreements, interest-rate and credit swaps, caps, floors and collars, various kinds of contingent contracts, as well as futures and options on an array of financial instruments. It may be quicker, easier, and cheaper, for example, for an investor to alter the risk profile of a portfolio by using derivatives than by buying and selling the underlying instruments. In modern wholesale financial markets, the ability to provide risk management services to clients depends heavily on a firm's role in the derivatives market, particularly over-the-counter (OTC) derivatives that allow structuring of what are frequently highly complex risk management products.

Advisory Services

Corporate finance activities of investment banks predominantly relate to advisory work on mergers, acquisitions, divestitures, recapitalizations, leveraged buyouts, and a variety of other generic and specialized corporate transactions. They generally involve fee-based assignments for firms wishing to acquire others or firms wishing to be sold (or to sell certain business units) to prospective acquirers.

The M&A business is closely associated with the market for corporate control. It may involve assistance to, and fund-raising efforts for, hostile acquirers or plotting defensive strategies for firms subjected to unwanted takeover bids. It may also involve providing independent valuations and "fairness opinions" for buyers or sellers of companies to protect against lawsuits from disgruntled investors alleging that the price paid for a company was either too high or too low. Such activities may be domestic, within a single national economy, or cross-border, involving parties from two countries. The global M&A marketplace has been extraordinarily active from time to time, with roughly half of the deal volume involving the United States.

As part of the M&A business, sales of state-owned enterprises (SOEs) to the private sector became a major component of global wholesale financial services beginning in the early 1980s. Such business generally involves the sale of the initial public offering of a large corporation but can also involve the sale of SOEs to corporate buyers, as well as advisory roles. And there are advisory assignments to governments on how the privatization processes should work in order to satisfy the public interests.

Businesses for sale have run the gamut from state-owned manufacturing and services enterprises to airlines, telecommunications, infrastructure providers, and so on. Sellers use various approaches such as sales to domestic or foreign control groups, local market flotations, global equity distributions, sales to employees, and others.

Principal Investing

So-called "merchant banking," a term used by American investment banks, involves financial institutions' placing their clients' and their own capital on the line in private investments of (usually) nonpublic equity securities, private equity, venture capital, real estate, and leveraged buyouts and certain other equity participations. It sometimes involves large, essentially permanent stakeholdings in business enterprises, including board-level representation and supervision of management. Or it may involve short-term subordinated lending such as bridge loans or mezzanine financing to assure the success of an M&A transaction. Firms began to participate in these investments in the late 1980s to take advantage of the opportunity to participate in the high expected returns emanating from their natural deal flow.

An important dimension of merchant banking involves venture capital and private equity investments, often through limited partnerships, with the idea that the investment banks would not only benefit from the success of the investment per se, they would also arrange the initial public offering and any other financial services needed afterwards. Virtually all of the global investment banks have now established private equity or venture capital units, although in the early 2000s many of them took massive losses in their private equity portfolios.

Securities Infrastructure Services

Finally, there is an array of services that lies between buyers and sellers of securities, domestically and internationally, that is critical for the effective operation of securities markets. These services center on domestic and international systems for trading and for clearing and settling securities transactions via efficient central securities depositories (CSDs). They are prerequisites for a range of activities, often supplied on the basis of quality and price by competing private-sector vendors of information services, analytical services, trading services and information processing, credit services, securities clearance and settlement, custody and safekeeping, and portfolio diagnostics.

Investor services represent financial market utilities that tend to be highly scale and technology intensive. Classic examples include Euroclear, a Belgian cooperative that was pioneered by (and had a longstanding operating agreement with) J. P. Morgan. Many banks and securities firms have stakes in investor services utilities, which can generate attractive risk-adjusted returns for financial services firms if all-important costs and technologies are well managed. There is an ongoing debate as to whether such utilities ought to be vertically integrated (with stock exchanges, for example) or independent and competing actively for transaction-flow.

Competition and Restructuring in Securities Services

All of these activities have to be organized in an effective structure that in most cases has come to form a so-called "full-service" global wholesale banking capability. Such a structure comprises market-assess services (debt and equity originations), trading and brokerage, corporate advisory services including M&A activities, principal investing, asset management, and (sometimes) investor services, and could take the form of an independent investment bank or the investment banking division of a universal bank or financial conglomerate. The top firms in the investment banking industry today comprise a relatively small number of U.S. independent firms such as Goldman Sachs, Lehman Brothers, Merrill Lynch, and Morgan Stanley, together with investment banking divisions of universal banks and financial conglomerates such as Citigroup, Crédit Suisse First Boston, Deutsche Bank, Dresdner Kleinwort Wasserstein, J.P. Morgan Chase, and UBS Warburg. There are also regional securities activities conducted by banks and independent or affiliated securities houses in the significant markets such as the United States, Canada, France, Spain, the Nordic countries, Japan, Hong Kong, China, Singapore, and a variety of others.

There is an active debate concerning the optimal organization of the securities industry. Some argue that its fast-moving, opportunistic nature in a mark-to-market environment and its heavy reliance on innovation and creativity make this industry best suited to independent firms that have relatively light and mobile structures, ideally with substantial equity ownership by management. Others argue that the industry has become increasingly capital intensive, both in supporting trading positions and financing deals, so that some of the most active firms may be found among investment banking divisions of financial conglomerates. Still others maintain that structural cohabitation is possible, with investment banking monoline specialists and generalists joined by smaller boutiques in a lively cocktail of firms competing for market share. So far, the jury remains out, although it seems likely that further M&A activity will characterize the shape of the industry going forward.

ASSET MANAGEMENT

As of 2002, the global total of assets under management was estimated at close to $56 trillion, comprising some $14 trillion in pension fund assets, about $9 trillion in mutual fund assets, another $9 trillion in fiduciary assets controlled by insurance companies, and perhaps $24 trillion in private client assets. Not only is this already massive industry likely to experience substantial growth in comparison with other segments of the financial services sector, but also cross-border volume—both regional and global—is likely to take an increasing share of that activity. Within this high-growth context, asset management attracts competitors from a broad range of strategic groups—commercial and universal banks, investment banks, trust companies, insurance companies, private banks, captive and independent pension fund managers, mutual fund companies, and various types of specialist firms. This rich array of contenders, coming at the market from several very different starting points, competitive resources, and strategic objectives, makes the market for institutional asset management a highly competitive one.

A schematic that is consistent with the overall dynamics of financial intermediation flows shown in Figure 1-1, which depicts the structure of asset management services, is presented in Figure 1-5. Retail investors have the option of placing funds directly with financial institutions such as banks or by purchasing securities from retail sales forces of broker-dealers, possibly with the help of fee-based financial advisers. Alternatively, retail investors can have their funds professionally managed by buying shares in mutual funds or unit trusts (again possibly with the help of advisers), which in turn buy securities from the institutional sales desks of broker-dealers (and from time to time maintain balances with banks).

Private clients are broken out as a separate segment of the asset management market, and are usually serviced by private bankers. The bankers bundle asset management with various other services such as tax planning, estates, and trusts, and place monetary assets directly into financial instruments, commingled managed asset-pools, or sometimes publicly

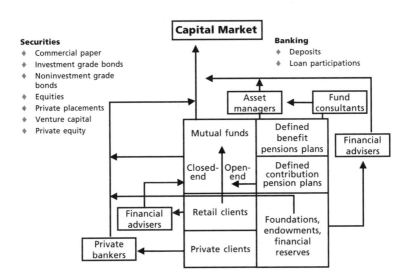

Figure 1-5. Organization of the Asset Management Industry.

available mutual funds and unit trusts. In between retail and private
clients is another category, *mass affluent*, that many financial institutions
have decided to target.

Foundations, endowments, and financial reserves held by nonfinancial
companies, institutions, and governments have several options regarding
asset management. They can rely on in-house investment expertise to
purchase securities directly from the institutional sales desks of banks or
securities broker-dealers, use financial advisers to help them build efficient portfolios, or place assets with open-end or closed-end mutual funds.

Pension funds take two principal forms, those guaranteeing a level of
benefits and those aimed at building beneficiary assets from which a
pension will be drawn (see below). Defined benefit pension funds can
buy securities directly in the market or place funds with banks, trust
companies, or other types of asset managers, often aided by fund consultants who advise pension trustees on performance and asset-allocation
styles. Defined contribution pension programs operate in a similar way
if they are managed in-house, creating proprietary asset pools and also
(or alternatively) providing participants with the option to purchase
shares in publicly available mutual funds.

The structure of the asset management industry encompasses significant overlaps among the four types of asset pools to the point where they
are sometimes difficult to distinguish. An example is the linkage between
defined contribution pension funds and the mutual fund industry, and
the association of the disproportionate growth in the former with the
expansion of mutual fund assets. There is a similar but perhaps more
limited linkage between private client assets and mutual funds, on the
one hand, and pension funds, on the other. This is particularly the case
for the lower bound of private client business (which is often commingled
with mass-marketed mutual funds) and pension benefits awarded high-
income executives (which in effect become part of high-net-worth portfolios).

The underlying drivers of the market for institutional asset management are well understood.

1. A continued broad-based trend toward professional management of discretionary household assets in the form of mutual
   funds or unit trusts and other types of collective investment
   vehicles, a development that has perhaps run much of its course
   in some national financial systems but has only begun in others.
2. The growing recognition that most government-sponsored pension systems, many of which were created wholly or partially
   on a pay-as-you-go (PAYG) basis, have become fundamentally
   untenable under demographic projections that appear virtually
   certain to materialize. These pension systems must be progressively replaced by asset pools that will generate the kinds of

returns necessary to meet the needs of growing numbers of retirees who are living longer.

3. Partial displacement of traditional defined benefit public and private sector pension programs backed by assets contributed by employers and working individuals. This displacement is a result of the evolving demographics, rising administrative costs, and shifts in risk-allocation by a variety of defined-contribution schemes.

4. Reallocation of portfolios that have been overweighted—for regulatory, tax, or institutional reasons—to domestic financial instruments (notably fixed-income securities) toward a greater role for equities and nondomestic asset classes. This shift not only promises higher returns but also may reduce the beneficiaries' exposure to risk due to portfolio diversification across both asset classes and economic and financial environments that are less than perfectly correlated in terms of total investment returns.

Mutual Funds

Competition among mutual funds can be among the most intense anywhere in the financial system. The competition is heightened by the aforementioned analytical services that track performance of funds in terms of risk and return over different holding periods and assign ratings based on fund performance. These fund-rating services are important, because the vast majority of new investments tend to flow into highly rated funds. For example, in the United States during the 1990s, about 85% of all new money was allocated to funds rated four-star or five-star by Morningstar, Inc. In addition, widely read business publications distribute regular scoreboards among publicly available mutual funds based on such ratings and, together with specialized investment publications and information distributed over the Internet, have made mutual funds one of the most intensely competitive parts of the retail financial services sector. These developments are mirrored to varying degrees in Europe as well, notably in the United Kingdom.

Despite clear warnings that past performance is no assurance of future results, a rise in the performance rankings often brings in a flood of new investments and management company revenues. The individual asset manager is compensated commensurately and sometimes moves on to manage larger and more prestigious funds. Conversely, serious performance slippage causes investors to withdraw funds, taking with them a good part of the manager's bonus and maybe his or her job, given that the mutual fund company's revenues are vitally dependent on new investments and total assets under management. With a gradual decline in the average sophistication of the investor in many markets as mutual funds become increasingly mass market retail–oriented and interlinked with pension schemes, performance ratings, name recognition, and "branding" appear to be progressively more important in defining competitive performance in the industry.

In addition to promoting their performance, when favorable, mutual fund companies and securities broker-dealers have aggressively added banking type services. These services include checking and cash management accounts, credit cards, and overdraft lines. The service providers offer user-friendly, integrated account statements and tax reporting. Client contact is based on easy access by telephone, mail, and the Internet. Commercial bank competitors in the mutual fund business have seen their retail competitive advantage become increasingly reliant on a fragile combination of high-cost branch networks and deposit insurance. Securities firms have likewise increased their mutual fund activity, presumably with the view that this part of the securities industry is more capable of supporting significant, sustained returns than is wholesale investment banking, such as debt and equity capital markets and corporate advisory services, where competition has become cutthroat, often capital-intensive, and subject to a high degree of earnings instability. Insurance companies have also considered the mutual fund business to be a strong candidate for strategic development, especially in the face of competition in their traditional annuities business and the cross-links that have emerged in some countries between the pension fund and mutual fund industries. There have also been successful examples of direct fund distribution even in heavily bank-dominated financial systems. Competition in the mutual funds business thus covers a rich array of players, ranging from commercial banks and securities broker-dealers to specialized mutual fund companies, discount brokerages, insurance companies, and nonfinancial firms. Such interpenetration of strategic groups, each approaching the business from a different angle, tends to make markets exceedingly competitive, especially with the growth of hedge funds.

Various observers have argued that consolidation in the mutual fund business is inevitable. Factors that seem to argue *for* greater industry concentration in the future are economies of scale and band-name concentration among progressively less sophisticated investors in taxable funds and mutual funds that are part of retirement accounts battling for attention among the enormous number of funds. Arguments *against* further concentration include shifts in performance track records and the role of mutual fund supermarkets in distribution, which increase the relative marketing advantage of smaller funds. One factor that may promote continued *fragmentation* of the mutual fund industry is that size itself can lead to significant performance problems. So far, at least, evidence of dramatically increased concentration remains elusive, although reshuffling via M&A transactions has been substantial.

Pension Funds

The pension fund market has proven to be one of the most rapidly growing sectors of the global financial system, and promises to be even more dynamic in the years ahead. Consequently, pension assets have been in the forefront of strategic targeting by all types of financial institutions, including banks, trust companies, broker-dealers, insurance companies, hedge funds, mutual fund companies, and independent asset management firms. Pension assets in 1995 in countries where consistent and comparable data are available (Australia, Canada, Japan, Switzerland, the United Kingdom, and the United States) were estimated to amount to $8.2 trillion, roughly two-thirds of which covered private sector employees; the balance covered public sector employees. By 2002, these had grown to $14.2 trillion. The basis for such growth is, of course, the demographics of gradually aging populations colliding with existing structures for retirement support, which in many countries carry heavy political baggage. These structures are politically exceedingly difficult to bring up to the standards required for the future, yet eventually doing so is inevitable.

The expanding role of defined-contribution plans in the United States and elsewhere has led to strong linkages between pension funds and mutual funds. Numerous mutual funds—notably in the equities sector—are strongly influenced by 401(k) and other pension inflows. These linkages are reflected in the structure of the pension fund management industry. For example in the United States in 2002, among the top-25 401(k) plan fund managers, three were mutual fund companies, ten were insurance companies, five were banks, one was a broker-dealer, two were diversified financial firms, and four were specialist asset managers. In Europe pension funds business has changed significantly over the years as well. In 1987 banks had a market share of about 95%, while insurance companies and independent fund managers split the rest about evenly. But by 2002 independent fund managers had captured over 40% of the market, banks were down to about 55%, and insurance companies accounted for the rest.

Private Clients

One of the largest pools of professionally managed assets in the world is associated with high-net-worth individuals and families, generally grouped under the heading of *private banking*. Total funds under management have been variously estimated at up to $27 trillion in 2003—significantly exceeding the size of the global pension asset pool—although the confidentiality aspect of private banking makes such estimates little more than educated guesses.

Private clients' asset management objectives are an amalgam of preferences across a number of variables, among which liquidity, yield, security, tax efficiency, confidentiality, and service level are paramount. Each of these plays a distinctive role. Traditional private banking clients were

concerned with wealth preservation in the face of antagonistic government policies and fickle asset markets. Clients demanded the utmost in
discretion from their private bankers, with whom they often maintained
lifelong relationships initiated by personal recommendations. Such high-
net-worth clients have to some degree given way to more active and
sophisticated customers. Aware of opportunity costs and often exposed
to high marginal tax rates, they consider net after-tax yield to be more
relevant than the security and focus on capital preservation traditionally
sought by high-net-worth clients. They may prefer gains to accrue in the
form of capital appreciation rather than interest or dividend income, and
tend to have a more active investment response to changes in total rates
of return.

The environment faced by high-net-worth investors is arguably more
stable today than it has been in the past. The probability of revolution,
conventional war, and expropriation has declined over the years in Europe, North America, the Far East, and Latin America, even as the financial markets themselves underwent serious turmoil. Nevertheless, a large
segment of the private banking market remains highly security conscious.
Such clients are generally prepared to trade off yield for stability, safety,
and capital preservation, although global terrorism may once again be
changing investor preferences.

Like everyone else, high-net-worth clients are highly sensitive to tax-
ation, perhaps all the more so as cash-strapped politicians target "the
rich" in a constant search for fiscal revenues. International financial markets have traditionally provided plenty of tax-avoidance and tax-evasion
opportunities, ranging from offshore tax havens to private banking services able to sidestep even sophisticated efforts to claim the state's share.
And secrecy is a major traditional factor in private banking—secrecy
required for personal reasons, for business reasons, for tax reasons and
for legal or political reasons. Confidentiality, in this sense, is a "product"
that is bought and sold as part of private asset management business
through secrecy and blocking statutes on the part of countries and high
levels of discretion on the part of financial institutions. The value of this
product depends on the probability and consequences of disclosure, and
is "priced" in the form of lower portfolio returns, higher fees, suboptimal
asset allocation, or reduced liquidity as compared with portfolios not
driven by confidentiality motives.

Finally, there is the level of service. While some of the tales of personal
services provided for private banking clients are undoubtedly apocryphal,
the "fringe benefits" offered to high-net-worth clients may well influence
the choice of and loyalty to a particular financial institution. Such benefits
may save time, reduce anxiety, increase efficiency, or make the wealth
management process more convenient. Personal service is a way for asset
managers to show their full commitment to clients accustomed to high
levels of personal service in their daily lives. The essence of private banking is to identify each client's unique objectives, and to have the flexibility

and expertise to satisfy these as fully as possible in a highly competitive marketplace.

Overall, the private banking business is highly fragmented. In 2002 the largest player was UBS AG, with $428 billion in private client assets under management, but accounting for only about 1.8% of the estimated global total. Indeed, the 11 top firms only accounted for 9.5% of total private client assets, indicating the degree of fragmentation in this business.

Competitive Restructuring in Asset Management

The foregoing discussion has noted that various kinds of financial firms have emerged to perform asset-management functions. Such firms include commercial banks, savings banks, postal savings institutions, savings co-operatives, credit unions, securities firms (full-service firms and various kinds of specialists), insurance companies, finance companies, finance subsidiaries of industrial companies, mutual fund companies, financial advisers, and various others. Members of each *strategic group* compete with one another, as well as with members of other strategic groups. There are two questions. First, what determines competitive advantage in operating distribution gateways to the end-investor? Second, what determines competitive advantage in the asset management process itself?

One supposition is that distribution of asset management services is both scope and technology-driven. That is, services can be distributed jointly with other types of financial services and thereby benefit from cost economies of scope as well as demand economies of scope (cross-selling). This joint distribution would tend to give retail-oriented financial services firms such as commercial and universal banks, life insurance companies, and savings institutions a competitive advantage in distribution. At the same time, more specialized firms may establish cost-effective distribution of asset management services by using proprietary remote-marketing techniques such as mail, telephone selling, or the Internet or by "renting" distribution through the established infrastructures of other financial intermediaries such as banks, insurance companies, or mutual fund supermarkets. They may also gain access through fund management consultants and financial advisers.

The asset management function itself depends heavily on portfolio management skills as well as economies of scale, capital investment, and technologies involved in back-office functions, some of which can be outsourced. Since fiduciary activities must be kept separate from other financial services operations that involve potential conflicts of interest, either through organizational separation or "Chinese walls," there is not much to be gained in the way of economies of scope.

Intersectoral competition, alongside already vigorous intrasectoral competition, is what will make asset management one of the most competitive areas of finance, even in the presence of rapid growth in the size of the market for asset management services. Certainly the dynamics of competition for the growing pools of defined-benefit and defined-contribution pension assets in various parts of the world, and its cross-linkage to the mutual fund business, has led to various strategic initiatives among fund managers. These initiatives include mergers, acquisitions, and strategic alliances among fund managers, as well as among fund managers, commercial and universal banks, securities broker-dealers, and insurance companies.

SUMMARY

This initial chapter has presented a conceptual profile of financial intermediation and related activities that can be used to frame the relevant questions that drive the industry's evolving structure. How can end users of the financial system optimize their own interests as sources or users of financial flows? How can financial intermediaries position themselves in the structure of financial flows in order to provide client value-added, secure acceptable market share, and achieve sustainable profitability? What is the activity space of each of the four major pillars of the financial services industry—commercial banking, investment banking, insurance, and asset management—and how do they interact as firms seek to position themselves in the most advantageous way possible?

The objective here has been to set the stage for understanding the industry's reconfiguration and the mergers and acquisitions deal flow that has become the principal vehicle for bringing it about.

2

The Global Financial Services
M&A Deal Flow

The previous chapter provided a structural framework within which the reconfiguration of the financial services sector can be explained in an historical context, assessed in terms of ongoing or rumored transactions, and sometimes predicted going forward. If a new financial intermediation channel opens up as a result of technological or regulatory change, it is virtually certain that end users of the financial system will sooner or later try out those channels, thereby rewarding the innovators. Established firms then have three choices: (1) they can stand and fight to beat back the threat of disintermediation by making an economic case that the new approach is not in clients' best interests or threatens to reduce access to other types of financial services of value to clients, perhaps coupled with appeals to the regulatory authorities for protection, (2) they can "go with the flow" and build their own capacity in the new areas that pose a competitive threat, (3) or they can acquire one or more of the firms that have developed a solid foothold in the new area of financial services activity.

Examples of each of these responses abound. Early in the 1990s, J.P. Morgan sponsored a new electronic Dutch auction platform for allowing large corporations to efficiently distribute conventional corporate bonds to institutional investors, which provided both the investors and the issuers with substantial savings in transaction costs without sacrificing efficient pricing or liquidity. Merrill Lynch and other major bond underwriters mounted a vigorous attack on this threat to their "bread and butter" bond underwriting business, pointing out various alleged shortcomings as well as torpedoing the whole exercise by "buying" the first couple of deals. The entrenched players' response to Dutch auction initial public offering (IPO) platforms pioneered by firms such as W.R. Hambrecht & Co. and Wit Soundview was not much different, although the innovators managed to obtain a small market share and may come back in a significant way in the future. In the late 1990s, when

e-brokerage threatened Merrill Lynch's vast sales force of "financial consultants"—the heart of its private client business—the firm publicly den-
igrated do-it-yourself e-brokerage as a "threat to clients' financial lives."
Within a year, Merrill and its retail brokerage competitors had developed
ways of integrating e-brokerage into their legacy distribution platforms,
providing clients with multiple options and providing the firms (through
"wrap" fees) with a presumably more stable source of revenues.

Technology shifts that make existing financial products or processes
obsolete represent one kind of stimulus to M&A transactions in the financial services sector. If the new technologies seem promising and exceed
the capabilities of a financial firm, a properly executed acquisition can
have substantial value in terms of both market share and profitability, as
in the case of Swiss Bank Corporation's acquisition of O'Connor Partners,
a derivatives specialist, in 1992. As various e-based transaction platforms
emerged in the 1990s, such as electronic communications networks
(ECNs), established players often acquired them or took equity participations. Technology-driven change can be both rapid and disruptive, with
uncertain outcomes. Some of this M&A activity takes on the character of
"strategic insurance."

Besides shifts in technologies, other external forces driving M&A activity in the financial services sector are linked to regulatory change. In 1974,
the so-called Mayday in the United States introduced negotiated stock
brokerage commissions and eroded the ability of many securities firms to
compete. Some went out of business, but most were bought by other firms
to form entities more capable of surviving in the new deregulated environment. In 1986 more or less the same thing happened in the United
Kingdom, with the so-called Big Bang, which eliminated the distinction
between brokers and dealers ("single-capacity firms") and the exclusivity
of narrow franchises. At the same time, a London Stock Exchange ruling
that outside ownership of LSE member firms could not exceed 29.9% was
lifted to 100%, which allowed all kinds of banks and other financial firms
to become registered broker-dealers.

The objective was to make London a far more competitive financial
center, and it succeeded. But in the process virtually all of the former
specialists were acquired by British merchant banks, British clearing
banks, and European and U.S. universal and commercial banks to form
multicapacity firms much better able to survive in the new deregulated
environment. Many banks turned out to have overpaid by overestimating
the quality of what they were buying or the sustainability of profit margins under the new conditions. The United Kingdom went through further consolidation a decade later, with all but two of the traditional British
firms in the securities industry acquired by foreigners (see below).

Regulatory triggers of financial sector M&A activity have been common in other regions as well. Examples include liberalization of market
access for foreign banks and insurers in countries such as Australia, Mexico and other Latin American countries, China, Korea, Taiwan, and many

others. Usually the policy objective is to create a leaner and more performance-oriented financial system by improving the management of local firms acquired by foreigners and forcing local firms that remain independent to face new competition and greatly improve performance. Sometimes this works so well—as in the Australian case in the 1980s— that the new foreign entrants do far worse than they anticipated.

Other changes in competitive barriers may be regional, as in the United States with the lifting in 1978 of the 1927 McFadden Act restrictions on interstate banking. The change in law made possible the creation of large regional, superrregional, and national banking companies through serial acquisitions of smaller banks by firms such as BancOne, Wells Fargo, Fleet Financial, Key Corp., and PNC Corp. As always, some have done much better than others. Nor have large banking companies succeeded in extinguishing small local and community banks. There remain almost 8,000 banks in the United States, and there is a constant flow of new bank charters awarded. Evidently banking entrepreneurs think they can survive against competition from the giants based on superior local information and relationships, better quality of service, and the ability of outsource some of the size-sensitive functions. New technologies often aid the entrepreneurs.

Another example of regulatory change is the liberalization of line-of-business barriers that existed for decades in the United States (the Glass-Steagall provisions of the Banking Act of 1933 and the Bank Holding Company Act of 1956) and in Japan (Article 65 of the Japan Financial Law of 1949). In the American case the Gramm-Leach-Bliley Act of 1999 effectively eliminated barriers and allowed qualified banks to acquire insurance companies as well as securities firms (and vice-versa), making it possible for the first time since the Great Depression to create (for better or worse) multifunctional financial firms such as Citigroup, Bank of America, and J.P. Morgan Chase. The idea was to create a level playing field where business logic and the demands of the marketplace, rather than regulatory dictates, determine the structural form of financial firms in a way that was consistent with safety and stability. Many people thought that the sweeping away of 36 years of barriers to competition between different types of financial services firms would lead to an immediate spate of cross-market mergers and acquisitions to form massive multifunctional financial services conglomerates. By 2003, they were still waiting.

Besides regulatory changes and technological change, the principal driver of financial sector M&A deal flow reflects the various strategies of the players involved. Somewhere along the line many firms in this industry decided that they were going to be "growth plays" from the perspective of investors and command the valuations commonly associated with growth stocks. But how to grow? One option is to expand geographically. Another is to add clients. And a third is to add products. These are not mutually exclusive, but they all have in common reliance on M&A

transactions as one of the principal tools. Whatever the M&A motivation, one has to ask whether the ultimate objective is indeed maximizing shareholder value or some other objective, such as executive compensation, firm size and market share, or just plain hubris. These issues will be discussed in the following chapter.

IN-MARKET AND CROSS-MARKET TRANSACTIONS

The basic M&A drivers in financial services described in the previous section have, to a significant extent, been reflected in the process of financial industry reconfiguration summarized in Figure 2-1.

First, in-market transactions have been most intense in the commercial banking sector, notably retail banking. Extensive banking overcapacity in some countries has led to substantial consolidation that has often involved M&A activity. Excess retail banking capacity has been slimmed down in ways that usually release redundant labor and capital. In some cases this process has been retarded by large-scale involvement of public sector institutions and cooperatives that operate under less rigorous financial discipline. Most of the shrinkage in U.S. commercial banking, from almost 15,000 banks to about 8,000 banks, has been the product of M&A deals that included periods of high-volume activity by regional and superrregional consolidators. In the process, the commercial banking industry has

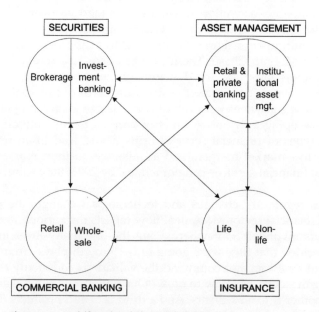

Figure 2-1. Multifunctional Financial Linkages.

become far more efficient, yet without precluding the continued existence and prosperity of small community banks.

In-market M&A activity has also occurred in the insurance sector, both life and non-life, as well as insurance brokerage. Insurance firms such as AIG in the United States and Aegon in the Netherlands are the products of sequential acquisitions, both domestically and around the world—although the fact that many of the world's leading life insurance companies were mutuals and had to make any acquisitions in cash arguably dampened M&A activity as a restructuring force in the life insurance business. The two global insurance brokerage firms Aon and Marsh & McLennan are both products of large numbers of acquisitions in what was once a highly fragmented business.

Similarly, in-market consolidation in investment banking had been a long-standing phenomenon—notably the accelerated consolidation triggered by deregulation in the United States and the United Kingdom noted earlier. Finally, asset management has also seen substantial in-market restructuring as larger fund managers acquired smaller ones unable to exploit scale economies or lacking sufficient marketing reach.

Another dimension of financial services consolidation is reflected in cross-market M&A transactions. At the retail level, commercial banking activity has been linked strategically to retail brokerage, retail insurance (especially life insurance), and retail asset management through mutual funds, retirement products, and private client relationships. Sometimes this product linkage has occurred selectively and sometimes by using multiple distribution channels coupled to aggressive cross-selling efforts. At the same time, relatively small and focused firms have sometimes continued to prosper in each of the retail businesses, especially where they have been able to provide superior service or client proximity while taking advantage of outsourcing and strategic alliances. In wholesale financial services, similar links have emerged. Wholesale commercial banking activities such as syndicated lending and project financing have often been shifted toward a greater investment banking focus, while investment banking firms have placed growing emphasis on developing institutional asset management businesses in part to benefit from vertical integration and in part to gain some degree of stability in a notoriously volatile industry.

The result has been M&A activity on the part of commercial banks and universal banks acquiring investment banks, exploiting the U.S. regulatory liberalization in 1999 that allowed them to do so. This activity paralleled to some extent the acquisition of brokers and jobbers as well as merchant banking firms in the United Kingdom, mostly by commercial and universal banks. Earlier, a number of insurance companies had likewise acquired investment banks. Most of these were later divested (one of the more recent being the sale by Groupe AXA of Donaldson Lufkin Jenrette to Crédit Suisse in 2000). Only Prudential Financial retains an in-house securities firm, Prudential Securities, which basically focuses on

Table 2-1 Disappearing Investment Banks, 1986–2003

• Kuhn Loeb (1986)	• Cowen & Co, (1998)
• E.F. Hutton (1987)	• Yamaichi Securities (1998)
• Morgan Grenfell (1989)	• Paribas (1998)
• Drexel Burnham (1990)	• Hambrecht & Quist (1998)
• Shearson Lehman American Express	• Charterhouse (1999)
(1993)	• Phoenix Securities (1999)
• Kidder Peabody (1994)	• Bankers Trust Company (1999)
• Baring Brothers (1995)	• Furman Selz (1999)
• Kleinwort Benson (1995)	• Schroders (2000)
• Alex Brown (1997)	• Robert Fleming (2000)
• Dillon Read (1997)	• PaineWebber (2000)
• Hoare Govett (1997)	• J.P. Morgan (2000)
• Robertson Stephens (1997)	• Donaldson Lufkin Jenrette (2000)
• Montgomery Securities (1997)	• Wasserstein Perella (2000)
• Peregrine Securities (1997)	• Beacon (2000)
• BZW (1998)	• ING Barings (2001)
• S.G. Warburg (1998)	• Dresdner Kleinwort Wasserstein (2001)
• NatWest Markets (1998)	• Robertson Stephens (2002)

Name drops: Dean Witter (2002), PaineWebber (2003), Salomon Smith Barney (2003).

retail brokerage, and even that business was partially sold to Wachovia Bank. Among the major banks there have been similar divestitures, for example Robertson Stephens by Fleet Financial in 2002. Outside the United States there were similar developments, including acquisition of Indosuez by Crédit Agricole, Banque Paribas by Banque Nationale de Paris, Morgan Grenfell by Deutsche Bank, Hoare Govett by ABN AMRO, Barings by ING Groep, Wasserstein Perella by Dresdner Bank, and a number of others. Again, some were later divested as firms such as Barclays and National Westminster Bank exited key investment banking activities and sold these businesses to Crédit Suisse and Bankers Trust, respectively. The latter was subsequently taken over by Deutsche Bank.

Table 2-1 and Figure 2-2 show the progressive disappearance of U.S. and U.K. securities firms, mostly though acquisitions but in some cases— such as Barings, Drexel Burnham Lambert, E.F. Hutton, and Kidder Peabody—due to malfeasance as a primary or contributory factor in their demise.

At the same time there has been substantial cross-market activity linking banking and insurance under the rubric of *Allfinanz* or *bancassurance*. Firms such as Citigroup, ING Groep, Allianz AG, Fortis Group, Lloyds TSB, and others offer both banking and insurance. In most cases these strategies involve acquisitions of insurance companies by commercial banking organizations or vice versa. The results have been decidedly mixed, ranging from considerable successes to unmitigated disasters. As always, the devil is in the details.

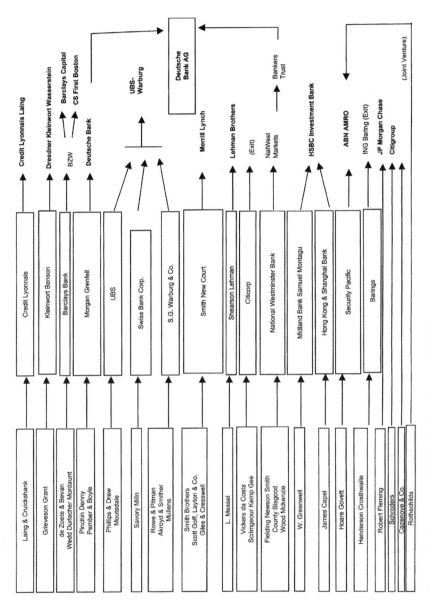

Figure 2-2. Evolution of British Merchant Banks 1986–2003.

**Table 2-2 Completed Global M&A Transactions 1985–2002
($ billions—thousands of transactions)**

	$ Value	%	#	%
U.S. Domestic				
All industries	8,103.7	45.1%	93.6	35.9%
All financial services	2,935.6	41.3%	33.0	37.4%
U.S. Cross-Border				
All industries	2,411.3	13.4%	28.2	10.8%
All financial services	589.6	8.3%	5.6	6.3%
Non-U.S.				
All industries	7,464.0	41.5%	138.8	53.3%
All financial services	3,588.8	50.4%	49.7	56.3%
Total				
All industries	17,979.0	100.0%	260.6	100.0%
All financial services	7,114.0	100.0%	88.3	100.0%

Data: Thomson Financial Securities Data, author calculations.

Finally, each of the other three types of financial firms have aggressively expanded their presence in asset management, often through cross-market M&A deals. Market valuations of asset management companies have consequently been quite high in comparison with other types of firms in the financial services industry, and this has been reflected in prices paid in M&A transactions.[1] Besides gaining access to distribution and fund management expertise, the underlying economics of this deal-flow presumably have to do with the realization of economies of scale and economies of scope, making possible both cost reductions and cross-selling of multiple types of funds, banking and/or insurance services, investment advice, high-quality research, and so on in a one-stop-shopping interface for investors.

Table 2-2 shows that mergers and acquisitions in the financial services sector have comprised a surprisingly large share of the total volume of M&A activity worldwide. Including only transactions valued in excess of $100 million, during the period 1985–2002 the cumulative total value of M&A transactions worldwide in all industries amounted to about $18 trillion. Of this total, M&A transactions in the financial services industry had a cumulative value of about $7 trillion, or 40% of the global total.

---

1. For example, at midyear 1996 in the United States, when the price to earnings ratio (based on expected 1996 earnings) for the S&P 500 stocks averaged 16.2, the price-earnings ratios of the top-ten domestic commercial banks with strong retail banking businesses averaged 10.3, the top life and casualty insurance companies averaged price-earnings ratios of about 10, the top-eight publicly owned investment banks (including J. P. Morgan and Bankers Trust) only 7.9, while the price-earnings ratios of the top-nine asset managers averaged about 14. The average share price to book value ratio for the top ten U.S. commercial banks in 1996 was 1.83, for the top investment banks it was only 1.27, while for the top-nine asset managers it was 4.64.

Tables 1–6 in Appendix 1 contain all of the major M&A deals in the financial services industry during 1990–2002 in the United States, Europe, and Asia and indicates when the transaction was announced and its value. From the deal list it is clear that the majority of the transactions occurred in the banking sector, followed by insurance. Indeed, as Figure 2-3 shows, the bulk of these transactions (by value) involved commercial banking— well over 60% of the total—with about 25% involving the insurance industry and the balance involving asset management companies, securities broker-dealers, and other types of financial firms. Relative to all other industries, commercial banking ranked second only to telecommunications in both the United States and Europe during the period 1985–2002, as shown in Table 2-3, with insurance ranked seventh in the United States and third in Europe.

As noted earlier, financial services M&A transactions can be either in-market or cross-market, in addition to being either domestic or cross-border. During the 1985–2002 period, most financial services M&A transactions were in-market (that is, *within* banking, insurance, securities, and so forth), with firms acquiring or merging with similar firms, rather than cross-market (*between* generic activities; for example, banks acquiring insurance companies), as Table 2-4 shows. As discussed, until late 1999 the United States had in place significant barriers to cross-market M&A activity—namely, the Glass-Steagall provisions of the Banking Act of 1933 and the Bank Holding Company Act of 1956. These barriers certainly contributed to the fact that such a large proportion (85%) of the M&A activity was *within* each of the sectors and rather than *between* them. Nevertheless, in Europe, where such restrictions have not limited the

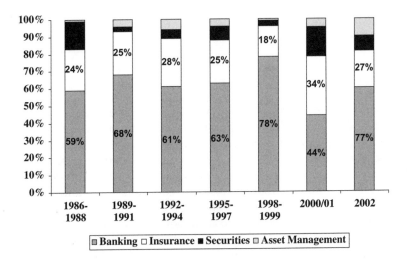

Figure 2-3. Worldwide Financial Services Merger Volume, 1986–2002.

Table 2-3 Merger-Intensity Rankings of Industry Groups of U.S. and European Buyers, 1985–2002

Acquirer Industry	U.S. Acquirer Rank	Rank Val. ($mils)	# of Deals	European Acquirer Rank	Rank Val. ($mils)
Investment and commodity firms/ dealers/exchanges	1	1886712.1	21427	1	1038258.7
Telecommunications	2	826320.7	2622	2	764393.1
Commercial banks, bank holding companies	3	797346.6	6615	3	729971.5
Business services	4	519058.4	12025	10	175877.4
Oil and gas; petroleum refining	5	512473.8	3539	6	255266.3
Radio and television broadcasting stations	6	492668.0	2280	22	55930.6
Electric, gas, and water distribution	7	441075.4	1745	5	441943.8
Insurance	8	388266.3	3283	4	464484.0
Drugs	9	297546.9	1599	9	214471.5
Electronic and electrical equipment	10	266854.2	3116	15	105363.9
Chemicals and allied products	11	216618.8	2044	8	234303.2
Prepackaged software	12	190625.3	3854	40	24468.9
Food and kindred products	13	185730.6	2135	7	247812.1
Computer and office equipment	14	164173.4	1778	52	4463.7
Measuring, medical, photo equipment; clocks	15	149222.1	3609	28	44632.1
Aerospace and aircraft	16	147746.9	579	24	47136.3
Transportation equipment	17	126989.6	1215	12	114772.1
Paper and allied products	18	125745.1	851	20	70869.1
Credit institutions	19	120169.4	893	46	10215.4
Printing, publishing, and allied services	20	117521.8	2703	14	109860.4
Health services	21	116291.7	3657	49	7731.6
Machinery	22	116029.8	2803	23	48727.6
Metal and metal products	23	114372.9	2225	18	94235.8

process of financial restructuring, over 74% of the transactions by value were likewise *within* the individual financial services sectors. This suggests that the dynamics of financial services industry restructuring in the United States and Europe may have been quite similar, driven by the economics of consolidation within the industry's various functional domains. It is interesting that the relative volume of insurance deals was substantially higher in Europe than in the United States.

Finally, the bulk of M&A transactions flow was domestic during the 1985–2002 period, that is, within national financial systems, as shown in Table 2-5. This suggests that much of the volume concerned the consolidation of domestic banking systems, with M&A transactions being the

Table 2-4 Volume of In-Market Mergers and Acquisitions in the United States and Europe, 1985–2002 (billions of U.S. dollars and percent)

Acquiring Institution	Target Institution								
	World Total			U.S.			Europe		
	Banks	Securities	Insurance	Banks	Securities	Insurance	Banks	Securities	Insurance
Commercial banks	1260 **(52.2%)**	71 (2.9%)	63 (2.6%)	594 **(50.9%)**	30 (2.6%)	0.3 (0.0%)	370 **(47.5%)**	24 (3.1%)	52 (6.7%)
Securities firms	111 (4.6%)	282 **(11.7%)**	96 (4.0%)	14 (1.2%)	182 **(15.6%)**	49 (4.2%)	53 (6.8%)	48 **(6.2%)**	39 (5.0%)
Insurance companies	128 (5.3%)	36 (1.5%)	365 **(15.1%)**	73 (6.3%)	19 (1.6%)	200 **(17.2%)**	50 (6.4%)	12 (1.5%)	131 **(16.8%)**
	79.0%			**83.7%**			**(70.4)**		

Source: Thomson Financial Securities Data.

Table 2-5 Volume of Cross-Border Mergers and Acquisitions in the United States and Europe, 1985–2002 (billions of U.S. dollars and percent)

Acquiring Institution	Target Institution											
	World Total			U.S.–non-U.S.			Intra-Europe			Europe–non-Europe		
	Banks	Securities	Insurance	Banks	Securities	Insurance	Banks	Securities	Insurance	Banks	Securities	Insurance
Commercial banks	185 (25.9%)	68 (9.5%)	11 (1.5%)	58 (19.1%)	44 (14.5%)	4 (1.3%)	79 (28.3%)	18 (6.5%)	4 (1.4%)	63 (22.7%)	40 (14.4%)	4 (1.4%)
Securities firms	31 (4.3%)	98 (13.7%)	17 (2.4%)	10 (3.3%)	61 (20.1%)	6 (1.8%)	8 (2.9%)	19 (6.8%)	4 (1.4%)	7 (2.5%)	40 (14.4%)	11 (4.0%)
Insurance companies	26 (3.6%)	28 (3.9%)	249 (34.9%)	1 (0.3%)	22 (7.2%)	98 (32.3%)	24 (8.6%)	3 (1.1%)	121 (43.4%)	2 (0.7%)	19 (6.9%)	90 (32.5%)

Source: DeLong, Smith, and Walter (1998) and Thomson Financial Securities Data. The first figure is the dollar value (in billions) of M&A activity and the second number in parentheses is the percentage of the total (these sum to 100 for each 3 × 3 matrix). Figures reported are the sum of the equity values of the target institutions.

principal vehicle for removing excess capacity and promoting domestic consolidation. The largest share of cross-border volume was in the insurance industry, suggesting that perhaps the underlying economics were somewhat different in that sector, with market-extension in the face of saturated domestic markets arguably representing an important motivation.

Whereas line-of-business and geographic restrictions have characterized the United States for all but the last several years covered by the M&A data, fostering a more narrow geographic and line-of-business focus to financial sector restructuring than might have occurred otherwise, this was not the case in Europe. The EU Second Banking Directive and directives covering investment services and insurance all had in common the "single passport," allowing financial firms to operate throughout the European Union (EU) in competition with local institutions. This did not mean a true level playing field, however, since the EU lacked a coherent set of takeover rules during this period and continued to be characterized by strong nationalism and the perceived need for "national champions" in the financial sector, particularly banking.

Cross-border restructuring in the United Kingdom was probably the most liberal, with most securities firms and a number of banks, insurance companies, and asset managers taken over by foreign players. The largest deal was the acquisition of Midland Bank by HSBC. Still, there were also a number of cross-border deals in France, Germany, Italy, Spain, Portugal, and the Nordic and Benelux countries.

SURVIVORSHIP

As one would expect, the financial services landscape around the world has been profoundly altered by M&A activity in all of the four sectors of the industry—banks, insurance companies, broker-dealers, and asset managers.

Table 2-6 shows the world's largest banks by asset size in 1989 and 2002. Note that none of the top-10 banks in 1989 remained on the list without at least one important merger or acquisition, sometimes several. Similarly all of the top-10 banks in 2002 had at least one important merger during the previous decade—a complete churning of this particular cohort of financial institutions.

Much the same is true in the life and non-life insurance industries, although the dynamic is quite different. In the life sector the largest firms were traditionally mutuals (owned by their policyholders). Over time many of them demutualized through initial public offerings, creating a cohort in 2001 in which all except the remaining Japanese life insurers and TIAA-CREF (a pension fund for university professors classified as an insurance company due to the guaranteed nature of some of its pension products) had become stock companies, benefiting from access to the capital markets and the strategic flexibility that goes with it (see Table

Table 2-6 The World's Largest Banks (assets in billions of U.S. dollars)

March 1989		February 2002	
1. Dai-Ichi Kangyo	$1,096	1. Mizuho[1]	$1,178
2. Sumitomo Bank	800	2. Citigroup	$1,051
3. Fuji Bank	751	3. Sumitomo-Mitsui Banking Corp[2]	840
4. Mitsubishi Bank	701	4. Deutsche Bank AG	809
5. Sanwa Bank	653	5. Mitsubishi Tokyo Fin. Group[3]	751
6. Industrial Bank of Japan	595	6. UBS	747
7. Credit Agricole	516	7. BNP Paribas	727
8. Citicorp	489	8. HSBC	696
9. Norinchukin Bank	483	9. J.P. Morgan Chase	694
10. Banque Nationale de Paris	468	10. Hypo Vereinsbank AG	642
Total Top 10	$6,552		$8,135

[1]Merger of Dai-Ichi Kangyo Bank, Fuji Bank, IBJ and Yasuda Trust established as a holding company in Sept. 2000.
[2]Announced October 14, 1999.
[3]Merger of Bank of Tokyo—Mitsubishi, Mitsubishi Trust and Banking, Nippon Trust and Tokyo created April 20, 2001.

2-7). In the non-life sector, however, most of the largest firms had been traditionally public companies, and the firms on the 2001 list (excepting State Farm, which remains a mutual) had been through at least one M&A transaction during the previous decade. Some firms had experienced many more (see Table 2-8).

Table 2-9 shows the world's largest asset managers in 2002, a rich array of contenders based in various financial services strategic groups. Some have a commercial banking background as trust companies, managing assets for defined benefit pension funds. Others are insurance companies undertaking third-party fiduciary business and leveraging off expertise

Table 2-7 World's Largest Life Insurance Companies, 2001

Ranking	Company	Country	Revenues ($mil)	Type
1	AXA	France	92,782	Stock
2	ING Group	Netherlands	71,206	Stock
3	Nippon Life	Japan	68,055	Mutual
4	CGNU	Britain	61,499	Stock
5	Generali	Italy	53,333	Stock
6	DAI-ICHI Mut. Life	Japan	46,436	Mutual
7	Prudential	Britain	43,126	Stock
8	TIAA-CREF	U.S.	38,064	Mutual
9	Sumitomo Life	Japan	37,536	Mutual
10	Metlife	U.S.	31,947	Stock

Table 2-8 World's Largest Non-life Insurance Companies, 2001

Rank	Company	Country	Revenues ($mil)	Type
1	Allianz	Germany	71,022	Stock
2	State Farm	U.S.	47,863	Stock
3	AIG	U.S.	45,972	Stock
4	Munich Re	Germany	40,672	Stock
5	Zurich	Switzerland	37,434	Stock
6	Berkshire	U.S.	33,976	Stock
7	Allstate	U.S.	29,134	Stock
8	Royal & Sun	Britain	25,570	Stock
9	Loews	U.S.	20,670	Stock
10	Swiss Re	Switzerland	18,688	Stock

gained in managing their own insurance reserves. Still others are independent asset managers such as mutual fund companies, some of which have become prominent in managing defined contribution retirement assets. Finally, investment banks have pushed aggressively into asset management, particularly mutual funds used for savings and retirement vehicles. Table 2-10 shows the pattern of M&A activity in the asset management industry, a pattern that is indicative of the degree to which fund managers have been acquired by banks, investment banks, and insurers over the years.

Among the various financial businesses that depend critically on human capital, M&A transactions have been especially problematic in asset management. History shows that it is very easy to overpay and that

Table 2-9 World's 20 Largest Asset Managers, 2001

Firm	Assets under management ($ billions)	Firm	Assets under management ($ billions)
UBS AG	1,438	Merrill Lynch	557
Kampo	1,230	Capital Group	556
Deutsche Bank AG	1,079	Mellon	510
Fidelity Investments	886	Morgan Stanley	472
Crédit Suisse	837	Citigroup	464
AXA	802	Vanguard	389
Barclays Global Inv.	801	Invesco	384
State Street	724	Putnam	370
Allianz AG	641	Amvescap	333
J.P. Morgan Fleming	638	Northern Trust	323

Source: *Institutional Investor*, July 2001 (U.S. data) and November 2001 (non-U.S. data).

Table 2-10 Merger and Acquisitions Activity in the Asset Management Industry (January 1985–June 2003, Millions of U.S. $ and Number of Transactions)

Total	Total Asset Managers	Open-end Mutual Fund Managers
Global Target	312,966 (7,821)	23,521 (459)
European Target	110,888 (3,171)	10,388 (204)
U.S. Target	117,703 (2,237)	5,366 (159)
Other Target	84,375 (2,413)	7,767 (96)

Total Asset Managers	Total	European Acquirer	U.S. Acquirer
U.S. Target	117,703 (2,237)	25,942 (181)	84,527 (1,931)
U.K. Target	55,295 (1,291)	41,055 (1,119)	10,241 (79)
Cont. Eur. Target	55,593 (1,880)	49,832 (1,685)	3,753 (128)

Open-end Mutual Fund Managers	Total	European Acquirer	U.S. Acquirer
U.S. Target	5,366 (159)	1,849 (8)	3,475 (148)
U.K. Target	3,490 (41)	3,455 (38)	0 (2)
Cont. Eur. Target	6,921 (163)	6,742 (148)	0 (3)

Data: Thompson Financial Securities Data, author calculations.

skill and judgment of individuals and teams in a highly fragmented industry is the key competitive variable. So many of the real success stories in the industry involve well-executed organic growth, such as Fidelity, Capital International, Vanguard, and TIAA-CREF, while some of the disasters involve acquisitions that have been difficult to integrate, control, and leverage—Zurich Financial Services, has provided one example. That hardly means it cannot be done, as Amvescap demonstrates. And asset management acquisitions can prove especially problematic to manage through the equity market cycle, when attractive revenue-driven deals executed in bull markets look very different in downturns, when attention turns to cost cutting, layoffs, and compensation cuts imposed on asset managers who in fact outperformed.

Finally, Table 2-1 and Figure 2-2 have already illustrated the disappearance of the vast majority of independent securities firms over the last several decades, mostly through being acquired by other securities firms or by commercial and universal banking organizations. Most of the activity has been in the United States (long hampered by the Glass-Steagall Act) and in the United Kingdom. Figure 2-4 is an illustration of how the major securities firms in today's competitive landscape got to where they

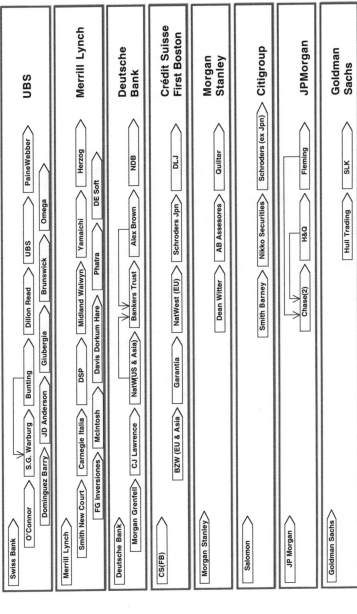

Figure 2-4. Global Investment Banking Consolidation (1). NOTES: (1) Not including insurance companies and asset management, (2) Chase includes Chemical Bank and Manufacturers Hanover. Data: UBS AG.

were as of 2002, such that the principal firms in terms of investment banking transaction flow in 2002 represented a varied group of major independent firms and investment banking divisions of commercial banks and financial conglomerates (Table 2-11). A favorite topic of conversation has been whether any of the independents in this industry will ultimately be able to survive, or whether all will eventually be absorbed into financial juggernauts, and what will be gained and lost in the process.

CROSS-HOLDINGS AND NONFINANCIAL SHAREHOLDINGS

One development in the restructuring of the financial services sector that has long been present in Europe, but not in the United States, involves cross-holdings among financial firms, as shown in Figure 2-5 as of 2002. Here banks and insurance companies have held minority shares in each other, both within and between their respective segments of the financial services industry. Sometimes these have been part of consortia, cooperation agreements, joint ventures, or strategic alliances, with cross-shareholdings used to cement such arrangements. Sometimes they have been defensive holdings to make sure significant blocks of shares are in friendly hands in case of hostile takeover attempts.

Sometimes, too, they have been strategic initiatives to give firms "a seat at the table" in the event that further restructuring developments and opportunities appeared. Most of the grander schemes along these lines have been judged failures. Joint ventures and strategic alliances rarely work for very long in this sector and usually develop a dynamic whereby one partner buys out the other or they go their separate ways. Nonetheless, the industry has seen a number of successful "tactical" alliances that helped cooperating firms achieve strategic goals in particular opportunistic situations. The classic example is the original alliance between Crédit Suisse and First Boston Corporation during the 1970s heyday of the Eurobond market.

Some cross-holdings, are the products of history, such as the one between Dresdner Bank, Allianz AG, and Munich Re. As the left-hand part of Figure 2-6 shows, there had been a structure of cross-holdings between the three firms, traceable in part to the fact that Allianz and Munich Re shared a cofounder and had a history of cooperation in areas such as reinsurance. Allianz and Dresdner Bank (long Germany's second largest) had reciprocal shareholdings as well, with cooperation including efforts to sell each other's products through their respective distribution networks. Another cooperation arrangement and shareholding involved Allianz with HypoVereinsbank, Germany's largest regional bank, based in Munich.

In 2001 Allianz agreed to acquire Dresnder Bank, following two unsuccessful attempts by Dresdner to merge, first with Deutsche Bank and then with Commerzbank. At the heart of the deal was the unbundling of the cross-shareholdings of Allianz AG, Munich Re, HypoVereinsbank, and

Table 2-11 Global Wholesale Banking Rankings, 2002 ($ million)

Firm Rank 2002*	Syndicated Bank Loans	Global Debt U/W & Private Placements	Global Equity U/W & Private Placements	M&A Advisory Completed	MTNS Arranged	Total	Market Share
J.P. Morgan (2)	419,326	262,193	17,491	182,831	25,093	906,935	11.28%
Citigroup/Salomon Smith Barney	228,004	349,156	46,286	208,220	20,115	851,780	10.59%
Goldman Sachs & Co (4)	8,651	197,037	40,324	320,750	15,801	582,562	7.24%
Deutsche Bank AG (8)	86,746	207,219	14,743	127,075	134,026	569,809	7.08%
Crédit Suisse First Boston (6)	24,142	262,111	38,916	211,999	16,479	553,648	6.88%
Merrill Lynch & Co Inc (3)	7,513	176,331	47,308	173,145	99,123	503,419	6.26%
Morgan Stanley (5)	12,626	216,483	26,703	195,095	15,822	466,729	5.80%
Banc of America Securities LLC	218,394	153,633	8,363	29,040	46,349	455,779	5.67%
Lehman Brothers (9)	20,724	257,572	15,988	133,664	18,217	446,165	5.55%
UBS Warburg (7)	9,447	223,434	16,226	133,064	15,162	397,333	4.94%
Bear Stearns & Co Inc (15)		140,398	4,036	83,806	18,989	247,228	3.07%
ABN AMRO (13)	37,337	74,041	2,819	29,636	64,529	208,361	2.59%
Barclays Capital (12)	70,379	87,935			30,094	188,407	2.34%
BNP Paribas SA (14)	41,887	44,276	3,147	55,088	41,062	185,459	2.31%
Lazard (17)				149,956		149,956	1.86%
HSBC Holdings PLC (16)	36,714	57,500	1,349	47,256	3,000	145,818	1.81%
Rothschild (26)				130,109		130,109	1.62%
Royal Bank of Scotland Group (19)	28,579	93,434			3,757	125,769	1.56%
Dresdner Kleinwort Wasserstein	25,436	47,153	359	28,722	8,264	109,934	1.37%

*2001 ranking in parentheses. Data: Thomson Financial Securities Data.

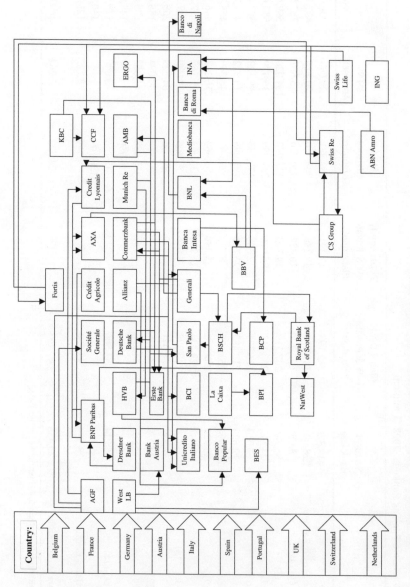

Figure 2-5. Financial Services Crossholdings in Europe. Data: UBS AG.

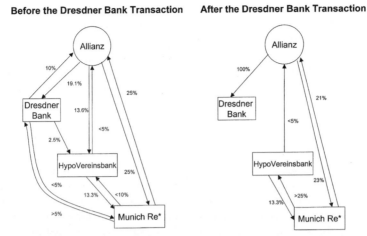

Before the Dresdner Bank Transaction   **After the Dresdner Bank Transaction**

Figure 2-6. Simplifying the Allianz Crossholding Structure. Source: Allianz AG.

Dresdner Bank. A 2001 German tax reform abolished a long-standing capital gains tax on liquidations of shareholdings in other companies, effective at the beginning of 2002, and was no doubt a catalyst for the merger. It allowed better utilization of capital while avoiding punitive taxes. Much of the €25 billion purchase price was paid for with asset trades of Allianz and Dresdner holdings amounting to €17 billion, or 68% of the deal value.

Allianz relinquished to Munich Re its interests in HypoVereinsbank, including its own 13.6% stake and a 2.5% interest that belonged to Dresdner. Allianz also re-acquired 10% of its own shares by buying Dresdner. As a consequence of the transaction, Munich Re and HypoVereinsbank, by then Germany's second largest bank, forged closer ties—with Munich Re emerging with an interest greater than 25% in the Bavaria-based bank. As part of the agreement to reduce its cross-holdings with Munich Re, Allianz intended to redeploy the released capital in its core businesses and in the process rationalize the domestic insurance businesses of both firms.[2]

In addition, European banks and insurance companies long had equity shareholdings in all kinds of business enterprises (see for example Figure 2-7). Some of these could be traced to rescue efforts by banks of their clients, which resulted in debt conversions into equity. Some had to do with how enterprises were financed in their early stages in the

2. Allianz purchased Munich Re's 45% interest in Bayerische Versicherungsbank and its 49.9% shareholding in Frankfurter Versicherung. Munich Re would in turn acquire the 36.1% interest held by Allianz in Karlsruher Lebensversicherung. Allianz also agreed with Munich Re in April 2001 to acquire its 40.6% stake in Allianz Lebenversicherung (Allianz Leben).

absence of broad and deep local capital markets. Simultaneously, investors needed to build sensible asset portfolios and find outlets for investable funds without the benefit of sophisticated capital markets. Governments often encouraged such shareholdings, and in some cases reinforced by them with public sector stakes in either financial institutions or corporations, or both. Not least, close *Hausbank* relationships between financial and nonfinancial firms reinforced and perpetuated such stakes.

As viable financial markets developed in various countries and the financial institutions themselves came under pressure to use their capital more efficiently, the institutions began to consider dissolving these stakes. The process is ongoing in Europe and is progressively having an impact on the industrial landscape as well as financial markets. Somewhat similar developments can be seen in Asia (notably in Japan and Korea), in these cases triggered by financial crises or prolonged economic stagnation.

In another joint venture example, Bank of America in 2002 undertook a $1.6 billion deal purchase of BSCH's Grupo Financiero Serfin in Mexico, the third largest bank in Mexico, in an effort to tap into the $10 billion in annual worker remittances by Mexicans employed in the United States, a flow that involves some $1 billion in fees annually. The deal improved Bank of America's competitive position against Citigroup and HSBC, which both have the necessary networks in both Mexico and the United States, and bolstered BSCH in competition with the Mexican activities of its main Spanish rival, BBVA, which controls Grupo Financiero Bancomer, the largest Mexican bank. BSCH (who also needed the $700 million capital gain to bolster its capital, impaired by losses in Argentina) obtained extensive U.S. distribution in the project, while Bank of America obtained a Mexican presence that would not have made sense on a stand-alone basis, and was able to better compete with Citigroup.

COHABITATION?

In terms of the leading firms (in terms of market capitalization) existing in the four principal sectors of the financial services industry today, Tables 2-12 and 2-13 show that the majority have been through at least one M&A transaction involving a minimum of 25% of the respective firm's market capitalization. That includes all of the top-10 banks and most of the others as well. Additionally, Zurich Financial Services made major acquisitions such as Scudder and BAT's financial services businesses, only to sell them a few years later to Deutsche Bank. Similar important acquisitions have been undertaken by Generali, Marsh McLennan, Merrill Lynch, and Schwab, while Goldman Sachs opened itself to public ownership in 1999 in part to take advantage of its shares as currency in possible future M&A deals.

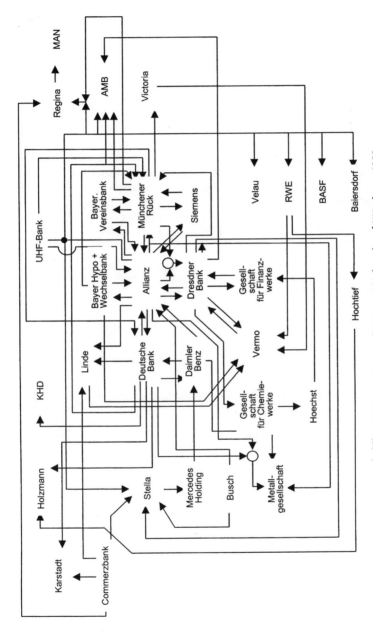

Figure 2-7. Legacy German Crossholding Structure. Source: E. Wenger, University of Würzburg, 1993.

Table 2-12 Top Financial Firms by Market Capitalization (in U.S. $ Billions)

1990		2003	
Industrial Bank of Japan	57.1	Citigroup	210.9
Fuji Bank	52.0	AIG	151.0
Mitsui Taiyo Kobe Bank	46.3	HSBC Holdings	127.0
Sumitomo Bank	46.0	Bank of America	111.1
Dai-Ichi Kangyo Bank	44.8	Berkshire Hathaway	109.0
Mitsubishi Bank	44.0	Wells Fargo	81.7
Sanwa Bank	41.2	RBS Group	75.1
Nomura Securities	25.5	Fannie Mae	73.2
Long-Term Credit Bank	24.8	UBS AG	67.6
Allianz AG	24.6	J.P. Morgan Chase	66.7
Tokai Bank	21.3	American Express	54.7
Mitsubishi Trust & Banking	17.2	Wachovia	54.2
Deutsche Bank	16.4	Morgan Stanley	49.6
AIG	16.3	Barclays	46.2
Bank of Tokyo	15.9	US Bankcorp	45.5

Data: Morgan Stanley Capital International, 2003.

Table 2-13 Global Financial Services Firms Ranked by Market Value (September 30, 2002, in U.S. $ Billions)

United States		Europe		Rest of World	
Citigroup	150.1	HSBC plc	95.7	Mitsubishi Tokyo	41.9
AIG	142.8	RBS Group plc	54.6	Sumitomo	31.5
GE Capital*	99.3	UBS AG	52.1	NAB	27.9
Berkshire Hathaway	97.4	Lloyds TSB plc	41.2	Nomura	25.7
Bank of America	95.9	Barclays plc	39.6	UFJ	23.3
Wells Fargo	81.8	HBOS Group plc	34.9	Royal Bank	22.4
Wachovia	44.9	BNP Paribas	29.1	Mizuho	22.0
BancOne	43.8	Deutsche Bank AG	28.2	Commonwealth	20.4
American Express	41.4	ING Group	27.6	ANZ	14.4
JP Morgan Chase	37.9	Grupo Santander	24.3	Scotiabank	14.2
Morgan Stanley	37.1	BBVA	23.8	WestPac	13.3
Fifth Third Bancorp	36.7	Crédit Suisse	23.3	Kookmin (Korea)	11.6
US Bancorp	35.6	Unicredito Italiano	22.5	Bank of Montreal	11.4
Goldman Sachs	31.8	Allianz AG	22.2	Toronto Dominion	11.2
Washington Mutual	30.4	Munich Re	18.8	CIBC	9.3

*Earnings volatility-adjusted GECS contribution to GE multiplied by GE market capitalization. Data: Bloomberg.

Moreover, the structural evolution of the industry cuts across both time and geography. Just about all of the top firms in 1990 went though such transactions in the following 10 years, and the same is true of the survivors on the 2002 list. The action is no less dramatic in Europe and Japan than in the United States, although the underlying causes have often been very different.

3

Why Financial Services Mergers?

The first chapter of this book considered how reconfiguration of the financial services sector fits into the process of financial intermediation within national economies and the global economy. The chapter also explored the static and dynamic efficiency attributes that tend to determine which channels of financial intermediation gain or lose market share over time. Financial firms must try to "go with the flow" and position themselves in the intermediation channels that clients are likely to be using in the future, not necessarily those they have used in the past. This usually requires strategic repositioning and restructuring, and one of the tools available for this purpose is M&A activity. The second chapter described the structure of that M&A activity both within and between the four major pillars of the financial sector (commercial banking, securities, insurance, and asset management), as well as domestically and cross-border. The conclusion was that, at least so far, there is no evidence of strategic dominance of multifunctional financial conglomerates over more narrowly focused firms and specialists, or vice versa, as the structural outcome of this process.

So why all the mergers in the financial services sector? As in many other industries, various environmental developments have made existing institutional configurations obsolete in terms of financial firms' competitiveness, growth prospects, and prospective returns to shareholders. We have suggested that regulatory and public policy changes that allow firms broader access to clients, functional lines of activity, or geographic markets may trigger corporate actions in the form of M&A deals. Similarly, technological changes that alter the characteristics of financial services or their distribution are clearly a major factor. So are clients, who often alter their views on the relative value of specific financial services or distribution interfaces with vendors and their willingness to deal with multiple vendors. And the evolution and structure of financial markets make it necessary to adopt broader and sometimes global execution capabilities, as well as the capability of booking larger transactions for individual corporate or institutional clients.

WHAT DOES THE THEORY SAY?

Almost a half-century ago, Miller and Modigliani (1961) pioneered the study of the value of mergers, concluding that the value to an acquirer of taking over an on-going concern could be expressed as the present value of the target's earnings and the discounted growth opportunities the target offers. As long as the expected rate of return on those growth opportunities is greater than the cost of capital, the merged entity creates value and the merger should be considered. Conversely, when the expected rate of return on the growth opportunities is less than the cost of capital, the merged entity destroys value and the merger should not take place.

To earn the above-market rate of return required for mergers to be successful, the combined entity must create new cash flows and thereby enhance the combined value of the merger partners. The cash flows could come from saving direct and indirect costs or from increasing revenues. Key characteristics of mergers such as *inter-industry* versus *intra-industry* mergers and *in-market* versus *market-extending* mergers need to be examined in each case.

Put another way, from the perspective of the shareholder, M&A transactions must contribute to maximizing the franchise value of the combined firm as a going concern. This means maximizing the risk-adjusted present value of expected net future returns. In simple terms, this means maximizing the following total return function:

$$NPV_f = \sum_{t=0}^{n} \frac{E(R_t) - E(C_t)}{(1 + i_t + \alpha_t)^t}$$

where $E(R_t)$ represents the expected future revenues of the firm, $E(C_t)$ represents expected future operating costs including charges to earnings for restructurings, loss provisions, and taxes. The net expected returns in the numerator then must be discounted to the present by using a risk-free rate i_t and a composite risk adjustment α_t, which captures the variance of expected net future returns resulting from credit risk, market risk, operational risk, reputation risk, and so forth.

In an M&A context, the key questions involve how a transaction is likely to affect each of these variables:

- Expected top-line gains represented as increases in $E(R_t)$ due to market-extension, increased market share, wider profit margins, successful cross-selling, and so forth.
- Expected bottom-line gains related to lower costs due to economies of scale or improved operating efficiency, usually reflected in improved cost-to-income ratios.

- Expected reductions in risk associated with improved risk management or diversification of the firm across business streams, client segment, or geographies whose revenue contributions are imperfectly correlated and therefore reduce the composite α_i.

Each of these factors has to be carefully considered in any M&A transaction and their combined impact has to be calibrated against the acquisition price and any potential dilutive effects on shareholders of the acquiring firm. In short, a transaction has to be accretive to shareholders of both firms. If it is not, it is at best a transfer of wealth from the shareholders of one firm to the shareholders of the other.

MARKET EXTENSION

The classic motivation for M&A transactions in the financial services sector is market extension. A firm wants to expand geographically into markets in which it has traditionally been absent or weak. Or it wants to broaden its product range because it sees attractive opportunities that may be complementary to what it is already doing. Or it wants to broaden client coverage, for similar reasons. Any of these moves is open to *build* or *buy* alternatives as a matter of tactical execution. Buying may in many cases be considered faster, more effective, or cheaper than building. Done successfully, such growth through acquisition should be reflected in both the top and bottom lines in terms of the acquiring firm's P&L account and reflected in both market share and profitability.

Figure 3-1A is a graphic depiction of the market for financial services as a matrix of clients, products, and geographies (Walter 1988). Financial institutions clearly will want to allocate available financial, human, and technological resources to those identifiable cells in Figure 3-1A that promise to throw off the highest risk-adjusted returns. In order to do this, they will have to appropriately attribute costs, returns, and risks to specific cells in the matrix. But beyond this, the economics of supplying financial

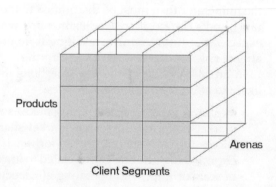

Figure 3-1A. Strategic Positioning.

Products

Arenas

Client Segments

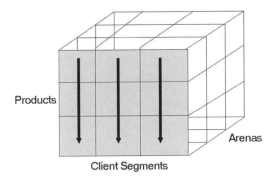

Products

Arenas

Client Segments

Figure 3-1B. **Client-Specific Cost Economies of Scope, Revenue Economies of Scope, and Risk Mitigation.**

services often depend on linkages *between* the cells in a way that maximizes what practitioners and analysts commonly call *synergies.*

Client-driven linkages such as those depicted in Figure 3-1B exist when a financial institution serving a particular client or client group can supply financial services—either to the same client or to another client in the same group—more efficiently. Risk mitigation results from spreading exposures across clients, along with greater earnings stability to the extent that earnings streams from different clients or client segments are not perfectly correlated.

Product-driven linkages depicted in Figure 3-1C exist when an institution can supply a particular financial service in a more competitive manner because it is already producing the same or a similar financial service in a different client dimension. Here again there is risk mitigation to the extent that net revenue streams derived from different products are not perfectly correlated.

Geographic linkages represented in Figure 3-1D are important when an institution can service a particular client or supply a particular service more efficiently in one geography as a result of having an active presence

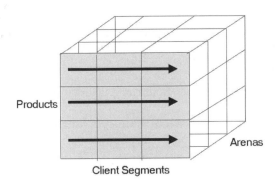

Products

Arenas

Client Segments

Figure 3-1C. **Activity-Specific Economies of Scale and Risk Mitigation.**

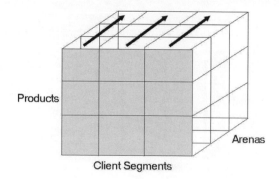

Products

Figure 3-1D. **Client, Product, and Arena-Specific Scale and Scope Economies, and Risk Mitigation.**

Arenas

Client Segments

in another geography. Once again, the risk profile of the firm may be improved to the extent that business is spread across different currencies, macroeconomic and interest-rate environments, and so on.

Even without the complexities of mergers and acquisitions, it is often difficult for major financial services firms to accurately forecast the value to shareholders of initiatives to extend markets. To do so, firms need to understand the competitive dynamics of specific markets (the various cells in Figure 3-1) that are added by market extension—or the costs, including acquisition and integration costs. Especially challenging is the task of optimizing the linkages between the cells to maximize potential joint cost and revenue economies, as discussed below.

ECONOMIES OF SCALE

Whether economies of scale exist in financial services has been at the heart of strategic and regulatory discussions about optimum firm size in the financial services industry. Does increased size, however measured, by itself serve to increase shareholder value? And can increased average size of firms create a more efficient financial sector?

In an information- and distribution-intensive industry with high fixed costs such as financial services, there should be ample potential for scale economies. However, the potential for diseconomies of scale attributable to disproportionate increases in administrative overhead, management of complexity, agency problems, and other cost factors could also occur in very large financial firms. If economies of scale prevail, increased size will help create shareholder value and systemic financial efficiency. If diseconomies prevail, both will be destroyed.

Scale economies should be directly observable in cost functions of financial services suppliers and in aggregate performance measures. Many studies of economies of scale have been undertaken in the banking, insurance, and securities industries over the years—see Saunders and Cornett (2002) for a survey.

Unfortunately, studies of both scale and scope economies in financial services are unusually problematic. The nature of the empirical tests used, the form of the cost functions, the existence of unique optimum output levels, and the optimizing behavior of financial firms all present difficulties. Limited availability and conformity of data create serious empirical problems. And the conclusion of any study that has detected (or failed to detect) economies of scale or scope in a sample selection of financial institutions does not necessarily have general applicability. Nevertheless, the impact on the operating economics (production functions) of financial firms is so important—and so often used to justify mergers, acquisitions, and other strategic initiatives—that available empirical evidence is central to the whole argument.

Estimated cost functions form the basis of most empirical tests, virtually all of which have found that economies of scale are achieved with increases in size among small banks (below $100 million in asset size). A few studies have shown that scale economies may also exist in banks falling into the $100 million to $5 billion range. There is very little evidence so far of scale economies in the case of banks larger than $5 billion. More recently, there is some scattered evidence of scale-related cost gains of up to 20% for banks up to $25 billion in size (Berger and Mester 1997). But according to a survey of all empirical studies of economies of scale through 1998, there was no evidence of such economies among very large banks (Berger, Demsetz, and Strahan 1998). The consensus seems to be that scale economies and diseconomies generally do not result in more than about 5% difference in unit costs.

The inability to find major economies of scale among large financial services firms also pertains to insurance companies (Cummins and Zi 1998) and broker-dealers (Goldberg, Hanweck, Keenan, and Young 1991). Lang and Wetzel (1998) even found diseconomies of scale in both banking and securities services among German universal banks.

Except the very smallest banks and non-bank financial firms, scale economies seem likely to have relatively little bearing on competitive performance. This is particularly true since smaller institutions are often linked together in cooperatives or other structures that allow harvesting available economies of scale centrally, or are specialists not particularly sensitive to the kinds of cost differences usually associated with economies of scale in the financial services industry. Megamergers are unlikely to contribute—whatever their other merits may be—very much in terms of scale economies unless the fabled "economies of superscale" associated with financial behemoths turn out to exist. These economies, like the abominable snowman, so far have never been observed in nature.

A basic problem may be that most studies focus entirely on firmwide scale economies. The really important scale issues are likely to be encountered at the level of individual financial services. There is ample evidence, for example, that economies of scale are both significant and important for operating economies and competitive performance in areas such as global custody, processing of mass-market credit card transactions, and institutional asset management but are far less important in other areas— private banking and M&A advisory services, for example.

Unfortunately, empirical data on cost functions that would permit identification of economies of scale at the product level are generally proprietary and therefore publicly unavailable. Still, it seems reasonable that a scale-driven M&A strategy may make a great deal of sense in specific areas of financial activity even in the absence of evidence that there is very much to be gained at the firmwide level. And the fact that there are some lines of activity that clearly benefit from scale economies while at the same time observations of firmwide economies of scale are empirically elusive suggests that there must be numerous lines of activity where *diseconomies* of scale exist.

COST ECONOMIES OF SCOPE

M&A activity may also be aimed at exploiting the potential for economies of scope in the financial services sector—competitive benefits to be gained by selling a broader rather than narrower range of products—which may arise either through cost or revenue linkages.

Cost economies of scope suggest that the joint production of two or more products or services is accomplished more cheaply than producing them separately. "Global" scope economies become evident on the cost side when the total cost of producing all products is less than producing them individually, whereas "activity-specific" economies consider the joint production of particular financial services. On the supply side, banks can create cost savings through the sharing of transactions systems and other overheads, information and monitoring cost, and the like.

Other cost economies of scope relate to information—specifically, information about each of the three dimensions of the strategic matrix (clients, products, and geographic arenas). Each dimension can embed specific information, which, if it can be organized and interpreted effectively within and between the three dimensions, could result in a significant source of competitive advantage to broad-scope financial firms. Information can be reused, thereby avoiding cost duplication, facilitating creativity in developing solutions to client problems, and leveraging client-specific information in order to facilitate cross-selling. And there are contracting costs that can be avoided by clients dealing with a single financial firm (Stefanadis 2002).

Cost diseconomies of scope may arise from such factors as inertia and lack of responsiveness and creativity. Such disenconomies may arise from increased firm size and bureaucratization, "turf" and profit-attribution conflicts that increase costs or erode product quality in meeting client needs, or serious conflicts of interest or cultural differences across the organization that inhibit seamless delivery of a broad range of financial services.

Like economies of scale, cost-related scope economies and diseconomies should be directly observable in cost functions of financial services suppliers and in aggregate performance measures.

Most empirical studies have failed to find cost economies of scope in the banking, insurance, or securities industries. The preponderance of such studies has concluded that some diseconomies of scope are encountered when firms in the financial services sector add new product ranges to their portfolios. Saunders and Walter (1994), for example, found negative cost economies of scope among the world's 200 largest banks; as the product range widens, unit-costs seem to go up. Cost-scope economies in most other studies of the financial services industry are either trivial or negative (Saunders & Cornett 2002).

However, many of these studies involved institutions that were shifting away from a pure focus on banking or insurance, and may thus have incurred considerable start-up costs in expanding the range of their activities. If the diversification effort in fact involved significant front-end costs that were expensed on the accounting statements during the period under study, we might expect to see any strong statistical evidence of diseconomies of scope (for example, between lending and nonlending activities of banks) reversed in future periods once expansion of market-share or increases in fee-based areas of activity have appeared in the revenue flow. If current investments in staffing, training, and infrastructure ultimately bear returns commensurate with these expenditures, neutral or positive cost economies of scope may well exist. Still, the available evidence remains inconclusive.

OPERATING EFFICIENCIES

Besides economies of scale and cost economies of scope, financial firms of roughly the same size and providing roughly the same range of services can have very different cost levels per unit of output. There is ample evidence of such performance differences, for example, in comparative cost-to-income ratios among banks and insurance companies and investment firms of comparable size, both within and between national financial services markets. The reasons involve differences in production functions, efficiency, and effectiveness in the use of labor and capital; sourcing and application of available technology; as well as acquisition of inputs, organizational design, compensation, and incentive systems—that is, in just plain better management—what economists call X-efficiencies.

Empirically, a number of authors have found very large disparities in cost structures among banks of similar size, suggesting that the way banks are run is more important than their size or the selection of businesses that they pursue (Berger, Hancock, and Humphrey 1993; Berger, Hunter, and Timme 1993). The consensus of studies conducted in the United States seems to be that average unit costs in the banking industry lie some 20% above "best practice" firms producing the same range and volume of services, with most of the difference attributable to operating economies rather than differences in the cost of funds (Akhavein, Berger, and Humphrey 1997). Siems (1996) found that the greater the overlap in branch office networks, the higher the abnormal equity returns in U.S. bank mergers, although no such abnormal returns are associated with increasing concentration levels in the regions where the bank mergers occurred. This suggests that any gains in shareholder-value in many of the financial services mergers of the 1990s were associated more with increases in X-efficiency than with merger-related reductions in competition.

If very large institutions are systematically better managed than smaller ones (which may be difficult to document in the real world of financial services), there might conceivably be a link between firm size and X-efficiency. In any case, from both a systemic and shareholder-value perspective, management is (or should be) under constant pressure through boards of directors to do better, maximize X-efficiency in their organizations, and transmit that pressure throughout the enterprise.

Table 3-1 presents cost savings in the case of three major U.S. M&A transactions in the late 1990s: Nations Bank–Bank of America, BancOne–First Chicago NBD, and Citicorp–Travelers. In each case the cost economies were attributed by management to elimination of redundant branches (mainly BancOne–First Chicago NBD), elimination of redundant capacity in transactions processing and information technology, consolidation of administrative functions, and cost economies of scope (mainly Citigroup). Despite the aforementioned evidence, each announcement also noted economies of scale in a prominent way, although most of the purported "scale" gains probably represented X-efficiency benefits. In any case the predicted cost gains on a capitalized basis were very significant indeed for shareholders in the first two cases, but less so in the case of the formation of Citigroup because of the complementary nature of the legacy Citicorp and Travelers businesses.

It is also possible that very large organizations may be more capable of the massive and "lumpy" capital outlays required to install and

Table 3-1 Purported Scale and X-Efficiency Gains in Selected U.S. Bank Mergers

Bank	Announced Savings	Blended Multiple	Potential Share Value Gains
BankAmerica	$1.3 billion over 2 years after tax	17× trailing earnings	$22.1 billion on $133 billion M-cap (17 %)
BancOne	$600 million	17×	$10.2 billion on $65 billion M-cap (16 %)
Citigroup	$930 million	15×	$14.0 billion on $168 billion M-cap (8%)

maintain the most efficient information-technology and transactions-processing infrastructures (these issues are discussed in greater detail in Chapter 5). If spending extremely large amounts on technology results in greater operating efficiency, large financial services firms will tend to benefit in competition with smaller ones. However, smaller organizations ought to be able to pool their resources or outsource certain scale-sensitive activities in order to capture similar gains.

REVENUE ECONOMIES OF SCOPE

On the revenue side, economies of scope attributable to cross-selling arise when the overall cost to the buyer of multiple financial services from a single supplier is less than the cost of purchasing them from separate suppliers. These expenses include the cost of the service plus information, search, monitoring, contracting, and other transaction costs. Revenue-diseconomies of scope could arise, for example, through agency costs that may develop when the multiproduct financial firm acts against the interests of the client in the sale of one service in order to facilitate the sale of another, or as a result of internal information transfers considered inimical to the client's interests.

Managements of universal banks and financial conglomerates often argue that broader product and client coverage, and the increased throughput volume or margins such coverage makes possible, leads to shareholder-value enhancement. Hence, on net, revenue economies of scope are highly positive.

Demand-side economies of scope include the ability of clients to take care of a broad range of financial needs through one institution—a convenience that may mean they are willing to pay a premium. Banks that offer both commercial banking and investment banking services to their clients can theoretically achieve economies of scope in several ways. For example, when commercial banks enter new activities such as underwriting securities, they may also be able to take advantage of risk-management techniques they have developed as a result of making loans. Moreover, firms that are diversified into several types of activities or several geographic areas tend to have more contact points with clients.

Commercial banks may also benefit from economies of scope by underwriting and selling insurance. Lewis (1990) emphasizes the similarities between banking and insurance by suggesting how the very nature of financial intermediation provides insurance to depositors and borrowers. In retail banking, for example, banks issue contracts to depositors that are similar to insurance policies. Both depositors and insured entities have a claim against the respective institution upon demand (in the case of depositors) or upon the occurrence of some event (in the case of those insured). The institution has no control over when the clients demand their claims and must be able to meet the obligations whenever they arise.

Both types of institutions rely on the law of large numbers. As long as the pool of claimants is large enough, not all will request payment simultaneously.

The banking-insurance cross-selling arguments have continued both operationally and factually. Credit Suisse paid $8.8 billion for Winterthur, Switzerland's second largest insurer, in 1997. The Fortis Group combines banking and insurance, albeit unevenly, in the Benelux countries. The ING Group is the product of a banking-insurance merger that has since acquired the U.S. insurer ReliaStar and the financial services units of Aetna. Allianz has acquired Dresdner Bank AG.

On the positive side, it is argued that there is real diversification across the two businesses, so that unit-linked life insurance is strong in bullish stock markets as funds flow out of bank savings products, and vice versa in down stock markets, for example. Capital can be deployed more productively in bancassurers, which are in any case less risky and less capital intensive than pure insurance companies. And it seems cross selling actually works well in countries like Belguim and Spain.

On the negative side, it is argued that banking and insurance are difficult and not particularly profitable to cross-sell, and that dual capabilities don't help much in building market share against pure banking or insurance rivals. They have very different time horizons and capital requirements, and it is hard to argue that there are major gains in scale economies or operating efficiencies. It is also suggested that there are hidden correlations that make bancassurers more risky than they seem—in the stock market of the early 2000s, for example, insurance reserves, asset management fees, and underwriting and advisory revenues all collapsed at the same time, causing massive share price losses among bancassurers. Citigroup's spinoff of its nonlife business in 2002 suggests that management sees little to be gained in retaining that business from a shareholder value perspective.

Most empirical studies of revenue gains involving cross-selling are based on survey data and are therefore difficult to generalize. For example, Figure 3-2 shows the results of a 2001 survey of corporate clients by Greenwich Research on the importance of revenue economies of scope between lending and M&A advisory services. The issue is whether companies are more likely to award M&A advisory work to banks that are also willing lenders or whether the two services are separable, so that companies go to the firms with the perceived best M&A capabilities (probably investment banking houses) for advice and to others (presumably commercial banks) for loans. Survey data seem to suggest that companies view these services as a single value-chain, so that banks that are willing to provide significant lending are also more likely to obtain M&A advisory work. Indeed, Table 3-2 suggests that well over half of the major M&A firms (in terms of fees) in 2001 were indeed investment banking units of commercial banks with substantial lending power.

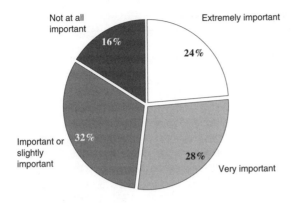

Figure 3-2. Importance of Lending to Earn M&A Business. Base: 626 U.S. Companies. Source: *Greenwich Associates, 2002.*

This process is sometimes called *mixed bundling*, meaning that the price of one service (for example, commercial lending) is dependent on the clients' also taking another service (for example, M&A advice or securities underwriting). However, making the sale of one contingent on the sale of the second (*tying*) is illegal in the United States. Modeling of client preferences is said to be easier in broad-gauge financial firms and provides the client with significantly lower search and contracting costs. But mixed-bundling approaches to client services probably contributed so some disastrous lending by commercial banks in the energy and telecom sectors in recent years. "Monoline" investment banks were derided by some of the large commercial banks with investment banking divisions as being

Table 3-2 Comparative Wholesale Banking Volumes (Cumulative 2000–2002)

Firm	Rank	Share	Volume
JP Morgan Chase*	1	11.99	3,980
Citigroup*	2	11.80	3,915
Merrill Lynch	3	9.92	3,292
Goldman Sachs	4	9.86	3,273
Morgan Stanley	5	9.85	3,146
CSFB*	6	8.37	2,812
Deutsche Bank*	7	5.67	1,882
UBS*	8	5.51	1,713
Lehman Brothers	9	5.16	1,713
Banc of America Securities*	10	4.81	1,596
Dresdner Kleinwort Wasserstein*	11	3.31	1,099
Barclays Capital*	12	2.28	757

*Denotes firms combining commercial banking and securities activities.

Table 3-3 Potential for Cross-selling: Citigroup Product Lines

Distribution Channels	Citibank Branches	Commercial Credit	Primerica Financial Services	Private Bank	Retail Securities	Insur. Agents	Tel. Marketing
Checking	CCI¹			CCI			TRV CCI
Credit cards	CCI		TRV	CCI	TRV		
Loans/mortgage	CCI	TRV	TRV	CCI	TRV		TRV CCI
Life insurance			TRV		TRV	TRV	TRV CCI
Home insurance		TRV	TRV			TRV	TRV CCI
Vehicle insurance		TRV	TRV			TRV	
Long-term care					TRV	TRV	
Mutual funds	CCI		TRV		TRV	TRV	
Annuities	CCI		TRV		TRV	TRV	
Wrap fee					TRV		
Securities broker-age				CCI	TRV		

¹CCI = Citicorp, TRV = Travelers.
Source: Citicorp, 1998.

incapable of providing the full value chain of investment banking services. The derision disappeared soon thereafter. The bankruptcies of Enron, WorldCom, Global Crossing, K-Mart, and Adelphia and credit problems in a host of other firms in the United States and elsewhere even led to speculation of future breakups of multiline wholesale financial services firms.

However, it is at the retail level that the bulk of the revenue economies of scope are likely to materialize, since the search costs and contracting costs of retail customers are likely to be higher than for corporate customers. As Table 3-3 suggests, the 1998 merger of Travelers and Citicorp to form Citigroup was largely revenue-driven to take maximum advantage of the two firms' strengths in products and distribution channels, as well as geographic coverage. In general, this is the basis of the European concept of *bancassurance* or *Allfinanz*—that is, cross-selling, notably between banking and insurance services.

A survey of U.S. households conducted at about the time of the Citigroup merger suggested that the apparent value of that deal in terms of revenue economies of scope was quite sound. Even though U.S. banking, securities, and insurance had long been separated by regulations dating back to the 1930s, a large-sample study of U.S. households revealed a willingness, perhaps enthusiasm, to have all financial needs provided by a single vendor (Figure 3-3). That is, the reduced search, transactions and contracting costs were perceived to yield substantial benefits to households.

Yet the same study also showed that respondents were concerned about

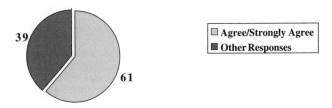

Figure 3-3. "I Would Prefer To Have All My Needs Met By One Financial Institution." Source: Council on Financial Competition Research, 1998.

whether they were in fact getting the best price, quality, and services from a single multifunction vendor, and whether that vendor would be able to cover all of the household's financial services needs. This is shown in Table 3-4. Whether justified or not, these kinds of concerns are perceptual ("the grass is always greener . . .") and may affect the prospects for revenue economies of scope in a particular financial services merger. The same survey suggested that the respondents were in fact using more rather than fewer financial services vendors, a finding that undercuts the argument that there is perceived client value in single-source procurement of financial services (Figure 3-4).

This sort of evidence suggests that U.S. households are more opportunistic and willing to shop around than the most ardent advocates of cross-selling would hope. Thus, the "share of wallet" that financial services vendors expect to achieve by broadening their product range may in the end be disappointing. This sort of conclusion may, of course, be different in other environments, particularly in Europe where universal banking and multifunctional financial conglomerates have always been part of the financial landscape. But even here the evidence of effective

Table 3-4 Perceived Benefits and Drawbacks of Cross-selling

Benefits (among households using more than one institution	Rank	%	Drawbacks (among households using more than one institution	Rank	%
It would be convenient to deal with one institution	1	54.2	The institution may not offer me the best prices	1	56.7
It would be easier to deal with one institution (would simplify my life)	2	45.7	The institution may not offer all the products my households need	2	46.6

Source: Council on Financial Competition Research, 1998.

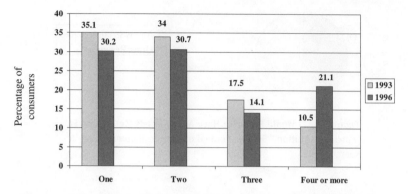

Figure 3-4. With How Many Financial Providers Do You Currently Hold Relationships? Source: Council on Financial Competition Research, 1998.

cross-selling and leveraging the value of firms through revenue economies of scope is spotty, at best.

Taken to its extreme, the future could well belong to a very different household financial services business model, perhaps one like that depicted in Figure 3-5. Here households take advantage of user-friendly interfaces to access Web service servers and integrated financial services platforms. These platforms, early versions of which are already in use, allow real-time linkages to multiple financial services vendors, such as Yodlee.com and Myciti.com. For the client, such platforms combine the "feel" of single-source purchasing of financial services while accessing best-in-class vendors on an open-architecture basis. The client, in other words, is cross-purchasing rather than being cross-sold.

Absent the need for continuous financial advice, such a business model can reduce information costs, transactions costs, and contracting costs while providing efficient access to the universe of competing vendors. Even advice could be built into the model through independent financial advisers (IFAs) or financial services suppliers who find a way to incorporate the advisory function through such delivery portals. If in the future such models of retail financial services delivery take hold in the market, some of the rationale for cross-selling and revenue economies of scope used to justify financial-sector mergers and acquisitions will clearly become obsolete.

Despite an almost total lack of hard empirical evidence, revenue economies of scope may indeed exist. But these economies are likely to be very specific to the types of services provided and the types of clients served. Strong cross-selling potential may exist for retail and private clients between banking, insurance, and asset management products, for example. Yet such potential may be totally absent between trade finance

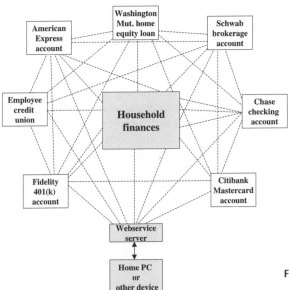

Figure 3-5. **Prototype On-Line Personal Finance Platform**.

and mergers and acquisitions advisory services for major corporate clients. So revenue-related scope economies are clearly linked to a firm's specific strategic positioning across clients, products, and geographic areas of operation as depicted in Figure 3-1 (Walter, 1988).

Indeed, a principal objective of strategic positioning is to link market segments together in a coherent pattern. Such *strategic integrity* permits maximum exploitation of cross-selling opportunities, particularly in the design of incentives and organizational structures to ensure that such exploitation actually occurs. Without such incentive arrangements, which have to be extremely granular to motivate people doing the cross-selling, no amount of management pressure and exhortation to cross-sell is likely to achieve its objectives. These linkages are often extraordinarily difficult to achieve and must work against corporate and institutional clients who are willing to obtain services from several vendors, as well as new-generation retail clients who are comfortable with nontraditional approaches to distribution such as the Internet. In cross-selling, as always, the devil is in the details.

Network economics may be considered a special type of demand-side economy of scope (Economides 1996). Like telecommunications, banking relationships with end users of financial services represent a network structure wherein additional client linkages add value to existing clients by increasing the feasibility or reducing the cost of accessing them. So-called "network externalities" tend to increase with the absolute size of the network itself. Every client link to the bank potentially complements every other one and thus potentially adds value through either one-way or two-way exchanges through incremental information or access to liquidity.

The size of network benefits depends on technical compatibility and coordination in time and location, which the universal bank is in a position to provide. And networks tend to be self-reinforcing in that they require a minimum critical mass and tend to grow in dominance as they increase in size, thus precluding perfect competition in network-driven financial services. This characteristic is evident in activities such as securities clearance and settlement, global custody, funds transfer and international cash management, forex and securities dealing, and the like. And networks tend to lock in users insofar as switching-costs tend to be relatively high, thus creating the potential for significant market power.

IMPACT OF MERGERS ON MARKET POWER AND PROSPECTIVE MARKET STRUCTURES

Taken together, the foregoing analysis suggests rather limited prospects for firmwide cost economies of scale and scope among major financial services firms as a result of M&A transactions. Operating economies (X-efficiency) seems to be the principal determinant of observed differences in cost levels among banks and nonbank financial institutions. Demand-side or revenue-economies of scope through cross-selling may well exist, but they are likely to be applied very differently to specific client segments and can be vulnerable to erosion due to greater client promiscuity in response to sharper competition and new distribution technologies. However, there are other reasons M&A transactions may make economic sense.

In addition to the strategic search for operating economies and revenue synergies, financial services firms will also seek to dominate markets in order to extract economic returns. By focusing on a particular market, merging financial firms could increase their market power and thereby take advantage of monopolistic or oligopolistic returns. Market power allows firms to charge more or pay less for the same service. In many market environments, however, antitrust constraints ultimately tend to limit the increases in market power. Managers of financial services firms often believe that the end game in competitive structure is the emergence of a few firms in gentlemanly competition with each other, throwing off nice sustainable margins. In the real world such an outcome can easily trigger public policy reactions that break up financial firms, force functional spinoffs, and try to restore vigorous competition. Particularly in a critical economic sector that is easily politicized, such as financial services, such reactions are rather likely, despite furious lobbying by the affected firms.

The role of concentration and market power in the financial services industry is an issue that empirical studies have not yet examined in great depth. However, suppliers in many national markets for financial services have shown a tendency toward oligopoly. Supporters have argued that high levels of national market concentration are necessary in order to provide a platform for a viable competitive position. Without convincing evidence of scale economies or other size-related gains, opponents argue that monopolistic market structures serve mainly to extract economic rents from consumers or users of financial services and redistribute them to shareholders, cross-subsidize other areas of activity, or reduce pressures for cost containment. They therefore advocate vigorous antitrust action to prevent exploitation of monopoly positions in the financial services sector.

A good example occurred late in 1998 when the Canadian Finance Ministry rejected merger applications submitted by Royal Bank of Canada and Bank of Montreal (Canada's largest and third-largest banks), as well as by Canadian Imperial Bank of Commerce and Toronto Dominion Bank (the second and fifth largest). Only Scotiabank (the fourth largest) did not apply to merge. The mergers would have left just three major banks in Canada, already one of the most highly concentrated banking markets in the world, two of which would have controlled over 70% of all bank assets in the country. The banks justified their proposed mergers in terms of prospective scale and efficiency gains and the need to compete with U.S. banks under the rules of the North American Free Trade Agreement (NAFTA), which would at the same time provide the necessary competitive pressure to prevent exploitation of monopoly power.

Concerns about the wisdom of the two mergers were expressed by the Ministry of Finance and the Canadian Federal Competition Bureau, specifically regarding access to credit by small businesses, branch closings in suburban and rural areas, excessive control over the credit card and retail brokerage businesses, concentration of economic power, reduced competition in banking generally, and problems of prudential control and supervision. Instead, a subsequent task force report noted that it was time to let foreign banks expand operations in Canada, allow banks and trust companies to offer insurance and auto leasing services, make the disclosure of service fees clearer and privacy laws stricter, and create an ombudsman to oversee the financial sector—hardly the reaction the banks proposing the mergers had in mind.

The key strategic issue is the likely future competitive structure in the different dimensions of the financial services industry. It is an empirical fact that operating margins tend to be positively associated with higher concentration levels. Financial services market structures differ substantially as measured, for example, by the Herfindahl-Hirshman Index (HHI), which is the sum of the squared market shares ($H=\Sigma s^2$), where $0<HHI<10,000$ and market shares are measured, for example, by deposits, assets, or capital. HHI rises as the number of competitors declines and as market share concentration rises among a given number of competitors. Empirically, higher values of HHI tend to be associated with higher degrees of pricing power, price-cost margins, and return on equity across a broad range of industries, as shown in Figure 3-6. HHI is, of course, highly

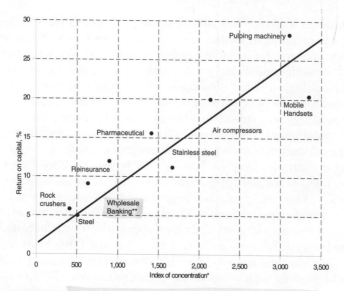

Figure 3-6. **Global Levels of Concentration and Return on Invested Capital Across Industries. (*Sum of the squares of competitors' market shares. **Ten-year average, estimated on allocated capital.) Source: J. P. Morgan and author estimates.**

sensitive to the definition of the market and pressuposes that this definition is measurable.

An interesting historical example of the effects of market concentration is provided by Saunders and Wilson (1999) and reproduced in Figure 3-7. During the 1920s, the U.K. government designated a limited number of clearing banks with a special position in the British financial system. Spreads between deposit rates and lending rates in the United Kingdom quickly rose, as did the ratio of market value to book value of the designated banks' equities. Both were apparently a reflection of increased market power, in this case conferred by the government itself. Then, in the 1960s and 1970s this market power eroded with U.K. financial deregulation, as did the market-to-book ratio.

Geographically, there are in fact very high levels of banking concentration in countries such as the Netherlands, Finland, and Denmark and low levels in relatively fragmented financial systems such as the United States and Germany. In some cases, public sector institutions such as postal savings banks and state banks tend to distort competitive conditions, as do financial services cooperatives and mutuals—all of which can command substantial client loyalty. But then, nobody said that the financial services industry has to be the exclusive province of investor-owned firms, and other forms of organization long thought obsolete (such as coopera-

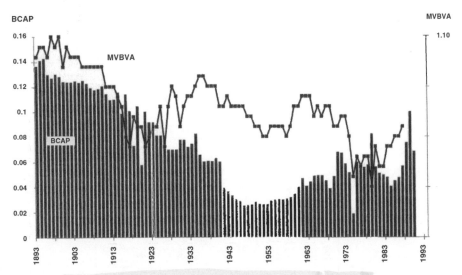

Figure 3-7. Market and Book Value of U.K. Bank Assets, 1893–1993. MVBVA = Ratio of the market value of assets to the book value of assets. BCAP = Book value of capital. Source: Anthony Saunders and Berry Wilson, "The Impact of Consolidation and Safety-Net Support on Canadian, U.S. and U.K. Banks, 1893–1992, *Journal of Banking and Finance*, 23 (1999), pp. 537–571.

tives in Europe and credit unions in the United States) have continued to exist and often to prosper.

Despite very substantial consolidation in recent years within perhaps the most concentrated segment of the financial services industry—namely, wholesale banking and capital markets activities—there is little evidence of market power. With some 80% of the combined value of global fixed-income and equity underwriting, loan syndications and M&A mandates captured by the top ten firms, according to Smith and Walter (2003) the Herfindahl-Hirshman index was still only 549 in 2002 (on a scale from zero to 10,000). (See Table 3-5.) This finding suggests a ruthlessly competitive market structure in most of these businesses, which is reflected in the returns to investors in the principal players in the industry.

Nor is there much evidence so far that size as conventionally measured (for example, by assets or capital base) makes a great deal of difference so far in determining wholesale banking market share. The result seems to be quite the opposite, with a long-term erosion of returns on capital invested in the wholesale banking industry, as suggested in Figure 3-8.

Furthermore, there are a variety of other businesses that combine various functions and show very few signs of increasing competition. An example of such a business is asset management, in which the top firms are European, American, and Japanese firms that function as banks,

Table 3-5 Global Wholesale Banking and Investment Banking Market Concentration

	1990	1991	1992	1993	1994	1995	1996	1997	1998	1999	2000	2001	2002
Top Ten Firms													
% of market share	40.6	46.1	56.0	64.2	62.1	59.5	55.9	72.0	77.9	77.0	80.0	74.12	71.3
Herfindahl Index	171.6	230.6	327.8	459.4	434.1	403.0	464.6	572.1	715.9	664.0	744.0	603.0	549.4
Number of Firms from													
United States	5	7	5	9	9	9	8	8	7	8	8	7	7
Europe	5	3	5	1	1	1	2	2	3	2	2	3	3
Japan	0	0	0	0	0	0	0	0	0	0	0	0	0
Top Twenty Firms													
% of market share			80.5	75.6	78.1	76.0	81.2	93.3	97.1	96.3	97.5	91.5	91.0
Herfindahl Index			392.7	478.4	481.4	439.5	517.6	620.9	764.0	709.0	784.0	639.0	591.1
Number of Firms from													
United States			8	15	15	14	14	13	11	12	9	8	10
Europe			11	4	5	5	6	7	8	8	11	11	10
Japan			1	1	0	1	0	0	1	0	1	1	0

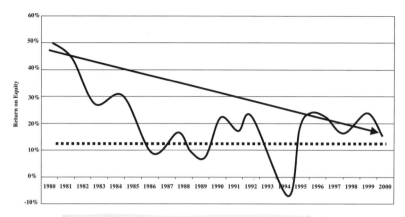

Figure 3-8. Large Investment Banks' Return on Equity (1980–2001). Source: Sanford Bernstein, 2002.

broker-dealers, independent fund management companies, and insurance companies. Asset management is among the most contestable in the entire financial services industry with a Herfindahl-Hirshman index of 540 for the top 40 firms in the industry, and shows very few signs of increasing concentration in recent years.

Although some national markets may be highly concentrated and exhibit signs that market power can be exploited by financial services firms to the advantage of their shareholders, there seems to be little sign of this in the United States, so far despite the decline in the number of banking organizations from almost 15,000 to about 8,000 over a decade or so and the development of a number of powerful national and regional players in areas such as credit cards, mortgage origination, and custody (see Figure 3-9).

In short, although monopoly power created through mergers and acquisitions in the financial services industry can produce market conditions to reallocate gains from clients to the owners of financial intermediaries, such conditions are not easy to achieve or to sustain. Sometimes new players—even relatively small new entrants—penetrate the market and destroy oligopolistic pricing structures, or there are good substitutes available from other types of financial services firms, and consumers are willing to shop around. Vigorous competition (and low Herfindahl-Hirshman indexes) seems to be maintained even after intensive M&A activity in most cases by a relatively even distribution of market shares among the leading firms, as in the case of global wholesale banking, noted earlier.

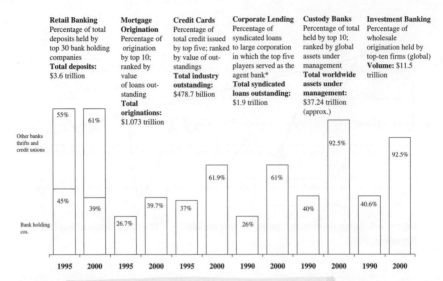

Figure 3-9. **Financial Services Concentration Ratios in the United States** (* the agent bank arranges a financing pool in which other banks participate). Sources: First Manhattan Consulting Group; Inside Mortgage Finance; the Nilson Report; Loan Pricing Corp.; Federal Reserve; Institutional Investor.

ASYMMETRIC INFORMATION, KNOW-HOW, AND EMBEDDED HUMAN CAPITAL

One argument in favor of mergers and acquisitions in the financial services industry is that internal information flows in large, geographically dispersed, and multifunctional financial firms are substantially better and involve lower costs than external information flows in the market that are available to more narrowly focused firms. Consequently, a firm that is present in a broad range of financial markets and geographies can find proprietary and client-driven trading and product-structuring opportunities that smaller and narrower firms cannot. Furthermore, an acquisition that adds to breadth of coverage should be value-enhancing by improving market share or pricing if the incremental access to information can be effectively leveraged.

A second argument has to do with technical know-how. Significant areas of financial services—particularly wholesale banking and asset management—have become the realm of highly specialized expertise. An acquisition of a specialized firm by a larger, broader, more heavily capitalized firm can provide substantial revenue-related gains through both market share and price effects. As noted in Chapter 2, in the late 1990s and early 2000s large numbers of financial boutiques and independent securities firms have been acquired by major banks, insurance companies, the major investment banks, and asset managers for precisely this purpose, and anecdotal evidence suggests that in many cases these acquisitions have been shareholder-value enhancing for the buyer. This success has also been seen in other industries, such as biotech. The key almost always lies in the integration process and in the incentive structures set in place to leverage the technical skills that have been acquired.

Closely aligned is the human capital argument. Technical skills and entrepreneurial behavior are embodied in people, and people can move. Parts of the financial services industry have become notorious for the mobility of talent, to the point that free agency has characterized employee behavior and individuals or teams of people almost view themselves as "firms within firms." Hiring of teams has at times become akin to buying small firms for their technical expertise, although losing them (unlike corporate divestitures) usually generates no compensation whatsoever. In many cases the default question is "Why stay?" as opposed to the more conventional, "Why leave?"

It is in this context of high-mobility of embedded human capital that merger integration, approaches to compensation, and efforts to create a cohesive "superculture" appear to be of paramount importance. These issues are discussed in the next chapter, and take on particular pertinence in the context of M&A transactions, where in the worst case the acquiring firm loses much talent after paying a rich price to buy a target.

DIVERSIFICATION OF BUSINESS STREAMS, CREDIT QUALITY, AND FINANCIAL STABILITY

One of the arguments for financial sector mergers is that greater diversification of income from multiple products, client-groups, and geographies creates more stable, safer, and ultimately more valuable institutions. Symptoms should include higher credit quality and debt ratings and therefore lower costs of financing than those faced by narrower, more focused firms.

Past research suggests that M&A transactions neither increase nor decrease the risk of the acquiring firm (Amihud et al. 2002), possibly because risk-diversification attributes (such as cross-border deals) have played a limited role in banking so far. Regulatory constraints that limit access to client-groups or types of financial services could have similar effects.

It has also been argued that shares of multifunctional financial firms incorporate substantial franchise value due to their conglomerate nature and their importance in national economies. However, Demsetz, Saidenberg, and Strahan (1996) suggest that this guaranteed franchise value serves to inhibit extraordinary risk taking. They find substantial evidence that the higher a bank's franchise value, the more prudent management tends to be. Thus, large universal banks with high franchise values should serve shareholder interests, as well as stability of the financial system and the concerns of its regulators, with a strong focus on risk management, as opposed to banks with little to lose. This conclusion, however, is at

variance with the observed, massive losses incurred by European universal banks in recent years in lending to highly leveraged firms, real estate
lending and emerging market transactions, and by U.S. financial conglomerates that in the early 2000s found themselves in the middle of an epic
wave of corporate scandals, bankruptcies, and reorganizations.

TOO BIG TO FAIL GUARANTEES

Certainly the failure of any major financial institution, including one that
is the product a string of mergers, could cause unacceptable systemic
consequences. Therefore, the institution is virtually certain to be bailed
out by taxpayers—as happened in the case of comparatively much smaller
institutions in the United States, France, Switzerland, Norway, Sweden,
Finland, and Japan during the 1980s and 1990s. Consequently, too-
big-to-fail (TBTF) guarantees create a potentially important public subsidy for the kinds of large financial organizations that often result from
mergers.

In the United States, this policy became explicit in 1984 when the U.S.
Comptroller of the Currency, who regulates national banks, testified to
Congress that 11 banks were so important that they would not be permitted to fail (see O'Hara and Shaw 1990). In other countries the same
kind of policy tends to exist and seems to cover more banks (see U.S.
GAO 1991). The policy was arguably extended to non-bank financial firms
in the rescue of Long-term Capital Management, Inc. in 1998, which was
arranged by the U.S. Federal Reserve. The Fed stepped in because, it
argued, the firm's failure could cause systemic damage to the global
financial system. The same argument was made by J.P. Morgan, Inc. in
1996 about the global copper market and the suggestion by one of its
then-dominant traders, Sumitomo, that collapse of the copper price could
have serious systemic effects. Indeed, the speed with which the central
banks and regulatory authorities reacted to that particular crisis signaled
the possibility of safety-net support of the global copper market, in view
of major banks' massive exposures in complex structured credits to the
copper industry. Most of the time such bail-out arguments are self-serving
nonsense, but in a political environment and apparent market crisis they
could help create a public-sector safety net sufficiently broad to limit
damage to shareholders of exposed banks or other financial firms.

It is generally accepted that the larger the bank, the more likely it is to
be covered under TBTF support. O'Hara and Shaw (1990) detailed the
benefits of being TBTF: without assurances, uninsured depositors and
other liability holders demand a risk premium. When a bank is not permitted to fail, the risk premium is no longer necessary. Furthermore, banks
covered under the policy have an incentive to increase their risk so as to
enjoy higher expected returns. Mergers may push banks into this desirable
category. The larger the resulting institution, therefore, the more attractive

will be an equity stake in the firm and the higher should be the abnormal return to shareholders upon the merger announcement.

Kane (2000) investigated the possibility that large bank mergers enjoy not only increased access to TBTF guarantees but also greater market power and political clout. He finds that the market reacts positively when two large U.S. banks announce a merger, especially if they are headquartered in the same state. Acquirers can increase the value of government guarantees even further by engaging in derivatives transactions. Such instruments increase the volatility of a bank's earnings, volatility that is not fully reflected in the share price if the institution is judged too big to fail. Although Kane's study did not distinguish between the market reacting to increased TBTF guarantees or increased efficiency, he pointed out that long-term efficiency has seldom materialized after mergers. He suggested further study to determine whether acquiring banks increase their leverage, uninsured liabilities, nonperforming loans, and other risk exposures, all of which would suggest that they are taking advantage of the TBTF guarantees.

One problem with the TBTF argument is to determine precisely when a financial institution becomes too big to fail. Citicorp was already the largest bank holding company in the United States before it merged with Travelers. Therefore, the TBTF argument may be a matter of degree. That is, the benefits of becoming larger may be marginal if financial firms already enjoy TBTF status.

CONFLICTS OF INTEREST

The potential for conflicts of interest is endemic in all multifunctional financial services firms (see Saunders and Walter 1994]. A number of reasons for this have been suggested.

First, when firms have the power to sell affiliates' products, managers may no longer dispense "dispassionate" advice to clients and have a salesman's stake in pushing "house" products, possibly to the disadvantage of the customer.

Second, a financial firm that is acting as an underwriter and is unable to place the securities in a public offering may seek to ameliorate this loss by "stuffing" unwanted securities into accounts over which it has discretionary authority.

Third, a bank with a loan outstanding to a client whose bankruptcy risk has increased, to the private knowledge of the banker, may have an incentive to encourage the corporation to issue bonds or equities to the general public, with the proceeds used to pay down the bank loan. One example is the 1995 underwriting of a secondary equity issue of the Hafnia Insurance Group by Den Danske Bank. The stock was distributed heavily to retail investors, with proceeds allegedly used to pay down bank loans even as Hafnia slid into bankruptcy (see Smith and Walter 1997b). The

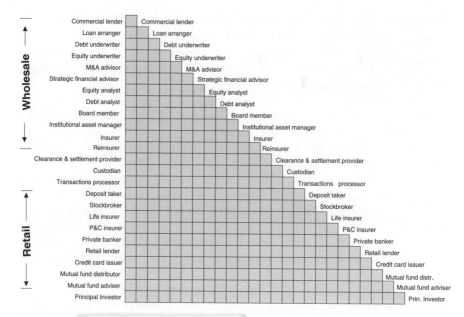

Figure 3-10. **Indicative Financial Services Matrix.**

case came before the Danish courts in successful individual investor litigation supported by the government.

Fourth, in order to ensure that an underwriting goes well, a bank may make below-market loans to third-party investors on condition that the proceeds are used to purchase securities underwritten by its securities unit.

Fifth, a bank may use its lending power activities to coerce a client to also use its securities or securities services.

Finally, by acting as a lender, a bank may become privy to certain material inside information about a customer or its rivals that can be used in setting prices, advising acquirers in a contested acquisition, or helping in the distribution of securities offerings underwritten by its securities unit (see Smith and Walter 1997a). More generally, a firm may use proprietary information regarding a client for internal management purposes, which at the same time harms the interests of the client.

The potential for conflicts of interest can be depicted in a matrix such as shown in Figure 3-10 (Walter 2003). Each of the cells in the matrix represents a different degree and intensity of interest conflicts. Some are serious and basically intractable. Others can be managed by appropriate changes in incentives or compliance initiatives. And some are not sufficiently serious to worry about. Using a matrix approach to mapping conflicts of interest clearly demonstrates that the broader the client and product range, the more numerous the potential conflicts of interest and the more difficult the resulting management problems become.

An interesting case of conflicts of interest in business client relationships came to light in 2003. A small Dutch commercial bank, SNS Bank NV, invested $15 million in a Citigroup offshore fixed-income investment vehicle, Captiva Finance Ltd., with the intent that this part of its portfolio be invested conservatively. The Captiva assets were under independent management, replaced in 1998 by another independent manager which, after allegedly poor performance, was in turn replaced by an asset management unit of Citibank. SNS claimed it never had the opportunity to vote on the management changes, as it was entitled to do, and that its requests to unload its Captiva stake were ignored by Citibank. By late 2001 the $15 million investment had dwindled to $3 million. The suit argued that most of the losses were incurred under Citibank management, which had failed to fire itself, and that some of the defaulted bonds had been underwritten by Citigroup's Investment Banking unit. Throughout, it appeared, Citigroup collected the fees as underwriter, fund manager, and fiduciary while SNS collected the losses.[1]

Shareholders clearly have a stake in the management and control of conflicts of interest in universal banks. They can benefit from conflict exploitation in the short term, to the extent that business volumes or margins are increased as a result. On the one hand, preventing conflicts of interest is an expensive business. Compliance systems are costly to maintain, and various types of walls between business units can have high opportunity costs because of inefficient use of information within the organization. Externally, reputation losses associated with conflicts of interest can bear on shareholders very heavily indeed, as demonstrated by a variety of "accidents" in the financial services industry. Indeed, it could well be argued that conflicts of interest may contribute to the price-to-book-value ratios of the shares of financial conglomerates and universal banks falling below those of more specialized financial services businesses.

The conflict of interest issue can seriously limit effective strategic benefits associated with financial services M&A transactions. For example, inside information accessible to a bank as lender to a target firm would almost certainly prevent the bank from acting as an adviser to a potential acquirer. Entrepreneurs may not want their private banking affairs dominated by a bank that is also involved in their business financing. A mutual fund investor is unlikely to have easy access to the full menu of available equity funds through a universal bank offering competing in-house products. These issues may be manageable if most of the competition is coming from other universal banks. But if the playing field is also populated by

---

1. Florence Fabricant, "Putting All the Eggs in a One-Stop Basket Can be Messy," *New York Times*, January 12, 2003.

aggressive insurance companies, broker-dealers, fund managers, and other specialists, these issues will prove to be a continuing strategic challenge for management.

Should a major conflict of interest arise, the repercussions for a firm's reputation could be quite detrimental. For example, J.P. Morgan, Inc. simultaneously served as commercial banker, investment banker, and adviser to the Spanish Banco Español de Crédito (Banesto), as well as being an equity holder and fund manager for co-investors in a limited partnership holding shares in the firm. In addition, Morgan's vice chairman served on Banesto's Supervisory Board. When Banesto failed and the conflicts of interest facing J.P. Morgan were revealed, the value of the firm's equity fell by 10% (see Smith and Walter 1995). And in 2002 Citigroup lost over 10% of its market capitalization on two separate trading days due to investors' worries about its involvement in a number of corporate scandals.

Another example focuses on the equity analyst conflicts of interest in the late 1990s and early 2000s. Analysts working for multifunctional financial firms wear several hats and are subject to multiple conflicts of interest. They are supposed to provide unbiased research to investors. But they are also expected to take part in the securities origination and sales process that is centered in their firms' corporate finance departments. The firms argue that expensive research functions cannot be paid for by attracting investor deal-flow and brokerage commissions, so corporate finance has to cover much of the cost. This fact and the compensation packages sometimes commanded by top analysts (occasionally exceeding $20 million per year) provide the best demonstration of which of the two hats dominates. Prosecution of Merrill Lynch by the Attorney General of the State of New York in 2002, a $1.4 billion "global" settlement, and a frantic scramble by all securities firms to reorganize how equity research is structured and compensated simply validated facts long known to market participants.

Mechanisms to control conflicts of interest can be market-based, regulation-based, or some combination of the two. Within large firms there appears to be a reliance on the loyalty and professional conduct of employees, both with respect to the institution's long-term survival and the best interests of its customers. Externally, reliance appears to be placed on market reputation and competition as disciplinary mechanisms. The concern of a bank for its reputation and fear of competitors are viewed as enforcing a degree of control over the potential for conflict exploitation. But conflicts that emerged during the corporate governance mess of the early 2000s suggested to many that tougher external controls over the activities of banks and other financial firms might be needed.

CONGLOMERATE DISCOUNT

It is often argued that the shares of multiproduct firms and business conglomerates tend to trade at prices lower than shares of more narrowly focused firms (all else equal). There are two basic reasons why this "conglomerate discount" is alleged to exist.

First, it is argued that, on the whole, conglomerates tend to use capital inefficiently. Empirical work by Berger and Ofek (1995) assesses the potential benefits of diversification (greater operating efficiency, less incentive to forego positive net present value projects, greater debt capacity, lower taxes) against the potential costs (higher management discretion to engage in value-reducing projects, cross-subsidization of marginal or loss-making projects that drain resources from healthy businesses, misalignments in incentives between central and divisional managers). The authors demonstrate an average value loss in multiproduct firms on the order of 13–15%, as compared to the stand-alone values of the constituent businesses for a sample of U.S. corporations during the period 1986–1991. This value loss turned out to be smaller when the multiproduct firms were active in closely allied activities within the same industrial sector.

The bulk of value erosion in conglomerates is attributed by the authors to overinvestment in marginally profitable activities and cross-subsidization. In empirical work using event-study methodology, John and Ofek (1995) show that asset sales by corporations result in significantly improved shareholder returns on the remaining capital employed, both as a result of greater focus in the enterprise and value gains through high prices paid by asset buyers.

Such empirical findings from event studies covering broad ranges of industry may well apply to diversified activities carried out by financial firms as well. If retail banking and wholesale banking are evolving more highly specialized, performance-driven businesses, one may ask whether the kinds of conglomerate discounts found in industrial firms may also apply to universal banking and financial conglomerate structures, especially as centralized decision making becomes increasingly irrelevant to the requirements of the specific businesses, run by specialists in markets demanding specialist standards of performance.

A second possible source of a conglomerate discount is that investors in shares of conglomerates find it difficult to "take a view" and add pure sectoral exposures to their portfolios. In effect, financial conglomerates prevent investors from optimizing asset allocation across specific segments of the financial services industry. Investors may avoid such stocks in their efforts to construct efficient asset-allocation profiles. This is especially true of highly performance-driven managers of institutional equity portfolios who are under pressure to outperform cohorts or equity indexes. So the portfolio logic of a conglomerate discount may indeed apply in the case of a multifunctional financial firm that is active in retail banking, wholesale commercial banking, middle-market banking, private banking, corporate finance, trading, investment banking, asset management, and perhaps other businesses. In effect, financial conglomerate shares mimic a closed-end mutual fund that covers a broad range of businesses. Consequently, both the portfolio-selection effect and the capital-misallocation effect may weaken investor demand for the firms' shares, lower equity prices, and produce a higher cost of capital than if the conglomerate discount were absent. This higher cost of capital would have a bearing on the competitive performance and profitability of the enterprise.

THE ISSUE OF NONFINANCIAL SHAREHOLDINGS

The financial conglomerate issue tends to be amplified when a bank or financial firm has large-scale shareholdings (including private equity stakes) in nonfinancial corporations. In such a case, the shareholder in the firm in effect obtains a closed-end fund that has been assembled by bank managers for various reasons over time and may bear no relationship to the investor's own portfolio optimization goals. The value of such a financial firm then depends on the total market value of its shares (to the extent they can be marked to market), which must be held by the investor on an all-or-nothing basis, plus the market value of the firm's own businesses.

There are wide differences in the role that banks and other financial firms such as insurance companies play in nonfinancial corporate shareholdings and in the process of corporate control (see Walter 1993a). These are stylized in Figure 3-11.

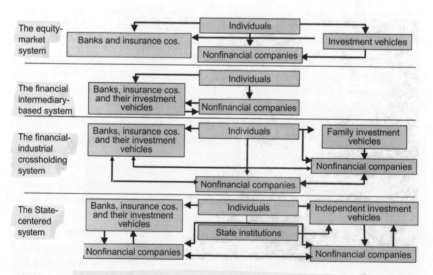

Figure 3-11. Alternative Financial–Nonfinancial Corporate Control Linkages.

- In the equity-market system, industrial firms are "semi-detached" from banks. Financing of major corporations is done to a significant extent through the capital markets, with short-term financing needs satisfied through commercial paper programs and bank facilities, longer-term debt through straight or structured bond issues and medium-term note programs, and equity financing through public issues or private placements. Research coverage tends to be extensive. Commercial banking relationships with major companies can be very important—notably through backstop credit lines and short-term lending facilities. These relationships tend to be between *buyer and seller*, with close bank monitoring and control coming into play mainly for small and medium-size firms or in cases of credit problems and workouts. Corporate control in such "Anglo-American" systems tend to be exercised through the takeover market on the basis of widely available public information, with a bank's function limited mainly to advising and financing bids or defensive restructurings. The government's role is normally arm's length in nature, with a focus on setting ground rules that are considered to be in the public interest. Relations between government, banks, and industry are sometimes antagonistic. Such systems depend heavily on effective governance, efficient monitoring, and conflict-resolution mechanisms, which is why the U.S. corporate scandals of 2001–2002 were so damaging: they called into question the key pillars of the system.
- The financial intermediary-based system centers on close bank–industry relationships, with corporate financing needs met mainly by retained earnings and bank financing. The role of banks carries well beyond credit extension and monitoring to share ownership, share voting, and board memberships in such systems. Capital allocation, management changes, and restructuring of enterprises is the job of nonexecutive supervisory boards on the basis of largely private information, and unwanted takeovers are rare. Mergers and acquisitions activity tends to be undertaken by relationship-based universal banks. Capital markets tend to be relatively poorly developed with respect to both corporate debt and equity, and there is usually not much of an organized venture capital market. The role of the state in the affairs of banks and corporations may well be arm's length in nature, although perhaps combined with some public sector shareholdings.
- In the financial-industrial crossholding approach, interfirm boundaries are blurred through equity crosslinks and long-term supplier–customer relationships. Banks may play a central role in equity crossholding structures—as in Japan's "keiretsu" networks—and provide guidance and coordination, as well as financing. There may be strong formal and informal links to government on the part of both the financial and industrial sectors of the economy.

Restructuring tends to be done on the basis of private information by drawing on these business-banking-government ties, and a contestable market for corporate control tends to be virtually nonexistent.

- The state-centered approach—perhaps best typified in the French tradition—involves a strong role on the part of government through national ownership or control of major universal banks and corporations, as well as government-controlled central savings institutions. Banks may hold significant stakes in industrial firms and form an important conduit for state influence of industry. Financing of enterprises tends to involve a mixture of bank credits and capital market issues, often taken up by state-influenced financial institutions. Additional channels of government influence may include the appointment of the heads of state-owned companies and banks, with strong personal and educational ties within the business and government elite.

These four stylized bank-industry-government linkages make themselves felt in the operation of banks and other financial firms in various ways. The value of any financial firm shareholdings in industrial firms is embedded in the value of the enterprise. The combined value of the bank or insurer and its industrial shareholdings, as reflected in its market capitalization, may be larger or smaller than the sum of their stand-alone values. For example, firms in which a bank or insurer has significant financial stakes, as well as a direct governance role, may be expected to conduct most or all significant commercial and investment banking or insurance activities with that institution, thus raising the value of the firm. However, if such "tied" sourcing of financial services raises the cost of capital of client corporations, this increased cost will in turn be reflected in the value of bank's or insurer's own shareholdings, and the reverse if such ties lower client firms' cost of capital. Moreover, permanent shareholdings may stunt the development of a contestable market for corporate control, thereby impeding corporate restructuring and depressing share prices, which in turn are reflected in the value of the bank or insurer to its own shareholders. Banks may also be induced to lend to affiliated corporations under credit conditions that would be rejected by unaffiliated lenders, and possibly encounter other conflicts of interest that may ultimately make it more difficult to maximize shareholder value.

MANAGEMENT AND ADVISOR INTERESTS IN M&A DEALS

Overinvestment is one reason managers may promote bank mergers and acquisitions that do not in the end create value. Managers may choose to overinvest for several reasons. They may want to expand the size of their organizations since managerial compensation tends to be positively related to firm size. Sometimes boards even compensate managers specifically for doing deals. Managers may also want to diversify their "employment risk"—that is, the risk of losing their professional reputations or jobs if the firm for which they are working has low earnings or enters bankruptcy. By engaging in diversifying projects, managers can learn a variety of transferable skills. This occurs even if such projects do not benefit stockholders (see Amihud and Lev 1981).

In his cash-flow theory, Jensen (1986) posits that managers with more cash flow than they need may engage in value-destroying diversification through overinvestment. When managers have access to free cash flow—defined as cash in excess of that needed for operations and positive-net present-value projects—they may choose not to return the cash to shareholders in the form of increased dividends. Instead, they invest in projects that do not necessarily have expected positive net-present values such as value-destroying mergers.

Investment bank advisors likewise have a strong desire for deals to be completed. Rau (2000) finds that an investment bank's market shares is in fact unrelated to the ultimate performance of acquirers advised by that bank in the past. What counts is that the investment bank has completed large numbers of deals in the past and is able to charge high success fees. The incentive to "get the deal done" can be quite strong regardless of long-term prospects of the deal itself.

HOW SHOULD SHAREHOLDERS THINK ABOUT FINANCIAL SERVICES M&A DEALS?

The chief executive of one particularly acquisitive U.S. bank has been quoted as saying, "With bank mergers . . . two plus two equals either three or five."[2] This statement nicely summarizes matters. The question is whether in an M&A situation the positives outweigh the negatives as discussed here—all balanced against the price paid either in cash or (if paid in stock) in terms of the dilutive effect on existing shareholders. There is usually no need to worry about the shareholders of the target firm. If boards are doing their jobs, they either receive an acceptable cash price or they can decide to sell their shares immediately after announcement. If they decide to hold, they are in the same boat as the shareholders of the acquiring firm, which is where the problem lies. So both old and new shareholders of the surviving entity must find a way to weigh the pluses and minuses discussed in this chapter, with all of the risks and uncertainties that this involves.

FROM BOOK VALUE OF EQUITY TO MARKET VALUE OF EQUITY

In any M&A deal that combines two publicly traded companies, it is easy to find out what the two firms were worth prior to the announcement of

---

2. Richard Kovacevich, CEO of Wells Fargo, as quoted in Davis (2000).

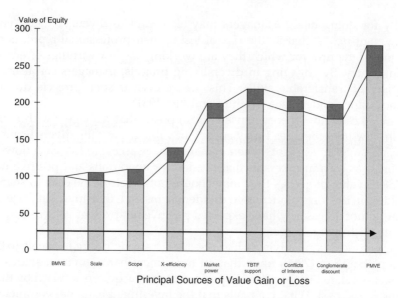

Figure 3-12. Loss-Recapture and/or Gain Augmentation in M&A Transactions.

the transaction, assuming the announcement effect was not already embedded in the share price. This is the pro forma, baseline market value of
equity (BMVE in Figure 3-12).

It is based on the pro forma combined book value of equity (BVE). In
the case of a bank, BVE is the sum of (1) the par value of shares when
originally issued, (2) the surplus paid in by investors when the shares
were issued, (3) retained earnings on the books of the bank, and (4)
reserves set aside for loan losses (Saunders & Cornett 2002). Depending
on the prevailing regulatory and accounting system, BVE must be increased or decreased by unrealized capital gains or losses associated with
assets such as equity holdings carried on the books of the bank at historical
cost and their prevailing replacement values (hidden reserves), as well as
the replacement values of other assets and liabilities that differ materially
from historical values due to credit and market risk considerations—that
is, their marked-to-market values.

This calculation gives the presumptive adjusted book value of equity
(ABVE). This value, however, is not normally revealed in bank financial
statements due to a general absence of market-value accounting across
broad categories of banking activities. Only a few commercial banking
products such as trading account securities, derivatives, and open foreign
exchange positions tend to be traded in liquid markets so that their market
value can be determined. Some loans and credit derivatives are today
also traded actively. Similar problems arise in insurance companies. However, the ABVE is a much more reliable guide in the case of investment

banks, where a much greater proportion of the balance sheet is marked to market on a real-time basis, and in the case of asset managers.

The franchise value of the firm can be defined as the difference between ABVE and BMVE. After all balance sheet values have been taken into account and priced out, there may still be a material difference between the resulting constructed value of equity and the current market value of equity. This difference represents the market's assessment of the present value of the risk-adjusted future net earnings stream, capturing all known or suspected business opportunities, costs, and risks facing the institution. Much of it is associated with reputation and brand value. Franchise value may be highly positive, as in the case of PepsiCo or Nestlé in the nonfinancial sector, or it could be significantly negative, with the firm's stock trading well below its adjusted book value—for instance, if there are large perceived losses embedded in the firm's internal or external portfolio of activities.

The franchise value can also affect the management of risk. As noted earlier, Demsetz, Saidenberg, and Strahan (1996) argue that the franchise value of banks also serves to inhibit extraordinary risk-taking. They find substantial evidence that the higher a bank's franchise value, the more prudent management tends to be. This suggests that large financial firms with high franchise values should serve shareholder interests (as well as the interests of the regulators) by means of appropriate risk management as opposed to banks with little to lose.

"Tobin's Q" is defined as the market value of a firm's equity divided by the book value. If the Q ratio is significantly below 1, for example, it may be that breaking up the firm can serve the interests of shareholders. That is, the adjusted book value of equity possibly could be monetized as a result of the breakup, in the same way as restructurings have raised shareholder value under the right circumstances in industrial companies. The Q ratio for well-run financial firms having a positive franchise value should normally be significantly in excess of 1 and is clearly susceptible to enhancement through managerial or shareholder action.

An M&A transaction can take place at the market price (no premium) or above the market price, representing a so-called "control premium." The economics of the combined entity centers on the price-to-book ratio paid for the target firm. As noted, the shareholders of the target firm capture the control premium. Whether the shareholders of the buying firm benefit depends on whether the net gains from the transaction over time exceed, on a present-value basis, the control premium paid for the target firm. The price recorded on the balance sheet of the acquiring firm reflects this "goodwill" and has to be amortized according to prevailing accounting rules against pretax earnings. It is easy to see why overpaying for acquisitions can be a real show-stopper for shareholders, if the economic gains of the transactions turn out to fall well short of expectations.

At least in the United States, commercial bank acquisitions during the period of intensive M&A activity in the 1990s have occurred at price-to-book value ratios of about 2.0, sometimes as high as 3.0 or even more. In eight of the eleven years covered by one study (Smith and Walter 1999), the mean price-to-book ratio for the U.S. banking industry acquisitions was below 2.0, averaging 1.5 and ranging from 1.1 in 1990 to 1.8 in 1985. In two years, the price-to-book ratio exceeded 2.0—in 1986 it was 2.8 and in 1993 in was 3.2. These values presumably reflect the opportunity for the acquired institutions to be managed differently and to realize the incremental value needed to reimburse the shareholders of the acquiring institutions for the willingness to pay the premium in the first place.

If in fact the potential to capture value for multifunctional financial firms exceeds that for the traditional U.S. type, separated commercial banks reflected in such studies, this should be reflected in higher merger premiums in banking environments outside the United States and within the United States after the 1999 liberalization of line-of-business restriction as a result of the Gramm-Leach-Bliley Act. Pressure for shareholder value optimization may not, of course, be triggered by an active and contestable market for corporate control, but in such markets it probably helps. Comparing cost, efficiency, and profitability measures across various national environments that are characterized by very different investor expectations and activism suggests that external pressure is conducive to realizing the potential value of shareholder equity in banking.

When financial firms engage in M&A transactions, managing for shareholder value means maximizing the potential market value of equity (PMVE) that the combined organization may be capable of achieving. The intent is to optimize the building-blocks that make up potential value of equity as depicted in Figure 3-12—economies of scale, economies of scope, X-efficiency, market power, and TBTF benefits, while minimizing value-losses from any diseconomies that may exist as well as avoiding to the extent possible conflict-of-interest problems and any conglomerate discount

SUMMARY

Assessing the potential effects of mergers or acquisitions in the financial services sector is as straightforward in concept as it is difficult to calibrate in practice. The positives include economies of scale, improvements in operating efficiency (including the impact of technology), cost economies of scope, revenue economies of scope, impact on market structure and pricing power, improved financial stability through diversification of revenue streams, improvements in the attraction and retention of human capital, and possibly presumptive TBTF support. The negatives include diseconomies of scale, higher operating costs due to increased size and complexity, diseconomies of scope on either the cost or revenue sides (or both), the impact of potential conflicts of interest on the franchise value of the firm, and a possible conglomerate discount that appears in the share price. Bigger is sometimes better, sometimes not. It all depends.

In terms of the evidence reviewed in this chapter, the relevant management lessons appear to include the following:

- Don't expect too much from economies of scale.
- Don't expect too much from *cost* economies of scope, and be prepared to deal with any cost diseconomies that may arise.
- Exploit *demand-side* economies of scope where cross-selling makes sense, most likely with retail, private, and middle-market corporate clients—and much more arguably with major corporate and institutional clients.
- Optimize operating economies or *X-efficiencies* through effective use of technology, reductions in the capital-intensity of financial services provided, reductions in the work force, incentive-compatible compensation practices, and other hallmarks of just plain better management.
- Seek out imperfect markets that demonstrate relatively low price elasticity of demand, ranging from private banking services to equity transactions that exploit "fault lines" across capital markets to leading-edge, emerging-market transactions that have not as yet been commoditized to dominant "fortress" market-share positions in particular national or regional markets, with particular client-segments, or in particular product lines. The half-lives of market imperfections in banking differ enormously, and require careful calibration of delivery systems ranging from massive investments in infrastructure to small, light, entrepreneurial, and opportunistic teams. A key managerial challenge for multifunctional financial firms is to accommodate a broad array of these activities under one roof.
- Specialize operations using professionals who are themselves specialists.
- Where possible, make the political case for backstops such as underpriced deposit insurance and TBTF support. Although this is a matter of public policy, shareholders clearly benefit from implicit subsidies that come without too many conditions attached.
- Pay careful attention to limiting conflicts of interest in organizational design, incentive systems, application and maintenance of Chinese walls, and managerial decisions that err on the side of caution where potential conflicts of interest arise.
- Minimize the conglomerate discount by divesting peripheral non-financial shareholdings and noncore businesses, leaving diversification up to the shareholder. The gain in market value may well outweigh any losses from reduced scope economies and earnings diversification. Pursuing this argument to its logical conclusion, of

course, challenges the basic premise of universal banks and financial conglomerates as structural forms.
- Pay careful attention to the residual "franchise" value of the firm by avoiding professional conduct lapses that lead to an erosion of the bank's reputation, uncontrolled trading losses, or in extreme cases criminal charges against the institution. It's never a good idea to cut corners on compliance or building an affirmative "culture" that employees understand and value as much as the shareholders.

If a strategic direction taken by the management a financial firm does not exploit every source of potential value for shareholders in M&A situations, then what is the purpose? Avoiding an acquisition attempt from a better-managed suitor, who will pay a premium price, does not seem as unacceptable today as it may have been in the past. In a world of more open and efficient markets for shares in financial institutions, shareholders increasingly tend to have the final say about the future of their enterprises.

4

Managing Financial Services Mergers and Acquisitions

The previous chapters of this book have provided the setting for M&A transactions in the financial sector: where they fit in the value-chain of financial services, the factual flow of deals, and their impact on the industry. The chapters have also detailed the underlying concepts and rationale regarding gains and losses with respect to market share and profitability. These considerations ought to determine strategic positioning, "doing the right thing," a strategic approach that provides good prospects for sustained financial performance. But even if a strategic plan is well conceived, it equally needs to be well executed, thus "doing the thing right."

In the traditional process of mergers and acquisitions, the post-merger integration phase is commonly applied after the deal is consummated. This approach, however, usually results in delays and frictions that diminish the benefits of the transaction. A more efficient approach used by firms that have engaged in numerous successful mergers and acquisitions seems to have applied the integration process early on and carried it out in a highly disciplined way.

This chapter centers on the issue of merger integration and its inevitable costs, which are important in a present-value sense because they are relatively certain and are incurred early in the process compared, for example, to revenue synergies, which may be quite speculative and take years to materialize. Even the best of mergers or acquisitions can be defeated by poor integration. Much of the thinking and evidence in this area falls in the realm of organizational behavior and business strategy and policy.

ORGANIZATIONAL STRUCTURE

Many M&A transactions are organizationally straightforward. The target firm is folded into the existing organizational structure of the acquirer and simply disappears. Others may require the acquiring firm itself to reorganize and, for example, to structure the acquired entity as a separately capitalized subsidiary. Reasons for such restructuring might include regulatory constraints, the design of management performance incentives, and branding and market-access issues. Reorganization requires some sort of new institutional profile that is appropriate for the activities of multifunctional financial firms. The broadest reorganizations target most or all client segments (at least in their home markets) and make an effort to provide each with a full range of the appropriate financial services. Outside the home market, firms may adopt a narrower competitive profile, perhaps focusing on wholesale banking and securities activities, asset management and private banking, or perhaps a self-standing retail presence abroad. This presents shareholders with an amalgam of more or less distinct businesses that are linked together in a complex network that draws on a set of centralized financial, information, human, and organizational resources. Such a profile can be extraordinarily difficult to manage in a way that achieves an optimum use of invested capital, as noted in the previous chapter.

Multifunctional financial firms may take a number of more or less distinct forms.[1] These are stylized in Figure 4-1.

- A fully integrated financial firm (Type-A) provides a broad range of financial services (banking, asset management, securities, and insurance) under a single corporate structure supported by a single capital base. This comes close to the classic European-style universal bank.
- A partially integrated financial firm (Type-B) conducts both commercial and investment banking within the same entity but undertakes insurance underwriting and distribution, as well as perhaps mortgage banking, asset management, lease financing, factoring, management consulting, and other specialized activities through separately capitalized subsidiaries, either because such activities are separately regulated or because they involve significant potential for exploitation of conflicts of interest, or a combination of such factors.
- In a Type-C financial firm, a commercial bank, whose core business as a credit institution is taking deposits and making commercial loans, forms the parent of subsidiaries engaged in a variety of other financial services ranging from investment banking to insurance.
- A final multiline financial firm structure (Type-D) involves creation of a holding company, which controls affiliates engaged in commercial banking, investment banking, insurance, and possibly other types of financial and nonfinancial businesses.

1. For a detailed discussion, see Saunders and Walter (1994).

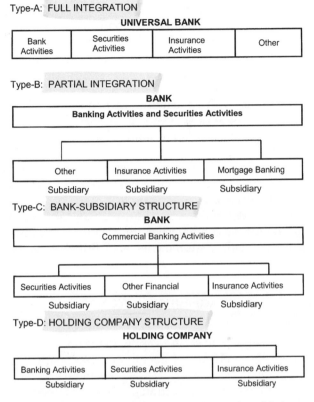

Figure 4-1. Organization Structures of Multiline Financial Firms.

The specific structures that financial firms adopt are driven by regulatory considerations, the characteristics of the financial services involved, and demand-side issues relating to market structure and client preferences. American regulation of multiline firms incorporating a commercial banking function, for example, mandates a Type-D form of organization. This was historically the case under the Glass-Steagall provisions of the Banking Act of 1933, requiring separation of banking (taking deposits and extending commercial loans) and most types of securities activities (underwriting and dealing in corporate debt and equities and their derivatives, as well as state and local revenue bonds). Permitted non-banking business had to be carried out through separately capitalized subsidiaries, and there were strict "firewalls" between them. U.S. bank holding companies were enjoined from most types of insurance underwriting and distribution. This changed with the 1999 Gramm-Leach-Bliley Act, which eliminated the securities and insurance prohibitions but continued to mandate the holding company structure.

British multifunctional financial firms have traditionally followed the

Type-C model, with securities and insurance activities (if any) carried out via subsidiaries of the bank itself. Most continental European countries seem to follow the Type-B model, with full integration of banking and securities activities within the bank itself (despite functional regulation), and insurance, mortgage banking, and other specialized financial and nonfinancial activities carried out through subsidiaries. The Type-A universal banking model, with all activities carried out within a single corporate entity, seems not to exist even in environments characterized by a monopoly regulator such as, for example, the Monetary Authority of Singapore.

From a strategic perspective, the structural form of multifunctional financial firms appears to depend on at least two factors: (1) the ease with which operating efficiencies and scale and scope economies can be exploited, which is determined in large part by product and process technologies, and (2) the comparative organizational effectiveness in optimally satisfying client requirements and bringing to bear market power.[2]

TYPOLOGY OF MERGERS AND ACQUISITIONS INTEGRATION

There are at least four strands to the conceptual basis for integrating mergers and acquisition that seem to apply to the financial services sector and that bear on the problems of integration. The first is the *strategic fit* (resource relatedness) view. M&A transactions in related sectors or markets that appear to demonstrate a strategic fit should perform better than in unrelated situations due to the possible benefits of economies of scale, scope, and market power that can be achieved. However, the empirical evidence in the management literature has produced inconsistent results (Lubatkin 1987; Haspelagh and Jemison 1991), indicating that resource relatedness may represent value *potential* but is not a *guarantor* of success in post-M&A performance. Strategic fit issues are more extensively dealt with in the economics literature, discussed in Chapter 3.

Second is the *organizational fit* view. The argument is that poor postacquisition performance of M&A transactions is linked to organizational problems encountered during the integration process. Several studies (Buono and Bowditch 1989; Datta 1991) have indicated that differences in human and organizational factors can have a severely negative impact on post-acquisition performance. The argument is essentially process-driven. Corporate performance is determined by the post-M&A integration process, in which value creation takes place through the transfer of particular skills (Kitching 1967; Porter 1987; Haspelagh and Jemison 1991). The au-

---

2. In this context, Switzerland presents an interesting case study, with the two major universal banks operating under a single set of domestic regulatory parameters having adopted rather different structural forms.

thors emphasize that deals are not one-off transactions, but rather a means for carrying out corporate renewal.

The entire M&A sequence in this view is split into two interactive processes: namely, the *decision-making* process in the pre-transaction stage and the *integration* process in the post-transaction stage. The justification for M&A deals is the transfer of strategic capabilities that provide a sustainable competitive advantage to the firm, thereby leading to long-term shareholder value creation for the combined enterprise. Strategic capabilities need to be aligned with the underlying motivation and contribution to a specific business strategy, as depicted in Table 4-1.

Third is the *resource-based* view, which attributes performance variances between firms to the difference in the way firm managers build, maintain, and defend their resources (Hamel, Prahalad, and Doz 1989; Crossan and Inkpen 1992). Resources are considered valuable not for their inherent characteristics but for the way in which they are used either individually or in combination (Penrose 1959).

Fourth is the *knowledge-based view*, which considers that human resources dominate the material resources of the firm. Such services tend to

Table 4.1 M&A Objectives in Corporate Renewal

Strategic Capabilities	Strategic Motivation	Contribution to Specific Business Strategy
Combination benefits Market share	*Domain strengthening* Strengthen existing areas of competencies, usually in restructuring situations [ex: horizontal acquisitions].	*Acquiring specific business capability* Piecemeal approach in acquiring different capabilities to build broad-based business strategy.
Resource sharing Economies of scope/ scale	*Domain extension* Apply existing capabilities to new adjacent business or vice versa.	*Acquiring a platform* Will only become integral part of business strategy with greater investment of resources.
Functional skills Processes	*Domain exploration* Move into new business needing new capabilities. Leverage industry specific learning, with goal of greater commitment to acquisition.	*Acquiring a business position* Acquisition implements the strategy.
General management skills Financial planning, HR		

Source: Philippe Haspeslagh and David Jemison, *Managing Acquisitions* (New York: Free Press, 1991).

vary according to changes in human capital and skills. So there is a strong link between the knowledge of employees and the benefits to be extracted from available material and financial resources (Penrose 1959). The uniqueness of employee knowledge is identified as the source of sustainable competitive advantage (Nonaka 1994). However, knowledge is tacit, difficult to replicate, and transferable through "learning by doing," observation, and imperfect imitation. If knowledge, embedded in human capital, is the most important element of value creation and is inherently difficult to manipulate (especially in the financial services industry), how can it be effectively transferred through the M&A integration process? "Firm learning" concepts may be especially applicable in this area, as discussed below.

PRE-MERGER INTEGRATION ISSUES

A number of managerial issues that can cause major integration problems must be considered in advance of an M&A transaction. First, is the "chemistry" right? Are the personalities of the senior executives from both firms compatible? The importance of complementarity needs to be stressed. In some financial mergers, such as Banco Santander–Central Hispano (BSCH) in 1999, a wide divergence in personalities and styles between the two CEOs can help minimize clashes during integration, since each may exercise a unique leadership role (see Appendix 2, Table 2). Possible leadership structures are depicted in Table 4-2. Optimally, key senior executive posts in the combined firm should be determined prior to the announcement of the transaction, with roles in the new leadership structure clarified as much as is realistically possible in order to minimize confusion, frictions, and turf battles during the integration process.

Second, as discussed later in this chapter, corporate culture is crucial to the integration process. It is also important to the success of the combined entity, since most of the key M&A benefits are tied to successful human interactions. This involves understanding the extent of cultural gaps that may exist. Determining whether a cultural gap is functional, social, or rooted in other causes needs to be clearly established in the pre-M&A stage and seriously addressed by senior management on both sides. If the cultural gap is deemed too wide and unlikely to be narrowed during integration, the transaction should be reconsidered. And the integration approach to be used should be determined by the extent of the cultural gap, the main purpose of the merger or acquisition, and the operating environment of the acquired firm or merger partner.

Personal interactions represent the main elements in the M&A integration process but provide some of the most serious challenges due poor acquirer information about the target firm, together with uncertainty about the acquisition's purpose and its perceived implications on the part of employees of the target firm (Haspeslagh and Jemison 1991). Symptoms include a lack of flexibility in implementing the integration process when

Table 4-2 Alternative Leadership Structures, Characteristics, Advantages, and Disadvantages

	Characteristics	Advantages	Disadvantages	Examples
Federal	1 overall CEO + subordinate (CEOs of acquired firms). The CEO and top senior management of acquired firm remains in place	Builds consensus	Need strong charisma to maintain authority	UniCredito
Collegiate	Triumvirate or quartet of Co-CEOs having equal power	Builds consensus Compromise solution	May be a negative in fast-paced I-banking. Personality clashes, with one or more CEOs actually leaving, causing disruption down the chain of command. Compromises leading to severe delays in deciding on key integration issues (conversion of IT platform, staff cuts).	Fortis, Dexia
Two Co-CEOs	One from each firm	Builds consensus Compromise solution		HypoVereinsbank, Banco Bilbao Vizcaya (where the Spanish govt. had to intervene to appoint a successor).
Single CEO	The CEO of dominant firm takes over, with other CEO forced/eased out before integration begins.	One voice Fast decision making	May cause disruption in acquired firm due to climate of uncertainty/ hostility	
Single CEO	The CEO of one firm takes over new CEO role, with a former CEO of other firm as the designated successor	Builds consensus Compromise solution One voice Fast decision making	If the most talented former CEO goes last, he may leave prematurely before his anticipated appointment date.	Landesgirokasse (Germany)

Source: Steven Davis, *Bank Mergers: Lessons for the Future* (London: Macmillan Press, 2000).

faced with new conditions, as well as psychic loss (morale erosion) and talent defections due to uncertainty and fear generated among the target firm's employees. This requires balancing expectations between determinism and excessive flexibility, providing quality and presence of institutional leadership, and selecting the appropriate level of gatekeeping (interface management) between the two firms in order to filter out interferences in the operations of the target company on the part of the acquirer.

The integration approach is viewed as a balance between two forces: (1) the strategic fit, that is, the relationship of target to the acquired firm or between merging partners, and the manner in which the value or strategic capability is to be extracted, and (2) the organizational fit—the need to preserve the target's strategic capability after the acquisition— which is dependent on how essential the preservation of the target firm's culture is to the survival of the strategic capabilities to be acquired.

ALTERNATIVE APPROACHES TO MERGER INTEGRATION

Three merger-integration approaches have been identified in the management literature, all based on clinical case studies. Ultimately, each of these approaches depends on the strategic intent underlying the specific M&A initiative being undertaken, as summarized for a number of cae studies in Appendix 2.

First, the *absorption approach* usually applies to M&A transactions within the same financial services sector (commercial banking, investment banking, insurance, asset management) in which one of the main justifications is the realization of economies of scale or operating efficiencies due to overlapping operations. The absorption approach can apply to both market strengthening (such as Wells Fargo and First Interstate Bank) and market extension (such as Deutsche Bank and Bankers Trust). The cultural gap needs to be bridged quickly due to the fast-paced nature of the absorption approach.

Second, the *symbiotic approach* generally applies to cross-sector transactions (for example, between commercial banking and investment banking, commercial banking and insurance), in which cultural differences and practices can be fairly wide, and therefore may take time to bridge. Examples include Citibank and Travelers, CIBC and Wood Gundy. However, a high level of integration at least in some functional areas is eventually necessary in order to benefit from scope-related M&A benefits such as cross-selling and leveraging of distribution channels. A symbiotic type of approach has also been used in market-strengthening situations (in-market deals) in which the cultural gap between the two organizations was deemed too wide to bridge quickly and therefore the slower symbiotic approach was chosen. A notable example is the Norwest–Wells Fargo transaction.

Table 4-3 Types of Integration Approaches

| | | Need for Strategic Interdependence | |
		Low	High
Need for Organizational Autonomy	High	Preservation	Symbiotic
	Low	[Holding]	Absorption

Source: Phillippe Haspeslagh and David Jemison, *Managing Acquisitions* (New York: Free Press, 1991).

Third, the *preservation approach* involves, as the main justification for a merger or acquisition, leveraging knowledge about the new business or industry area of the acquired firm and/or specific skills and business competencies ("best practices") that could be transferred back to the parent or to the parent's other affiliates. In most cases, the cultural gap between the two firms is wide due to cross-sector differences, and is therefore kept separate from that of the acquiring firm by granting a high level of autonomy. In financial services, a preservation approach can be used when the acquiring firm is interested in obtaining a platform in a new sector of the industry or in a new national market, but does not yet itself have those activities within which to integrate the acquired firm. Some banks, such as Banc One, in the past have used a preservation approach in order to leverage knowledge about possible best practices. Banc One also used a preservation approach to facilitate the negotiation process for their acquisitions because of the non-threatening nature of this approach—that is, the target firm is left more or less intact after the acquisition.

A mapping of each of these approaches onto the need for strategic interdependence and the need for organizational autonomy is provided in Table 4-3. The context, characteristics, and challenges for each type of integration approach are highlighted in Table 4-4. The key issues that need to be addressed are

- Client retention and extension (client franchise)
- Geographic presence in major markets
- Product coverage and branding
- Revenue economies of scope, distribution channel leveraging and broadening (cross-selling)
- Economies of scale and operating efficiencies
- Human resources, redundancies, retention, and skill leveraging

Table 4-4 Integration Approaches—Context, Characteristics, and Challenges

	Applicable Context (Capabilities)	Applicable Context (Acquisition Purpose)	Examples	Approach Characteristics
Absorption	Resource sharing (economies of scope/ scale). General management skills.	Domain strengthening. Domain extension.	Electolux's acquisition of Zanussi in 1984 to broaden its product range.	Much overlap (same sector, same geographic area). Rationalization of resources is usually the primary M&A motive. A high level of integration does not mean centralization (Zanussi was absorbed into Electrolux's decentralized operations)
Symbiotic	Resource sharing (economies of scope/ scale). General management skills. Functional skills.	Domain strengthening. Domain extension.	ICT's acquisition of Beatrice Chemicals.	Usually a large gap in culture differences (sector, cross-border). First co-exist and then become increasingly interdependent as the cultural gap narrows. The most complex integration approach due to its gradual nature, requiring capability transfer (for ex: synergies), while preserving those capabilities. Therefore, there is a need for boundary preservation while providing permeability ("semi-permeable membrane").
Preservation	Functional skills	Domain exploration.	BP's 1979 acquisition of Hendrix, a Dutch animal feed company. Desire to diversify away from oil, yet in a field (protein) where BP wanted to increase its learning, BP had made earlier forays into synthetic protein production from oil.	Main acquisition motive is to accumulate learning: (1) learn about an industry as a possible new domain; (2) expose acquiring firm to a different business that may be relevant to its core activities. Complete need to preserve different identity & culture

Source: Philippe Haspeslagh and David Jemison, *Managing Acquisitions* (New York: Free Press, 1991).

Approach Challenges		
Balancing Expectation	Institutional Leadership	Interface Management
Less flexibility required due to programmed nature of approach.	Senior management of acquired firm to create conditions for staff of acquired firm to transfer allegiances.	Gate-keeping temporarily needed to monitor pace, timing, and nature of interactions.
Difficulty in assessing accruing benefits from skill transfer, therefore continuous need for reassessment, but flexibility runs against managerial instincts. Resistance of target firm increases if expected benefits are too clearly specified.	Even-handedness is crucial regardless of size.	Complexity in striking the right balance between preserving the identity of the acquired firm and promoting the appropriate flow of information exchange
Excessive flexibility (autonomy) results in reduced learning opportunities.	Failure to reconfirm acquired firm's purpose will not provide reassurance.	Gate-keeping is crucial to preserve boundary (autonomy) around acquired firm.

- Capital base and debt rating
- Technology platform
- Physical infrastructure
- Leveraging of institutionalized know-how

Clearly, the overall integration process will be driven by the underlying objective of the transaction. Mistargeted approaches can be disastrous in this sector, since the financial services industry depends critically on human capital, which is often highly mobile.

DECIDING ON THE INTEGRATION LEVEL BY IMPACT AREA

The integration level targeted for each M&A impact area may not be the same as the overall level of integration. Table 4-5 depicts this and also notes implications for the BSCH and Banc One merger sequences. For example, in the *preservation* approach a few impact areas such as information technology (IT) and data-processing functions, as well as accounting and audit systems, may be targeted for high integration while the remaining areas may remain autonomous or only loosely aligned with those of the acquiring firm.

Since the *absorption* and *symbiotic* approaches both aim at a high overall level of integration—although achieved at different speeds—most impact areas should be targeted similarly (see Table 4-5). However, there may be some exceptions, especially in *symbiotic* acquisitions in which some areas are intentionally *not* targeted for a high degree of integration. This appears to have been the case, for example, with the Banco Santander–Central Hispano merger, in which management decided after the merger to integrate and align most of the two predecessor banks' functions, systems, policies, and procedures progressively but to maintain separate retail brands and product groups. Nevertheless, exceptions to high levels of integration-specific impact areas may just represent caution on the part of management, which could eventually move to fully integrate all aspects of the combined business.

Given that a *preservation-type* of acquisition aims at maintaining a high degree of autonomy in the acquired firm, one would expect that integration levels across most impact areas would be relatively low, therefore mostly occupying the space in the low integration column in Table 4-5. The acquirer may nevertheless want to aggressively integrate some functional areas in order to introduce effective financial and operational control. For example, in the case of Banc One's numerous acquisitions up to the mid-1990s, high integration levels were targeted for IT, accounting, and auditing functions and systems, although this was usually a very slow process. Branding was also rapidly integrated, since the Banc One name was effectively "franchised" to acquire institutions. All remaining areas were not initially targeted for high integration, as indicated in Table 4-5.

Table 4-5 Targeted Integration Level by Impact Area

Impact Area	Integration Level		
	High	Medium	Low
IT & data processing functions			
Operations (back-office) functions			
Front-office functions			
Physical facilities			
HR policies			
Operating procedures			
Accounting/audit systems			
IT and data processing systems			
Product range			
Brands			

BSCH

Impact Area	Integration Level		
	High	Medium	Low
IT & data processing functions	X		
Operations (back-office) functions	X		
Front-office functions	?		
Physical facilities	?		
HR policies	?		
Operating procedures	X		
Accounting/audit systems	X		
IT and data processing systems	X		
Product range			X
Brands			X

Banc One through the mid-1990s

Impact Area	Integration Level		
	High	Medium	Low
IT & data processing functions	X		
Operations (back-office) functions			X
Front-office functions			X
Physical facilities			X
HR policies			X
Operating procedures	X		
Accounting/audit systems	X		
IT and data processing systems	X		
Product range			X
Brands			X

Key issues in merger integration are speed and communication. The decision process and communication of the actions affecting key integration impact areas should be as rapid as possible in order to minimize uncertainty confronting staff and clients. Management often has to contend with several different integration schedules and priorities relating to individual impact areas:

- Front-office and client coverage functions
- Accounting and audit systems
- Human resources and compensation policies
- Operating procedures and reporting lines
- Product range and delivery
- Branding and marketing
- IT systems, data processing, and back-office functions

The last of these issues will be discussed separately in the following chapter.

THE ISSUE OF PERSONNEL RETENTION

The replacement or retention of personnel in M&A situations is in part determined by the integration approach used, and especially by the degree of existing overlap between the two firms. In-market deals such as the consolidation of two commercial banks operating in the same geographic area usually involve considerable personnel redundancies, especially in the branch network and operations.

The firm's leadership has to aim to strike the right balance between the need for reducing personnel and the need for minimizing employee disruptions that often accompany restructurings during the integration process. As discussed, a high degree of replacement in human resources of the acquired firm tends to negatively impact the post-acquisition performance of the combined firm through the departure of key talent and the demoralization of the remaining employees down the chain of command. Although empirical findings in this area have been limited so far to senior management replacement in U.S. commercial banking acquisitions, aggressive personnel replacement in the acquired firm is a frequent pitfall in many mergers or acquisitions due to a strong pressure to slash costs. This can lead to severe damage to employee morale, with negative repercussions on personnel retention, customer service, and customer retention, as well as loss of focus on possible synergies such as cross-selling.

Alternative selection approaches in human resource retention and replacement are presented in Table 4-6. Firm-level research suggests several important methods to deal with human resources.

1. The key individuals in the acquired firm should be quickly identified for retention.

Table 4-6 Alternative Selection Approaches in Human Resources Retention/Replacement

	Characteristics	Advantages	Disadvantages	Examples
"Our team takes over"	Loyalty to personnel of acquiring firm.	Trust in known and tested managers.	Limiting, if additional talent will be required to foster long-term growth. Strong chance of demoralizing staff of acquired firm.	First Union (USA)
Meritocracy	Selection based on fairness and transparency. Based on view that human talent is the main resource of the firm.	Fairness may help to push through layoffs and minimize personnel disruptions. Alternative could be disastrous (best people leaving to other firms with desire of revenge).	Process can be time-consuming (3–4 months in Lloyds TSB merger). May not be popular with staff of acquiring/dominant firm, as it may accuse management of actually favoring the other (weaker) side.	Chase, Lloyds TSB
Maintaining balance/ equality	Maintain balance in staff between both firms. Solution often favored in Europe and Japan.	Compromise solution, builds consensus. Easier to implement if labor laws are more inflexible.	Could cause disruption if staff from one side feels that their counterparts from other side are less talented.	ABN/Amro, Bank Austria/ Creditanstalt, Merita/ Nordbanken

Source: Steven Davis, *Bank Mergers: Lessons for the Future* (London: Macmillan Press, 2000).

2. The selection process for redundancy, replacement, or retention should be fair and transparent. Ideally, the staff from both firms should be placed in the same evaluation pool for selection.
3. Human resources decisions should be done quickly, for example within the first 100 days after the M&A announcement, in order to avoid uncertainty, which would lead employee morale erosion and the exit of key talent.
4. The managers of the acquired firm who were opposed to the merger or acquisition should be terminated.

These initiatives ought to help minimize future conflicts and may require the development of a process that will bring conflicts to the surface and help identify at an early stage the less-cooperative employees of the acquired firm.

An example is Swedbank, which used this approach in its integration of acquired banks. Over a period of several days, it brought together the employees of the acquired firm and exposed them to the bank's vision. Each employee was asked whether he or she agreed with the vision of the new combined firm, and those who disagreed were either retired early or offered help in outplacement. The approach was relatively costly, however, and did provoke some perhaps unnecessary employee disruptions.

The way in which the personnel selection, retention, and separation process is performed needs to be effectively communicated to staff, emphasizing the degree of transparency and fairness applied, in order to establish credibility. This credibility, along with the extent of retention packages for the surviving staff of the acquired firm or merger partner, need to be quickly set in order to minimize the departure of key personnel. The need for a realignment of compensation structures between the two firms must also be evaluated early on, especially in integrations that attempt to bring together staff from different sectors in cross-selling initiatives.

DEALING WITH CULTURAL CHANGE

Whereas many of the factors determining whether an M&A transaction in the financial services sector is accretive to shareholders have been explored extensively in the literature, little attention has been paid to issues surrounding corporate culture. This is a "soft" factor that arguably explains some of the differences observed between expected and actual shareholder value gains and losses. In some cases, clashes of cultures within the merged entity appear to have been the reason for M&A disasters. Corporate culture has certainly become one of the most actively debated issues distinguishing successful from lackluster performers in the financial services sector.

Culture is something every financial services firm has, even if it is weak. It is central to the institutional environment in which people have to work. If a financial services firm wants to get the most out of its people, the first thing management has to give them is a highly desirable and effective workplace, which is where they spend more of their time than anywhere else. Some key ingredients are

- High-quality peers and role models from whom to learn, and with whom to compete.
- A sufficiently nonhierarchical, loose organizational structure that permits ideas to rise, be taken seriously, considered carefully on the basis of merit, acted upon quickly—that is, a structure that protects high-potential individuals from bureaucratic stifling.
- An *esprit de corps* that thrives on measurable competitive success—such as significantly increasing market share or profit margins—in a business where winners and losers are not difficult to distinguish and where valuable franchises are difficult to build but easy to lose.

- A performance-based compensation and advancement system that is generally respected as being fair and right not less than about 80% of the time. This must be an integral part of a benign form of ruthless Darwinism, one that includes a reasonably high level of involuntary turnover, in which only the best survive and progress.

In short, there has to be a climate in which bright people, if they are found suitable, will *want* to spend their careers. This climate requires a sense of continuity, admired and respected seniors, and a serious, consistent commitment to careful recruitment, management development, and training. Qualified people who are not from the institution's home country must be considered for high office. Such people cannot automatically be deemed unworthy just because they come from a different background.

Corporate culture in a highly competitive industry like financial services has to be regarded by management and boards as an important competitive weapon, centered on grasping and preserving the qualities of winning. This includes

- Sound strategic direction and leadership from the top—senior managers who know the right thing to do, then get it done promptly by providing sufficient resources.
- An overriding attention to teamwork, avoiding becoming dependent on so-called "stars" and stamping-out arrogance. Some apparently "strong" cultures are really not much more than institutionalized arrogance.
- The selection of hundreds of loyal and efficient "squad and platoon leaders" to carry out day-to-day activities at high levels of quality and professionalism, to include a fine, ingrained sense of what is unacceptable conduct, including conduct that does not violate law or regulation but nevertheless could impair the reputation of the firm and compromise its responsibility to clients.
- A high level of adaptability by the whole organization in an industry subject to rapid change—*sic transit gloria*. Senior management must be keenly aware of the need for adaptability and communicate it effectively by word and deed. A certain amount of corporate angst helps keeps people on their toes.

Leadership is important. The evidence suggests that the culture of a financial institution can be strongly influenced by one or two individuals at the top of their organizations, either to push forward and improve upon a core culture that already exists or to dramatically change it. But most financial services firms are run by committees on the basis of shared responsibility and power by people, however capable, who reached their positions largely by bureaucratic progression within the system. This may be less true in smaller institutions than in larger ones, and less true in investment banks than in commercial and universal banks. As products of the system, they tend to promote the shared values and behavior patterns characteristic of that system. Sometimes "outsiders" with quite different perspectives are included on the top management team, often with great catalytic effect, but other times they seem to have only limited impact on institutions. There may be several origins of a firm's culture, which, individually or together, can form a strong competitive asset.

First) the history of an organization is often a useful cultural anchor, particularly if that history includes a strongly positive social and political as well as economic impact. Employees quickly identify with a "proud" history and the cultural attributes associated with it, and leverage this history in a productive way in client relationships. Business setbacks, strategic errors, and even scandals may be more easily overcome with a strong historical anchor embedded in the corporate culture. The problem with a history-linked cultural identity is that it either exists or it does not, and represents a factual basis that cannot be altered in the short-run. Most established firms have long and honorable histories, but few are so distinguished that this provides a powerful cultural asset.

Second) is the firm's overall "franchise," the cumulative product of its business successes and failures in the relatively recent past. In the case of market successes or dominance, the positive lessons can permeate the entire firm. In the case of failures, the demoralization effect on corporate culture can far exceed the direct impact of the failure itself. Financial institutions that are repeatedly successful in financial innovation, for example, often acquire resonance in the market, which can positively affect corporate culture over a relatively short time span. People are generally proud to be considered innovative or to be associated with innovators, and this can pay cultural dividends. It is also well known that entrepreneurial and start-up ventures often have extremely positive cultures that place a premium on hard work well beyond formal responsibilities, self-motivation, attention to quality, and the like. The problem is that the excitement can dissipate fairly quickly, after which routine takes over and its cultural value is lost.

Third) a sense of institutional self-perception. Mission statements can be helpful in the development of strong cultures as long as they are both realistic and "alive" in the sense that management "walks the talk," to use a popular phrase. Among the most useless and indeed damaging efforts can be mission statements intended to weld together a coherent corporate culture but that turn out to be opportunistic, unrealistic, frequently violated, and pious. These mainly serve to create a sense of cynicism, dissent, and disinterest. Many firms have a powerful corporate culture without a mission statement, only a strong sense of vision on the part of senior management.

Finally) there ought to be a "partnership" approach. In this industry, employees are indeed the most important assets. They must be trained, led, and given role models to emulate. They must be compensated well and fairly, but not excessively relative to what they contribute. The question is whether certain cultural attributes specific to partnerships can be synthetically introduced into corporate organizations in order to derive some of the benefits. Sometimes it can be achieved in part through well-designed and credible management information and profit attribution systems, which allocate earnings into "pools" where they are properly generated, whether directly or indirectly. This system must then be sold to employees as being both "accurate" and "fair," so that those doing the performing trust it as much as possible. Lateral information flows across the organization and cooperative behavior intended to leave as little business on the table as possible may thus be encouraged far more effectively than any amount of exhortation by management.

One question that constantly arises among financial services firms is whether a single culture is appropriate for an organization that covers a very broad range of activities, extending from foreign exchange dealing to mass-market retail banking to M&A advisory transactions in investment banking. But there may be some over-arching cultural attributes (a superculture) that can be an effective umbrella covering widely different business cultures and national cultures within an organization (see Figure 4-2). If this is considered impossible to achieve, it is likely that a holding company form of organization—where unit cultures are closely aligned to the respective businesses—is superior to more integrated structural forms among financial services firms. However, cultural fragmentation in such a structure has potential drawbacks, including the fragmentation of market delivery and quality control, that are not to be taken lightly.

A decentralized federation will permit and sometimes even encourage multiple cultures. A cultural takeover, in which the dominant partner imposes its own culture, can be direct or indirect. In a *direct* cultural

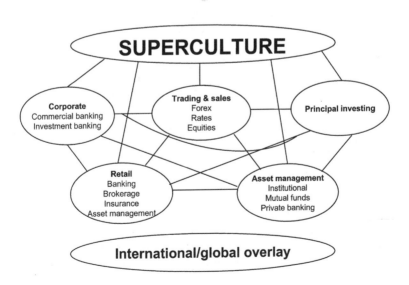

Figure 4-2. Cultural Overlays.

imposition, the dominant firm squarely imposes its own culture (for example, Fleet Bank, Svenska Handelsbanken). This approach forces people to focus on where they are going, not where they have come from. However, the culture of the dominant firm is itself continuously evolving. In an _indirect_ cultural integration, the dominant firm chooses a subculture from within its own organization if it deems that its core culture is not well suited to the other company. In order not to repeat the mistakes made with the Morgan Grenfell acquisition, for example, Deutsche Bank adopted a softer cultural approach when acquiring Bankers Trust in 1999 by handling the acquisition through its line investment bankers based in London office rather than by its German-based entities.

In building a new culture, management has to focus personnel on the future by adopting new values, most of which tend to be performance-related. This approach (for example, as adopted by HypoVereinsbank) is based on the assumption that behavior characteristics, rather than values, must be changed, since the adoption of new behavior is easier than the alteration of existing beliefs. In contrast to the performance-related approach, the _soft-value_ approach focuses on shaping a new culture around certain specific ideals such as integrity, collaboration, and meritocracy. Another version of the soft-value approach is to blend the best of both firms—for example, the high-touch client-relationship approach of Norwest blended with the high-tech electronic and phone-banking approach of Wells Fargo.

Senior management should not bury cultural differences, but rather encourage open discussion of any such differences in order to raise awareness. The goal is to foster mutual understanding. The message must be truthful. Statements to avoid include

- _It's a natural fit._ No matter how complementary the cultures of two firms may be, it should never be assumed that they could easily be merged into a seamless combined entity.
- _Nothing is going to change._ All mergers and acquisitions are highly disruptive. A false pretense will only cause unrealistic expectations among employees, which can lead to subsequent disappointments and disruptions.
- _It's a merger of equals._ Such statements can lead to wholly unrealistic expectations, resulting in turf battles and staff disruptions—as in the NationsBank–BankAmerica merger, in which case BankAmerica staff soon found out that they had, in fact, not been merged, but simply acquired.

Persistent communication throughout the integration process is an essential ingredient of success in bridging the cultural gap, especially when attempting to forge a new culture. Among communication vehicles available to senior management are mission statements, in-house continuing education, and the like.

CONCEPTS OF "FIRM LEARNING" AND FINANCIAL SERVICES M&A TRANSACTIONS

The firm is viewed as a set of so-called "routinized behaviors" developed over time through knowledge accumulation that has been formed from either direct or indirect experience (Zollo and Singh 1997; Zollo 2000). Post-integration decisions and the learning process to implement those decisions—*integration capabilities*—are ultimately influenced by routines developed by the acquiring firm and will tend to have an impact on the firm's postmerger performance. A firm's learning experience from past M&A deals is either tacit (learning by doing) or codified in manuals, blueprints, and the like.

Knowledge codification represents the ways in which individuals involved in implementing the merger integration process discuss and share their experience and develop process-specific tools. These tools include the creation and updating of integration manuals, checklists and decisions support software, the analysis of post-performance metrics, and the writing of postmortem evaluation reports. Knowledge codification should positively affect post-acquisition performance by (1) serving as a repository of organizational memory, (2) facilitating diffusion of knowledge to other parts of the firm, for example through manuals, (3) clarifying the roles, responsibilities, and deadlines for those executing the integration process, and (4) helping understand the causality between decisions taken and performance outcomes.

A recent survey of U.S. banking M&A transactions measured the impact on post-acquisition impact of (1) preacquisition attributes, for example target firm performance, acquirer size, and market overlap, (2) postintegration decisions, in terms of the extent of integration required and degree of senior management replacement involved; and (3) tacit learning and knowledge codification applied. Some of the results of the survey are the following (Zollo 2000).

Target quality had a significant negative impact on post-acquisition performance. This negative impact suggests that the transfer of capabilities and resources between the acquirer and the target firm was a better way to create shareholder value than the opposite—that is, learning from the target. However, acquirer size did not have a significant impact on post-acquisition performance. Market overlap (defined as measured market relatedness in terms of geographical locations and types of customers served) also did not significantly impact post-acquisition performance. This seems surprising, given the greater potential for significant economies of scale in horizontal acquisitions than in market-extension acquisitions due to the rationalization of the geographic coverage and the cost savings of closing redundant branches. The finding suggests that the possibilities for value creation (mainly cost efficiencies) or destruction in horizontal mergers and acquisitions are equivalent to those achieved in market-extension M&A deals. Value creation in such mergers relies on revenue-enhancing opportunities, mainly through cross-selling and organizational learning.

The degree of post-acquisition integration (defined in terms of the alignment and centralization of systems, procedures, and products) had a significantly positive impact on post-acquisition performance. The degree of replacement of the target firm's senior management had a significantly negative impact on post-acquisition performance. This finding suggests that the replacement of the target's top management tended to destroy shareholder value rather than enhance it. Value destruction appeared to result from the loss of human and social capital associated with the departure of managers and from the noncooperative or antagonistic attitude of the remaining employees due to a perception of unfair treatment in the integration phase, thereby increasing the complexity involved in the integration process.

The amount of prior acquisition experience did not have a significant impact on post-acquisition performance. Prior acquisition experience by itself did not seem to be sufficient to affect firm performance due to the low frequency, high heterogeneity, and level of ambiguity (the risk of applying the lessons in one context to a seemingly similar but very different one) inherent in the acquisition process. This finding invalidates the benefits associated with the "learning by doing" mechanism.

The extent of knowledge codification did have a significantly positive impact on post-acquisition performance. The development of M&A integration capabilities seemed to have a strong positive effect on firm performance but not without costs—for example, investments in time and energy to create and update these tools. At some point there is a risk that the marginal costs of building and maintaining knowledge codification may outweigh the benefits of developing collective competencies for integrating M&A transactions. At higher levels of integration, the degree of knowledge codification did have a very significant positive impact on performance. This finding suggests that with increasing degrees of complexity due to higher integration levels, knowledge codification is a predictor of successful post-acquisition performance.

INTERFACE MANAGEMENT IN THE INTEGRATION PROCESS

The objective of interface management depends on the integration approach that is adopted. For an "absorption" acquisition, only a temporary interface management structure is likely to be necessary, whereas more permanent structures will be needed in symbiotic and especially preservation approaches. Interface management staff can be drawn from personnel of the parent firm, the acquired firm, or from the outside. Outsiders are valuable especially in preservation acquisitions, where objectivity and neutrality are key issues. Important quality characteristics of an interface manager include a high degree of fairness, excellent interpersonal and cross-cultural abilities, and a good understanding of the business of the acquired firm. Effective interface management should be capable of warding off undue interference from the parent, providing guidance, and delivering on commitments. During the interface management process, the acquiring firm needs to refocus the attention of the target's staff on operational issues, for example by providing performance targets. It also needs to provide a new vision and incentives to employees, for example through realistic and coherent mission statements. As the tables in Appendix 2 suggest, the integration tasks to be performed vary in accordance with the integration approach used.

The evidence suggests that knowledge codification does have a significant impact on postacquisition performance in certain instances. Thus, a frequent acquirer may want to consider developing integration tools of its own in areas such as systems conversion (conversion and training manual), human resources integration (staffing models, training, and integration packages), sales and marketing integration (product mapping, product training manuals), and possibly other areas as well. There appear to be some limits to codification, however. Some U.S. non-bank financial firms have had apparent success in using knowledge codification in integrating their acquisitions, notably the former GE Capital Services (see Appendix 2, Table 6). And the empirical findings linking knowledge codification to post-acquisition performance are so far limited to acquisitions only—that is, no mergers of equals—mostly among U.S. commercial banks; the data do not yet cover investment banks, asset managers, insurance companies, or other types of financial services firms.

BENCHMARKING M&A INTEGRATION PERFORMANCE

In the end, the integration effort must be judged against a number of benchmarks set by management and consistent with extracting maximum shareholder value accretion from the acquisition or merger. Figure 4-3 is one way to depict the integration process. The key questions revolve around how it affects the following impact areas:

- Client retention and extension—that is, the firm's core franchise.
- Presence in major product and geographic markets achieved, as measured by market share, industry rankings, and similar indicators
- Human resources disruptions encountered, resulting in defections of key personnel, cultural conflict, and erosion of morale
- Economies of scale and operating efficiencies achieved as measured, for example in cost-to-income ratios
- IT disruptions encountered and their impact on revenue generation and cost structures

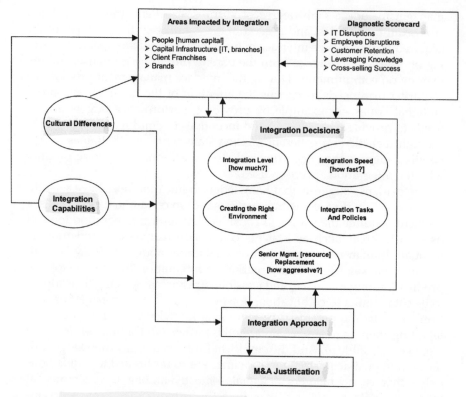

Figure 4-3. The Integration Process: A Framework.

- Revenue economies of scope achieved, including leveraging of distribution channels and cross-selling gains achieved
- Leveraging of knowledge and specialist expertise across the firm

The relevant integration tasks for the three major types of M&A transactions—the absorption, preservation and symbiotic approaches identified earlier—are presented in Tables 4-7, 4-8, and 4-9. Each merger or acquisition has unique features and can easily go wrong (or leave a great deal of value on the table) if the integration process is mishandled.

As noted, the tables in Appendix 2 summarize a series of case studies intended to benchmark M&A integration approaches in a series of transactions based on available deal information. These include the acquisition of a regional investment bank by a nationwide commercial bank (CIBC–Wood Gundy), a major domestic European commercial banking merger (Banco Santander–Banco Central Hispano), a highly acquisitive serial dealmaker in U.S. commercial banking (Banc One), acquisition of a major wholesale bank by a European universal bank (Deutsche Bank–Bankers Trust), acquisition of a technology-based investment bank by a major

Table 4-7 Integration Tasks—Absorption Approach

Task	Purpose	Actions and Methods
Preparing the blueprint for consolidation	Work out the integration plan in detail over a precise time-line, with deadlines and targets provided.	• *Choose a single leader* [avoid a board]. • *Choose the management team* [senior managers from both sides, and involve them in choosing the choice of individuals at the next level]. Selection must be rather quick, otherwise creates employee disruptions [value destruction]. • *Install a transition structure with specific tasks for key integration areas* to identify and evaluate potential synergies and ways to achieve them. Task forces should be used selectively using criteria of critically and compatibility [how compatible is integration in this area?]. Focus on critical functions, where firms have used different approaches [high criticality/low compatibility]. Strongly recommended not to postpone solutions in these areas. Second priority of task forces is to focus on critical but compatible functions. Here the payoff will be to demonstrate merger benefits. Decisions on what trade-offs [what areas to focus on] should be made on factual evidence/analysis not on political grounds. • *Manage to an integration calendar*: announce and stick to a workable/realistic calendar for maintaining pressure for progress. • *Communication*: preparation of integration plan requires much preparation along the way. The logic and timing must be sold to employees, usually in a confused and turbulent environment. Communication must be frequent, clear, and transparent.
Managing the rationalization process	Crux of the integration process, as a number of areas must be merged within a certain time span.	• *Weigh clear benefits and costs of rationalizing a function*. Sometimes the costs include intangible ones of compromise such as diminished moral . . . • *A determined and fast-paced execution is needed*: avoid danger of slowing down the speed because of a perceived difficulty or resistance. *(continued)*

Table 4-7 Integration Tasks—Absorption Approach (continued)

Task	Purpose	Actions and Methods
		• *Get acceptance of the integration:* (1) focus on real issues [what creates real improvements on results such as investments], not on principles; (2) *communicate* integration goals clearly and allow debate; (3) and *co-opt managers of acquired firm* [are winners as well].
Move to best practice	Search and adopt areas of "best practice" [aside from benefits of resource sharing, absorption can provide functional skill transfers as well]. This may be the main source of value creation.	• Implement a systematic program determining best practice on the basis of technical parameters. • Share and transfer that practice.
Harnessing the complementarity	Focus also on complementarities [differences] rather than just similarities [resource sharing benefits]. Focus on cultural differences.	• *Ensure uniformity on some dimensions and encourage complementarity on other dimensions* [allow for different brand spaces and allocate responsibilities]. This will foster innovation and drive.

Source: Philippe Haspeslagh and David Jemison, *Managing Acquisitions* (New York: Free Press, 1991).

commercial bank (NationsBank–Montgomery Securities), and a serial non-bank financial services acquirer (the former GE Capital Services) that has grown rapidly in multiple niches by using both roll-ups and major acquisitions and has arguably perfected the acquisitions process better than any other firm.

SUMMARY

This chapter has considered key issues involved in the post-M&A integration process with specific reference to the financial services industry. Most of them are given by the nature and objective of the transactions themselves and the organizational design into which they are intended to fit. Sequencing is important, as are human relations and cultural aspects. In a human capital-intensive business like financial services, problems related to incentives, morale, and leadership have probably destroyed more shareholder value than probably any other. Each integration

Table 4-8 Integration Tasks—Preservation Approach

Task	Purpose	Actions and Methods
Continued boundary protection	Permanent need for vigilance of non-interference from parent company.	• Gatekeepers may constantly need to use their influence to ward off interference. • Gatekeepers have to also meet corporate staff needs (deal personally with planning and control forms).
Nurturing to accelerate business development	*Create value by nurturing the acquisition to accelerate business development.* Fallacies are to think that this is accomplished by leaving it alone and generous funding. This is not really the case.	Three key actions to be taken in nurturing process: • *Instilling ambition:* key is not to throw resources at acquired firm but to increase horizons, raise ambitions of acquired management, and change risk perceptions. The small size of acquired firm may have caused "vision blindness." This can be done by using a policy statement (e.g., BP and Hendrix). The issue is not the use of the parent's resources but the fact that they are there. • *Practical support:* an ambitious vision must be accompanied by practical support that vision is strategically sound and that capabilities for implementation are there. What is critical here is the informal transfer of managerial expertise (not imposition of formal systems but one-on-one dialogue). At Hendrix, IM staff continuously clarified strategic objectives and furthered the professional development of management. • *Staying vigilant:* gatekeeping becomes harder to enforce once acquired company is becoming successful or expanding (e.g., Hendrix acquiring in Spain]. Non-interference principles should be reiterated.
Accumulate business learning	*To accumulate learning about the business and from the business (justification of the acquisition).* Industry and business knowledge will influence parent's decision whether to further move into an area.	• *Learning about the business:* gatekeepers play a key role in accumulating, sifting through, and disseminating this knowledge (learn the acquired business from an insider's perspective). However, learning must take place. For this, there must be a restrained environment (only a few people) and also the position of the acquired firm in the overall industry context must be understood. • *Learning from the business:* this learning provides long-term benefits to the parent's current domain (cultural and organizational change process through exposure to a very

(continued)

Table 4-8 Integration Tasks—Preservation Approach *(continued)*

Task	Purpose	Actions and Methods
		different business, such as CIBA-Geigy's entry into household products). This is more complex than learning about a business, as the base business can be hostile/suspicious about this sort of transfer. Solution lies with top management of parent to balance demands of host structure (IM) of champion status with that of equal treatment by base business of parent firm. Balance is function of parent to provide financial support for both (equal treatment) and IM structure to attract managerial talent to acquired firm and willingness to maybe lose them to parent.
Organizational championing	*Due to their platform type, viability within the parent is rarely stable (too small to represent a durable commitment). Momentum must come from IM structure, which must act as champions and persuade parent to commit resources.*	*What is needed:* (1) strong leadership; (2) demonstrate early control over operating performance; (3) ability to maintain good rapports with corporate staff units (strategic planning), who are the "friends at court." • *Possible pitfall of expanding acquired firm through acquisitions:* can put pressure on IM structure to focus on short-term operational results of acquired firm than on issues needed to promote internal growth (investment in people).

Source: Plilippe Haspeslagh and David Jemison, *Managing Acquisitions* (New York: Free Press, 1991).

Table 4-9 Integration Tasks—Symbiotic Approach

Task	Purpose	Actions and Methods
Starting with preservation	*All contacts need to be channeled through gatekeeping structure.* However, attention needs to be paid to managers of acquirer and organizational reporting of new unit.	• *Need for patience:* minimize the pressure the acquired firm (due to the premiums paid for the transaction). Allay fears by focusing managers of acquired firm on own budgets and long-term performance. Clear need for understanding between corporate level and IM on strategic objectives, time-horizons, and type of organizational path. • *Hold back acquirer's managers:* claims for involvement by acquiring firm's managers are stronger, especially those who worked on the acquisition process and identified the potential synergies. Will have to agree to a delay but also prepare their own organization as a receptor of the intended capability. • *Both companies are adjacent (side by side):* report to a single executive, who will provide vision and pressure both companies to prepare for change.
Reaching out rather than reaching in	*Achieve the capabilities transfer between both sides.*	• *Boundary to be transformed into a semipermeable membrane:* key determining success factors were the style and direction of initial and subsequent contacts. Initial contacts should originate from managers in acquired firm. To facilitate this, acquiring firm to put at the disposition of acquired firm experienced individuals to help to identify resources in parent organization that would solve their problems. This will help convince acquired firm of accruing benefits from early interactions.
Trading operational responsibility for strategic control	*Overtime, need to increase the influence of parent.*	• *Entrust managers of acquired firm with more responsibilities* (giving product lines). At operating level, both companies remain distinct. • Yet strategy is increasingly developed to parent, as resources and people move over to it.
Amalgamating the organizations	*End-goal to become a new, unique entity, without losing the character underlying capabilities of acquired firm.*	• *Senior executives in both organizations assigned double roles:* guardian of their own unit and an involvement in broader strategy decisions. • *Regroup the individuals physically or geographically:* for example, invest in new buildings, facilities. Lessening the physical distance, lessens the demand for maintaining differences (separate compensation structure).

Source: Pilitppe Haspeslagh and David Jemison, *Managing Acquisitions* (New York: Free Press. 1991).

exercise presents a series of "war stories" that range from virtually seam-less exercises to abject failure. And it appears that firms can learn to integrate. In an industry as dynamic as financial services, this is not a bad skill to develop. The following chapter continues the integration story with one of its most critical dimensions, information technology.

5

The Special Problem
of IT Integration

Information technology (IT) systems form the core of today's financial institutions and underpin their ability to compete in a rapidly changing environment. Consequently, integration of information technology has become a focal point of the mergers and acquisitions process in the financial services sector. Sometimes considered largely a "technical" issue, IT integration has proved to be a double-edged sword. IT is often a key source of synergies that can add to the credibility of an M&A transaction. But IT integration can also be an exceedingly frustrating and time-consuming process that can not only endanger anticipated cost advantages but also erode the trust of shareholders, customers, employees and other stakeholders.

IT spending is the largest non-interest-related expense item (second only to human resources) for most financial service organizations (see Figure 5-1 for representative IT spend-levels). Banks must provide a consistent customer experience across multiple distribution channels under demanding time-to-market, data distribution, and product quality conditions. There is persistent pressure to integrate proprietary and alliance-based networks with public and shared networks to improve efficiency and service quality. None of this comes cheap. For example, J.P. Morgan was one of the most intensive private-sector user of IT for many years. Before its acquisition by Chase Manhattan, Morgan was spending more than $75,000 on IT per employee annually, or almost 40% of its compensation budget (Strassmann 2001). Other banks spent less on IT but still around 15–20% of total operating costs. Moreover, IT spend-levels in many firms have tended to grow at or above general operating cost in-

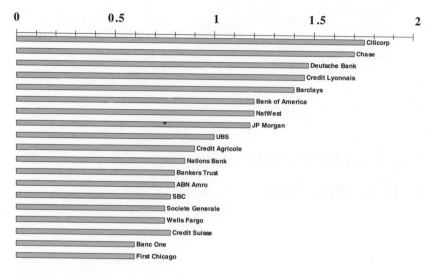

Figure 5-1. Estimated Major Bank IT Spend-Levels ($ billions).
Source: The Tower Group, 1996.

creases, as legacy systems need to be updated and new IT-intensive products and distribution channels are developed.

As a consequence, bank mergers can result in significant IT cost savings, with the potential of contributing more than 25% of the synergies in
a financial industry merger. McKinsey has estimated that 30–50% of all
bank merger synergies depend directly on IT (Davis 2000), and The Tower
Group estimated that a large bank with an annual IT budget of $1.3 billion
could free up an extra $600 million to reinvest in new technology if it
merged, as a consequence of electronic channel savings, pressure on suppliers, mega-data centers, and best-of-breed common applications.[1] However, many IT savings targets can be off by at least 50% (*Bank Director*
2002). Lax and undisciplined systems analysis during due diligence, together with the retention of multiple IT infrastructures, is a frequent cause
of significant cost overruns.

Such evidence suggests that finding the right IT integration strategy is
one of the more complex subjects in a financial industry merger. What
makes it so difficult are the legacy systems and their links to a myriad
applications. Banks and other financial services firms were among the
first businesses to adopt firmwide computer systems. Many continue to
use technologies that made their debut in the 1970s. Differing IT system
platforms and software packages have proven to be important constraints
on consolidation. Which IT systems are to be retained? Which are to be
abandoned? Would it be better to take an M&A opportunity to build a

1. "Merger Mania Catapults Tech Spending," *Bank Technology News*, December 6, 1998.

completely new, state-of-the-art IT infrastructure instead? What options are feasible in terms of financial and human resources? How can the best legacy systems be retained without losing the benefits of a standardized IT infrastructure?

To further complicate matters, IT staff as well as end users tend to become very "exercised" about the decision process. The elimination of an IT system can mean to laying off entire IT departments. In-house end users must get used to new applications programs, and perhaps change work-flow practices. IT people tend to take a proprietary interest in "their" systems created over the years—they tend to be emotionally as well intellectually attached to their past achievements. So important IT staff might defect due to frustrations about "wrong" decisions made by the "new" management. Even down the road, culture clashes can complicate the integration process. "Us" versus "them" attitudes can easily develop and fester.

Efforts are often channeled into demonstrating that one merging firm's systems and procedures is superior to those of the other and therefore should be retained or extended to the entire organization. Such pressures can lead to compromises that might turn out to be only a quick fix for an unpleasant integration dispute. Such IT-based power struggles during the integration process are estimated to consume up to 40% more staff resources than in the case of straightforward harmonization of IT platforms. (Hoffmann 1999).

At the same time, it is crucial that IT conversions remain on schedule. Retarded IT integration has the obvious potential to delay many of the non-IT integration efforts discussed in the previous chapter. Redundant branches cannot be closed on time, cross-selling initiatives most be postponed, and back-office consolidations cannot be completed as long as the IT infrastructure is not up to speed. In turn, this can have important implications for the services offered by the firm and strain the relationship to the newly combined client base.

An Accenture study, conducted in summer 2001, polled 2,000 U.S. clients on their attitude toward bank mergers. It found, among other things, that the respondents consider existing personal relationships and product quality to be the most important factors in their choice of a financial institution. When a merger is announced, 62% of the respondents said they were "concerned" about its implications and 63% expected no improvement. Following the merger, 70% said that their experience was worse than before the deal, with assessments of relationship and product cost registering the biggest declines. Such bleak results can be even worse when failures in IT intensify client distrust. The results are inevitably reflected in client defections and in the ability to attract new ones, in market share, and in profitability.

But successful IT integration can generate a wide range of positive outcomes that support the underlying merger rationale. For instance, it can enhance the organization's competitive position and help shape or enable critical strategies (Rentch 1990; Gutek 1978). It can assure good quality, accurate, useful, and timely information and an operating platform that combines system availability, reliability, and responsiveness. It can enable identification and assimilation of new technologies, and it can help recruit and retain a technically and managerially competent IT staff (Caldwell and Medina 1990; Enz 1988) Indeed, the integration process can be an opportunity to integrate IT planning with organizational planning and the ability to provide firmwide, state-of-the-art information accessibility and business support.

KEY IT INTEGRATION ISSUES

As noted, information technology can be either a stumbling block or an important success factor in a bank merger. This discussion focuses on some general factors that are believed to be critical for the success of IT integration in the financial services industry M&A context. Unfortunately, much of the available evidence so far is case-specific and anecdotal, and concerns mainly the technical aspects treated in isolation from the underlying organizational and strategic M&A context.

Whether an IT integration process is likely to be completed on time and create significant cost savings or maintain and improve service quality often depends in part on the acquirer's pre-merger IT setup (see Figure 5-2). The overall fit between business strategies and IT developments focuses on several questions: is the existing IT configuration sufficiently aligned to support the firm's business strategy going forward? If not, is the IT system robust enough to digest a new transformation process resulting from the contemplated merger? Given the existing state of the IT infrastructure and its alignment with the overall business goals, which merger objectives and integration strategies can realistically be pursued? The answers usually center on the interdependencies between business strategy, IT strategy, and merger strategy (Johnston and Zetton 1996).

Once an acquirer is sufficiently confident about its own IT setup and has identified an acquisition target, management needs to make one of

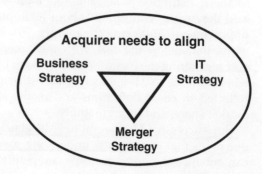

Figure 5-2. Alignment of Business Strategy, IT Strategy, and Merger Strategy.

the most critical decisions: to what extend should the IT systems of the target be integrated into the acquirer's existing infrastructure? On the one hand, the integration decision is very much linked to the merger goals—for example, exploit cost reductions or new revenue streams. On the other hand, the acquirer needs to focus on the fit between the two IT platforms. In a merger, the technical as well as organizational IT configurations of the two firms must be carefully assessed. Nor can the organizational and staffing issues be underestimated. Several tactical options need to be considered as well: should all systems be converted at one specific and predetermined date or can the implementation occur in steps? Each approach has its advantages and disadvantages, including the issues of user-friendliness, system reliability, and operational risk.

ALIGNMENT OF BUSINESS STRATEGY, MERGER STRATEGY, AND IT STRATEGY

Over the years, information technology has been transformed from a process-driven necessity to a key strategic issue. Dramatic developments in the underlying technologies plus deregulation and strategic repositioning efforts of financial firms have all had their IT consequences, often requiring enormous investments in infrastructure (see Figure 5-3). Meeting new IT expectations leads to significant operational complexity due to large numbers of new technology options affecting both front- and back-office functions (*The Banker* 2001). This evolution is often welcomed by the IT groups in acquirers who are newly in charge of much larger and more expensive operations. At the same time, however, they also face a very unpleasant and sometimes dormant structural problem—the legacy systems.

Most European financial firms and some U.S. firms continue to run a patchwork of systems that were generally developed in-house over several decades. The integration of new technologies has added further to the complexity and inflexibility of IT infrastructures. What once was considered decentralized, flexible, multi-product solutions became viewed as a high-maintenance, functionally inadequate, and incompatible cost item. The heterogeneity of IT systems became a barrier rather than an enabler for new business developments. Business strategy and IT strategy were no longer in balance.

This dynamic tended to deteriorate further in an M&A context. Being a major source of purported synergy, the two existing IT systems usually require rapid integration. For IT staff this can be a Herculean task. Bound by tight time schedules, combined with even tighter budget constraints and an overriding mandate not to interrupt business activities, IT staff has to take on two challenges—the legacy systems and the integration process. Under such high-pressure conditions, anticipated merger synergies are difficult to achieve in the short term. And reconfiguring the entire

IT infrastructure to effectively and efficiently support new business strategies does not get any easier.

(1)   The misalignment of business strategy and IT strategy has been recognized as a major hindrance to the successful exploitation of competitive advantage in the financial services sector. (Watkins, 1992). Pressure on management to focus on both sides of the cost-income equation has become a priority item on the agenda for most CEOs and CIOs (*The Banker* 2001). Some observers have argued that business strategy has both an external view that determines the firm's position in the market and an internal view that determines how processes, people, and structures will perform. In this conceptualization, IT strategy should have the same external and internal components, although it has traditionally focused only on the internal IT infrastructure—the processes, the applications, the hardware, the people, and the internal capabilities (see Figure 5-3). But external IT strategy has become increasingly indispensable.

For example, if a retail bank's IT strategy is to move aggressively in the area of Web-based distribution and marketing channels, the management must decide whether it wants to enter a strategic alliance with a technology firm or whether all those competencies should be kept internal. If a strategic alliance is the best option, management needs to decide with whom: a small company, a startup, a consulting firm, or perhaps one of the big software firms? These choices do not change the business strategy, but they can have a major impact on how that business strategy unfolds over time. In short, organizations need to assure that IT goals and business goals are synchronized (Henderson and Venkatraman 1992).

(2)   Once the degree of alignment between business strategy and IT strategy has been assessed, it becomes apparent whether the existing IT infrastructure can support a potential IT merger integration. At this point, alignment with merger strategy comes into play. As noted in Figure 5-4, much depends on whether the M&A deal involves: horizontal integration (the transaction is intended to increase the dimensions in the market), vertical integration (the objective is to add new products to the existing production chain), diversification (if there is a search for a broader portfolio of individual activities to generate cross-selling or reduce risk), or consolidation (if the objective is to achieve economies of scale and operating cost reduction) (Trautwein 1990). Each of these merger objectives requires a different degree of IT integration. Cost-driven M&A deals usually lead to a full, in-depth IT integration.

(3)   Given the alignment of IT and business strategies, management of the merging firms can assess whether their IT organizations are ready for the deal. Even such a straightforward logic can become problematic for an aggressive acquirer; while the IT integration of a previous acquisition is still in progress, a further IT merger will add new complexity. Can the organization handle two or more IT integrations at the same time? Shareholders and customers are critical observers of the process and may not

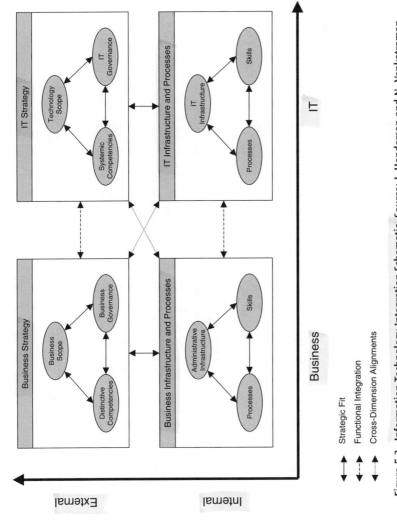

Figure 5-3. Information Technology Integration Schematic. Source: J. Henderson and N. Venkatraman, "Strategic Alignment: A Model for Organizational Transformation through Information Technology," in T. Kochon and M. Unseem, eds., *Transformation Organisations* (New York: Oxford University Press, 1992).

Business Strategy

Business Scope: *Determines where the enterprise will compete* – market segmentation, types of products, niches, customers, geography, etc.

Distinctive Competencies: *How will the firm compete in delivering its products and services* – how the firm will differentiate its products/services (e.g. pricing strategy, focus on quality, superior marketing channels).

Business Governance: Will the firm enter the market as a single entity, via alliances, partnership, or outsourcing?

IT Strategy

IT Scope: *Types of ITs that are critical to the organization* – knowledge-based systems, electronic imaging, robotics, multimedia, etc.

Systemic Competencies: *Strengths of IT that are critical to the creation or extension of business strategies* – information, connectivity, accessibility, reliability, responsiveness, etc.

IT Governance: Extent of ownership of ITs (e.g. end user, executive, steering committee) or the possibility of technology alliances (e.g. partnerships, outsourcing), or both; application make-or-buy decisions; etc.

Business Infrastructure and Processes

Administrative Structure: *Roles, responsibilities, and authority structure* – Is the firm organized around product lines? How many management layers are required?

Processes: *Manner in which key business functions will operate* – Determines the extent to which work flows will be restructured, perhaps integrated, to improve effectiveness and efficiency.

Skills: *Human resource issues* – Experience, competencies, values, norms of professional required to meet the strategy? Will the business strategy require new skills? Is outsourcing required?

IT Infrastructure and Processes

IT Architecture: Choices, priorities, and policies that enable the synthesis of applications, data, software, and hardware via a cohesive platform

Processes: Design of major IT work functions and practices – application development system management controls, operations, etc.

Skills: Experience, competencies, commitments, values, and norms of individuals working to deliver IT products and services.

External

Internal

Business

IT

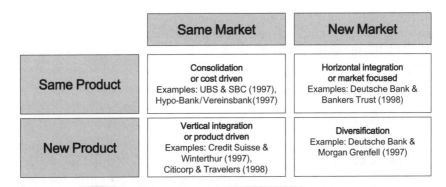

	Same Market	New Market
Same Product	Consolidation or cost driven Examples: UBS & SBC (1997), Hypo-Bank/Vereinsbank(1997)	Horizontal integration or market focused Examples: Deutsche Bank & Bankers Trust (1998)
New Product	Vertical integration or product driven Examples: Credit Suisse & Winterthur (1997), Citicorp & Travelers (1998)	Diversification Example: Deutsche Bank & Morgan Grenfell (1997)

Figure 5-4. Mapping IT Integration Requirements, Products, and Markets. Source: Penzel. H.-G., Pietig, Ch., *MergerGuide—Handbuch für die Integration von Banken* (Wiesbaden: Gabler Verlag, 2000).

be convinced, so early analysis of a firm's IT merger capability can be a helpful tool in building a sensible case.

In recent years, outsourcing strategies have become increasingly popular. With the aim of significantly reducing IT costs, network operations and maintenance have been bundled and placed with outsourcing firms. This has the advantage of freeing up resources to better and more efficiently handle other IT issues, such as the restructuring of legacy systems. However, critics argue that there is no evidence that financial firms really save as a result of outsourcing large parts of their IT operations. On the contrary, they argue that firms need to be careful not to outsource critical IT components that are pivotal for their business operations. Outsourcing may also sacrifice the capability of integrating other IT systems in mergers going forward. In this case, the business and IT strategies might well be aligned, but they may also be incompatible with further M&A transactions.

Lloyds TSB provided an example of a pending IT integration process that made it difficult to merge with another bank. Although Lloyds and TSB effectively became one bank in October 1995, the two banks did not actually merge their IT systems for five years. In fact, three years after the announcement, the bank was still in the early stages of integrating its IT infrastructure. The reason was not the cost involved or poor integration planning, but rather the fact that the Act of Parliament that allowed Lloyds to merge its customer base with TSB's was not enacted until 1999. During the intervening period it would have been difficult for Lloyds TSB to actively pursue any other potential M&A opportunities. The subsequent integration process would have added even more complexity to the existing situation. Not only would the ongoing internal integration process have been disrupted, but customers might have faced further inconveniences as well. During the five years of system integration, customers of the combined bank experienced different levels of service, depending on from which bank they originally came. For example, if a former TSB customer deposited a check and then immediately viewed the balance at an ATM, the deposit was shown instantly. But if a former Lloyds customer made the same transaction at the same branch, it did not show up until the following day.

THE CHALLENGE OF IT INTEGRATION

At the beginning of every merger or acquisition stands the evaluation of the potential fit between the acquiring firm and the potential target. This assessment, conducted during the due diligence phase, forms the basis for IT synergy estimates as well as IT integration strategies.

Take, for example, two Australian Banks—the Commonwealth Bank of Australia (CBA) and the State Bank of Victoria (SBV), which CBA acquired for A$1.6 billion in January 1991.[2] CBA was one of Australia's largest, with its head office in Sydney and spanning some 1,400 branches across the country with 40,000 staff and assets of A$67 billion. The bank was owned at the time by the Australian government. SBV was the largest bank in the State of Victoria, with its head office in Melbourne. It encompassed 527 branches, 2 million customer records, 12,000 staff (including 1,000 IT staff), and assets of A$24 billion.

CBA had a solid, centralized, and highly integrated organizational setup, whereas SBV was known for its more decentralized and business-unit driven structure. CBA's IT organization was more efficient, integrated, and cost-control oriented. Its centralized structure and tight management approach were geared toward achieving performance goals, which were reinforced by a technological emphasis on high standards and a dominant IT architecture reflecting its "in-house" expertise. IT staffing was mainly through internal recruitment, training and promotion, and rewarded for loyalty and length of service. This produced a conservative and risk-averse management style. CBA's IT configuration was well suited to its business environment, which was relatively stable and allowed management to have a tight grip on IT costs within a large and formalized IT organization that was functionally insulated from the various businesses.

SBV's IT organization, on the other hand, was focused on servicing the needs of the organization's business units. Supported by a decentralized IT management structure and flexible, project-based management processes, the IT organization concentrated on how it could add value to each business unit. Because it was highly responsive to multiple business divisions, SBV ran a relatively high IT cost structure, with high staffing levels and a proliferation of systems and platforms. The IT professional staff was externally trained, mobile, and motivated by performance-

2. This example is taken with permission from Johnston and Zetton (1996).

driven pay and promotion. This structure was a good match for the bank's overall diversified, market-focused business environment. The corporate IT unit coordinated the business divisions' competing demands for IT services in cooperation with IT staff located within the various business divisions.

Based on its due diligence of SBV, CBA identified the integration of the computer systems and IT operations of the two banks as a major source of value in the merger. However, it was clear that the two banks' IT setups were very different, as is evident in Figure 5-5.

To address these differences, CBA decided as a first step to build a temporary technical bridge between the two banks' IT systems so that customers of either bank could access accounts at any branch of the newly merged institution. To retain SBV customers, CBA decided to proceed carefully rather than undertaking radical IT rationalization. Emphasis was on keeping the existing IT shells operational until a full-scale branch systems conversion could be undertaken. CBA decided to pursue a best-of-both-worlds approach: identify best practice in each area of the two banks' IT platforms, which could then be adopted as the basis for building a new integrated IT structure.

Integration meetings between each bank's IT specialist areas did not

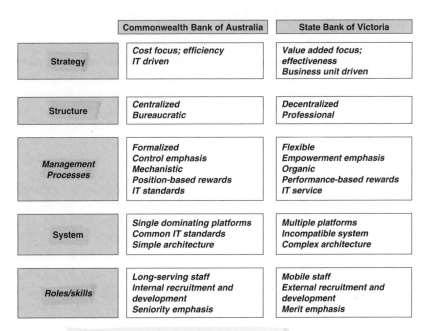

	Commonwealth Bank of Australia	State Bank of Victoria
Strategy	Cost focus; efficiency IT driven	Value added focus; effectiveness Business unit driven
Structure	Centralized Bureaucratic	Decentralized Professional
Management Processes	Formalized Control emphasis Mechanistic Position-based rewards IT standards	Flexible Empowerment emphasis Organic Performance-based rewards IT service
System	Single dominating platforms Common IT standards Simple architecture	Multiple platforms Incompatible system Complex architecture
Roles/skills	Long-serving staff Internal recruitment and development Seniority emphasis	Mobile staff External recruitment and development Merit emphasis

Figure 5-5. Comparing IT Integration in a Merger Situation. Source: K.D. Johnston and P.W. Zetton, "Integrating Information Technology Divisions in a Bank Merger—Fit, Compatibility and Models of Change," *Journal of Strategic Information Systems*, 5, 1996, 189.

succeed for long. Agreeing on what was best practice became increasingly difficult. Fueled by technical differences as well as by the emotional and political atmosphere of the takeover, strategy disagreements between IT teams mounted, and there were extensive delays in planning and implementation.

Meanwhile, CBA faced increasing pressure to complete the IT integration. Competitors were taking advantage of the paralysis while the two banks' were caught in the integration process. And it became expensive for CBA to run dual IT structures. Shareholders were becoming concerned whether the promised IT synergies could actually be realized and whether the merger economics still made sense. CBA decided to replace the best-of-both-worlds approach by an absorption approach that would fully convert all of SBV's operations into CBA's existing IT architecture. For the IT area, this meant the rationalization and simplification of systems and locations and the elimination of dual platforms. Indeed, the merger was completed on time and IT synergies contributed significantly to the anticipated value creation of the merged bank.

Traditionally, potential technical incompatibilities of two IT systems receive most of the attention during the due diligence phase and the subsequent merger integration process. But resolving technical incompatibilities alone usually does not take care of key integration problems stemming from underlying dissonance among IT strategy, structure, management processes, or roles and skills in each organization. Regardless of the technology differences, the incompatibility of two organizational cultures (which in the CBA-SBV case emerged from the particular evolution of organizational components within each configuration) can itself be sufficient to cause problems during integration. Each IT configuration evolves along a different dynamic path involving the development of organizational resources and learning specific to that path. In this case, CBA was technology-centered and efficiency-driven, whereas SBV was business-centered and sought to add value. The two IT configurations, while internally congruent and compatible within their own organization, were incompatible with each other.

This incompatibility between the two IT configurations helps explain the dynamics of the IT integration process in this particular example. The strategic planning for IT integration after the takeover of SBV by CBA envisaged a two-step process. First, a technical bridge was to be built between the banks, enabling the separate IT configurations to be maintained. This was a temporary form of coexistence. Second, a new configuration based on a best-of-both-worlds model of change was developed. Eventually that model was abandoned, and an absorption model was adopted that integrateed the SBV platform into the CBA structure.

In a classic view, the firm's choice of strategy determines the appropriate organizational design according to which the strategy is implemented—structure follows strategy (Chandler, 1962). A parallel argument can be made in the case of IT integration. Given a sensible merger strategy and the existing IT setups of the merging firms, four IT integration strategies can be distinguished (see Figure 5.6):

- Full integration or absorption of one firm's IT systems into the other's existing systems
- Keeping systems separated and running the two IT platforms in parallel
- Combining the most efficient systems of both firms
- Developing a new, state-of-the-art IT system, possibly coupled to partial outsourcing IT operations

The difference between IT configurations might explain the shift from a best-of-both-worlds approach to an absorption model in the CBA-SBV case. A political view might explain the absorption of one bank's IT configuration as a function of the relative power of the (usually larger) acquiring organization's IT units (Linder 1989). An alternative explanation is that the IT configuration of the dominant firm in an M&A transaction is a product of established organizational fit between the acquiring organization and its IT units—a fit that supports the stated goals of the merger. In this case SBV had a decentralized IT management structure and flexible, project-based management processes as opposed to CBA's centralized structure that very much valued efficiency, integration, and cost control. A reverse absorption by SBV would therefore have resulted in a misfit between its IT configuration and that of its new parent orga-

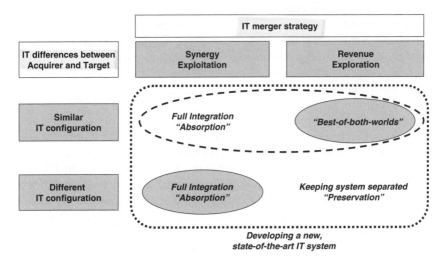

Figure 5-6. Schematic of Principal Drivers of IT Integration. Source: Author's diagram based on inputs from K.D. Johnston and P.W. Zetton, "Integrating Information Technology Divisions in a Bank Merger—Fit, Compatibility and Models of Change," *Journal of Strategic Information Systems*, 5, 1996, 189–211, as well as P. Haspeslagh and D. Jeminson, *Managing Acquistions* (New York: Free Press, 1991) and own thoughts.

nization. Although SBV might have many characteristics that were attractive to CBA, the "reverse takeover" would have created the need for multiple and complex changes in CBA's operations to reestablish alignment of IT and its organization. However, it might be feasible to do a reverse takeover where there is only slight overlap or the target's IT systems are significantly stronger than the acquirer's.

The Full Integration: The "Absorption" Approach

When an organization's strategy is intent on cost reductions from IT integration, the absorption of one IT system by another is almost a foregone conclusion. In this case, all business processes are unified and all applications standardized. Central data processing centers are combined. Network connections are dimensioned to support data flow to and from the centralized data-processing center. Databases may also have to be converted to new standards as well as new software packages.

The major problems associated with the integration of two incompatible IT configurations are thus avoided. Complexity can be significantly reduced, as can time to completion. But this strategy is not without its risks. One risk concerns the management of the downsizing process. The length of downsizing initiatives becomes important when redundant IT systems need to be maintained for a longer period in order to ensure full service capabilities until all system components are converted onto the dominant platform. To keep this time as short as possible and avoid any unintended disruptions, key IT staff members need to be kept on board. Another potential risk relates to scaling up existing systems to cover increased transaction volumes. The platform that absorbs the redundant IT system must be capable of handling the increased data volumes from the outset. Obviously, the integration process will be much easier and faster if only relatively minor adjustments are required in two systems that are already quite similar. However, IT integration can also be a good opportunity to improve or even extend current IT capabilities.

When Union Bank of Switzerland and Swiss Bank Corporation merged in 1997 to form the present UBS AG, the two banks hoped to achieve annual cost savings of some $2.3 billion by eliminating duplication in distribution, product development, and especially IT infrastructure. SBC had been a loyal user of IBM-compatible mainframes, supplied by Hitachi, whereas the Union Bank of Switzerland was a long-time user of Unisys mainframes. The two hardware platforms were incompatible. An added complication was that both banks were using custom software to run their respective retail banking operations (Nairn 1999).

The SBC software, called Real-Time Banking (RTB), consisted of 25,000 programs that only ran on its IBM-compatible mainframes. UBS had its own Abacus suite of 15,000 programs that only worked on the Unisys computers. The two banks had invested decades in the development of their respective programs and the IT staff of each bank, naturally, claimed their technology was superior. "The conflict was less about the hardware platform and more a question of which was the best software application," according to Dominic Fraymond, head of large accounts for Unisys Switzerland (Nairn 1999). The bank knew it had to make a clean choice.

To counter charges of favoritism, an external consultant was retained to evaluate the competing systems. Unisys won the battle, and a crop of new ClearPath servers was acquired to expand capacity at the UBS datacenter in Zurich, where IT operations for the whole group were centralized. SBC's legacy datacenter in Basle continued to support those SBC branches that had not yet abandoned the RTB software, but the bank had all its branches running on the common IT platform in Zurich by the end of 1999.

In February 2001, Citigroup announced a deal to buy the $15.4 billion (assets) European American Bank for $1.6 billion from ABN Amro Holdings NV. Observers were quick to call it a defensive move. The deal, completed five months later, kept a 97-branch franchise in Citi's home market, the New York City area, from the clutches of such aggressive competitors as FleetBoston Financial Corp. and North Fork Bancorp. of Melville, New York. Although Citigroup had gained a great deal of experience in acquisition integration, it had not been an active buyer of U.S. banks. European American, headquartered in Uniondale, gave Citigroup executives a chance to test their acquisition, merger, and integration skills on an acquired branch banking system.

European American Bank's earnings were almost invisible on Citigroup's bottom line. But 70% of its branches were on Long Island, as were $6.2 billion of deposits, and this gave Citigroup a 10.3% local market share, second only to J.P. Morgan Chase's 13.1%. Still, the average former European American branch lagged other Citigroup branches by 17% in revenue and 23% in net income, although the European American branches were ahead in terms of growth. Citigroup intended to bring its own consumer banking expertise to former EAB branches and focus the latter's skills on serving small and mid-size business on established Citigroup markets.

One reason for the growth in branch revenue after Citigroup bought EAB was the use of Citipro—essentially a questionnaire about customers' financial needs that is offered as a free financial planning tool. In addition to helping point customers in the right direction financially, it identified opportunities for the bank to make sales—investments and insurance in addition loan and deposit accounts.

The Best-of-Both-Worlds Approach

If the strategic intent is to add value through capitalizing on merger-driven cost synergies, the best-of-both-worlds model could be appropriate. It aims to identify each aspect of the two firms' IT practices that could be adopted as the basis for building a new integrated IT structure. At the same time, this approach requires a lengthy process of meetings between each firm's IT teams. The best systems and processes of both need to be identified, analyzed, and finally adopted. The key question is whether the two IT platforms are compatible. Where this is the case, synergies can be realized by incremental adjustments, capitalizing on possibilities for learning among the individual elements in the IT organization. However, where the configurations are incompatible, high costs associated with a long period of systems realignment are likely to be encountered.

An example of this approach was the acquisition of a Chicago derivatives boutique, O'Connor & Associates, in 1994 by Swiss Bank Corporation. O'Connor used very sophisticated front-end IT applications in its derivatives business, whereas SBC used fairly standard software packages that were not as flexible and not as up-to-date with respect to the latest business developments. As a consequence, SBC decided to keep O'Connor's IT applications and progressively integrate them into the existing SBC (later UBS) platforms. Having chosen the best-of-both-worlds approach, the bank was at the same time able to absorb knowledge about the derivatives business and its IT implications.

Preservation: Keeping IT Systems Separate

Here the acquirer's strategy does not provide for any integration of the IT systems of the two companies. All components are intentionally kept independent. The only linkages are those for transmission of the data necessary for corporate management. The two organizations remain separate.

This setup is usually only selected for acquisitions of unrelated or geographically distinct businesses. Maintaining separate IT configurations is likely to be low risk and minimizes integration complexity. Whether the two premerger IT configurations fit or not is irrelevant. The individual IT platforms are sustained, interdependencies minimized, and integration limited to establishing interfaces between the systems. This avoids the organizational complexities associated with attempting to combine the two configurations. Although it is low-risk, the preservation option generally produces a higher overall IT cost structure, since there are few gains from economies of scale and reduced levels of resource duplication.

When Citicorp and Travelers announced their merger in 1998, it was clear that this was not supposed to be a cost-driven deal, but rather a revenue-driven transaction. With relatively limited overlap in activities and markets, there was less duplication and, as a result, less cost takeouts that were likely to occur. Indeed, Citicorp CEO John Reed and his counterpart at Travelers, Sandy Weill, did not emphasize cost cutting in their April 1998 announcement of the transaction. They planned on boosting their share of wallet through cross-selling between Citibank's 40 million U.S. customers and Travelers 20 million clients. Analysts estimated that the greatest advantage in cross-selling would go to the former Citicorp, which would integrate customers' account information, including insurance, banking, and credit cards, onto one statement. Facing incompatible IT configurations and the mandate to generate new revenue streams through cross-selling, Citi and Travelers decided not to follow the traditional absorption approach, but rather to keep their IT systems decentralized to promote the advantage of specialized configurations.

Development of New, State-of-the-Art IT Systems

The most attractive solution following a merger sometimes seems to be the development of a new, state-of-the-art IT platform. The firm can then scrap all legacy systems and realize its hopes for a true world-class system. Highly integrated IT platforms can fully support the client managers, trading floors, risk management, and top management requirements. Still, a complete buildup from scratch takes a long time and will absorb most IT resources for an extended period. Moreover, the firm risks being incapable of reacting to new market developments requiring an IT response. Besides, a *de novo* IT platform may be difficult to manage and to finance.

COMPARATIVE GAINS AND COSTS

The four integration options reviewed here can be seen from an IT strategy and configuration perspective. In a merger with two incompatible IT configurations, the implementation of a best-of-both-worlds approach is difficult. Attempting to adopt individual components from each configuration and then blend them into a new and more powerful system can easily fail, so the absorption model can often be more appropriate. In contrast, in a merger with two compatible IT configurations the absorption approach could result in large cost savings. It can also provide the opportunity for the value-added via the best-of-both-worlds approach.

Evidence shows that there is an exponential increase in resource requirements associated with moving across the spectrum from the most economic integrated platform to the development of a new state-of-the-art IT system. For example, when Bayerische Vereinsbank and Vereins- und Westbank merged in 1990, the integration team tried to calculate how many man-years it would take to complete each IT integration approach (Penzel and Pietig 2000). According to management estimates:

- Building a completely new state-of-the-art IT network would have absorbed about 3,000 man-years, or about seven to ten years of implementation efforts.
- An integration in which about half of the IT systems of each bank were combined would have required about 1,000 man-years.
- A straightforward absorption of the Vereins- und Westbank into the IT configuration of Bayerische Vereinsbank would have required the least resources, with about 200 man-years.
- Another solution would have been to integrate most of the Vereins- und Westbank systems into Bayerische Vereinsbank, but keep a few peripheral systems from Vereins- und Westbank running.

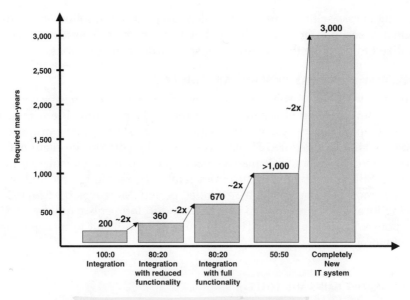

Figure 5-7. **Potential Resource Requirements in IT Integration.** Source: Penzel.
H.-G., Pietig, Ch., *MergerGuide—Handbuch für die Integration von Banken* (Wiesbaden: Gabler Verlag, 2000).

Some of the former's functionalities would have been lost due to standardization. This approach was estimated to require 360 man-years, or about four years of integration time in total.
• The same integration, but with the effort to preserve all the functionalities of both banks, would have increased the integration requirements to 670 man-years (see Figure 5-7).

IMPLEMENTATION OF IT INTEGRATION

Once the integration approach has been decided, critical timing decisions need to be made. Should the actual data conversion be gradual or in a "Big Bang"? If gradual, what are the appropriate steps and sequencing?

The Big Bang approach often seems to be the most attractive on the surface. At one pre-determined time all infrastructure systems, databases, application software, and processing units convert and run on one common platform. Though convenient, this approach is also risky, since all logistical, administrative, technical, and personnel issues need to be resolved in tandem. At the time of the conversion, the stress on systems and staff can be enormous. Keeping control of the entire integration process can become difficult, especially when the IT configurations are large and incompatible. As a consequence, major financial firms usually avoid the Big Bang approach.

In a stepwise integration, things are a bit more relaxed, but still far from easy. Temporary links first need to be established to allow basic data migration. The IT configurations need to exchange high-priority information such as trading data already in the process. Once the individual systems have been properly evaluated, conversion preparation begins and may extend to the development of additional software. In contrast to the "Big Bang" approach, data and system conversion occur in individual steps to ensure that each system will be implemented in a timely way, with minimal disruption for the business areas. For example, the conversion of branch networks might be undertaken regionally to reduce complexity. Individual applications within operating units might also be converted sequentially. IT management must balance the safety and reliability of stepwise integration with the disruption and inconvenience caused for other bank internal units, staff, and clients. New systems require extensive training for the end-users. And all this needs to occur at a time when the organization is already stressed by other merger integration issues.

There is little available evidence on the optimum speed of integration, which seems to be best determined on a case-by-case basis. Functionally, IT integration is usually best accomplished by a project manager who has unquestioned authority and operates with minimum interference, reporting directly to the CEO and the firm's executive committee. (Alternative IT conversion choices were presented earlier in Figure 5-2.) IT integration can easily be compromised by unfinished IT conversions from prior acquisitions.

IT conversion can create a significant operational risk for banks and other financial firms. If the IT configurations cannot be merged smoothly into a stable and reliable platform, without causing major disruptions or operational integrity, the firm could face severe consequences. Not only can it delay the integration process as a whole, but the firm could also become liable for damages incurred by trading partners. There could be client defections. Regulatory concerns could also weigh heavily. Operational risks need to be incorporated into the calculation of the required minimum equity base of a bank under revised regulatory accords. Any major problems in a conversions process could lead to higher risk levels and higher capital requirements.

When Wells Fargo completed its hostile takeover of First Interstate Bank of Los Angeles in 1996 for $11 billion, it was a record deal in the U.S. banking industry, and it drew rave reviews from Wall Street analysts. But they soon changed their views. Stung by IT problems and what some outsiders said was a heavy-handed approach to pushing customers into new types of accounts, the banks saw angry business and retail clients head out the door. The expected 7,500 job losses soon turned into nearly 13,000 as revenues dwindled. The embarrassment reached a climax in summer 1997, when Wells Fargo admitted it incorrectly posted customer deposits to the wrong accounts and was unable to find the money—

although customers were quickly made good on the missing balances (Silverstein and Vrana 1998).

Mizuho: How Not to Approach IT Integration

Mizuho Bank and Mizuho Corporate Bank were launched in April 2001 by the Mizuho Financial Group, following the group's reorganization of its three former core banks—Dai-Ichi Kangyo Bank (DKB), Fuji Bank and the Industrial Bank of Japan (IBJ)—into the two Mizuho holding company subsidiaries. After the merger Mizuho Group was the worlds largest banking company in terms of assets.

On April 1, 2000, Mizuho Bank announced that it had encountered major IT problems, causing most of its 7,000 automated teller machines (ATMs) to malfunction across the country (*Journal of Japanese Trade and Industry* 2002). The retail banking arm was also troubled by delays in money transfers for customers' utility and other household payments. The total number of pending money transfer orders reached 2.5 million at the peak of the problem. Similar problems that plagued Mizuho Bank also impacted Mizuho Corporate Bank. Customers were often double-billed for various charges. Mizuho's ATMs had recovered by the morning of the following day, but the backlog of money transfer orders could not be cleared until April 18.

It was the first time that payments systems at a major bank in Japan had been so extensively disrupted. Some business clients using Mizuho as their clearer for their customers' bill payments had to send their clients blank receipts or apology letters because many money transfers had not been completed by the due dates. Although the bank reimbursed customer losses in certain cases, some corporate clients announced their intention to seek damages from Mizuho Financial Group. The problems were compounded because Mizuho's IT system integration coincided with the April 1 start of a new fiscal year, when the volume of financial transactions usually spikes. There had already been payment delays at the end of the previous fiscal year.

Mizuho's relay computers connecting the various operations went down, overloaded by the massive volume of data processing. Human errors, such as erroneous programming and false data inputs, compounded the problem. It soon became clear that the Mizuho fiasco was not simply the result of an unfortunate coincidence, but was caused by a combination of management mistakes such as insufficient computer tests, programming defects, and human error. It also raised questions about the role played by the Financial Services Agency (FSA) and the Bank of Japan as financial regulators and supervisors. And it suggested the need for strengthened bank inspections focusing on IT operations.

One cause of the Mizuho debacle seems to have been power struggles among the three legacy banks in anticipation of the IT integration, a massive reorganization project stretching over three years. One of the key challenges was how to integrate the three banks' respective computer systems. DKB cooperated with Fujitsu Ltd., Fuji Bank with IBM, and IBJ with Hitachi. In December 1999, four months after the announcement of the three-way merger, the banks decided that a merged retail bank would adopt the DKB's Fujitsu-based computer system. That plan was rescinded in November 2000 due to strong opposition from Fuji Bank, which was concerned that the DKB would turn out to play the leadership role in developing the combined retail banking platform—a vital issue for any commercial bank. As a result, the banks reached a compromise: they would install relay computers connecting the three separate IT platforms while keeping the existing systems for one year after the April 2000 launch before eventually integrating them fully.

Evidently the integration plan had some fundamental problems, such as delays in decision making and insufficient computer load tests. Mizuho had turned down requests by Tokyo Electric Power Co. to conduct computer tests beforehand.

The series of episodes suggested that Mizuho did not seem to have a clear information technology strategy within the framework of the overall merger integration plan. Moreover, Mizuho management may not have been fully aware of the associated operational risks. Japanese banks, whose credit ratings continued to be under pressure due to slow progress in disposals of nonperforming loans, were concerned that the Mizuho debacle could further undermine the confidence in the Japanese banking industry's credibility. This was especially important in light of Bank for International Settlement's plans to include banks' preparedness for operational risk in a new set of guidelines to be adopted in 2006 ("Basel 2") to promote operational integrity and soundness. The fallout of the Mizuho fiasco developed into a political issue and ultimately led to a reprimand from Japanese Prime Minister Koizumi, a highly unusual event.

WHY DOES IT INTEGRATION SUCCEED OR FAIL?

At the end of the 1980s, in a study conducted by the American Management Association (AMA), two-thirds of the companies involved in M&A transactions indicated that there was an inadequate basis for making informed decisions concerning IT issues (Bohl, 1989). Half of the respondents reported that this information was unavailable because no one thought to inquire. IT professionals were often not involved in (or even told of) pending structural changes until an official merger announcement was made (Bozman, 1989). With little warning, IT personnel were expected to reconcile system incompatibilities quickly so that the flow of information was minimally disrupted.

Although this survey was conducted more than ten years ago, mergers of IT configurations remain just as challenging today. The need to quickly integrate new IT systems can be an extremely difficult task for a number of reasons. First, corporate decision making still does not always systematically include IT staff in the planning process. IT integration-related planning typically does not occur until the merger is over, thus delaying the process. Second, the new corporate structure must cope with the cultural differences (Weber and Pliskin 1996) and workforce issues involving salary structures, technical skills, work load, morale, problems of retention and attrition, and changes in IT policies and procedures (Fiderio 1989). Third, the lack of planning results in shifting priorities relative to the development of application projects. Fourth, technology issues relating to compatibility and redundancy of hardware and software, connectivity, and standards must be resolved. However, the integration of non-compatible systems is time consuming and cannot occur overnight if done properly. Corporate expectations relative to IT integration during the M&A process are often unrealistic. All of these factors can impede the successful integration of IT during merger activities, create information shortages and processing problems, and disrupt the normal flow of business.

In a survey of 44 CIOs of companies that had undergone corporate mergers during 1989–1991, an attempt was made to examine the relationships between the measures of IT integration success and the components that affect it (Stylianou, Jeffries, and Robbins 1996). According to the study, the quality of merger planning appears to be an important contributor to the success of the integration process, contributing to the ability to exploit merger opportunities while avoiding problems in merging the IT processes. This could often be achieved by including IT personnel in pre-merger planning activities and performing an IT audit prior to the merger.

Data sharing across applications and programming language incompatibilities also plays a role. There seems to be greater success in the integration process when there is a high level of cross-application data-sharing. Not surprisingly, programming language incompatibilities have a negative impact on the success of the integration process. A large number of changes in IT policies and procedures also have a negative impact on personnel. Decreases in IT salaries or benefits surely leads to a decline in morale, and this reduces the chances of successful integration. Redundancies and defections also reduce the ability of the IS workforce to avoid merger problems.

The results of this study indicate that in addition to past integration experience, outcomes in the IT area following a merger or acquisition are managerial in nature and largely controllable. Successful integration requires high-quality merger and IT integration planning, positive support by senior management, good communications to the IT systems' end users, and a high level of end-user involvement in strategic decision making during the process. In addition, as expected, an emphasis on IT standardization is a positive factor.

In another study commissioned by applications development specialist Antares Alliance in 1997, senior IT managers from 45 U.K. organizations, including financial services, were surveyed. All of the organizations in the survey had experienced a £25 million or larger merger or acquisition. When it came to financial services, the research found that banks, building societies, and insurers appeared to suffer more from postmerger IT problems than their nonfinancial counterparts. Dealing with legacy data and the integration of IT staff following a merger or acquisition were seen as major problems—far more so than for nonfinancial institutions. In addition, despite the inevitable change that follows mergers and acquisitions, fewer than half of the respondents said they would use M&A as an opportunity to review overall IT strategy. Only 20% took the opportunity to move packaged applications, 17% to scrap legacy data, and around 12% to migrate from central mainframe computers to distributed client-server systems. In contrast, 60% of the organizations surveyed said they would use an M&A deal as an opportunity to review IT applications software (Green, 1997).

Although the synergy potential of M&A deals is widely promoted, attempts to exploit such synergy in IT are often unsuccessful. One of the most important factors is organizational culture (Weber and Schweiger 1992). Culture clash in M&A deals is marked by negative attitudes on the part of the acquired management toward the acquiring management. (Pliskin et al. 1993; Romm et al. 1991). These attitudes reduce the commitment of the acquired managers to successful integration of the merging companies and inhibit their cooperation with the acquiring firm's management. Moreover, when there is intense and frequent contact, such as under high levels of IT integration, cultural differences increase the likelihood of conflict between the two top management teams involved in the merger. Since financial firms hope to harvest IT integration synergies, this will most likely be associated with more contact between the two top management cultures, setting the groundwork for culture clashes whose negative performance effects may offset some of the potential positive effects of IT integration.

In a study of 69 companies that completed an M&A process, 40 of which were banks, Weber and Pliskin (1996) investigated the potential contribution of IT integration to the effectiveness of merger and acquisitions. The findings provide systematic evidence that organizational culture plays an important role in the effective implementation of IT integration. Specifically, for banks, strong culture differences between the two merging IT units are negatively associated with merger effectiveness. For such firms, internal management processes associated with the level of fit between the organizational cultures may determine whether investment in IT integration can be effectively translated into better performance. The study found that banks, as opposed to other industries represented in the sample, engaged in higher levels of IT integration in an attempt to realize the potential synergy from integration. The results do not support the view that the *degree* of IT integration following an M&A transaction is associated with effectiveness of the merger.

WHAT ARE THE KEY LESSONS?

Information technologies represent a critical resource for the financial services industry. Mergers and acquisitions, and the resulting task of integrating diverse systems, have the potential to disrupt and throw out of alignment the smooth operation of even the best-managed IT systems. However, an IT organization can use the opportunities offered by an M&A event to achieve a positive net impact on its capability to perform and contribute to the organizational objectives. Important lessons are the following.

First, financial institutions should deal with potential IT integration issues as early as possible, as soon as merger talks start. If a firm has not solved its own internal IT problems, an acquisition decision will only further complicate the situation. The underlying business strategy and IT strategy should be aligned and not stand in sharp contrast in a potential merger situation.

Second, IT integration is not only a technical issue. Management should pay as much attention to questions of cultural fit during premerger search processes as they do to issues of potential synergy from IT integration. Problems during integration can be the consequence of a more complex organizational misfit between the merging IT configurations (Johnson, 1989). The effectiveness of the strategic planning process can be enhanced by early diagnosis of organizational and technical fits. Some of the failures can be attributed to premerger discussions that tend to focus on the financial components of the deal while ignoring the problems associated with integrating the technical architecture and organizational infrastructure of the two separate entities. So IT tends to be ignored in the M&A planning process. To minimize the disruptive nature of integrating them, the acquirer and target's technical architecture and organizational infrastructure should be assessed prior to the acquisition. As a result, IT professionals should be fully involved in the entire process, including premerger discussions, so that potential integration problems can be identified early (Johnson 1989; McCartney and Kelly 1984).

Third, even if an acquirer is aware of the technical and organizational IT issues, the integration of IT following a merger must proceed carefully in order to reap any anticipated synergies. Cultural clashes may severely damage the cooperation and commitment of the very group that may be instrumental in determining the success of the IT integration and ultimately the merger itself (Buck-Lew et al. 1992; Weber and Pliskin 1996).

Finally, the cost and the risk of IT integration should always be taken into account when evaluating the feasibility of a merger or acquisition, although it will rarely be the determining factor. Companies merge for many reasons, and if margins are so tight that one cannot incorporate the cost of appropriate IT integration, the deal itself might not be sustainable.

6

What Is the Evidence?

The previous five chapters of this book have considered, in sequence (1) reconfiguration of the financial services sector and its impact on strategic positioning and execution in financial intermediaries, (2) the importance of M&A transactions in that reconfiguration process, in terms of the structure of the global transaction flow, (3) where the gains and losses from M&A transactions in the financial services sector are likely to come from, and (4) the all-important issues centering on post-merger integration.

Chapters 6 and 7 of this book seek to answer a simple question: So what? Does all of the intense and sometimes frantic M&A activity actually serve to benefit shareholders by improving their firms' competitive performance and long-term, risk-adjusted equity returns? And does it create a leaner, more efficient, more creative, more globally competitive, and more stable and robust financial system? This chapter deals with the first of these questions, and Chapter 7 deals with the second. Neither question is easy. To come up with defensible answers, it is necessary to come up with plausible stories of what would have happened in the absence of the M&A activity that occurred. Since such an exercise inevitably deals in hypotheticals, the conclusions are always subject to further debate.

There are two approaches to this issue. One is a clinical examination of case studies in an effort to understand the rationale and execution of individual M&A transactions in the context of a firm's overall strategy, in order to determine whether and how they helped move that strategy along in the achievement of improved and sustained market share and profitability. A second approach is to focus on the universe of M&A transactions captured in a large dataset and, by using various statistical techniques, try to separate characteristics that seem to distinguish successes from failures.

This chapter begins with three illustrative case profiles—Allianz AG, J.P. Morgan Chase, and GE Capital Services—to ascertain what management thought they were achieving by undertaking specific or sequential acquisitions, how they presented the various cases to the market, and evidence as to what was actually accomplished. This is followed by a data-based survey of available quantitative studies on the evidence.

CASE STUDIES

In a very useful discussion based extensive interviews with senior managers at some 30 financial services firms, Davis (2000) concludes that the impact of mergers and acquisitions on the shareholders of acquiring firms seems to have little bearing on the proclivity of managements to engage in M&A deals. In 11 of 33 transactions examined, the presumed synergies were minimal and not rigorously quantified in advance. Moreover, in some cases potential benefits were lost in excessively hasty execution of the integration process. In other cases, the integration process was too protracted, with much the same end result. In some cases as well, there were nasty surprises that were not caught in the due diligence phase of the transactions. Especially cross-border deals seemed to be problematic, due to greater difficulty in quantifying gains and extracting synergies. A key issue in many cases appears to be overpayment, so where value was in fact extracted from an acquisition it ended up with the shareholders of the target firms, who have the additional benefit of getting paid up-front and escaping the downside risk.

Davis takes care to identify some exceptions. Examples include Chemical Bank's acquisition of Manufacturers Hanover Trust Company under Walter Shipley, and its subsequent acquisition of Chase Manhattan, and Sandy Weill's imaginative and opportunistic construction of Citigroup though sequential acquisitions, each apparently well targeted and executed and creating an apparent "Weill premium" for a time in the Citigroup share price. Richard Kovacevich's creation of a silk purse out of a sow's ear at Wells Fargo and Angel Corcostegui's role in the shaping of Banco Santander Central Hispano (BSCH) in Spain also attract praise, as does Sir Brian Pitman's role in the creation of Lloyds TSB.

Of course, things do change, and the proof of the pudding may not become evident for a while. Two years after these cases were examined and positive conclusions drawn, J.P. Morgan Chase and Citigroup had come under a massive cloud and were busy rethinking their various businesses, caught in the middle of the Argentine, telecoms, and corporate governance disasters. BSCH, too, suffered large losses in its Latin America strategy, and Corcostegui was gone. Lloyds TSB and Wells Fargo continued to do well, although even here observers were asking: "Where next?" Evidently reaching conclusions based on individual cases is a hazardous business, even without falling into the trap of trying to generalize from them.

A much more informal way of making this point is simply listing each year's winner of "Banker of the Year" awards in the various trade publications (the selections usually being influenced by recent M&A transactions), and then tracking what happened to their firms' share prices in the ensuing period. The conclusions are rather sobering.

According to Davis (2000), the reasons for the apparent paradoxes in management behavior in financial-sector M&A case studies seem to be related to preoccupation with (1) a presumed overriding industry consolidation process and the herd-like desire to be part of it, (2) the notion that the current deal is an exception to the decidedly mixed track record of others, based on factors such as management superiority and creativity, and (3) the fact that management's own gains and losses are in the end rather distinct from those of ordinary shareholders due to compensation arrangements approved by their boards—compensation arrangements that may not have very much to do with long-term risk adjusted total return objectives. One could perhaps add the catalytic impact of management consultants and investment bankers, who may instill fears of being "caught in the middle," "eat or be eaten," or tagged as being "out of the flow." Combined with an overreliance on external advice in the press of daily business and the desire to tell a "growth story" to the market, this kind of self-reinforcing, herd-like behavior in corporate strategic actions among financial firms is not too difficult to imagine.

Plenty of other case-related evidence on financial sector M&A transactions also exists. Most of it comes from financial analysts focusing on the financial services sector, who diagnose the positives and negatives of individual M&A transactions on announcement, and then try to assess how they are likely to contribute to the value of the franchise over a period of time. They are, after all, supposed to be providing unbiased, expert advice to investors. But since some of the best analyst coverage of financial services firms comes from the major investment banks, their objectivity has been heavily compromised in recent years by conflicts of interest relating to their firms' capital-raising and advisory businesses.

These conflicts of interest arguably contribute a systematic positive bias to their assessments of financial services deals, as it does in other sectors. For example, in the April 1998 announcement of the Citicorp-Travelers merger-of-equals that formed today's Citigroup, every analyst covering the two firms had either "strong buy" or "buy" recommendations on the two stocks. Although a survey of the analyst coverage shows plenty of pluses and minuses, the balance was overwhelmingly weighted in favor of the pluses. Maybe this was objective. Maybe not. Still, many of the recommendations looked as though they had emanated from the two firms' investor relations departments. One way to avoid this problem is to rely more heavily on analysis emanating from buy-side firms such as Sanford Bernstein or Prudential Securities. Another option is to review of the work of consultants and academics that are (one hopes) distanced from commercial relationships with parties to the deal.

Judging from anecdotal evidence reported in innumerable media reports, there are plenty of examples of financial firms that have both succeeded and failed in M&A transactions in recent years, each of which could be the subject of a clinical case study. Among the most actively reported deals are the following:

- Deutsche Bank's 1989 acquisition of the U.K. merchant bank and asset manager Morgan Grenfell & Co. at a cost of $1.5 billion. In a transaction that many felt was overpriced, Morgan Grenfell was allowed to pursue an independent course for years without Deutsche forcing through effective integration or leveraging its corporate finance capabilities through its own broad client base. Then the bank was blindsided in 1996 by a Morgan Grenfell Asset Management rogue employee scandal in London that cost the bank $600 million to restore client assets plus $330 million in client restitution paid by Morgan Grenfell Asset Management and $1.5 million in fines to British regulators. Later, Deutsche acquired a wounded U.S. money center bank, Bankers Trust Company, and appeared to do a much better job of making the most of the acquisition, gradually pulling itself to within striking range of the world's top-tier wholesale banks.
- Crédit Suisse Group's acquisition of Winterthur insurance for $8.51 billion in 1997 and U.S. investment bank Donaldson Lufkin Jenrette from Groupe AXA for $12.8 billion in 2000. In the Winterthur case, cross-selling of banking and insurance seemed to be less successful than hoped, and as a diversification move failed miserably as crashing equity markets in 2001 and 2002 hit both the Group's insurance and investment banking businesses simultaneously. All of this occurred against the backdrop of critical management problems in its investment banking unit, Crédit Suisse First Boston, including a series of regulatory sanctions and fines around the world—symptomizing a culture that was clearly out of control and that needed some serious reining in. These problems came on top of overpriced, badly timed, and poorly executed acquisition of Donaldson Lufkin Jenrette. In 2002 the Crédit Suisse Group was forced to inject $1.1 billion into its Winterthur insurance unit in order to prevent capital impairment due to investment losses. At the same time, its CS First Boston unit was suffering from the same revenue collapse as its investment banking competitors and, as it was trying to right itself from its long string of management snafus and excessive costs, CSFB found itself in the middle of U.S. regulatory and Congressional investigations into the role of banks in Enron and other corporate governance scandals—as well as $100 million and $200 million settlements over IPO practices and analyst conflicts of interest, respectively. Maybe it was bad luck. Maybe bad management. Maybe bad strategy. Maybe a bit of each. In any case, CS shares dropped by 60% in the eight months ending December 2002, and rumors identified the firm as a possible takeover candidate for a large international

group particularly interested in its private banking and investment banking franchises.

- Fortis attempted one of the more ambitious among European M&A-driven strategies by merging Dutch and Belgian banking and insurance groups into a financial conglomerate that was at once cross-functional, cross-border, and cross-cultural (and with shares listed in both the Belgian and Dutch markets). Following such acquisitions as the Dutch merchant bank MeesPierson from ABN-AMRO for $1.12 billion in 1996 and the Dutch insurer ASR from the City of Rotterdam for $3.5 billion in 2001, Fortis remained largely a Belgian-dominated conglomerate with a massive home market share but indifferent share price performance.

- A Dutch group, AEGON NV, executed a much more focused acquisitions-driven strategy concentrating on life insurance, serially acquiring control of Hungarian state-owned insurer Allami Biztosito in 1992, U.K. life insurer Scottish Equitable in 1993, Providian's U.S. insurance business in 1997, and in 1999 both Transamerica Corporation in the United States and the life insurance business of Guardian Royal Exchange in the United Kingdom. In the process it became the world's third largest insurer in terms of assets. The highly focused, rapid, and apparently disciplined growth by acquisition was combined with strong profitability and impressive share price performance until the Transamerica transaction, which many regarded as overpriced and beset with difficulties in unloading the target's peripheral businesses. This, together with management change and general problems in the insurance sector, caused AEGON shareholders to give back much of their earlier gains and required a capital increase in 2002.

- UBS AG is likewise the product of a targeted strategy executed via sequential acquisitions, large and small, mostly initiated by the former Swiss Bank Corporation (SBC), then the country's third largest bank. The most important strategic acquisitions among them include the former Union Bank of Switzerland's purchase of U.K. fund manager Philips & Drew in 1984, SBC's creation of a joint venture and later acquisition of the U.S. derivatives firm O'Connor & Partners in 1992, U.S. institutional asset manager Brinson in 1994, the U.K. merchant bank S.G. Warburg in 1995, the U.S. corporate finance specialist Dillon Read in 1997, and later that year the merger of SBC and UBS—from a management perspective a takeover of the larger UBS by the smaller SBC—to form the new UBS AG. Thereafter there were two more strategic acquisitions by the combined firm—Global Asset Management in 1999 and U.S. retail broker PaineWebber in 2000. Looking back, the strategy appeared to be consistent and well-executed to focus on three pillars: global private banking and asset management, wholesale and investment banking, and leadership in domestic retail banking. Most of the acquisitions appeared to be carried out in a targeted and disciplined way, especially the integration process, so that by 2002 UBS had become the largest bank in Switzerland and the world's largest asset manager, and was closing in on the top players in global wholesale and investment banking.

- Royal Bank of Scotland, having taken over National Westminster Bank in a hotly contested battle with the Bank of Scotland, in 1991 acquired the retail banking operations of Mellon Bank in the United States to supplement its 1989 acquisition of Citizens Bank, active in New England, plus 19 smaller acquisitions. Management argued that the bank's U.S. technology platform was not fully utilized, and that more acquisitions would be sought. Evidently the RBS U.S. business was a well-managed, profitable, stand-alone venture capable of competing effectively against both large and small domestic rivals in a number of regional markets.

- Citigroup's M&A history is probably the most dramatic of any financial institution in the world. Primerica Corp. (itself an amalgam of several predecessor firms under CEO Sandy Weill), acquired Smith Barney in 1987 and Travelers Corp. in 1992–1993, and as Travelers Inc. acquired Shearson Lehman Brothers Inc. in 1993, the property insurance business of Aetna in 1996, Salomon, Inc. in 1997, Citicorp in 1998, and then as Citigroup Inc. acquired Travelers Property Casualty in 2000, Associates First Capital Corp. in 2000, and European-American Bank, Bank Handlowy in Poland, the investment banking business of Schroders PLC and Peoples Bank Cards in the UK, Fubon Group in Taiwan and Banamex-Accival in Mexico, all during 2001, in addition to an array of smaller acquisitions in the United States and abroad. This remarkable track record and what by all appearances was effective and rapid integration created a financial conglomerate that seemed to deliver the goods for shareholders until the U.S. financial and corporate governance scandals of 2001–2002. Given the breadth and depth of its reach, it was a virtual certainty that Citigroup would end up in the middle of such a problem, which cost the firm and its shareholders dearly (on one day alone the stock lost 16% of its value). This, plus the earlier decision to spin off Citigroup's property and casualty business to shareholders, raised questions about when big is too big and broad is too broad.

It is not easy to determine success or failure from such case profiles. No doubt the firms involved would have had very different competitive configurations if they had not engaged in extensive M&A activity, or perhaps if they had engaged in different ones. But would the shareholder have done any better? Who knows. Should Deutsche Bank have moved more aggressively to integrate Morgan Grenfell? Sure, and they did just that with the takeover of Bankers Trust. Should Crédit Suisse have used a premier banking franchise to fritter away resources on an investment bank that had become semidetached? Probably not. Nor should AEGON have violated its own return on equity hurdle rate to acquire Transamerica, which many at the time considered "one step too far." And even UBS, which seemed to go about things in a disciplined, transparent, and purposeful way, may have overstepped with PaineWebber—a solid U.S. retail brokerage firm but fully priced and with little in common with the bank's "core affluent" target global client base in its most important business, private banking. Even Citigroup, amply rewarded by the market after its 1998 creation, was blindsided by events. When mistakes are made, they are not too difficult to diagnose after the fact.

Perhaps the most dramatic M&A deal in recent years that did *not* actually take place was the $30 billion merger of Deutsche Bank AG and Dresdner Bank AG, with heavy involvement by Allianz AG, announced in March 2000. The deal would have created the world's largest bank, with $1.2 trillion in assets. The idea was to merge the two banks' troubled retail businesses into a single entity, taking the name of Deutsche Bank's "Bank 24." This entity would be the product of a three-way exchange of shares under which Allianz would swap its 5% holding in Deutsche Bank and its 21.7% holding in Dresdner Bank for a 49% stake in the new Bank 24. Initially the retail business was to be run by Deutsche Bank, but it would also provide Allianz with a bank-based platform for the sale of insurance products. Bank 24 would then be floated in an IPO as an independent firm, with Deutsche Bank selling its shares and Allianz reducing its stake to about one-third. As part of the deal, Deutsche's mutual fund business, DWS, would also be sold to Allianz, together with Deutsche Herold (Deutsche's insurance business) for about $5.8 billion.

Meantime, the Deutsche and Dresdner retail businesses would undergo far-reaching cost savings, estimated to be worth about $2.5 billion, through branch closings and job cuts. The two banks' remaining asset management businesses would create one of the world's largest fund managers at a time when managed asset pools, notably in the pension sector, were expected to grow rapidly in Europe. The combined investment banking operations of Deutsche and Dresdner were intended to provide a stronger base for competing with the dominant American firms, although the deal seemed to do little to broaden the combined firm's footprint in areas such as M&A advisory work, initial public offerings, and some other parts of the equities business. Nor did it help create a pan-European banking and securities platform. The plan was that Rolf-Ernst Breuer and Bernhard Walther, heads of the two banks, would become co-heads of the combined entity and that Dresdner shareholders would own 39% of the new firm.

Initial reactions to the announcement were highly negative. Analysts and shareholders basically concluded that Deutsche Bank had been taken to the cleaners by Dresdner and especially Allianz. One estimate was the Deutsche was getting about $5.5 billion too little for asset disposals while paying about $5.5 billion too much for Dresdner Bank. The announcement that there were $2.6 billion in synergies expected beginning in 2003 was seen as unrealistic, given that most of the cost cuts were likely to come in Bank 24, which was to be divested. Observers also expected that restructuring charges would exceed the announced $2.7 million. And there was concern about how the co-CEO plan would work out, particularly in light of the very different corporate cultures of the two firms.

So both the strategy and the structure of the Deutsche-Dresdner deal raised plenty of doubts. Shares of Deutsche Bank dropped 6% on announcement day, and Dresdner shares dropped 6% as well. The deal never happened. Deutsche's investment bankers were clearly unhappy with the merger of the wholesale businesses, taking the view that they were making good progress in investment banking on their own after the acquisition of Bankers Trust Company and that Dresdner's investment banking operation, Dresdner Kleinwort Wasserstein, was mainly excess baggage—much of which would eventually be "torched." Certainly they were unwilling to see the inevitable redundancies in the securities business come from their own ranks. Nor did the word "torch" do much to boost morale at Dresdner Kleinwort Wasserstein. Faced with insurrection among his investment bankers, Breuer backtracked. Feeling betrayed, Walther resigned. The deal was off, with plenty of bruised egos left in its wake.

From case-based evidence, the key seems to be a well thought-through strategy that promises sustainable risk-adjusted excess returns to shareholders under plausible market developments, which is then carefully carried out with the help of selected corporate actions. One of the key factors is realistically priced M&A deals. In other words: *doing the right thing, at the right price, and then doing it right.* Everyone strives for this, but some do it better than others. Here we shall look in somewhat greater detail at three merger-intensive financial services firms with very different characteristics and equally different patterns in use of M&A transactions for strategic development—Allianz AG, J.P. Morgan Chase, and the former GE Capital Services.

Allianz AG–Dresdner Bank AG

Founded in 1890, the Allianz Group at the end of 2000 was the world's largest property and casualty insurer in terms of premium income. It was ahead of U.S. rival AIG and was the third largest European life insurer. Property and casualty insurance represented 55% of its total premium income, with life/health insurance making up the remaining 45%. P&C traditionally accounted for 80–85% of total group net earnings. Moreover, the importance and profitability of its German home market, in which Allianz was the P&C and life insurance market leader, were equally striking, with a third of Allianz's total premium income coming from Germany. Allianz, in short, was the leading German insurer and the leading P&C insurer worldwide. Management was determined to turn the firm into a high-performance global supplier of a diverse set of financial services, and so several of M&A transactions were launched in order to implement this strategic vision.

Table 6-1 shows the sequence of major Allianz acquisitions from 1984 to 2001. Announced in early April 2001, the most important of these was the $24 billion acquisition of Dresdner Bank AG. This created a multi-functional financial firm with a market capitalization of $98 billion and combined revenues of about $90 billion. The merged company employed 182,000 and spanned businesses ranging from insurance to asset management, and from mass-market retail financial services to wholesale commercial and investment banking. In terms of asset size, the Allianz Group at the time ranked as Germany's largest—and the world's fourth largest—financial services firm, with over $900 billion in assets.

The key justification for the Allianz acquisition of Dresdner Bank was to position the combined firm for a capital markets windfall that German pension reform was expected to generate. Success was dependent on developing strong distribution (asset-gathering) capabilities, as well as having an asset management (production) platform with sufficient scale and expertise. The acquisition aimed to exploit cross-selling opportunities in long-term savings products (for example, whole life insurance, annuities, and mutual funds) by using both its own agent-based insurance distribution platform and Dresdner's extensive retail branch network. In order to tap the promising German institutional pension market, the merged firm intended to leverage Dresdner's roster of corporate banking relationships. In asset management, Dresdner contributed about $230 billion in assets under management—raising total Allianz Group AUM to more than $600 billion at the end of 2001 and $1.1 trillion if unit-linked products (annuities) and the Group's own investments are included. The merged fiduciary asset management platform, renamed ADAM (Allianz Dresdner Asset Management), promised significant scale economies and offered a broad diversity in investment styles. Finally, Dresdner's investment banking division, Dresdner Kleinwort Wasserstein (DKW), had a good record in M&A advisory work, although it remained a mid-size player in the industry.

At the time of announcement, Allianz management estimated the acquisition would contribute about $285 million in net synergies, starting in 2002, to eventually reach about $1 billion by 2006 (see Figure 6-1). Cumulative net synergies were to amount to about $3 billion during this period, including $360 million in restructuring costs. The bulk of synergies would be provided by distribution (46%) and asset management (33%), and to a lesser extent by organizational restructuring and IT (21%). Most of the identified synergies were revenue-based, rising from only 11% in 2002 to 70% by 2006.

Allianz already owned 21% of Dresdner prior to the acquisition, so the outstanding 79% interest was valued at $24 billion, including a 25% premium of $5.8 billion. The terms of the $30 billion transaction were one Allianz share and $185 in cash for every 10 Dresdner shares ($52 per

Table 6-1 Chronology of Key M&A Transactions of Allianz AG (1984–2001)

Target (100% unless noted)	Deal Announcement Date	Industry Focus of Target	Target Geographic Market	Acquired Stake	Acquisition Price (In €)
RAS (51%)	1984	Insurance	Italy	51%	585 million
Cornhill Plc. (98%)	1986	Insurance	United Kingdom	98%	524 million
Deutsche Versicherung (51%)	1990	Insurance	Germany (Former GDR)	51%	138 million
Fireman's Fund	1991	Insurance	United States	100%	3.6 billion
Elvia[1]	1995	Insurance	Switzerland	N/A	N/A
Lloyd Adriatico[1]	1995	Insurance	Italy	100%	556 million
Vereinte Health[1]	1995	Insurance	Germany	N/A	N/A
Elementar[1]	1995	Insurance	Austria	N/A	N/A
AGF (51%)	1997	Insurance	France	51%	4.6 billion
First Life	1999	Insurance	South Korea	100%	297 million
PIMCO (70%)	2000	Asset management	United States	70%	3.7 billion
Nicholas Applegate	2001	Asset management	United States	100%	1.1 billion
Dresdner Bank AG	2001	Diversified Financial services	Germany/Global	80%	24.8 billion

Source: Allianz AG.
[1] These acquisitions were part of the same transaction with Swiss Re.

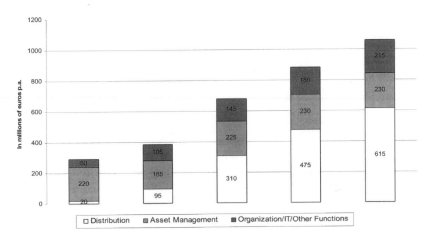

Figure 6-1. Allianz-Dresdner, Expected Annual Net Synergies from Business Segments and Functional Areas (2002–2006).

Dresdner share). In structuring the deal, Allianz intended to unwind its cross-shareholdings in a tax-efficient way (see Figure 2-6 in Chapter 2), minimize new debt, and avoid the dilutive effects of net capital increases. As part of the agreement to reduce its cross-holdings with Munich Re, Allianz also planned to restructure its joint holdings in their German insurance enterprises. This step allowed Allianz to redeploy the released capital in its core businesses.

Upon announcement, Allianz projected the deal to be earnings-accretive starting in 2001 even without synergies. The insurer was then forecasting a combined 2001 net income of $2.7 billion after deducting $540 million in goodwill and financing charges—an increase in earning per share of 13%. Allianz also anticipated that the reduction in cross-shareholdings would increase the firm's free-float from 65% to 80% and would positively influence its share price. The Allianz shareholding structure after the Dresdner Bank acquisition is shown in Figure 6-2.

The main Allianz objectives in the Dresdner transaction included the achievement of better competitive positioning in both production and distribution of a broad array of financial services, particularly at the retail level. Scale (driven by market share) and scope (range of products) increasingly mattered. Larger market share not only seemed to allow lower fees due to scale economies, but also fed the perception of better reliability (brand awareness). Wider product choice was important to enhance client share-of-wallet, business volume, and premium pricing. Moreover, due to low barriers to entry, production of financial services represented the "commoditized" end of the value chain, in which branding and performance were key competitive advantages. Financial services firms relying mainly on production operations were likely to be increasingly vulnerable

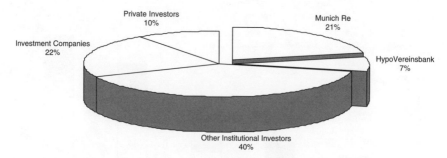

Figure 6-2. Allianz AG Shareholder Structure (Dec. 31, 2001)—Free Float 72%, Major Long-Term Investors, 28%.

to margin pressure. In contrast, margins were thought to be increasingly attractive in distribution and advice. The combination with Dresdner would create a flexible multichannel distribution platform, leveraging the complementary distribution strengths of both firms in each of the principal target markets.

Allianz believed that this model could only work through an actual merger or acquisition, as opposed to relying on cooperative distribution agreements. "Owning" was perceived better than "renting," since it allowed "in-house" retention of production and distribution and a better realization of synergies through business integration. Management felt that prior distribution agreements for long-term savings products with banks in which it held minority stakes (for example, Dresdner Bank and HypoVereinsbank) had been ineffective. These banks were often competitors as both distributors and producers in this same segment. For its part, Dresdner viewed the acquisition by Allianz as an opportunity to restructure its retail banking business. The potential generation of fee income from cross-selling life and P&C insurance and the intensified culling of branches and staff planned by Allianz was seen to help improve the retail segment's high cost-to-income ratio and its overall profitability.

By creating a multichannel distribution platform, the merged firm would be well positioned across three retail channels and one institutional distribution channel (see Figure 6-3). The key attraction of this model was extensive access to both German institutional and individual clients. In addition to a broad corporate reach, the combined entity would have the second largest financial services retail customer base in Germany, with 20 million clients. The other main justification for the Allianz-Dresdner deal was to build its combined fund management business, ADAM, into a world-class asset management platform serving as an in-house "factory" of diverse, high-performance financial products.

As expected, a great deal of speculation followed the Allianz acquisition of Dresdner Bank about the future of its investment banking business, Dresdner Kleinwort Wasserstein.

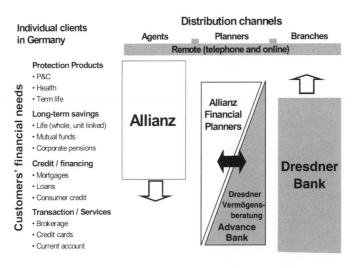

Figure 6-3. Allianz-Dresdner Multichannel Distribution (Germany).

On the one hand, it was argued that an investment banking business could be a useful part of the kind of multifunctional financial conglomerate the Allianz Group had become—as a potentially profitable unit to serve corporate and institutional investor clients (and with low correlations of returns with the remaining Allianz businesses) and as an in-house source of superior products and investment ideas for Allianz clients. Conversely, the Allianz capital base and distribution platform would make Dresdner Kleinwort Wasserstein a firm to be taken much more seriously in the world of global investment banking.

On the other hand, having an investment bank as part of the Allianz Group could add substantially to earnings volatility. In addition, building Dresdner Kleinwort Wasserstein into one of the top five or six firms globally would require massive doses of capital, talent, risk tolerance, and endurance. Furthermore, most investment banking businesses were enormously competitive, without particularly attractive sustained profitability for most of the players. Besides, after the merger Allianz had become such an important asset manager that the best ideas and execution were likely to flow from just about all of the major investment banks. So the value of an in-house investment banking firm could be quite limited.

In the fall of 2001 Allianz announced that Dresdner Kleinwort Wasserstein was not for sale. The decision was probably facilitated by the low value of investment banking franchises at the time. Co-CEO Bruce Wasserstein subsequently resigned to become head of Lazard Frères and took with him several talented senior bankers. Allianz reiterated publicly that Dresdner Kleinwort Wasserstein would remain part of the Group.

Allianz management style was largely decentralized, reflecting the leadership's view of the firm as "a financial holding with a reserved right of intervention." This meant that senior managers of acquired businesses usually kept their positions, and subsidiaries retained considerable latitude in their own operations, for example product design, underwriting, and distribution. Allianz only intervened directly in the activities of subsidiaries when they underperformed and required management changes or restructuring. The Group also provided various levels of centralized support, notably in the areas of financial and strategic planning, investment management, firmwide marketing initiatives and information technology, and management training. Given the diversity of its operations, the culture of Allianz was not monolithic. Instead, it represented a loosely defined umbrella for an array of subcultures associated with very different businesses, ranging from insurance to investment banking. As with other large financial services firms that grew rapidly through acquisitions, Allianz faced the challenge of moving to a common corporate superculture, discussed in Chapter 4.

Following the Dresdner acquisition, Allianz made a number of adjustments to its long-term strategic goals. Senior management emphasized five strategic objectives: (1) optimize the economic value added (EVA) of the Group, (2) capitalize on high-growth property and casualty insurance (P&C) market opportunities by leveraging the Group's risk management expertise, (3) build on the Group's leading position in long-term savings and protection products by focusing on its clients' old age provision (pension) requirements, (4) expand the firm's asset gathering capabilities by building customer-specific, multichannel distribution platforms; and (5) continue to strengthen the firm's capital markets expertise.

Figure 6-4 provides the pro-forma Allianz Group revenue breakdown by businesses for 2000, the year prior to the Allianz-Dresdner deal. Allianz seemed to be in a position to challenge some of its principal rivals such as Groupe AXA, AIG, and Citigroup, each of which had a global footprint but exhibited significant differences in strategic targeting and execution. The question remained whether management could translate this impressive platform into a seamless global financial services player that would be able to combine exploitation of both revenue and cost synergies with sufficiently large market shares to create durable excess returns. The stock market seemed to be unconvinced, as Figure 6-5 suggests. At a time when all insurance companies were under substantial performance pressure due to sinking equity returns and serious losses related to the terrorist attacks of September 11, 2001, in New York, Allianz shares significantly underperformed what was arguably its closest peer, the U.S.-based global insurer AIG.

A year after the Dresdner Bank acquisition many of the Allianz's expectations had not yet materialized. Revenues had indeed grown, although Dresdner Bank alone was estimated to have lost more than $2 billion in 2002 (loan losses of $600 million plus investment banking losses

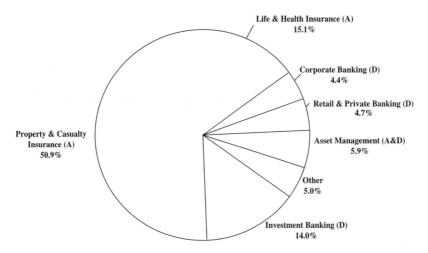

Figure 6-4. Allianz–Dresdner Pro Forma Earnings Distribution, 2000 (total = $6.1 billion). Source: *Wall Street Journal,* April 2, 2001.

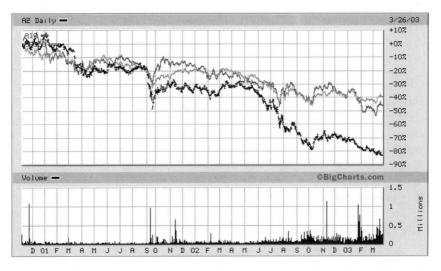

Figure 6-5. Allianz AG Share Price 2001–2002 (compared to AIG and S&P 500 Index).

of $1.4 billion at DKW). In addition, investment losses in the insurance business were encountered owing to weak stock markets. In March of 2003 Allianz announced its first annual loss since 1945, totaling EUR 1.2 billion after tax for 2002 (dropping from net earnings of EUR 3.5 billion in 2000 and EUR 1.6 billion in 2001), while the share price dropped roughly 70% from the announcement of the Dresdner acquisition—a decline of roughly 50% against the German Xetra Dax index. Management continued to defend the competitive model, however, although the future of DKW as part of the Group was increasingly called into question.

J.P. Morgan Chase & Co.

In January 1995, the share price of Chase Manhattan Corp. was $34, with a return on assets a bit under 1%, a return on equity of about 15%, a price-to-book ratio of about 1.2 and a price-to-earnings multiple of 7.0. In the view of some at the time, this was decidedly mediocre for a financial services firm that incorporated a number of first-rate business franchises in areas such as New York retail banking, custody, private banking, credit cards, corporate lending, and a number of others, as well as a global presence that seemed to embody numerous unrealized possibilities.

In April 1995, investment manager Michael Price, Chairman of Mutual Series Fund, Inc., announced that funds under his management had purchased 6.1% of Chase's stock, and that he believed the Chase board should take steps to realize the inherent values in its businesses in a manner designed to maximize shareholder value. At the bank's subsequent annual meeting, Price aggressively challenged the bank's management efforts: "Dramatic change is required. It is clear that the sale of the bank is superior to the company's current strategy . . . unlock the value, or let someone else do it for you."[1] Chase's chairman at the time, Thomas Labreque, responded that Price's assertions were unfounded and that he had no intention of selling or breaking up the bank. By mid-June 1995, Michael Price and other institutional investors, convinced that Chase stock was undervalued, were thought to have accumulated approximately 30% of the bank's outstanding shares, and the stock price had climbed to about $47. Labreque announced that the bank was continuing its efforts to refocus its businesses and to reduce costs going forward.

During June and July of 1995, Chase and BankAmerica talked seriously about a merger in which the BankAmerica name would be retained. Then BankAmerica suddenly backed out for reasons that were not totally clear. Chemical Bank followed quickly with a proposal for a "merger of equals." According to Chemical's then CEO, Walter Shipley, "This combined company has the capacity to perform at benchmark standards. And when we say benchmark standards, we mean the best in the industry."[2] Labreque agreed, and the negotiations were completed on August 28, 1995. Chem-

---

1.. *The Wall Street Journal*, May 19, 1995.
2. *ABC Evening News*, August 28, 1995.

ical would exchange 1.04 shares of its stock for every Chase share out-standing, an offer reflecting a 7% premium over the closing price of Chase shares on the day before the announcement.

The combined bank, retaining the Chase name, thus became the largest bank in the United States and thirteenth largest in the world in terms of assets. The new Chase also became the largest U.S. corporate lending bank, one of the largest credit card lenders, and the largest player in trust, custody, and mortgage servicing. Shipley became chief executive, and Labreque became president. Substantial cost-reduction efforts were quickly launched (including large-scale layoffs and branch closings) aimed at reducing the combined overhead of the two banks within three years by 16%. In the month following the announcement of the merger, Chemical Bank's stock rose 12%.

Labreque denied that shareholder pressure had anything to do with the merger. Michael Price asserted that he had not played a major role, but was happy to have been in the "right place at the right time." Nevertheless, adjusting for the exchange offer and the postmerger run-up in Chemical's share price, Chase shares more than doubled in a little over six months based on the market's assessment of the potential value embedded in the merger (see Figure 6-6).

Following Chemical Bank's acquisition of Chase, the new Chase (CMB) had become a broadly diversified global banking and financial services company, and conducted its business through various bank and non-bank

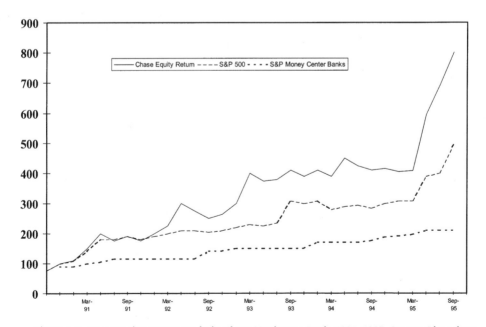

Figure 6-6. Comparative Return Analysis: Chase Manhattan Bank, 1991–1995. Source: Bloomberg.

subsidiaries, including Chase Manhattan Bank, a New York bank holding corporation, Chase Manhattan Bank USA National Association, a national bank, and Chase Securities Inc., a securities broker-dealer engaged in all aspects of investment banking. Chase's activities were internally organized into five major business franchises: (1) national consumer services (retail banking and credit cards), (2) investment banking, (3) private equity investments through Chase Capital Partners, (4) global services (information and transaction processing), and (5) wealth management and private banking.

By 2000, Chase's wholesale banking competitor J.P. Morgan (JPM) was a leading global financial services firm that operated mainly in corporate and institutional business segments: syndicated bank credits, corporate finance, equities and equity investments, interest rate and currency markets, asset management services, and proprietary trading. As the commercial banking product of the 1930s breakup of the House of Morgan due to the Glass-Steagall Act, many long considered J.P. Morgan the best bank in the United States.

Both JPM and CMB had been struggling to establish themselves in the securities underwriting and M&A advisory businesses, areas that were much more profitable than traditional commercial banking. For it's part, Chase had never made a secret of its desire to buy an equities franchise to complete the lineup of its wholesale and investment banking operations. In a bid to strengthen equities underwriting, Chase chose a path of successive acquisitions (Hambrecht & Quist in 1998, the Beacon Group and Robert Fleming in 2000) to strengthen its investment banking capabilities. But although it made some progress off the back of its enormous wholesale lending and loan syndication business, Chase had been unable to break into the top-10 ranks of key corporate finance areas such as equity underwriting and M&A advisories.

According to many observers, J.P. Morgan's future had become increasingly uncertain. Starting from an enviable base as the top U.S. corporate bank in the 1980s, its costly transformation from a wholesale commercial bank into a leading investment bank failed to bear as much fruit as intended. Despite a stellar client list and good progress in building market share in a number of areas (including mergers and acquisitions), Morgan found it very difficult to compete in critical areas such as equity originations and non-investment grade bonds—especially given its tradition of wholesale banking for top corporates, its lack of relationships with smaller companies in "hot" sectors, and its insignificant presence in retail banking or securities distribution. With the benefit of hindsight, a merger with one of the major securities houses or even one or two targeted acquisitions along the way could have made Morgan a viable and indeed formidable competitor. Perhaps the terms would have been unattractive. Or an unwillingness to contaminate the bank's strong culture, together with a certain degree of arrogance, may have precluded this. It is difficult to

Table 6-2 J.P. Morgan–Chase Pro-forma Revenues and Pretax
Cash-flow, 1999 ($ billions)[1]

	Revenues	Pretax Cash Earnings
Investment banking	$15.9	$5.9
Wealth management	3.7	1.0
Private equity	3.4	3.0
Operating services	3.3	0.9
U.S. consumer services	9.9	2.6

[1] Last twelve months (LTM) ending June 30, 2000; pro forma, including Robert
Fleming.

judge from the outside. But by 2000 Morgan seemed to be floundering,
and this was clearly reflected in the share price.

Together with a cost structure that was stubbornly high for an investment bank, J.P. Morgan's stock price reflected the firm's disappointing
performance. Once the most valuable bank in America, its capitalization
fell to the $30 billion range, far short of its one-time peers such as Citi-
group ($247 billion in December 2000). Rumors intensified that Morgan
was finished as an independent firm. Amidst takeover speculation, its
stock had already seen a gain from about $110 in early July to $177.75 on
September 12, 2000, the day of the Chase-Morgan merger announcement.
From that perspective, J.P. Morgan's sellout was not surprising. Still, one
of the greatest institutions in American finance was gone, and many
thought that it did not necessarily have to turn out this way.

The merger took the form of an all-stock offer by Chase of 3.7 shares
of the new firm for each share of JPM, which valued each JPM share at
$207 based on the pre-announcement CMB share price of $56.06—a premium of about 16%. The deal cost Chase shareholders $30.9 billion. Ac-
cording to Chase CEO William B. Harrison at the time of the merger
announcement, "It's a very fair deal. . . . And most importantly, when we
look at the overall transaction two years from now, it should be accretive
to shareholders."[3]

The J.P. Morgan–Chase (JPMC) combination, said the press release issued jointly by the companies, would create an organization with un-
paralleled client base, global capabilities, and product leadership in
growth markets. The purported strategic considerations centered around
complementary strengths in clients, geographies, and services (see Tables
6-2 and 6-3, Figure 6-7). This included the addition of Chase's non-
investment grade clients, middle-market clients, and clients engaged in

3. As quoted in Andrew Ross Sorkin, "Those Sweet Trips to the Merger Mall," *New York Times*, April
7, 2002.

Table 6-3 J.P. Morgan–Chase Comparative Product Strengths

J.P. Morgan	Chase
Equity underwriting	New economy and Asian equities
Equity & structured derivatives	FX & interest rate derivatives
Global M&A—Europe	Global M&A
Europe fixed income	Syndicated & leveraged finance
U.S. asset management	European & Asian asset mgmt.
LabMorgan (e-banking applications)	Chase.com (e-banking)
	Operating services

"new-economy businesses" to J.P. Morgan's first-rate client base comprising mainly large, blue-chip, investment grade companies. The combination was to provide increased opportunities for cross-marketing the company's full product array. The new firm would be a massive, globally balanced wholesale financial services company focusing on corporations and institutions.

The combined company would in addition have a total of $720 billion of fiduciary assets under management, making JPMC the second largest active asset manager in the United States, behind Fidelity Investments. These assets were well diversified in terms of major categories (equities 52%, fixed income 25%, cash and other classes 23%), by geographic region (U.S. 65%, non-U.S. 35%), and by client type (institutional investors 60%, private clients 40%).

The merger thus created a very broad firm with leading positions in fixed income underwriting and trading, syndicated lending, risk management, private equity, asset management and private banking, custody,

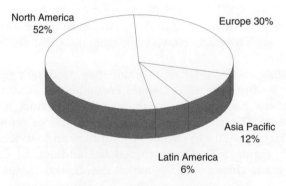

Figure 6-7. J.P. Morgan Chase pro forma 1999 global revenue distribution. Source: Company filings.

and several key areas of retail banking. The core value propositions at the time of the merger were purported to be the following:

- Greater diversification of business lines. The combined company would be broadly diversified to encompass an array of financial services businesses, which could be expected to provide a more stable revenue stream than those experienced by a pure wholesale bank.
- Enhanced scale and global reach. The combined company would be among the top five global financial institutions in terms of market capitalization (about $95 billion) at the time of the merger announcement, ranking third in the United States after Citigroup and Morgan Stanley Dean Witter, respectively.
- Synergies and cost savings. On a pretax basis, the cost savings and incremental revenue accruing to the combined entity, by the end of the second year, was estimated at $1.5 billion and $400 million, respectively. The two merging banks had already made significant progress on their own. Fee income had attained almost 70% of total earnings, while efficiency and credit problems of both banks had improved substantially. This progress had contributed to pushing combined pro forma return on equity above 20%.

In addition, the deal was intended to leverage Chase's integration track record. While J.P. Morgan had mainly pursued a "build" strategy, Chase had an array of acquisitions under its belt carried out by the legacy Chemical Bank team, including difficult ones like Manufacturers Hanover and the old Chase itself, and people-sensitive ones like Hambrecht & Quist and Robert Fleming.

Despite the track record, purported common cultural attributes, and inclusive approach to integration (see Table 6-4), the deal soon turned into an outright Chase takeover of J.P. Morgan. Within two years most of the key Morgan managers were gone, as were many of the important line bankers and specialists. Divisions of responsibility in various units between people from the two predecessor banks were usually short-lived, with the ex-Chase individuals winning most of the time. This was foreseeable, perhaps inevitable, in the light of experience with most financial

Table 6-4 J.P. Morgan Chase: Purported Capacity to Integrate

Track record of successful integrations
Inclusive approach to integration
Common cultural elements
More focused, less complex than prior mergers
Staff retention driven by opportunity and incentives

industry mergers, but it might have been disproportionately important here because of the unusually high quality of the J.P. Morgan staff and its teamwork-oriented culture. That culture itself was a powerful attribute of J.P. Morgan. The Chase culture was also strong, but very different. The two evidently did not mix well.

From a cost standpoint the deal was a disappointment as well. A $3.2 billion restructuring charge indicated by management on announcement of the deal in September 2000 was intended to make possible $1.5 billion in annual savings. In fact, the restructuring charge later turned into $4.5 billion in order to "right-size" the business given the weaker than expected economic conditions.

The Chase-Morgan merger is often compared with the Travelers–Citicorp merger two years earlier. Analysts were universally bullish on Citigroup based on possible revenue synergies, efficiency gains, and the expectation of a ruthless integration process in the Sandy Weill tradition—integration that would nevertheless retain and motivate the best people. They were much more cautious about the J.P. Morgan–Chase deal, less about the strategy itself than about management's ability to pull it off and the persistence of missing resources in important areas of investment banking.

The JPMC board, however, had no such doubts and awarded special bonus payments of some $50 million to senior managers for getting the deal done. Shareholders of both firms did less well, as roughly 40% of the stock's value disappeared in the two years following the deal's announcement in September 2000. By late 2002 the combined firm was worth little

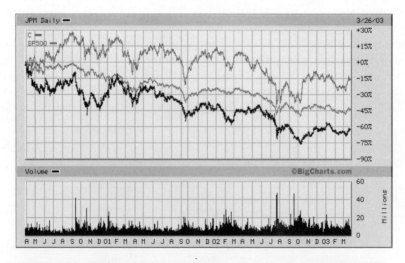

Figure 6-8. Share Prices of Citigroup and J.P. Morgan Chase in the Two Years Following the JPMC Merger.

more than Chase alone prior to the merger. It was perhaps a hallmark of the times that managers got paid for doing deals rather than delivering value to shareholders.

Figure 6-8 describes the stock prices of J.P. Morgan Chase and Citigroup against the S&P 500 index during this period. Both companies suffered from adverse developments in the equity market, as reflected in the S&P 500 index, as well as emerging market problems, and financial distress and bankruptcies during this period. Both found themselves in the middle of Enron and other corporate scandals. But the market seemed to persist in its differentiation between the two stories.

General Electric Capital Services

Few financial services organizations demonstrated as consistent a degree of success in sustaining high rates of risk-adjusted profit growth as did General Electric Capital Services (GECS), the financial services subsidiary of GE, until its dissolution in 2002.

Formed over 70 years ago to finance customers of GE household appliances, GECS had assets of $490 billion at the end of 2001—the largest non-bank financial institution in the world. It contributed net income of $3.6 billion on revenues of $58.2 billion to GE's 2002 total of $134 billion—almost half of GE's total revenues and (in a bad year) about 20% of its profits (see Figure 6-9). With about 91,000 employees worldwide, it produced after tax returns on invested capital between 20% and 25% for over 20 years, a consistent record of growth and profitability that very few other financial firms could match. GECS was, in effect, a financial conglomerate within a conglomerate. It was also the highest-growth business

Segment Revenues $131,698 million

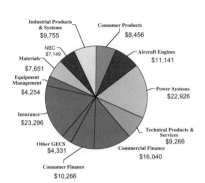

**Segment Pre-Tax Profit
$18,780 million
(after-tax ROE 25.8%)**

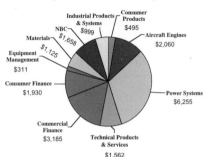

Figure 6-9. General Electric, 2002.
Note: Insurance (loss $509), other GECS (loss $291).

among GE's stable of businesses. To the extent that GE was a growth story for investors over the years, GECS played a disproportionately important role in that process.

Shareholders of General Electric in effect own a "closed-end mutual fund." The fund consisted of aircraft engines, plastics, power generation and distribution equipment, broadcasting, diesel locomotives, large household appliances, medial equipment, and a variety of other industrial activities, plus one of the world's largest financial services businesses. They are therefore confronted with all the pluses and minuses associated with conglomerates, including, most important, the evidence of a conglomerate discount that is almost always embedded in the share price, as discussed in Chapter 2. Even if GECS had been an independent company, it would still have been a massive financial conglomerate. So how did GE and GECS produce both impressive and consistent returns, which in the end made GE the most valuable company in the world?

The classic GE management principles appeared to account for this apparent anomaly. To rephrase Jack Welch's insistent messages: seek to dominate fast-growing but highly concentrated markets and combine that with "six-sigma" targets in quality control and fierce attention to costs, leadership development, and leveraging know-how. In short, try to create an internal market for capital that functions more efficiently than the external market—something most economists would deny can be done on a sustained basis. No doubt Jack Welch would have argued that the same thing applies to the market for human capital, where the legendary GE approach to promoting and optimizing the use of talent seemed to operate in tandem with the highly disciplined pattern of in financial optimization.

Tables 6-5 and 6-6 reproduce two pages out of the GE playbook designed to highlight not only the purposeful way GE went about its business but also the notion that these are real businesses that carry the firm profitably through economic cycles and produce real returns without

Table 6-5 GE Leadership Based on Financial Visibility and Accountability

Diverse set of #1 franchises in global markets	Business initiatives with visible financial benefits	Strong balance sheet to capitalize on change and opportunity
↓	↓	↓
Every business executes and contributes	Accelerating impact from Digitization	Disciplined approach to investment and risk
Portfolio produces growth through every cycle	All initiatives deliver operational improvements	Core competence in acquisition and integration

Source: General Electric Company, Annual Report 2001.

Table 6-6 Key GE Operating Principles

[We] are passionately focused on driving customer success.
Live Six Sigma quality . . . ensure that the customer is always its first beneficiary . . . and use it to accelerate growth.
Insist on excellence and be intolerant of bureaucracy.
Act in a boundaryless fashion . . . always search for and apply the best ideas regardless of their source.
Prize global intellectual capital and the people who provide it . . . build diverse teams to maximize it.
Create a clear, simple, customer-centered vision . . . and continually renew and refresh its execution.
Create an environment of "stretch," excitement, informality, and trust . . . reward improvements . . . and celebrate results.

Source: General Electric Company, Annual Report 2001.

smoke and mirrors. Ultimately the story has to be effectively sold to the market. Of course, the devil is in the details. Yet the results suggest that the broad objective was largely achieved for many years.

What about GECS? Figure 6-10 shows the organizational structure of GE's financial services activities at the beginning of 2002—representing 28 "independent businesses," of which 11 were considered global leaders. Each was managed according to the GE principles of growth, market concentration, service quality, and attention to costs. There were relatively few cross-links between these businesses, so the structure and its sustained profitability did not depend heavily on cross selling, as would usually be true in universal banking or other financial conglomerate structures. The key linkages between GECS and its parent were managerial and financial. The GE management philosophy was clearly manifest in the development and success of GECS, and GE's deep pool of talent was used to support GECS's rapid growth.

That growth was itself the result of a rapid-fire series of acquisitions (Ashkenas, DeMonaco and Francis 1998). Those over $100 million completed during 1999–2002 in the United States and internationally are listed in Table 6-7. During the 1992–2001 decade, GECS completed a total of over 400 acquisitions, and in the year 2001 alone closed 27 deals worth $42 billion, including its largest single acquisition, Heller Financial at a cost of $ 5.3 billion.

The firm's acquisition process has been a topic of interest for years. The GECS structure of high-performance specialists evidently allowed the firm to be extremely opportunistic and aggressive in actively soliciting acquisitions. The managers of each of the relatively narrow financial businesses knew that particular part of the industry and the key players very

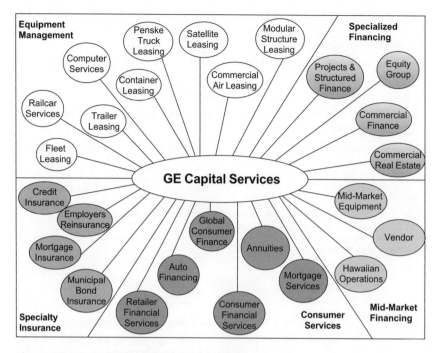

Figure 6-10. GE Capital Services Legacy Structure.

well, and knew them globally. So when acquisitions opportunities pre-sented themselves, perhaps resulting from economic or financial devel-opments, management could move quickly and decisively. Management was able to understand the target, value it, undertake due diligence with the help of GE teams who were expert in the process, and conclude transactions that were highly favorable to the firm. The opportunistic $2.3 billion acquisition of most of beleaguered ABB's structured finance arm in September 2002 was a case in point.

Figure 6-11 presents a stylized version of the highly disciplined, logical, and codified GECS acquisition process—some have called it a virtual "acquisition machine." Done right at the right prices and integrated quickly and well, it is clear how this machine could fuel both top-line growth and bottom-line profitability. GECS acquisition activities in Japan in the late 1990s, depicted in Figure 6-12, constitute a good example of this unique institutional skill, executed through highly focused business units within the GECS group. All of this clearly came at a cost, however, in terms of the transparency of GE financials. GE's legendary internal financial discipline and audit process may have understood things, but it was certainly difficult for outsiders—professional analysts and fund man-agers, as well as ordinary investors—to follow along. So the Jack Welch, GE, and GECS "mystique" probably became a major factor driving the

Table 6-7 GE Financial Services Acquisitions Exceeding $100 Million in The United States, 1990–2002

Date Announced	Date Effective	Value ($mil)	Target Name	Target Business Description	Target Country
01/02/90	01/31/90	350.00	McCullagh Leasing Inc.	Provide vehicle leasing services	
03/30/90	04/30/90	1193.60	Ellco Leasing Corp	Provide commercial leasing services	
10/11/90	05/10/91	1600.00	Macy Credit, Macy Receivables	Provide personal credit services	
06/02/92	06/02/92	560.00	Chrysler Capital-Diversified	Provide business credit services	
01/06/93	04/15/93	750.00	GNA Corp (GE Capital Corp)	Life insurance company	
02/04/93	12/31/93	500.00	First Chicago Corp-Commercial	Real estate loan portfolio	
04/05/93	07/14/93	550.00	United Pacific Life Insurance	Life insurance company	
05/27/93	07/16/93	215.00	Verex Corp (GFC Financial)	Insurance company	
06/30/94	11/01/94	400.00	Harcourt General Inc-Insurance	Insurance company	
12/27/94	04/03/95	1800.00	ITT-Equip Fin, Small Bus Fin	Mnfr communications equip	
11/13/95	04/03/96	400.00	Union Fidelity Life Insurance	Insurance holding company	
12/26/95	04/03/96	960.00	Life Insurance Co of Virginia	Life, health insurance company	
05/20/96	07/23/96	454.785	AmeriData Technologies Inc	Whl computers, peripherals	
08/02/96	11/29/96	1799.24	First Colony Corp	Insurance holding company	
01/23/97	05/30/97	450.00	Coregis Insurance	Insurance company	
06/30/97	11/04/97	1081.10	Colonial Penn P&C Group	Insurance company	
07/31/98	10/29/98	500.00	Kemper Reinsurance Co	Fire, marine, casualty insurance company	
10/12/98	12/31/98	800.00	Colonial Pacific Leasing	Provide external financing services	
05/17/99	10/29/99	3961.00	LTCB-US Loan Assets Portfolio	Mortgage security finance co	
09/15/99	11/19/99	200.00	Crown Castle International	Provide wireless transmission services	
03/30/01	08/01/01	2118.663	Franchise Finance Corp of Amer	Real estate investment trust	
06/29/01	06/29/01	100.00	NTL Inc	Provide communications services	
07/30/01	10/25/01	5321.532	Heller Financial Inc	Provide business finance services	
08/01/01	08/01/01	120.00	Crescent Real Estate Equities	Real estate investment trust	
12/14/01	05/14/02	5541.921	Security Capital Group Inc	Provide real estate research services	

(continued)

02/26/90	04/27/90	239.98	Wang International Finl Ltd	Provide computer leasing services	Ireland-Rep
07/18/90	07/18/90	331.692	Burton Group Financial Svcs	Provide financial services	United Kingdom
05/17/91	07/02/91	450.125	Mercantile Cred-Vehicle Loans	Provide vehicle credit services	United Kingdom
07/23/91	05/08/92	140.00	Banco Bilbao Vizcaya SA	Bank	Spain
04/06/93	11/01/93	1350.018	GPA Group PLC-43 Planes	Manufacture airplanes	Ireland-Rep
04/06/93	08/31/93	107.227	TIP Europe PLC	Provide trailer rental services	United Kingdom
08/16/93		385.64	Finax	Provide credit card services	Sweden
01/23/95	02/28/95	145.424	Credit de l'Est	Bank	France
02/03/95	02/04/95	140.054	United Merchants Finance Ltd	Provide financing services	Hong Kong
02/04/95	02/28/95	162.269	Societe Gestion Financiere et	Investment holding company	France
02/28/95	08/31/95	132.624	Australian Retail Finl Network	Provide credit card finl services	Australia
07/28/95	12/13/95	1515.085	Sovac(Eurafrance)	Bank; holding company	France
10/12/95	09/02/96	277.14	Marubeni Car System Co	Provide car leasing services	Japan
08/21/96	11/24/97	192.175	Central Transport Rental Group	Provide RR car rental services	United Kingdom
07/29/97	01/09/98	815.182	Woodchester Investments PLC	Investment bank	Ireland-Rep
09/22/97	11/03/97	502.71	MEPC PLC-Small Commercial(191)	Own, operate office property	United Kingdom
11/03/97	04/01/98	593.871	Toho Mutual-New Bus Op & Sales	Insurance company	Japan
02/18/98	05/29/98	599.899	UIS	Own and operate buildings	France
05/29/98	11/23/98	273.999	GPA Group-9 Aircrafts	Provide aircraft leasing services	Ireland-Rep
06/08/98	06/25/98	497.029	Financial Sector-Tranche ABCD	Provide financial services	Thailand
01/26/99	03/05/99	6565.60	Japan Leasing Corp	Provide business credit services	Japan
05/21/99	06/30/99	493.00	Avco Financial Services Ltd	Provide financial services	Australia
12/20/99	03/01/00	2323.68	Toho Mutual Life	Life insurance company	Japan
05/26/00	10/20/00	269.034	Nissen-Consurmer Credit Bus	Provide consumer credit services	Japan
05/29/01	06/12/01	312.51	Malvern House Acquisition Ltd	Investment company	United Kingdom
06/22/01	04/08/02	522.44	National Mutual Life Assurance	Provide insurance services	United Kingdom

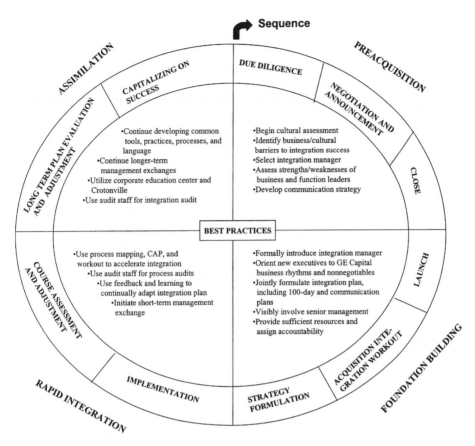

Figure 6-11. The GECS Acquisition Process. Source: Ronald Ashkenas, Lawrence J. DeMonaco, and Suzanne C. Francis, "Making the Dean: How GE Capital Integrates Acquisitions," *Harvard Business Review,* January–February 1998, p. 167.

GE share price to what some argued were improbable levels over a long period of time.

In financial matters, the various GECS units clearly benefited from the low cost of capital associated with a high corporate share price and a AAA GE debt rating—from which GECS benefited through a "comfort letter" from the parent to its finance subsidiary, which covered GECS's capital market issues. GECS borrowings in 1999 were $200 billion, for example, most of which were involved in financing receivables. In this sense there was a "cross-subsidy" that GECS received from its parent, whose value would be eroded if GECS's weight in GE's overall business became sufficiently large to endanger the corporations' overall credit quality. This weight (in terms of revenues) increased steadily from about 37% in 1995 to over 45% in 2001.

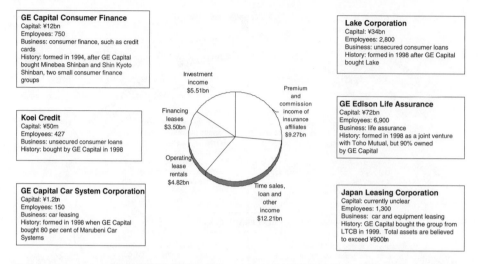

GE Capital Consumer Finance
Capital: ¥12bn
Employees: 750
Business: consumer finance, such as credit cards
History: formed in 1994, after GE Capital bought Minebea Shinban and Shin Kyoto Shinban, two small consumer finance groups

Koei Credit
Capital: ¥50m
Employees: 427
Business: unsecured consumer loans
History: bought by GE Capital in 1998

GE Capital Car System Corporation
Capital: ¥1.2bn
Employees: 150
Business: car leasing
History: formed in 1998 when GE Capital bought 80 per cent of Marubeni Car Systems

Lake Corporation
Capital: ¥34bn
Employees: 2,800
Business: unsecured consumer loans
History: formed in 1998 after GE Capital bought Lake

GE Edison Life Assurance
Capital: ¥72bn
Employees: 6,900
Business: life assurance
History: formed in 1998 as a joint venture with Toho Mutual, but 90% owned by GE Capital

Japan Leasing Corporation
Capital: currently unclear
Employees: 1,300
Business: car and equipment leasing
History: GE Capital bought the group from LTCB in 1999. Total assets are believed to exceed ¥900bn

Investment income $5.51bn

Premium and commission income of insurance affiliates $9.27bn

Financing leases $3.50bn

Operating lease rentals $4.82bn

Time sales, loan and other income $12.21bn

Figure 6-12. GE Capital Services Acquisitions in Japan in the 1990s. Source: General Electric (the chart shows Japan revenues for 1998).

Although it was clearly a financial services conglomerate embedded within a parent that was itself a conglomerate, GECS was almost the antithesis of the way the major banks and financial conglomerates have traditionally been managed—often operating in highly competitive markets with bloated costs, bureaucratic organizations structured as generalists not specialists, and often with mediocre or poor service quality. Overall, the top 10 global banks have produced about one-half the growth and operating performance of GECS during the decade of the 1990s and beyond. And although it is impossible to determine total returns to shareholders (since GECS is not a listed company), those returns would no doubt reflect this fact. GECS was considerably smaller than the world's largest banks but would certainly qualify as one of the most valuable financial services franchises.

A comparison of GECS and Citigroup is instructive in this regard (see Table 6-8). Citigroup in 2001 was much larger in terms of assets and somewhat ahead in terms of return on assets, but GECS was ahead in terms of return on equity, assuming comparable accounting. Although GECS was not a bank, its leverage actually exceeded that of Citigroup, yet it benefited from a higher debt rating. Although they are similar only to the extent that they are conglomerates, the similarity in stock price performance after the 1998 formation of Citigroup is striking. Both dramatically outperformed the market (for example, the S&P 500 index) for an extended period, although Citigroup shares appeared more volatile. Both were hard-hit by the equity market declines of 2001 and 2002 and (for somewhat different reasons) by the corporate scandals and loss of

Table 6-8 GE Capital Versus Citigroup 2001

	GE Capital	Citigroup
Total Assets	$426 billion	$1.05 trillion
Total Debt	$240 billion	$399 billion
Return on Assets	1.36%	1.43%
Return on Equity	21.0%	20.4%
Debt to Capital Ratio	87.96%	81.87%
LT Debt Rating	AAA	AAA

Date: Bloomberg Financial Markets, Standard & Poor's, company reports.

market credibility that began with the 1991 Enron disaster (as depicted in (Figure 6-13). Although the GE share price lagged somewhat.

As noted, concerns in the case of GE had long centered on the growing importance of GECS within the GE structure and the potential threats it posed for the parent's AAA debt rating, as well as the massive exposure of GECS to the commercial paper market—that is, allegedly using uncommitted short-term financing for long-term funding requirements. Together with lack of transparency and the retirement of Jack Welch, this may help explain the rapid erosion of GE's extraordinary valuation multiples that had prevailed for such a long time. In response, GE moved quickly in 2002 to add committed bank lines to its financing armory, significantly increased disclosure of the internal financial affairs, and broke GECS into four separate businesses that were, according to GE CEO Jeffrey Immelt, easier to understand and easier to manage from the corporate center (see Figure 6-14 for detail on the four businesses). It was the end of a rather

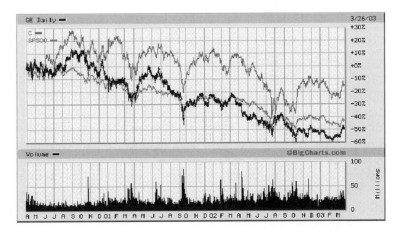

Figure 6-13. General Electric versus Citigroup (share prices after the Citigroup merger on April 6, 1998).

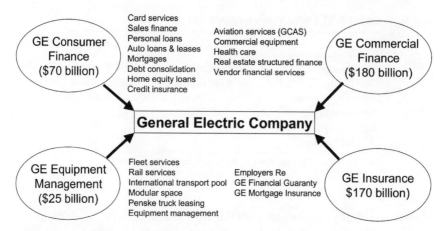

Figure 6-14. Breakup of GE Capital Services, July 2002 (August 2002—total assets $445 billion).

impressive chapter in the annals of the financial services industry. Whether the breakup of GECS will make a difference in the remarkable returns achieved by GE's financial businesses remains to be seen. If the disciplined GE approach to capital allocation and risk management can be sustained, there is reason for optimism.

As indicated earlier, case studies and clinical analyses all suffer from the unobservable counterfactual, as well as possible biases in the analysis. So case-based conclusions are basically impossible to generalize. Sooner or later one has to proceed to statistical studies that are based either on cross-sectional or time-series data. Assuming the availability of reliable data, definitive conclusions are at least in the realm of the possible, and in some cases may be highly instructive.

WHAT DOES THE EMPIRICAL EVIDENCE SHOW?

Most studies of financial sector mergers examine either market reaction to merger announcements or long-term performance measures against various kinds of benchmarks. Market reaction studies attempt to gauge whether the market sees the announcement of a merger as a positive or negative event. In general, market reaction to the announcements of financial-sector mergers is neutral or slightly negative for the acquirer but highly positive for merger targets. Combined returns to both partners are usually around zero. Conditions in the M&A market can influence those returns, however. For example, James and Weir (1987) find that acquirer returns go up when acquirers have more potential targets, but go down when more potential acquirers exist.

Studies evaluating the long-term performance of merged banks produce mixed results. Cornett and Tehranian (1992) found that merged banks outperformed the industry in terms of return on equity but not return on assets. They concluded that better performance appears to be the result of attracting more loans and deposits to a given equity base, as well as employee productivity and asset growth. DeLong (2001a) found that average return on assets does not improve as a result of M&A transactions, but industry-adjusted efficiency increases.

An examination of the world's 200 largest banks during the 1980s (Saunders and Walter 1994) found evidence that the very largest banks grew more slowly than the smaller banks in the sample. Limited economies of scale did appear to exist among the banks included in the study.

A study of 72 financial services M&A deals exceeding $500 million during 1990–1999 conducted by Accenture (2000) found that one third of the deals created significant shareholder value during the two years after merger completion. Top deals were HSBC-Midland Bank, Lloyds-TSB, and Morgan Stanley- Dean Witter (see Figure 6-15). Two-thirds of financial services M&A deals destroyed shareholder value within two years against local benchmarks. However, the best-performing one-third of the deals outweighed the rest to produce a 7% two-year excess return. Important factors in the Accenture study included a premerger integration plan, a premerger succession plan, top-line (revenue) focus, and an emphasis on consistent and effective branding. Less important factors were found to

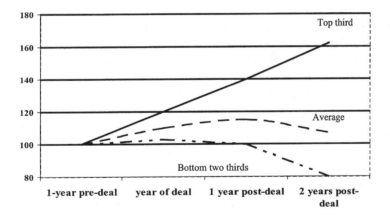

•Two thirds of financial services M&A deals destroy shareholder value within two years (against local benchmarks).
•One third create significant shareholder value – top deals HSBC-Midland, Lloyds-TDB, and MSDW.
•Best third outweighs the rest to produce 7% two-year excess return.
•Important factors: premerger integration plan, succession plan, top-line focus and branding.
•Less important factors: cost take-out, IT integration

Figure 6-15. Long-Term Performance in Financial Services M&A Transactions (cumulative total return to shareholders from 72 deals exceeding $500m each, 1990–1998). Data: Accenture, 2000.

Table 6-9 Post-Acquisition Returns in Selected U.S. Financial Sector Mergers

| | | | | | Returns‡ | | |
| | | | | | Seller | Buyer | Buyer |
Acquirer	Target	Date	Value†	Premium#	1 wk*	1 wk*	1 year**
Travelers	Citicorp	4/98	70.0	10.4%	8%	6%	2%
NationsBank	B of A	4/98	59.3	48.4%	2%	4%	4%
Chase	Morgan	9/00	36.3	59.7%	24%	−19%	14%
Norwest	Wells Fargo	6/98	33.6	0.9%	−3%	−11%	10%
Conseco	Greentree	4/98	7.1	85.9%	35%	−15%	−55%
M&T Bank	Keystone	5/00	1.0	41.6%	29%	−4%	54%
Star Banc	Firstar	7/98	7.0	44.1%	44.1%	−2%	44%
NY Community	Richmond	3/01	0.8	7.2%	11%	7%	43%

* Price change one week pre- and post-announcement. ** Price change one week pre-announcement to one year post-announcement. † Value of offer when announced. # Difference between offer price and market price one week before offer. ‡ Percentage point differences over specified periods relative to S&P 500 peers. Data: Standard & Poor's, Mergerstat, Boston Consulting Group, Thomson Financial.

be cost takeout and IT integration. This mixed record is reflected in Table 6-9, which depicts deal premiums and returns to buyers and sellers over a one-week and one-year period following announcement of each transaction in the case of a number of American deals during the 1998–2001 period.

A few empirical studies look at both market reaction and long-term performance to determine whether the market can correctly predict successful bank mergers. Evidence from these studies is mixed. Pilloff (1996) found no relationship between abnormal returns upon the announcement of a merger and subsequent performance of the publicly traded banks examined. That is, the market does not seem to be able to predict which bank mergers will improve performance. However, Cornett and Tehranian (1992) found significant correspondence between market reaction and several more indicators (operating efficiency, pretax cash flow, ROE, deposits-to-equity, loans-to-assets, and asset growth).

As noted in Chapter 2, active debate has persisted in banking concerning the benefits and costs of universal banking and financial conglomerates (Saunders and Walter 1994). Proponents suggest that banks that are permitted to serve all the financial needs of individuals and companies are more efficient than institutions that provide only one or a few of the services. Arguments against universal banks and conglomerates suggest that such institutions tend to be less innovative than segmented financial firms. With regard to mergers, the pertinent question is, should a merger combine two entities engaged in the same activity, or should it extend the product line of the acquirer? Intra-industry mergers are those where the acquirer targets a firm that is engaged in similar activities. The main advantages of intra-industry mergers are that they could improve efficiency as well as enjoy economies of scale. Inter-industry mergers, or mergers where the partners are engaged in different activities, allow the acquirer to realize economies of scope as well as lower the risk and cost of bankruptcy.

DeLong (2001a) found that the market reacts positively to bank mergers that focus activities and geography but that different facets of focusing actually improve long-term performance. The study concluded that inefficient acquirers tend to improve the efficiency of the merged entity more than other acquirers. This finding suggests that acquirers use mergers as an excuse to improve efficiency within their current organizations by eliminating unprofitable activities or letting go less productive staff. Indeed, in an early study Jensen and Ruback (1983) suggested that in-market or focusing mergers are a good mechanism to replace inefficient managers with efficient ones. In a later work, Jensen [1986] contended that this could enhance value only if partners come from the same industry, since managerial skills are not transferable between industries.

Focusing Mergers: Improved Efficiency and Scale-Effects

Extensive research has shown that activity-focusing mergers could improve efficiencies either through the transfer of skills or changing the mix of outputs. Berger and Humphrey (1992b) found that acquiring banks tend to be significantly more efficient than the acquired banks, suggesting that the acquirer may potentially improve the efficiency of the target. Akhavein, Berger, and Humphrey (1997) found that megamergers between U.S. banks increase revenues by improving efficiency rather than increasing prices. They found that increased revenues come in part from a shift in asset allocation after the merger from government securities to loans, which earn more for the bank. They also found evidence consistent with both partners being inefficient. This low-efficiency hypothesis again suggests that acquiring banks use mergers as an excuse to improve efficiency within their own organizations.

Findings on merger-related improvements in return on equity are contradictory. Linder and Crane (1992) and Pilloff (1996) found that return on equity (ROE) does not improve for merged banks. Cornett and Tehranian (1992) did find a significant increase in industry-adjusted ROE (but not in industry-adjusted return on assets). Berger and Humphrey (1992b) pointed out that Cornett and Tehranian looked at mergers that occurred from 1982 to 1987. The final year of their study, however, was an unusual one for the banking industry; most large banks made sizable loss provisions for their loans to developing countries. Such provisions greatly reduced equity and thus increased ROE. Perhaps their finding was mainly a result of unusual circumstances and not robust with regard to other periods.

In-market mergers seem to allow the acquirer to reduce redundant operations that both partners were performing before the merger. Houston and Ryngaert (1994) and DeLong (2001) found that the market rewards mergers where geographic overlap exists between acquirer and target. Houston, James, and Ryngaert (1999) found that geographic overlap is positively related to the estimated present value of mergers, as well as estimated cost savings. Cornett, Hovakimian, Palia, and Tehranian (1998) found that mergers of partners headquartered in the same U.S. state earn higher returns than mergers with partners in different U.S. states. Furthermore, corporate governance mechanisms appear to work better for in-market mergers than market-extending ones. For example, CEO equity ownership tends to align CEO and shareholder interests in intrastate mergers but less so for interstate mergers.

Evidence on long-term performance of focusing mergers is mixed. Cornett and Tehranian (1992) found that improvement is greater for bank mergers within U.S. states than between U.S. states. However, using a more specific measure of geographic overlap, DeLong (2001) found that common geography does not lead to long-term performance enhancement.

As noted in Chapter 2, most empirical studies of financial services mergers do not find evidence of economies of scale. Some studies of bank scale economies (see Berger and Humphrey [1993] for an overview) have found economies of scale in banking in small banks. Other studies (see Clark [1988] and Berger, Hunter, and Timme [1993]) found the relationship between size and average cost to be U-shaped. This suggests that small banks can benefit from economies of scale, but that large banks seem to suffer from diseconomies of scale, resulting in higher average costs as they increase in size. Although Kane (2000) found that the stock market reacts positively when big banks merge, he suggested that the merged entity was taking greater advantage of government guarantees, not taking advantage of economies of scale.

Despite the lack of much empirical evidence showing the existence of significant scale economies in banking based on overall firms size, the argument is so pervasive in the financial community and the media that the market may believe scale economies actually do exist. If so, it will reward bank mergers that it considers more likely to reduce average costs by virtue of size, and thereby enhance equity values upon announcement. Long-term realization of economies of scale, however, could be elusive.

Focusing Mergers: Monopoly Power

Geographically broadening mergers could also take advantage of monopoly rents by entering areas that are protected from competition. To create new value from the target, the acquirer must employ resources to increase the market share, introduce new activities, or change the mix of activities to include those that extract the most rents of the firm in the protected market. Empirically, banks seem to seek out monopolistic or oligopolistic markets. Beatty, Santomero, and Smirlock (1987) found that the higher the market concentration of the banking industry in a given area (as reflected by the Herfindahl-Hirschman index), the higher the premium paid to acquire a bank in that area; the higher concentration is a proxy for regulatory protection.

Although various studies find that banks in concentrated markets tend to charge higher interest rates or pay lower deposit rates than banks in less concentrated markets, antitrust policy seems to prevent banks that merge from taking advantage of their increased market power. Berger and Hannan (1996) found that loan rates were higher and deposit rates were lower when banks operated in concentrated markets. These increased revenues, however, did not result in higher profits. The study also showed evidence consistent with managers pursing a "quiet life" and incurring higher costs than their counterparts in less concentrated markets.

Akhavein, Berger, and Humphrey (1997) found that banks that merge charge more for loans and pay less on deposits before they merge than other large banks. Specifically, they found that banks that merged charged 17 basis points more for loans than the average large bank prior to merging. After the merger, however, this difference fell to about 10 basis points. This suggests that merging banks do not tend to take advantage of their increased market power. The authors contend that antitrust policy is effective in preventing mergers that would create market power problems.

Siems (1996) reached a similar conclusion. In his study of 19 bank megamergers (partners valued over $500 million) in 1995, he rejected the market power hypothesis, although he found that in-market mergers create positive value for both the acquirer and the target upon announcement. He found no relationship between the abnormal returns and the change in the Herfindahl-Hirschman index that measures market concentration.

Diversifying Mergers: Economies of Scope

As noted in Chapter 3, there is very little empirical evidence regarding cost economies of scope—whether unit costs of financial services firms go down or up, all else equal, in response to a broader product range achieved, for example, through mergers or acquisitions.

Giddy (1984) showed how underwriting and commercial lending risks are similar in that both are comparable to put options. Both incur limited upside gains: in the case of underwriting, it is the difference between the offer price and the net cost; and in commercial lending the gains come from the spread between the cost of funds and the interest rate on the loan. Both also incur substantial downside risks: if the market price of a security is below the offer price, buyers will be scarce and the underwriter might have to sell at a price below the net price. The risk in commercial lending is that some or the entire loan will not be repaid. The limited upside gain coupled with substantial downside risks is similar to writing puts on stocks. Having learned to assess and price this risk, commercial bankers could transfer some of the knowledge and experience they have to underwriting securities. Furthermore, banks offering both commercial and investment banking services minimize not only information-gathering costs but also monitoring costs. The monitoring of a bank loan, for example, is similar to the monitoring of a corporate investment.

In his survey of the literature on economies of scope in banking, Clark (1988) found no consistent evidence. Of the 11 studies that examined global economies of scope, only one presented significant evidence of scope economies when it examined the relationship among several products. Berger and Humphrey (1992a) found scope economies could lower the costs of a commercial bank by 10 to 20%. Moreover, Mitchell and Onvural (1995) examined the cost structure of over 300 large banks—with assets between $0.5 and $100 billion—in both 1986 and 1991 and found extremely weak evidence for the existence of economies of scope.

Empirical evidence concerning the existence of certain product-specific economies of scope is more substantial. Yu (2001) provided interesting support for the economies of scope argument. The U.S. equity market responded favorably to stocks in the financial services sector as a whole with the Financial Services Modernization Act (the Gramm-Leach-Bliley Act) of 1999. This allowed U.S. commercial banks to engage in securities and insurance activities and vice versa. Among other things, the legislation repealed the Glass-Steagall Act of 1933 that separated commercial from investment banks in the United States. The Act allowed Citigroup—a firm created from the commercial bank holding company of Citicorp and the Travelers insurance and financial services company, which also owned the Salomon Smith Barney securities firm—to stay in business. Yu's study found that the market reacted most favorably to large securities firms, large insurance companies, and bank holding companies already engaged in some securities businesses (those with Section 20 subsidiaries allowing limited investment banking activities). The study suggested that the market expected gains from product diversification, possibly arising from cross-product synergies or perhaps extension of "too-big-to-fail" guarantees. Another study by Lown et al. (2000) similarly found that both commercial and investment bank stocks rose on announcement by President Clinton on October 22, 1999, that passage of the Gramm-Leach-Bliley Act was imminent.

A study of U.S. bank mergers in the 1990s by Brewer et al. (2001) found that merger premiums increased by about 35% as a result of deregulation—specifically, the passage of the 1997 Riegle-Neal Act, which eliminated geographic restrictions for U.S. bank operations. The study found that bid premiums were higher, and the better-performing were the targets as measured by return on average assets, the lower the embedded risk of the targets, the greater the diversification represented by the acquisition, and the larger the representation of independent directors on the boards of the target banks. The latter observation is consistent with other research in finance, which suggests that independent directors contribute materially to obtaining the best possible price for the shareholders of target firms.

Other examples of economies of scope exist in history. During the 1920s, U.S. commercial banks were permitted to have securities affiliates. Kroszner and Rajan (1994) found that U.S. bank affiliates typically underwrote better-performing securities than specialized investment banks. Perhaps commercial banks obtained knowledge about firms contemplating selling securities through the deposit and borrowing history of the firm. If so, commercial banks could then select the best risks to bring to market. Investors seem to take such arrangements into consideration: Puri (1996) found that securities underwritten by commercial banks generated higher prices than similar securities underwritten by investment banks. This suggests lower *ex ante* risk for those underwritten by commercial banks.

What little empirical evidence there is suggests that economies of scope seem to exist for specific combinations of products in the realm of commercial and investment banking as well as insurance. However, they are often difficult to extract and require well-designed, incentive-compatible, cross-selling approaches.

Diversifying Mergers: Tax-Efficiency

Geographically diversifying mergers may reduce taxes by lowering both the expected and actual tax burden of the combined entity. If effective marginal tax rates increase with the value of firm's pretax revenue, Smith and Stulz (1985) showed that lowering the variability of a firm's pretax value can reduce the expected tax burden and thereby increase the expected value of the firm. For example, if there are two firms with expected earnings of $600, one with certain earnings of $600 and one with expected earnings of $600, it has a 50% chance of earning $1,200 and a 50% chance of earning nothing. Assume an increasing tax rate: the tax rate is 10% for the first $750; for larger earnings it climbs to 12%. The expected taxes of the first firm are $60; for the second firm, they are $64.50 (0.5 × (0.10 × $750 + 0.12 × $450 + 0). Even though the firms have the same expected earnings ($600), the one with the less volatile earnings has lower expected taxes. Over time, firms can lower their actual tax burdens by lowering the volatility of their earnings.

Not much empirical evidence, however, exists to support the tax-reduction argument. Santomero (1995) pointed out that if the tax argument holds, American firms would be less interested in reducing the volatility of their earnings as a result of lower marginal U.S. corporate tax rates. But he found no evidence to support this contention. He also pointed out that tax reduction depends on *taxable* income, not reported book income. Since discretion exists concerning the reporting book profit, real economic decisions, such as the decision to merge, would tend not to depend on profits reported to the market. The more discretion exists concerning the reporting book profits, the less valid the tax reason for wanting to reduce earnings volatility.

Diversifying Mergers: Financial Stability

As noted in Chapter 2, diversification can reduce the risk embedded in a firm's share price and therefore improve value. Bankruptcy costs include the direct costs of legal, accounting, and administrative fees, as well as the indirect costs of lower sales, worse terms for purchasing supplies or obtaining credit, reduced employee morale, and other opportunity costs. James (1991) finds banks lose about 30% of the value of their assets when they declare bankruptcy. Since bankruptcy costs can be high, lowering expected default would be beneficial to a financial firm. By reducing the volatility of a bank's share value, activity diversification could reduce the expected risk of failure and thereby reduce the expected costs associated with bankruptcy. The lower the correlation between cash flows from different businesses, the greater the benefits of diversification. That is, the more differently the activities react to an external and internal shocks, the more beneficial is diversification.

A drawback to stockholders of reducing the probability of bankruptcy is that the value of current debt increases at the expense of equity holders. This wealth redistribution occurs because bond-holders receive payment with greater probability and the market value of the current debt increases. Israel (1991) presented a model that shows that higher debt levels of potential merger targets result in lower profitability for the acquirer. Billett (1996) tested this theory and finds evidence to support the existence of a wealth transfer from bidder and target-equity holders to target-debt holders. He found that the more noninvestment grade debt a firm has, the less likely it is to be acquired. Acquirers seem to want to avoid co-insuring debt.

Studies that test the risk reduction hypothesis often look at how hypothetical combinations could have reduced risk by using actual industry averages. Using accounting and market data, Boyd, Graham, and Hewitt (1993) tested whether hypothetical mergers between bank holding companies and non-bank financial firms decrease risk. In a sample of data from 1971 to 1987, they found that mergers between bank holding companies and insurance firms could have reduced risk, whereas mergers between bank holding companies and securities firms or real estate firms could have increased risk.

There is some additional evidence that a positive link exists between diversification and financial stability. Saunders and Walter (1994) carried out a series of simulated mergers between U.S. banks, securities firms, and insurance companies in order to test the stability of earnings of the pro-forma "merged" firm as opposed to separate institutions. The opportunity-set of potential mergers between existing firms and the risk-characteristics of each possible combination were examined. The findings suggest that there are indeed potential risk-reduction gains from diversification in multi-activity financial services organizations, and that these gains increase with the number of activities undertaken. The main risk-reduction gains appear to arise from combining commercial banking with insurance activities, rather than with securities activities. These studies may exaggerate the risk-reduction benefits of cross-market mergers because they ignore many of the operational costs involved in setting up and managing these activities—that is, only the financial firms in existence for the full 1984–1988 period are considered.

Santomero and Chung (1992) likewise created hypothetical bank holding companies comprising of various combinations of banking, insurance, and securities firms to test whether activity diversification could reduce risk. The authors found that bank holding companies that existed from 1985 to 1989 could have reduced their probability of failure had they been permitted to diversify into insurance and securities. Of the ten combinations the authors examined, the best combination was the bank holding company with both insurance and securities firms. The only combination that would have increased the probability of bankruptcy over the stand-alone bank holding company was one encompassing a large securities firm. The findings are particularly interesting in light of the turbulence during the late 1980s in both the securities and insurance industries. That is, volatility should have increased as a result of the macroeconomic environment.

CROSS-BORDER MERGERS AND ACQUISITIONS

A special case of market-extending mergers involves crossing borders. Examples cited earlier include UBS–PaineWebber, Deutsche Bank–Bankers Trust, and HSBC–Republic–CCF in banking and securities and a large number of transactions in insurance and asset management. Interest in cross-border deals presumably responded to the EU's 1988 Second Banking Directive and the U.S. 1999 Gramm-Leach Bliley Act, which made such mergers easier.

In a very early study Grubel (1977) examined the phenomenon of multinational banks in an attempt to find the advantages banks have by locating in a foreign country that enables them to overcome the inherent disadvantages they face vis-à-vis indigenous financial institutions. Product differentiation, he suggested, is not an advantage, since products can be copied. Foreign banks' main advantage is knowledge of operations and needs of clients from their home countries. This information is difficult for host country banks to acquire, unless the local banks work with the multinational firms. Even then, the banks do not know entire operations. When banks move abroad, therefore, they do so defensively so that the host country banks do not have the opportunity to obtain this special knowledge.

In another early study, Gray and Gray (1981) observed that multinational banks gain their comparative advantage from market imperfections. The two most important "raw materials" of banks were found to be funds and knowledge; by expanding their presence abroad, banks were able to enhance both. A stay-at-home bank was constrained by the need to obtain global funds through correspondent banks, which means that the information such a bank receives is second-hand. When banks were able to obtain funds more cheaply by cutting out the middleman and obtain information less expensively by being there, they may have had a comparative advantage. So, as clients expand their operations, banks may want to follow them to provide all the services they need. Although DeLong (1993) finds that foreign banks tend to locate in countries where there is a great deal of direct investment, the study was unable to show whether banks were leading or following their clients.

A study by Buch and DeLong (2001) found that cross-border bank mergers are in fact still quite rare. When they did occur, how did they perform? In a paper that comprehensively examines theory and evidence about cross-border bank mergers, Berger, DeYoung, Genay, and Udell (2000) explored the causes and consequences. Managerial motives seem to play an important role in cross-border bank mergers, as does deregulation that allows such mergers. Although the authors find that foreign institutions tend to be less efficient than their local counterparts on average, banks from certain countries are able to overcome the local market advantage of their domestic rivals. Banks from some countries such as Spain are as efficient as their local counterparts, and banks from one country, the United States, are more efficient than their domestic counterparts. The results suggest that domestic institutions will continue to be important for the provision of financial services despite foreign competition. However, banks that provide services as well as, or more efficiently than, their local counterparts may work to increase global consolidation.

The study does not explore why U.S. banks tend to be successful internationally. The authors cautioned that they looked only at developed countries, that the results may differ for emerging markets, and that financial institutions could alternatively provide international services through means other than acquisitions. Furthermore, the study involved accounting data, which are very difficult to compare internationally and may not accurately reflect the condition of the banks. What is interesting, the authors found that banks that perform well at home tend to perform well outside their home countries, and those that do not perform well at home tend to be international laggards as well.

The finding that competitive efficiency in a bank's home market influences efficiency in the affiliate is supported by Berger and DeYoung (2001), who examined the effects of geographic expansion on bank efficiency. They found that parent organizations have a great influence on the efficiency of their affiliates. Control by headquarters appears to be more difficult as distance increases, but well-run parents seem to have well-run affiliates regardless of distance.

Buch (2002) found that regulations, as well as information costs (measured by distance), common language, and common legal systems, induce banks to engage in international investments. The importance of each of these factors varies from country to country. The results suggest that banks may choose different paths for internationalization. Banks from some countries, such as Spain, prefer markets that are similar to their own, whereas others want markets with low entry barriers.

Most of the empirical works on cross-border M&A deals in the financial services industry have focused on banks. There is virtually no empirical work available on securities firms, asset managers, or insurance companies. In the first two industries, there have arguably been too few deals to devise a large enough dataset suitable for analysis, although this is hardly the case in the insurance sector, as discussed in Chapter 2.

Event Studies

Event study methodology (Brown and Warner 1985) can be used to determine investor reaction to events such as the announcement of a merger or an earnings report. The technique controls for conditions in the general market. For example, if the market is doing poorly (well), a stock may do poorly (well) because of the market environment and not because of the event. Therefore, one needs to determine the relationship a particular stock has with the market during "normal" times—that is, before the event occurs. This relationship can be determined by regressing the returns of the stock on the market index and a constant.[4] One then determines what the stock "should" have earned (total returns) given the state of the general market, as well as the stock's past relationship with the general market. These hypothetical returns are compared with actual returns to determine the abnormal returns, that is, how much more or less the stock earns as a result of the announcement.[5]

Abnormal returns are added together over various periods, usually several days before the announcement to several days after. It is important to look at a few days before the event in case any news about the event itself has leaked and has already affected the value of the stock. Looking at the abnormal returns for a few days after the announcement allows event studies to take "second thoughts" into account. The market may be so surprised about an announcement that it may need a few days to digest the news. One cannot know with certainty the ideal length of the pre-or post-event periods. Extending either period leads to problems, since other events, such as earnings reports or changes in management, could occur and the market could be reacting to those events instead.

As an example of how the event study approach can be used, we applied it to the seven strategic M&A deals, cited earlier, that were undertaken by UBS AG and its predecessor organizations during the period 1984–2000. These include the Swiss Bank Corporation acquisition of

---

4. We obtain the following relationship: $R_i = a_i + b_i R_{Mt}$ where R_{Mt} = the return on the market at time t; a_i = regression result on the constant; b_i = relationship between the market and stock i, also known as the beta of stock i.

5. That is, $AR_{it} = R_{it} - (a_i + b_i R_{Mt})$, where AR_{it} = abnormal return for stock i at time t; R_{it} = return on stock i at time t; and R_{Mt} = the return on the market at time t.

O'Connor (January 9, 1992), the SBC acquisition of Brinson (August 31, 1994), the SBC acquisition of S.G. Warburg (May 2, 1995), the SBC takeover of Dillon Read (May 15, 1997), the merger of Swiss Bank Corporation and Union Bank of Switzerland to form the present UBS AG (December 8, 1997), the UBS acquisition of Global Asset Management (GAM) announced in September 13, 1999, and the UBS acquisition of PaineWebber announced on July 11, 2000. The first four deals were undertaken by Swiss Bank Corporation and can therefore be viewed in terms of SBC share price impacts; the SBC-UBS merger in 1997 can be examined in terms of both the SBC and UBS cumulative abnormal returns, and the GAM and PaineWebber deals would have affected the shares of the new UBS AG.

We estimated alpha and beta using daily returns from 500 to 10 days before the merger announcement by regressing the returns of the stock on the returns of the Swiss SMI index. To determine the extent to which a particular merger was perceived by the market to have created or destroyed value, we cumulated the abnormal returns for various event windows for each SBC and UBS transaction beginning with O'Connor in 1992 and ending with PaineWebber in 2000. As mentioned above, no scientific way of determining the ideal event window exists, although no confounding events (earnings reports, changes in management, other major mergers) occurred around the time of the various merger announcements. We therefore conclude that the market was reacting only to the announcement of the particular merger. Table 6-10 summarizes the respective calculated abnormal returns.

No regularity is obvious from the market's reactions to SBC or UBS merger or acquisition announcements based on the seven cases examined here. That is, the market appears to judge each merger on its own merits. Market reaction to the merger of UBS and SBC, for example, was highly positive for shareholders of both firms, possibly reflecting expected cost cuts (especially in their domestic banking businesses) that could be made

Table 6-10 Abnormal Returns Associated With Selected UBS Transactions

Merger	Date	Event Date	Abnormal Returns for Acquirer		
			[−1,+1] window	[−3,+3] window	[−5,+5] window
SBC O'Connor	9-Jan-92	0.444%	0.930%	−2.587%	0.902%
SBC Brinson	31-Aug-94	−0.713%	1.084%	−3.704%	−5.205%
SBC Warburg	2-May-95	−0.012%	−2.515%	−5.170%	−7.127%
SBC Dillon Read	15-May-97	−0.413%	−1.551%	−1.842%	5.231%
SBC-UBS (for SBC)	8-Dec-97	4.108%	7.756%	5.929%	4.936%
SBC-UBS (for SBC)	8-Dec-97	9.368%	13.133%	12.813%	10.256%
UBS-GAM	13-Sep-99	−0.082%	0.977%	1.452%	−0.899%
UBS-PaineWebber	11-Jul-00	−0.244%	−7.306%	−2.795%	−3.509%

possible by the mergers—together with the presumably stronger competitive position of the new UBS AG in its various areas of activity (notably private banking and investment banking). However, market reaction to the UBS acquisition of PaineWebber was strongly negative, possibly a reaction to of the high price paid, the absence of short-term cost reductions, lack of major PaineWebber contributions to strengthening the UBS investment banking platform in the United States, and uncertainly about how the PaineWebber capabilities would be leveraged into UBS operations outside the United States—the latter uncertainty was noted in a subsequent Moody's downgrade of UBS debt in 2001.

Specifically in the positive market reaction to the announcement of the SBC-UBS merger, the good reputation of SBC as a serial acquirer may have had a positive influence. By mid-1997, SBC had cultivated a strong reputation concerning its ability to target acquisitions, integrate them successfully, and ultimately extract value for its shareholders. For example, *The Economist* (1999) had noted that "SBC's handling of its previous— i.e., prior to the UBS merger—acquisitions had been hard to fault," and Davis (2000) wrote that SBC had a "track record of successfully blending and shaping different cultures in a meritocractic environment" (p. 105). Market reaction to the announcement of the SBC merger with UBS was also in line with conclusions from the empirical M&A literature cited earlier.

EUROPEAN VERSUS U.S. FINANCIAL SECTOR MERGERS

Event studies in the empirical M&A literature have been heavily concentrated U.S.-based transactions. Among the reasons for this bias are limitations in international data availability, consistency, and equity market characteristics in various countries such as large, concentrated blocks of shareholdings, multiple share classes, slowness in dissemination of M&A information, the role of governments as regulators, and holders of "golden shares."

Nevertheless, research concerning European bank mergers has been growing. Cybo-Ottone and Murgia (1997) examined market reactions to European financial-sector mergers while Vander Vennet (1998) examined at long-term performance.

Cybo-Ottone and Murgia (1997) assessed stock market reaction to the announcement of several bank mergers in Europe. Contrary to studies of U.S. mergers that find neither positive nor negative reaction on average, their study found that the combined return to bidders and targets is positive, and also found weak evidence of a positive response to acquirers. The authors suggest that their results could be capturing possible economies of super-scale (European mergers on average tend to be much larger than U.S. mergers), as well as a regulatory environment that was historically friendlier to universal banking. European bank mergers could thus take advantage of more revenue synergies than U.S. mergers.

Vander Vennet (1998) attempted to determine which European banks were more likely to be active in their domestic takeover markets and why, and further investigated long-term performance to understand whether the banks' expectations were fulfilled. For mergers of equals, both partners tend to be underperformers, in terms of operational efficiency and profitability. This finding suggests that acquirers want to merge to in order take advantage of presumed synergies. Operational efficiency and, to a lesser extent, profitability improve in the three years after the merger. The long-term performance of merged European banks suggests that the synergies were to a large extent realized.

Although DeLong (2001b) and Houston, James, and Ryngaert (1999) found that in-market mergers tend to create value upon announcement based on the U.S. financial services deal flow, such findings may not be true for non-U.S. mergers, since in-market takeovers are expected to cut costs faster and more dramatically than market-extending acquisitions, and in addition may do so more dramatically in the United States than elsewhere. Especially in Europe, where strong unions and social legislation prevent large-scale personnel layoffs, even in-market mergers may not be able to cut costs as effectively as in the United States.

Moreover, according to Vander Vennet (1998), event studies are seldom used to study European bank mergers because many European banks involved in takeovers are not publicly traded in liquid equity markets. One comprehensive study (Cybo-Ottone and Murgia 1997) finds that the announcements of European bank mergers, like U.S. bank mergers, generally result in no gains or losses to combined stockholders of the partners. However, U.S. acquirers tend to lose value slightly, whereas U.S. targets gain 7 to 14 percent (Cornett and Tehranian 1992; Houston and Ryngaert 1994). European acquirers tend not to lose value, but European targets do not appear to make great gains. Although mergers of equals surveyed in the latter study range from megamergers to combinations of small banks, a common problem exists in blending the dissimilar corporate philosophies. Results for *takeovers*, defined as a larger institution acquiring a smaller one, are different. Market power and increasing size appear to be the driving forces. Large universal banks tend to acquire targets that are relatively small and inefficient. Takeovers do not lead to long-term improvement in return on assets or efficiency, perhaps because the targets are too small to have much influence on the large organization.

In a study of Dutch and Belgian financial services firms, Verweire and Van den Berghe (2002) found a negative and linear relationship between the degree of diversification of business streams and performance in terms of total returns to shareholders. This is attributed to the costs of integration complexity carried by the firms involved, which more than outweighed the positive scope economies that tend to appear mainly on the revenue side. Davis (2000) points out several ways that European bank mergers differ from U.S. mergers. In a series of case studies, he finds Europeans are much more concerned about unions, and that cost-cutting is a much smaller source of any joint gains than in the United States.

SUMMARY

The empirical literature on mergers and acquisitions in the financial services sector surveyed in this chapter broadly validates the conclusions suggested in the conceptual discussion that preceded it. Mergers and acquisitions that work tend to focus the activities of the acquiring firm, either geographically or by product or by client, which allows the realization of operating efficiencies and maximizes the firm's market footprint. Those gains in market share and cost-cutting efforts may then translate into improved returns on capital invested. How the transaction is implemented is as important as the transaction itself, notably the price, the integration process, and persistent careful attention to quality and service. An overpriced acquisition can be hard to overcome. And merger integration in this industry has to be rapid and transparent: people need to know where they stand, and those who remain on board have to be enthusiastic about their own and the firm's prospects going forward. Not least, clients have to be convinced that the transaction is in their interest as well, either by delivering better pricing or better service. Still, a 1999 report by the Bank for International Settlements (1999) concluded: "Studies continue to indicate that the experience of a majority of mergers is disappointing, as organizational problems are systematically underestimated and acquirers tend to overpay for targets."

The same lessons hold when firms pursue mergers in other regions or try to *broaden* the client base or scope of activity through acquisitions. Such transactions have to be conducted according to the same rulebook that applies to *focusing* transactions. GECS has been noted as one firm that has tried to do this, often with impressive success. And some financial firms, such as National Australia Bank and HSBC, have shown that close attention to the rulebook can lead to a portfolio of profitable stand-alone businesses in some very diverse markets. This does not deny that scope economies are achievable, notably on the demand side through cross-selling. But in such cases the incentives to cross-sell have to be examined at an extremely granular level. Employees and clients need to believe that cross-selling is in their own interests. Anything else tends to be just exhortation.

It is worthwhile to note that determining whether the mergers and acquisitions in the financial services sector were successful, partially successful, or failed might be difficult to assess in terms of shareholders' value creation in the early 2000s. One needs to distinguish between the company-related implications (that is, unsystematic implications) and the effects of the market at large (that is, the systematic implications). There are numerous instances of successful mergers and acquisitions in financial services, but unfavorable business cycles and other adverse circumstances could render the best-conceived deal economically unfeasible. Apparently, the jury is still out on the merits of mergers in the industry, but they nevertheless go on, albeit a slower rate due to a lackluster economy in the early 2000s as well as declines in share prices that limited the attractiveness of stock-for-stock swaps.

In a survey paper written at the peak of the U.S. financial M&A wave, Pilloff and Santomero (1997), point out the paradox that there appeared to be no net economic gain from all of this activity. Self-delusion and self-enrichment by management were rejected as implausible over the long term. The devil, in fact, seems to be in the details. How effectively is the integration if carried out, and how disciplined is the internal capital-allocation process applied going forward?

7

Mergers, Acquisitions, and the Financial Architecture

Merger and acquisitions activity in the financial sector has been one of the major vehicles in the transformation of a key set of economic activities that stand at the center of the national and global capital allocation and payments system. It can therefore be argued that the outcome of the M&A process in terms of the structure, conduct, and performance of the financial sector has a disproportionate impact on the economy as a whole.

There are three issues here. The first relates to how well the financial system contributes to economic efficiency in the allocation of resources, thereby promoting a maximum *level* of income and output. The second relates to how it affects *the rate of growth* of income and output by influencing the various components of economic growth—the labor force, the capital stock, the contribution of national resources to growth, as well as efficiency in the use of the factors of production. The third issue concerns the safety and stability of the financial system, notably systemic risk associated with crises among financial institutions and their propagation to the financial system as a whole and the real sector of the economy.

A financial structure that maximizes income and wealth, and promotes the rate of economic growth together with continuous market-driven economic reconfiguration, and achieves both of these with a tolerable level of institutional and systemic stability would have to be considered a "benchmark" system.

The condition and evolution of the financial sector is therefore a matter of public interest. Outcomes of the financial-sector restructuring process through M&A activity or in other ways that detract from its contribution to efficiency, growth, and stability can therefore be expected to attract the attention of policymakers. For example, nobody seriously believes that a dynamic market-driven economy that hopes to be competitive on a global scale can long afford a financial services industry that is dominated by one or two mega-conglomerates that are able to extract monopoly rents from their clients and shield themselves from competition by new entrants. Long before that happens, the high political profile of the financial industry and its institutions would trigger a backlash felt in legislative initiatives, judicial decisions, and regulatory changes, reflecting efforts to restore higher levels of competitive discipline to the industry.

This chapter examines the public policy issues affecting the structure of the financial system and therefore the M&A process, and vice versa. The issues range from competition policy to the design of the financial safety net and the potentially intractable problems of assuring the safety and soundness of massive financial conglomerates that are active in a wide range of financial businesses and sometimes extend across the world.

IMPACT ON THE STRUCTURE OF THE FINANCIAL SYSTEM

One way to calibrate the so-called "static" efficiency properties of a financial system is to use the all-in, weighted average spread (differential) between ① rates of return provided to ultimate savers and investors and ② the cost of funds to the ultimate users of finance. This stylized gross spread can be viewed as a measure of the total cost of financial intermediation, and is reflected in the monetary value of resources consumed in the financial intermediation process. In particular, it reflects direct costs of financial intermediation (operating costs, cost of capital, and so on). It also reflects losses incurred in the financial process that may ultimately be passed on to end users, as well as liquidity premiums and any excess profits earned. In this framework, financial processes that are considered *statically inefficient* are usually characterized by high all-in margins due to high overhead costs, high losses not ultimately borne by shareholders of the financial intermediaries themselves, excess profits due to concentrated markets and barriers to entry, and the like.

Dynamic efficiency is characterized by high rates of financial product and process innovation through time. Product innovations usually involve creation of new financial instruments along with the ability to replicate certain financial instruments by bundling or rebundling existing ones (synthetics). There are also new approaches to contract pricing, new investment techniques, and other innovations that fall under this rubric. Process innovations include contract design and methods of trading, clearance and settlement, transactions processing, custody, techniques for efficient margin calculation, application of new distribution and client-interface technologies such as the Internet, and so on. Successful product and process innovation broadens the menu of financial information and services available to ultimate borrowers and issuers, ultimate savers, and various other participants in the financial system.

A healthy financial system exerts continuous pressure on all kinds of financial intermediaries for improved static and dynamic efficiency. Structures better able to deliver these attributes eventually supplant those that do not, and this is how financial markets and institutions have evolved and converged through time. For example, global financial markets for foreign exchange, debt instruments, and to a lesser extent equities have already developed various degrees of "seamlessness." It is arguable that the most advanced of the world's financial markets are approaching a theoretical, "complete" optimum where there are sufficient financial instruments and markets, and combinations, thereof, to span the whole state-space of risk and return outcomes. Conversely, financial systems that are deemed inefficient or incomplete tend to be characterized by a high degree of fragmentation and incompleteness that takes the form of a limited range of financial services and obsolescent financial processes.

Both static and dynamic efficiency in financial intermediation are of obvious importance from the standpoint of national and global resource allocation. That is, since many kinds of financial services can be viewed as "inputs" into real economic processes, the level of national output and income—as well as its rate of economic growth—are directly or indirectly affected, so that a "retarded" financial services sector can represent a major impediment to an economy's overall economic performance. Financial system retardation represents a burden on the final consumers of financial services and potentially reduces the level of private and social welfare; it reduces what economists call *consumer surplus*, an accepted measure of consumer welfare.[1] It also represents a burden on producers by raising their cost of capital and eroding their competitive performance in domestic and global markets. These inefficiencies ultimately distort the allocation of labor as well as capital and affect both the level of income and output, as well as the rate of economic growth, by impeding capital formation and other elements of the growth process.

As noted in earlier chapters, in retail financial services extensive banking overcapacity in many countries has led to substantial consolidation—often involving the kind of M&A activity detailed in the tables found in the Appendix 1. Excess retail production and distribution capacity in banking has been slimmed down in ways that usually release redundant labor and capital. This is a key objective of consolidation in financial services generally, as it is in any industry. If effective, surviving firms tend to be more efficient and innovative than those that do not survive. In some cases this process is retarded by restrictive regulation, by cartels, or by large-scale involvement of public sector financial institutions that operate under less rigorous financial discipline or are beneficiaries of public subsidies.

Also at the retail level, commercial banking activity has been linked

---

1. Consumer surplus is the difference between what consumers would have paid for a given product or service according to the relevant demand function and what they actually have to pay at the prevailing market price. The higher that price, the lower will be consumer surplus.

strategically to retail brokerage, retail insurance (especially life insurance), and retail asset management through mutual funds, retirement products, and private-client relationships. At the same time, relatively small and focused firms have sometimes continued to prosper in each of the retail businesses, especially where they have been able to provide superior service or client proximity while taking advantage of outsourcing and strategic alliances where appropriate. Competitive market economics should be free to separate the winners and the losers. Significant departures from this logic need to be carefully watched and, if necessary, redressed by public policy.

In wholesale financial services, similar links have emerged. Wholesale commercial banking activities such as syndicated lending and project financing have often been shifted toward a greater investment banking focus, whereas investment banking firms have placed growing emphasis on developing institutional asset management businesses in part to benefit from vertical integration and in part to gain some degree of stability in a notoriously volatile industry. Vigorous debates have raged about the need to lend in order to obtain valuable advisory business and whether specialized "monoline" investment banks will eventually be driven from the market by financial conglomerates with massive capital and risk-bearing ability. Here the jury is still out, and there is ample evidence that can be cited on both sides of the argument.

The United States is a good case in point. Financial intermediation was long distorted by regulation. Banks and bank holding companies were prohibited from expanding geographically and from moving into insurance businesses and into large areas of the securities business under the Glass-Steagall provisions of the Banking Act of 1933. Consequently banks half a century ago dominated classic banking functions, independent broker-dealers dominated capital market services, and insurance companies dominated most of the generic risk management functions, as shown in Figure 7-1. Cross-penetration between different types of financial intermediaries existed mainly in the realm of retail savings products.

A half century later this functional segmentation had changed almost beyond recognition, despite the fact that full *de jure* deregulation was not fully implemented until the end of the period with passage of the Gramm-Leach-Bliley Act of 1999. Figure 7-2 shows a virtual doubling of strategic groups competing for the various financial intermediation functions. Today there is vigorous cross-penetration among all kinds of strategic groups in the U.S. financial system. Most financial services can be obtained in one form or another from virtually every strategic group, each of which is, in turn, involved in a broad array of financial intermediation services. The system is populated by mega-banks, financial conglomerates, credit unions, savings banks, saving and loan institutions, community banks, life insurers, general insurers, property and casualty insurers, insurance brokers, securities broker-dealers, asset managers, and financial advisers

Institution \ Function	Payment Services	Savings Prod.	Fiduc. Services	Lending: Business	Lending: Retail	Underwriting Issuance of: Equity	Underwriting Issuance of: Debt	Insurance and Risk Mgt. Products
Insured Depository Institutions	✓	✓	✓	✓	✓			
Insurance Companies		✓		(✓)				✓
Finance Companies				(✓)	✓			
Securities Firms		✓	✓			✓	✓	
Pension Funds		✓						
Mutual Funds		✓						

(✓) Minor involvement

Figure 7-1. The U.S. Financial Services Sector, 1950. Figures 7-1 and 7-2 courtesy of Richard Herring, The Wharton School, University of Pennsylvania.

Institution \ Function	Payment Services	Savings Prod.	Fiduc. Services	Lending: Business	Lending: Retail	Underwriting Issuance of: Equity	Underwriting Issuance of: Debt	Insurance and Risk Mgt. Products
Insured Depository Institutions	✓	✓	✓	✓	✓	✓	✓	✓
Insurance Companies	✓	✓	✓	✓	✓	✓	✓	✓
Finance Companies	✓	✓	✓	✓	✓	(✓)	(✓)	✓
Securities Firms	✓	✓	✓	✓	✓	✓	✓	✓
Pension Funds		✓	✓	✓	✓			
Mutual Funds	✓	✓	✓		✓	(✓)		✓
Diversified Financial Firms	✓	✓	✓	✓	✓	✓	✓	✓
Specialist Firms	✓	✓	✓	✓	✓	✓	✓	✓

(✓) Selective involvement of large firms via affiliates

Figure 7-2. The U.S. Financial Services Sector, 2003.

mixing and matching capabilities in ways the market seems to demand. It remains a highly heterogeneous system today, confounding earlier conventional wisdom that the early part of the twenty-first century would herald the dominance of the European style universal bank or financial conglomerate in the United States. Evidently their time has not yet come, if it ever will.

If cross-competition among strategic groups promotes both static and dynamic efficiencies in the financial system, the evolutionary path of the U.S. financial structure has probably served macroeconomic objectives— particularly growth and continuous economic restructuring—very well indeed. Paradoxically, the Glass-Steagall limits in force from 1933 to 1999 may have contributed, as an unintended consequence, to a much more heterogeneous financial system than otherwise might have existed—certainly more heterogeneous than prevailed in the United States of the 1920s or that prevail in most other countries today.

Specifically, Glass-Steagall provisions of the Banking Act of 1933 were justified for three reasons: (1) the 8,000-plus bank failures of 1930–1933 had much to do with the collapse in aggregate demand (depression) and asset deflation that took hold during this period, (2) the financial-sector failures were related to inappropriate activities of major banks, notably underwriting and dealing in corporate stocks, corporate bonds, and municipal revenue bonds, and (3) these failures were in turn related to the severity of the 1929 stock market crash, which, through asset deflation, helped trigger the devastating economic collapse of the 1930s. The available empirical evidence generally rejects the second of these arguments, and so financial economists today usually conclude that the Glass-Steagall legislation was a mistake—the wrong remedy implemented for the wrong reasons.

Political economists tend to be more forgiving, observing that Congress only knew what it thought it understood at the time and had to do something dramatic to deal with a major national crisis. The argumentation presented in the 1930s seemed compelling. So the Glass-Steagall provisions became part of the legislative response to the crisis, along with the 1933 and 1934 Securities Acts, the advent of deposit insurance, and other very positive dimensions of the regulatory system that continue to evolve today.

The Glass-Steagall legislation remained on the books for 66 years, reconfiguring the structure of the financial system into functional separation between investment banking and securities, commercial banking, and "commerce" (which included insurance) was later cemented in the Bank Holding Company Act of 1956. European-type universal banking became impossible, although some restrictions were later eased by allowing Section-20 investment banking banking subsidiaries of commercial bank holding companies to be created with progressively broader underwriting and dealing powers and 10% (later 25%) "illegal-activity" revenue limits.

Very few financial institutions actually took advantage of this liberalization, however.

What happened next? Independent securities firms obtained a long-lasting monopoly on Glass-Steagall-restricted financial intermediation activities—mainly underwriting and dealing in corporate debt and equity securities and municipal revenue bonds—which they fought to retain through the 1990s via a wide range of vigorous rear-guard political lobbying and legal tactics. Firms in the securities industry included legacy players like Lehman Brothers and Goldman Sachs, as well as firms forcibly spun off from what had been universal banks, such as Morgan Stanley.

All of the U.S. securities firms were long organized as partnerships, initially with unlimited liability—thus fusing their ownership and management. This did not change until almost a half-century later, when many converted to limited liability companies and later incorporated themselves—the last being Goldman Sachs in 1999. Arguably, the industry's legacy ownership-management structure caused these firms to pay extraordinary attention to revenue generation, risk control, cost control, and financial innovation under high levels of teamwork and discipline. Some of this may have been lost after their incorporation, which the majority of the partners ultimately deemed necessary in order to gain access to permanent capital and strategic flexibility.

Unlike banks, independent U.S. securities firms operate under relatively transparent mark-to-market accounting rules, a fact that placed management under strict market discipline and constant threat of capital impairment. There was also in many firms a focus on "light" strategic commitments and opportunism and equally "light" management structures that made them highly adaptable and efficient. This was combined with the regulatory authorities' presumed reluctance to bail out "commercial enterprises" whose failure (unlike banks) did not pose an immediate threat to the financial system.

When Drexel Burnham Lambert failed in 1990 it was the seventh largest financial firm in the United States in terms of assets. The Federal Reserve supplied liquidity to the market to help limit the systemic effects but did nothing to save Drexel Burnham. When Continental Illinois failed in 1984 it was immediately bailed out by the Federal Deposit Insurance Corporation—including all uninsured depositors. In effect, the bank was nationalized and relaunched after restructuring under government auspices. Shareholders, the board, managers, and employees lost out, but depositors were made whole. The lack of a safety net for U.S. securities firms arguably reinforced large management ownership stakes in their traditional attention to risk control.

The abrupt shake-out of the securities industry started in 1974. The independent securities firms themselves were profoundly affected by deregulation (notably elimination of fixed commissions, intended to improve the efficiency of the U.S. equity market). Surviving firms in the end proved to be highly efficient and creative under extreme competitive pressure (despite lack of capital market competition from commercial banks), dominating their home market (which accounted for around 60% of global capital-raising volume and on average about the same percentage of M&A activity) and later pushing that home-court advantage into the international arena as well. Alongside the independent securities firms grew a broad array of independent retail and institutional fund managers, both generalists and specialists, and brokers with strong franchises that were not full-service investment banks, such as like Charles Schwab and A.G. Edwards, as well as custodians such as State Street, Bank of New York, and Northern Trust Company.

The regulation-driven structure of independent U.S. capital market intermediaries may have had something to do with limiting conflict of interest and other problems associated with involvement of financial firms in multiple parts of the financial services business. There was also a general absence of investment bankers (but not commercial bankers) on corporate boards. There were few long-term holdings of corporate shares by financial intermediaries. That is, there were few of the hallmarks of universal banking relationships that existed elsewhere in the world.

The structure also had much to do with the process of U.S. financial disintermediation on the borrower-issuer side as well as the savings and asset management side of the flow of funds, with financial flows through the capital markets showing better static and dynamic efficiency properties and drawing off financial activities from banks and thrifts. Nonetheless, many small community banks and thrifts continued to thrive by virtue of client proximity, better information, better service, or some combination of these.

Finally, legacy effects of the Glass-Steagall provisions, through the resulting financial intermediation structure, also had much to do with U.S. reliance in matters of corporate governance on a highly contestable market for corporate control. For better or worse, in the absence of Glass-Steagall the U.S. economic performance story though the end of the twentieth century might have been very different from what it actually was. It proved to be very good at producing sustained economic dynamism compared with most other parts of the world. It did not, however, prove to be a good guardian against the kinds of fiduciary violations, corporate governance failures, and outright fraud that emerged in the U.S. financial scandals in 2002.

Still, consolidation has proceeded apace in the United States, although the 1999 deregulation did not in fact produce a near-term collapse of the highly diversified financial structure depicted in Figure 7-2. However, consolidation has been accompanied in recent years by higher concentration ratios in various types of financial services, except in retail banking, where concentration ratios have actually fallen. None of these concentrations seem troublesome yet in terms of preserving vigorous competition and avoiding monopoly pricing, as suggested in Figure 3-9 in Chapter 3.

A similar framework for discussing the financial structure of Europe is not particularly credible because of the wide structural variations among countries. One common thread, however, given the long history of universal banking, is that banks dominate most financial intermediation functions in much of Europe. Insurance is an exception, but given European *bancassurance* initiatives that seem to be reasonably successful in many cases, some observers still think a broad-gauge banking-insurance convergence is likely.

Except for the penetration of continental Europe by U.K. and U.S. specialists in the investment banking and fund management businesses, many of the relatively narrowly focused continental financial firms seem to have found themselves sooner or later acquired by major banking groups. Examples include Banque Indosuez and Banque Paribas in France, MeesPierson and Robeco in the Netherlands, Consors in Germany, and Schroders, Flemings, Warburgs, and Gartmore in the United Kingdom. Figure 7-3 may be a reasonable approximation of the European financial services industry structure, with substantially less "density" of functional coverage by specific strategic groups than in the United States and correspondingly greater dominance of major financial firms that include commercial banking as a core business.

It is interesting to speculate what the European financial services industry-structure matrix in Figure 7-3 will look like in ten or twenty years. Some argue that the impact of size and scope is so powerful that the financial industry will be dominated by large, complex financial institutions in Europe, especially in the euro-zone. Others argue that a rich array of players, stretching across a broad spectrum of strategic groups,

Institution \ Function	Payment Services	Savings Prod.	Fiduc. Services	Lending		Underwriting Issuance of		Insurance and Risk Mgt. Products
				Business	Retail	Equity	Debt	
Insured Depository Institutions	✓	✓	✓	✓	✓	✓	✓	✓
Insurance Companies		✓	✓					✓
Finance Companies				✓	✓			✓
Securities Firms			✓			✓	✓	✓
Pension Funds			✓					
Mutual Funds		✓	✓					
Diversified Financial Firms								
Specialist Firms	✓	✓	✓	✓	✓	✓	✓	✓

✓ Selective involvement of large firms via affiliates

Figure 7-3. The European Financial Services Sector, 2003.

will serve the European financial system and its economic future better than a strategic monoculture based on massive universal banking organizations and financial conglomerates. Consolidation is often to the good, but it has its limits.

Besides the United States and Europe, there is the perennial issue of the role of Japan's financial system. Like the United States, it was long distorted by competitive barriers such as Article 65 of the Japan Financial Law, promulgated during U.S. occupation after World War II. But it also had distinctive Japanese attributes, such as the equity crossholdings between banks and industrial companies in *keiretsu* structures. Major Japanese City banks such as Sumitomo and Bank of Tokyo existed alongside four major and numerous minor securities firms, trust companies, finance companies, and the like. Competitive dynamics were hardly transparent, and government ministries—notably the Ministry of Finance and the Ministry of International Trade and Industry—wielded extraordinary influence.

The good years of the 1970s and 1980s covered up myriad inefficiencies and inequities in Japan's financial system until they ended abruptly in the early 1990s. The required Japanese financial-sector reconfiguration was not impossible to figure out (see for example Walter and Hiraki 1994). Mustering the political will to carry it out was another matter altogether, so that a decade later the failed Japanese system still awaited a new, permanent structural footing. Meanwhile, life goes on, and some of the key Japanese financial business in investment banking, private banking, and institutional fund management have seen substantial incursions by foreign firms. In other sectors, such as retail brokerage, foreign firms have had a much more difficult time.

Structural discussions of Canada, Australia, and the emerging market economies, as well as the transition economies of eastern Europe, have been intensive over the years, particularly focusing on eastern Europe in the 1990s and the Asian economies after the debt crisis of 1997–1998 (see Claessens 2000; Smith and Walter 2000). Regardless of the geographic venue, some argue that the disappearance of small local banks, independent insurance companies in both the life and nonlife sectors, and a broad array of financial specialists is probably not in the public interest, especially if, at the end of the day, there are serious antitrust concerns in this key sector of the economy. And as suggested in Figure 7-4, the disappearance of competitors can have significant transactions cost and liquidity consequences for financial markets—in this case non-investment grade securities.

At the top of the financial industry food-chain, at least so far, the most valuable financial services franchises in the United States and Europe in terms of market capitalization seem far removed from a financial-intermediation monoculture (see Tables 2-12 and 2-13 in Chapter 2). In fact, each presents a rich mixture of banks, asset managers, insurance companies, and specialized players.

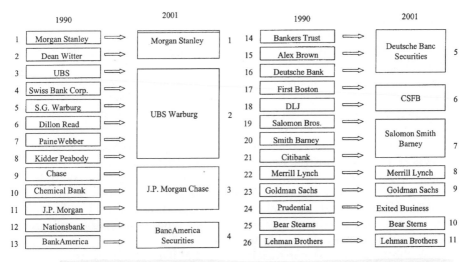

Figure 7-4. Active underwriters and dealers: high-yield bonds. The consolidation of many securities firms combined with the dealers' reduced willingness to take risk have drastically reduced all firms' market-making activities. Source: J.P. Morgan Chase.

An interesting facet of Tables 2-12 and 2-13 is that no single strategic group seems to have come to dominate the playing field. Some of the most valuable firms in the business are generalists, even financial conglomerates. Some are international, even global, while others are mainly domestic or regional. And some are specialists, focusing on only part of the financial services spectrum but obviously doing something right. So far it does not seem that multifunctional financial conglomerates, most created through extended periods of M&A activity, have been successful in driving the more specialized firms from the playing field. Nor does the reverse seem to be the case, although creation of today's cohort of specialists has usually involved equally intense M&A activity. And so it seems that in terms of structural survivorship and dominance, the jury remains out.

How the institutional structure of the financial services sector will evolve is anybody's guess. Those who claim to know often end up being wrong. As noted in the previous chapter, influential consultants sometimes convince multiple clients to do the same thing at the same time, and this spike in strategic correlation can contribute to the wrongness of their vision. What is clear is that the underlying economics of the industry's competitive structure will ultimately prevail, and finance will flow along conduits that are in the best interests of the end users of the financial system. The firms that constitute the financial services industry will have to adapt and readapt to this dynamic in ways that profitably sustain their *raison d'être*.

THE REGULATORY OVERLAY

This discussion has argued that on the whole, M&A activity in the financial services industry is driven by straightforward, underlying economic factors in the financial intermediation process dominated by a constant search for static and dynamic efficiency. If bigger is better, restructuring will produce larger financial services organizations. If broader is better, it will give rise to multifunctional firms and financial conglomerates. If not, then further restructuring activity will eventually lead to spin-offs and possibly breakups once it becomes clear that the composite value of a firm's individual businesses exceeds its market capitalization. Along the way, it is natural that mistakes are made and a certain herd mentality that exists in banking and financial services seems to cause multiple firms to get carried away strategically at the same time. Still, in the end, the economic fundamentals tend to win out.

At the same time, the financial services industry is and always will be subject to regulation by government. First, as noted earlier, problems at financial institutions—especially commercial banks—can create impacts that broadly affect the entire financial system. These problems, in turn, can easily have an impact on the economy as a whole. The risks of such "negative externalities" are a legitimate matter of public interest and justify regulation. If the taxpayer is obliged to stand by to provide safeguards against systemic risks, the taxpayer gets to have a say in the rules of the game.

Additionally, financial services firms are dealing with other people's money and therefore have strong fiduciary obligations. Governments therefore try to make sure that business practices are as transparent and equitable as possible. Besides basic fairness, there is a link to financial system efficiency as well in that people tend to desert rigged markets and inequitable business practices for those deemed more fair. Regulators must therefore keep the three goals—efficiency, stability, and equity—in mind at all times as the core of their mandate. This is not a simple matter, and mistakes are made, especially when the financial landscape is constantly changing, as are the institutions themselves.

Markets and institutions tend, perhaps more often than not, to run ahead of the regulators. Regulatory initiatives sometimes have consequences that were not and perhaps could not have been foreseen. The regulatory dialectic in the financial services sector is both sophisticated and complex, and often confronts both heavily entrenched and politically well-connected interests (as well as some of the brightest minds in business). The more complex the industry—perhaps most dramatically in the case of massive, global financial services conglomerates where comprehensive regulatory insight (and perhaps even comprehensive management oversight) is implausible—the greater the challenge to sensible regulation (Cumming and Hirtle 2001). Here the discussion will be limited to some of the basic regulatory parameters that are consistent with the financial services industry dynamics—leaving aside the question whether of a small country is in fact capable of bailing out a major global bank under its regulatory jurisdiction.

As noted, we presuppose that the financial services industry worldwide has been, and will continue to be, subject to significant public authority regulation and supervision due to the fiduciary nature of the business, the key role of financial systems in driving economic performance, the potential for financial fraud, and the possibility of serious social costs associated with financial failure. Indeed, we know from experience that even small changes in financial regulation can bring about large changes in financial system activity. We also know that, to the extent information flows among counterparties in financial activities are imperfect, regulation can significantly improve the operation of financial systems. The greater the information asymmetries and transaction-cost inefficiencies that exist, the greater will be the value of regulation quite apart from its benefits in terms of safety and soundness. And it sometimes seems that the more the financial intermediaries complain, the better the regulators are doing their jobs.

Edward Kane (1987) is one of the pioneers in thinking about financial regulation and supervision as imposing a set of "taxes" and "subsidies" on the operations of financial firms exposed to them. On the one hand, the imposition of reserve requirements, capital adequacy rules and certain financial disclosure requirements can be viewed as imposing "taxes" on a financial firm's activities in the sense that they increase intermediation costs. On the other hand, regulator-supplied deposit insurance, information production and dissemination, and lender-of-last resort facilities serve to stabilize financial markets, reduce information and transaction inefficiencies, improve liquidity, and lower the risk of systemic failure—thereby improving the process of financial intermediation. They can therefore be viewed as implicit "subsidies" provided by taxpayers.

The difference between these tax and subsidy elements of regulation can be viewed as the "net regulatory burden" (NRB) faced by particular types of financial firms in any given jurisdiction. All else equal, financial flows tend to migrate toward those regulatory domains where NRB is lowest. NRB differences can induce financial-intermediation migration when the savings realized exceed the transaction, communication, information and other economic costs of migrating. Indeed, it has been argued that a significant part of the financial disintermediation discussed in Chapter 1—and its impact on various types of financial firms—has been due to differences in NRB, which is arguably highest in the case of commercial banks. Competition triggers a dynamic interplay between demanders and suppliers of financial services, as financial firms seek to reduce their NRB and increase their profitability. If they can do so at acceptable cost, they will actively seek product innovations and new avenues that avoid cumbersome and costly regulations by shifting them either functionally or geographically.

REGULATORY TRADEOFFS

The right side of Figure 7-5 identifies the policy tradeoffs that invariably confront those charged with designing and implementing a properly structured financial system. On the one hand, they must strive to achieve maximum static and dynamic efficiency with respect to the financial system as a whole, as defined earlier, as well as promote the competitive viability of the financial industry. On the other hand, they must safeguard the stability of institutions and the financial system, in addition to helping to assure what is considered acceptable market conduct—including the politically sensitive implied social contract between financial institutions and unsophisticated clients. The first problem, safety-net design, is beset with difficulties such as moral hazard and adverse selection, and becomes especially problematic when products and activities shade into one another, when on- and off-balance sheet activities are involved, and when domestic and foreign business is conducted by financial firms for which the regulator is responsible. The second problem, market conduct, is no less difficult when end users of the system range across a broad spectrum of financial sophistication from mass-market retail clients to highly sophisticated trading counterparties.

In going about their business, regulators continuously face a dilemma. On the one hand, there is the possibility that "inadequate" regulation will result in costly failures. On the other hand, there is the possibility that "overregulation" ' will create opportunity costs in the form of financial efficiencies not achieved, or in the relocation of firms and financial transactions to other regulatory regimes offering a lower NRB. Since any improvements in financial stability can only be measured in terms of damage *that did not occur* and costs that were *successfully avoided*, the argumentation surrounding financial regulation is invariably based on "what if" hypotheticals. In effect, regulators are constantly compelled to rethink the balance between financial efficiency and creativity on the one hand, and safety, stability and suitable market conduct in the financial system on the other. They face the daunting task of designing an "optimum" regulatory and supervisory structure that provides the desired degree of stability at minimum cost to efficiency, innovation, and competitiveness—and to do so in a way that effectively aligns such policies among regulatory authorities functionally and internationally and avoids "fault lines" across regulatory regimes. There are no easy answers. There are only "better" and "worse" solutions as perceived by the constituents to whom the regulators are ultimately accountable.

Regulators have a number of options at their disposal. These range from "fitness and properness" criteria under which a financial institution may be established, continue to operate, or be shut-down to line-of-business regulation as to what types business financial institutions may engage in, adequacy of capital and liquidity, limits on various types of exposures, and the like, as well as policies governing marking-to-market

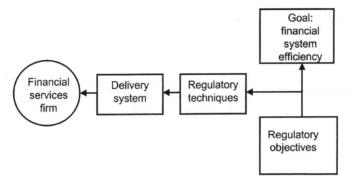

Figure 7-5. Regulatory Tradeoffs, Techniques, and Control.

of assets and liabilities (see Figure 7-6). Application of regulatory techniques can also have unintended consequences, as discussed in the first part of this chapter, which may not all be bad. And as noted, regulatory initiatives can create financial market distortions of their own, which become especially problematic when financial products and processes evolve rapidly and the regulator can easily get one or two steps behind.

A third element involves the regulatory machinery itself. Here the options range from reliance on self-control on the part of boards and senior managements of financial firms concerned with protecting the value of their franchises through financial services industry self-

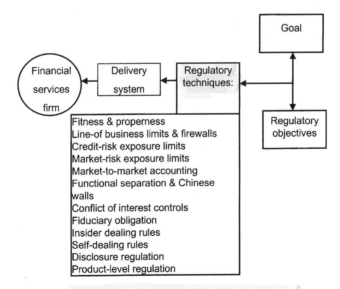

Figure 7-6. Regulatory Tradeoffs, Techniques, and Control.

regulation via so-called self-regulatory organizations (SROs) to public oversight by regulators with teeth—including civil suits and criminal prosecution. The options are listed in Figure 7-7

Self-regulation remains controversial, since financial firms seem to persistently suffer from incidents of business losses and misconduct—despite the often devastating effects on the value of their franchises. Management usually responds with expensive compliance infrastructures. But nothing is perfect, and serious problems continue to slip through the cracks. And "ethics" programs intended to assure appropriate professional conduct are often pursued with lack of seriousness, at worst creating a general sense of cynicism. People have to be convinced that a good defense is as important as a good offence in determining sustainable competitive success. This is something that is extraordinarily difficult to put into practice in a highly competitive environment and requires an unusual degree of senior management leadership and commitment (Smith and Walter 1997).

Control through self-regulatory organizations (SROs) is likewise subject to dispute. Private sector entities that have been certified as part of the regulatory infrastructure in the United States, for example, have repeatedly encountered problems. For instance, in 1996 one of the key U.S. SROs, the National Association of Security Dealers (NASD), and some of its member firms were assessed heavy monetary penalties in connection with member firms' rigging over-the-counter (OTC) equity markets. A vigorous attempt to refute empirical evidence of improprieties eventually yielded to major changes in regulatory and market practices. The Financial Accounting Standards Board, an SRO populated with accountants and dependent on the major accounting firms for funding, was clearly incapable of preventing audit disasters and the collapse of Arthur Andersen. Nor did the New York Stock Exchange, the American Stock Exchange, the NASD, the Investment Company Institute (covering mutual funds), the Securities Industry Association (representing investment

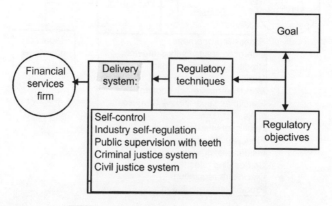

Figure 7-7. **Regulatory Tradeoffs, Techniques, and Control.**

banks), and broad-gauge business organizations such as the Business Round Table do much to head off the widespread governance failures in the early 2000s that called into question some of the basic precepts of U.S. market capitalism.

The U.S. corporate scandals hardly speak well of either firm or industry self-regulation, with systematic failures across the entire "governance chain" ranging from corporate management along with boards of directors and their various committees to the external control process including commercial banks, investment banks, public accountants, rating agencies, institutional investors, and government regulators. In some cases the regulators seem to have been co-opted by those they were supposed to regulate, and in others (especially banks and accounting firms) they actively facilitated and promoted some of the questionable activities of management at the expense of shareholders and employees.

Commercial and investment banks were right in the middle of the mess, actively facilitating some of the most egregious shenanigans. It was not until the launching of legal proceedings by the Attorney General of the State of New York, Congressional hearings, and belated enforcement action by the Securities and Exchange Commission that the various SROs and industry associations were stirred into action. Probably the equity market collapse in 2000–2002, and the view that this had become a major political issue did as much as anything to get serious corrective action underway.

Other well-known examples occurred in the United Kingdom, which relied heavily on the SRO approach. In 1994, the self-regulatory body governing pension funds, The Investment Management Regulatory Organization (IMRO), failed to catch the disappearance of pension assets from Robert Maxwell's Mirror Group Newspapers, and the Personal Investment Authority (PIA) for years failed to act against deceptive insurance sales practices at the retail level. In the Maxwell case, a 2001 report of the Department of Trade and Industry (DTI) described the conduct of the firms involved as beset with "cliquishness, greed and amateurism."

Inevitable in self-regulation are charges of the fox watching the henhouse. As in the Maxwell case, the City of London came in for a good deal of criticism for the "easygoing ways" that did much to contribute to its competitive success in the global marketplace. And Americans have cut down on lecturing others about the superiority of the market-driven U.S. corporate governance system.

But reliance on public oversight for financial regulation has its own problems, since virtually any regulatory initiative is likely to confront powerful vested interests that would like nothing better than to bend the rules in their favor (Kane 1987). The political manipulation of the savings and loan regulators in the United States during the 1980s is a classic example and created massive incremental losses for taxpayers. So were the efforts by Enron and other corporations, as well as some of the financial firms, to use their government contacts to further their causes. Even the judicial process, which is supposed to arbitrate or adjudicate matters of regulatory policy, may not always be entirely free of political influence or popular opinion.

Just as there are tradeoffs implicit in Figure 7-6 between financial system performance and stability, there are also tradeoffs between regulation and supervision. Some regulatory options (for example capital adequacy rules) are fairly easy to supervise but full of distortion potential due to their broad-gauge nature. Others (for example fitness and properness criteria) may be highly cost-effective but devilishly difficulty to supervise. Finally, there are tradeoffs between supervision and performance, with some supervisory techniques far more costly to comply with than others. Regulators must try to optimize across this three-dimensional set of tradeoffs under conditions of rapid market and industry change, blurred institutional and activity demarcations, and functional as well as international regulatory fault lines.

THE AMERICAN APPROACH

One observation from U.S. experience is that, on balance, commercial banks clearly carry a net regulatory burden, which, in terms of the actual requirements and costs of compliance, has been substantially greater than that which applies to the securities industry and other nonbank intermediaries. This has arguably had much to do with the evolution of the country's financial structure, generally to the detriment of commercial banking. Institutional regulation of nonbank intermediaries is relatively light, but regulation of business conduct is relatively heavy and sometimes not particularly successful, as the financial scandals of 2001–2002 demonstrated.

For example, when Congress passed the Securities Act of 1933 it focused on "truth in new issues," requiring prospectuses and creating underwriting liabilities to be shared by both companies and their investment bankers. It then passed the Securities Act of 1934, which set up the Securities and Exchange Commission and focused on the conduct of secondary markets. Later on, in the 1960s, it passed the Securities Investor Protection Act, which provided for a guarantee fund (paid in by the securities industry and supported by a line of credit from the U.S. Treasury) to protect investors who maintain brokerage accounts from losses associated with the failure of the securities firms involved. None of these measures, however, provided for the government to guarantee deposits with securities dealers, nor did it in any way guarantee investment results. So there was less need to get "inside" the securities firms—the taxpayer was not at risk. Where the taxpayers were at risk, in commercial banking and savings institutions, regulation was much more onerous and compliance much more costly, ultimately damaging these institutions' market shares in the financial evolution process.

Although the SEC developed into a forthright regulator, often willing to use its powers to protect individual investors and ensure the integrity of the markets, most of the discipline to which U.S. nonbank financial firms have been subject since 1934 is provided by the market itself. Prices have risen and fallen. Investors have often lost money. Many securities firms have failed or have been taken over by competitors. Others have entered the industry with a modest capital investment and succeeded. Firms are in fact "regulated" by the requirements of their customers, their creditors, and their owners—requirements demanding marked-to-market accounting, adequate capitalization, and disclosure of all liabilities. Customers presumably require good service and honest dealings or they will change vendors.

Together with the ever-present threat of massive class-action civil suits, these market-driven disciplines, many would argue, have proven to be as effective regulators of business conduct as any body established by government, particularly in the securities industry. The approach forces independent securities firms (or separately capitalized securities firms that are part of bank holding companies) to pay great attention to managing risks, managing costs, and ensuring profitability. There is no lender of last resort for the individual firm. In addition, they are subject to the costs of maintaining expensive compliance systems, and since they are dependent on banks for much of their funding, they have to meet acceptable credit standards. Even in the case of massive failures like Drexel Burnham Lambert, regulators allowed the failure to run its course, taking care only to provide sufficient liquidity to the market during the crisis period.

Since multifunctional financial firms began to emerge in the United States during the 1990s and particularly after 1999, the basic approach has been regulation by function, requiring holding company structures with separately capitalized banking and non-banking affiliates and a lead regulator, the Federal Reserve, responsible for the holding company as a whole.

Functional regulation in the United States has been carried out through a crazy-quilt of agencies, including the Federal Reserve, Federal Deposit Insurance Corporation, Office of the Comptroller of the Currency, and Securities and Exchange Commission, plus SROs such as the NASD, FASB, CFTC, and the major financial exchanges. Sometimes nonfinancial regulators get involved, such as the Department of Labor, the Special Trade Representative, the antitrust and consumer protection agencies, and various Congressional committees. In addition there are the courts, with particular importance accorded the Chancery Court of the State of Delaware.[2] The whole regulatory structure is replicated to some extent at the state level, with state banking and securities commissions as well as insurance regulation, which rests entirely with the states.

2. See for example "Top Business Court Under Fire," *New York Times*, 23 May 1995.

The system is certainly subject to unnecessary complexity and excessive regulatory costs. In recognition of this, it was partially streamlined in the 1999 Gramm-Leach-Bliley deregulation. However, there is a sense that regulatory competition may not be so bad in fostering vigorous competition and financial innovation. "Regulator shopping" in search of lower NRBs can sometimes pay economic dividends. And some of the major regulatory problems of the past—notably the BCCI debacle in 1991, theft of client assets in the custody unit of Bankers Trust Company in 1998, and evasion of banking regulations in the case of the Crédit Lyonnais–Executive Life scandal in 2001—were all uncovered at the state, not federal, level. Similarly, conflicts of interest involving sell-side research analysts among investment banks in 2002 were pursued aggressively by the Attorney General of the State of New York, with the SEC becoming active only when the political heat was turned up. This suggests that sometimes more eyes are better than fewer.

Mistakes have certainly been made in U.S. financial regulation, and there have doubtless been significant opportunity costs associated with overregulation. A possible example is the self-dealing prohibition under the Employee Retirement Income Security Act of 1974 (ERISA), which prohibits transactions between the investment banking and pension fund management units of the same financial firm. The prohibition is designed to prevent conflicts of interest in multifunctional financial firms handling retirement funds, but at the cost of less-than-best execution in securities transactions (Srinivasan, Saunders and Walter, 2002). Furthermore, the way the LTCM collapse was handled by the Federal Reserve in 1998 continues to be widely debated. And as noted, few of the regulatory and quasiregulatory organizations covered themselves with glory during the financial scandals of 2002.

But by and large, the system has delivered a reasonably efficient and creative financial structure that has been supportive of U.S. growth and development and at the same time has been tolerably stable. Maybe this is as good as can be expected. If there are lessons, they are that regulatory messiness and competition are not always bad and can lead to unexpected dynamism as solutions are left to the market instead of the regulators. There are accidents embedded in this approach, but so far they have been reasonably tolerable.

EUROPE IS DIFFERENT

As discussed earlier, in Europe there has been no tradition of separation of commercial banking, investment banking, and insurance of the type that existed in the United States from 1933 to 1999. Instead, the *universal banking* model predominated from Finland to Portugal, and banks have for the most part been able to engage in all types of financial services— retail and wholesale, commercial banking, investment banking, asset management, as well as insurance underwriting and distribution. Savings banks, cooperative banks, state-owned banks, private banks and in a few cases more or less independent investment banks have also been important elements in some of the national markets. Reflecting this structure, bank regulation and supervision has generally been in the domain of the national central banks or independent supervisory agencies working in cooperation with the central banks, responsible for all aspects of universal bank regulation. The exception is usually insurance, and in some cases specialized activities such as mortgage banking, placed under separate regulatory authorities. And in contrast to the United States, there was little history or tradition of regulatory competition *within* national financial systems, with some exceptions, such as Germany and its regional stock exchanges.[3]

Given their multiple areas of activity centered around core commercial banking functions, the major European players in the financial markets can reasonably be considered too big to fail in the context of their national regulatory domains. This means that, unlike the United States or Japan, significant losses incurred in the securities or insurance business could bring down a bank that, in turn, is likely to be bailed out by taxpayers through a government takeover, recapitalization, forced merger with a government capital injection, or a number other techniques. This means that European financial regulators may find it necessary to safeguard those businesses in order to safeguard the banking business. Failure to provide this kind of symmetry in regulation could end in disaster. No bank failure in Europe has so far been triggered by securities or insurance losses. But it can easily happen. Despite the disastrous trading activities, which ultimately brought it down, it was the responsibility of the Bank of England, as home country regulator, to supervise Baring's global activities, a case that was an object lesson in how difficult such oversight can be.

The European regulatory overlay anchored in EU directives cover the right of banks, securities firms, asset managers, and insurers to engage in business throughout the region, the adequacy of capital, as well as the establishment and marketing of collective investment vehicles such as mutual funds. One can argue that the "single passport" provisions and home-country responsibility for institutional fitness and properness were a necessary response to reconciling the single-market objectives in the European Union with appropriate regulation of the financial services sector.

All EU regulation was supposed to be in place at the beginning of 1993. But delays and selective implementation by member governments dragged out the process so that, almost a decade later, the benefits of the single-market initiatives in this sector were probably a fraction of what they might have been. There remain important problems with respect to regulatory symmetry between banks and non-bank financial services

---

3. See for example "A Ragbag of Reform," *The Economist*, March, 1 2001.

firms. Perhaps most seriously, there remain persistent dissonance in conduct-of-business rules across the European Union.

The latter continue to be the exclusive responsibility of host-country authorities. Financial institutions doing business in the European Union must deal with 16 sets of rules (if the offshore Eurobond market is included)—26 after enlargement in 2005. These have gradually converged toward a consensus on minimum acceptable conduct-of-business standards, although they remain far apart in detail. Areas of particular interest include insider trading and information disclosure. For example, the view that insider trading is a crime, rather than a professional indiscretion, has been new in most of Europe. Few have been jailed for insider trading, and in several EU countries it is still not a criminal offense. On information disclosure in securities new issues, there has been only limited standardization of the content and distribution of prospectuses covering equity, bond, and Eurobond issues for sale to individuals and institutions in the member countries. The devil is in the details.

If a sound regulatory balance is difficult to strike within a single sovereign state, it is even more difficult to achieve in a regional or global environment where differences in regulation and its implementation can lead to migration of financial activities in accordance with relative net regulatory burdens. In a federal state like the United States, there are limits to NRB differences that can emerge—although there are some. A confederation of sovereign states like the European Union obviously has much greater scope for NRB differences, despite the harmonization embedded in the EU's various financial services directives. Each of these represents an appropriate response to the regulatory issues involved. But each leaves open at least some prospect for regulatory arbitrage among the participating countries and "fault lines" across national regulatory systems—particularly as countries strive for a share of financial value-added. Players based in the more heavily regulated countries will successfully lobby for liberalization, and the view that there ultimately has to be a broad-gauge consensus on common sense, minimum acceptable standards has gained momentum (Dermine and Hillion, 1999; Walter and Smith 2000).

So far, progress in Europe on financial market practices has been painfully slow. As a result, the cost and availability of capital to end users of the financial system (notably in the business sector) has remained unnecessarily high, and the returns to capital for end users (notably households and most importantly pension investors) remains unnecessarily low. This has doubtless had an adverse overall impact on Europe's economic performance, both in terms of static welfare losses to consumers and producers and dynamic underperformance reflected in the process of structural adjustment and the rate of growth.

The most promising European response to this regulatory drag on economic welfare was the Lamfalussy Committee's final report (2001). Its goals were straightforward and essentially performance-driven: (1) modernizing financial market regulations, (2) creating open and transparent markets that facilitate achieving investor objectives and capital-raising, (3) encouraging the development of pan-European financial products that are easily and cheaply traded in liquid markets, and (4) developing appropriate standards of consumer protection.

Judging from the Lamfalussy Committee's report, European convergence is likely to involve centralized regulatory structures at the national level. Emphasizing efficiency and accountability, the structure is similar to that of the U.K. Financial Services Authority (FSA), which was created in 2000 as a result of reforms that began in 1997. It covers both institutions and market practices. The idea is that national regulatory convergence along these lines will contribute to reducing fragmentation of financial markets. Denmark, Sweden, Belgium, Luxembourg, and Finland are reportedly moving in this direction. In Germany, a debate persisted about regulatory domains of the federal and state level. France has apparently focused on the merits of separate regulators, one for wholesale business and institutional soundness and the other for retail activities. The French approach tries to be responsive to consumer protection and potential conflict of interest problems, as well as to the criticism that omnibus market regulators like the SEC lean too heavily to the retail side and that this can lead to overregulation of interprofessional wholesale markets.

This general convergence on a more or less consistent regulatory approach at the national level still leaves open the question of pan-European regulation, with wide differences of opinion as to necessity and timing.

The Lamfalussy Report simply recommended a fast-track "securities committee" intended to accelerate the process of convergence based on a framework agreed by the EU Commission, Council of Ministers, and European Parliament. As noted earlier, small changes in regulation tend to trigger big changes in the playing field. Some win and some lose, and the losers' political clout can postpone the day of reckoning—especially if the "common interest" is hard to document. So the Lamfalussy Committee also had more concrete recommendations on investment rules for pension funds, uniformity in accounting standards, access to equity markets for financial intermediaries on a "single passport" basis, the definition of investment professionals, mutual recognition of wholesale financial markets, improvements in listing requirements for the various exchanges, a single prospectus for issuers throughout the European Union, and improvements in information disclosure by corporations.

This led to proposals for a "single financial passport" that would let companies raise capital in any of the EU debt and equity markets via a single prospectus approved by regulators in the firm's home country in most cases (in any EU country for large-denomination issues), and a uniform, simplified prospectus for smaller companies. Individual exchanges would retain the power to reject prospectuses. The plan remained controversial because of its reliance on home-country approval even when the necessary level of regulatory competence may not exist, as well as the decision to classify as "wholesale" investments exceeding €50,000 with a simplified prospectus, although many institutional investors often buy less than that amount.

Many of the Lamfalussy recommendations were already incorporated in the EU's 1992 Investment Services Directive but were implemented unevenly or sometimes not at all. The Committee made a compelling case for accelerated and forthright implementation, hardly too much to ask a decade after launch. So a "regulators committee" was foreseen in order to assure that enabling legislation and market rules are actually implemented. The European Securities Committee (ESC) was created in June 2001 to accelerate progress in line with the Lamfalussy Report's end-2003 target. Made up of representatives of the member states, the ESC was ultimately to be transformed into a pan-EU regulatory body charged with implementing securities legislation.[4] The European Parliament immediately demanded the power to review decisions of the ESC. In June 2001 the draft single-prospectus directive was generally welcomed, although the "market abuse" draft directive was highly criticized for being excessively broad. The reception of both suffered from a lack of consultation by the Commission with national financial regulators and the financial community.

All of the Lamfalussy recommendations made a great deal of sense. The best features of the Anglo-American approach are adopted and those that might not work well in the European context (including perhaps a central SEC with substantial enforcement powers) are de-emphasized. The proposals, if vigorously implemented, will go a long way toward achieving the efficiency and growth objectives that the Committee targeted in its initial report. Within the financial sector itself, if European firms are eventually to gain on the current American market share of roughly 65% in global capital raising and corporate advisory revenues, who could disagree?

JOINING THE PUBLIC POLICY ISSUES

Mergers and acquisitions in the financial sector are driven by the strategies of individual management teams who believe it is in their organization's best interests to reconfigure their businesses, hoping to achieve greater market share and profitability and therefore higher valuations of their firms. As discussed in previous chapters, they believe that these gains will come from economies of scale, improved operating efficiencies, better risk control, the ability to take advantage of revenue synergies and other considerations, and are convinced they can overcome whatever economic and managerial disadvantages may arise. Sometimes they are right. Sometimes they are wrong, and net gains may turn out to be illusory or the

4. *The Economist* (ibid.) quotes the case of Lernout & Hauspie, a Belgian tech firm under investigation for fraudulent accounting, where local investigators had to rely on the US SEC's EDGAR system for financial reports on the company.

integration process may be botched. In the end, the market will decide. And when the markets are subject to shocks, such as changes in economic fundamentals or technologies, they usually trigger a spate of M&A transactions that often seem to be amplified by herd-like behavior among managements of financial firms. Public policy comes into the picture in several more or less distinct ways.

First, policy changes represent one of the key external drivers of the M&A process. These may be broad-gauge, such as the end of the Bretton Woods fixed exchange rate regime in 1971, or the advent of the euro in 1999, or the liberalization of markets through the European Union or NAFTA or trade negotiations covering financial services under the auspices of the World Trade Organization. Other general policies designed to improve economic performance, ranging from macroeconomic policy initiatives to structural measures affecting specific sectors, can have profound effects on M&A activity in the financial services industry by affecting market activity and the client base.

In addition, there are specific policy initiatives at the level of financial institutional and markets that can have equally dramatic effects. U.S. examples mentioned earlier include the 1933 Glass-Steagall Act, the 1956 Bank Holding Company Act, the McFadden Act (limiting geographic scope) among regulatory constraints, or the 1974 U.S. "Mayday" introduction of negotiated brokerage commissions and the 1999 Gramm-Leach-Bliley Act, among the important regulatory initiatives. European examples include the EU's banking, insurance, and investment services directives, the 1986 U.K. "Big Bang" deregulation and a host of "mini-bangs" that followed on the Continent in efforts to improve the efficiency and competitiveness of national financial systems. Japan followed the deregulation trend in its unique way, creating substantial opportunities (and some risks) for strategic moves by domestic as well as foreign-based financial firms.

In short, changes in public policies at the broad-gauge and financial-sector levels have been among the most important drivers of M&A activity among financial firms—whether they are based in legislation, judicial decisions, or actions of regulatory agencies. As noted, even small changes in the policy environment can have large effects on financial markets and the financial services industry and trigger M&A activity.

Conversely, the general public is vitally concerned with the results of financial services M&A activities. We have identified static and dynamic efficiency of the financial sector alongside safely and soundness as the twin public-interest objectives, and M&A activity affects both.

Deals that threaten to monopolize markets are sure to trigger public policy reactions sooner or later. A manager's nirvana of comfortable oligopolies with large excess returns is unlikely to be sustained for long as a matter of public interest—or as a result of market reactions, as clients flee to other forms of financial intermediation or other geographic venues where they can get a better deal. What the public needs is a highly creative

and vigorously competitive and perhaps diverse set of financial intermediaries that earn normal risk-adjusted returns for their shareholders
and generate minimum all-in financing costs for the business sector and
maximum consumer surplus for the household sector, all the while contributing to continuous market-driven economic restructuring in accordance with global competitive advantage. A tall order. But M&A transactions in the financial services sector that hold promise of moving things
in that direction are clearly in the public interest.

At the same time, we have discussed safety and soundness of the
financial system as a second public interest objective, one that often requires a delicate balancing against the aforementioned efficiency objective.
Normally safety and soundness is defined in terms of the stability of the
financial system. But it has been defined more broadly in this chapter to
encompass market conduct, transparency, governance and corporate control, fairness, and even safeguarding of the stability of individual institutions when that involves explicit or implicit backstops borne by taxpayers. M&A transactions that alter the financial landscape can clearly affect
this broad definition of safety and soundness. Deals can easily create firms
that are in fact too big to fail. Or the resulting entities are so broad and
complex as to defy managerial oversight, much less regulatory insight.
Or they become so politically connected that they coopt the regulators.
Or the M&A deals are driven by the regulations themselves, triggering
unintended consequences or moral hazard.

There may be concerns that regulatory arbitrage internationally could
cause firms to exploit "regulatory fault lines" or perhaps exceed the ability
of the home-country regulator and its central bank to assure financial
stability. This puts a premium on international coordination in the regulatory overlay. A great deal of progress has been made in this regard
through the Bank for International Settlements (BIS)—notably with respect to consolidated financials and capital adequacy—although often in
fits and starts, accompanied by a great deal of debate and disagreement.
Less dramatic international policy alignment has occurred in insurance,
asset management and securities, and certainly in general issues such as
transparency and corporate governance. So the emergence through the
acquisitions process of massive multinational, multifunctional financial
firms like Citigroup, HSBC, J.P. Morgan Chase, Deutsche Bank AG, Allianz AG, BNP Paribas, Crédit Suisse Group, and a host of others presents
special public policy challenges. Appropriate responses are not always
easy to identify or implement.

The point is that mergers and acquisitions in the financial sector carry
with them a substantial public interest element. Sometimes they are driven
by measures taken in the public interest. Sometimes they themselves drive
those measures. It is an unstable equilibrium that will surely persist as a
key facet of the national and global financial environment in the years
ahead.

8

The Key Lessons

This book has portrayed the contours of the mergers and acquisitions landscape in financial services. It identified (1) what drives the broad structure of the industry, (2) how the patterns of financial takeovers have transformed it and are likely to continue reshaping the industry going forward, (3) what motivates financial sector M&A deals and what they are supposed to achieve, (4) what it takes to execute them successfully, (5) whether they actually "work" in terms of market share and shareholder value, and (6) whether the outcomes are good for the efficiency and stability of the financial system. An effort was made to link the basic underpinnings of competitive advantage in this unique industry to the observed outcomes based on available performance data and individual case studies. So what have we learned?

HOW DO SHAREHOLDERS FARE?

As in most other industries, shareholders of target companies in the financial services industry consistently do well. They normally receive a premium to the premerger market price of their stock (or the intrinsic value of the firm if it is not publicly traded) and usually have the option to cash out quickly if they don't like the prospects of the combined firm. This option is valuable, as shareholders who have held their shares in merged financial firms too long can painfully attest.

On the other hand, shareholders of financial services acquirers on average do far less well. They can gain if the strategic rationale behind the acquisition makes sense, if the price is right, and if the integration is handled effectively. Unless they bail out on announcement, they can risk losing heavily if the underlying rationale of the deal is flawed, the acquisition is overpriced, or the process of integration ends up destroying much of the value of the deal.

On balance, restructuring of the financial services industry through mergers and acquisitions tends to redistribute wealth among shareholders of acquiring and target firms. But it is not necessarily a zero-sum game. Indeed, market-driven restructuring in the financial services sector should, as in other industries, increase both the efficiency and dynamism of the sector as a whole. In some transactions two plus two does equal five—or even more—in which case both buyers and sellers get to carve up the joint gains. So on balance, financial industry restructuring through M&A transactions should throw off plenty of net benefits, which makes it all the more curious that shareholders of acquiring firms tend to do so poorly. It seems that the owners of targets in many mergers tend to get the lion's share of the joint gains. But in well conceived and well executed deals stockholders of the buying firms do in fact share in the bounty. As always, the devil is in the details.

COMPETITIVE GAINS AND LOSSES: COST AND EFFICIENCY

The evidence suggests that the net gains from M&A transactions, come either on the cost and efficiency side or the revenue side of the combined businesses. The key lessons from the evidence, on the cost side, appear to be the following.

For entire financial firms there appear to be few *economies of scale* (unit cost reductions associated with larger size, all else remaining the same) to be harvested in the banking, insurance, and securities industries beyond relatively small firm size. Moreover, cost differences attributable to economies of scale tend to be relatively small compared to total costs and compared to cost differences between the most and least efficient firms in these sectors. Nor is there much evidence of *diseconomies of scale* beyond optimum-size firms. So cost economies of scale are not likely to be an appropriate motivation for M&A deals, especially large ones, nor is the possibility of diseconomies of scale likely to represent a compelling argument against them.[1]

However, since financial firms usually consist of an amalgam of scale-sensitive and non-scale-sensitive activities, M&A transactions can add significant value if product-level scale economies are aggressively exploited. Obvious candidates include various kinds of mass-market consumer financial services, securities custody, trade financing, and the like.

Besides economies of scale, there is plenty of evidence that operating efficiencies can be harvested as a result of M&A transactions. It has been noted repeatedly that financial services firms of roughly the same size can have very different efficiency levels, as measured for example by cost-to-income ratios, and that the largest observed firmwide economies of scale

---

1. A possible exception is asset management specialists, where economies of scale in production and distribution of fiduciary services may be substantial over broad levels of assets under management.

seem to pale by comparison to operating efficiency differences—perhaps by a factor of four or five. So M&A transactions can lead to major gains in operating efficiency regardless of size, particularly where there are significant overlaps in production or distribution infrastructures (for example, branch offices, IT systems) that permit significant downsizing of the workforce and more productive redeployment of capital. Improved operating efficiencies mean a great deal to shareholders of acquiring firms because, after the necessary restructuring charges, they show up early in the evolution and their risk-adjusted net present value can be very high indeed—the so-called "low-hanging fruit" in M&A deals.

IT has clearly grown in importance as a focus of operating economics in financial services firms over the years, as have annual IT budgets. If those budgets are "lumpy" in terms of minimum critical mass in order to achieve state-of-the-art platforms, and if only large financial firms can support the spend-levels required, it could be that the IT channel provides a link to improved operating efficiency—so that mergers or acquisitions that generate greater size may also generate larger operating efficiency. However, outsourcing and pooling of IT capabilities may help smaller firms limit this potentially adverse effect on their competitive performance.

Working against possible scale and efficiency gains in mergers and acquisitions are costs associated with complexity. Larger firms are harder to manage than smaller ones. It is not easy to instill compelling cost discipline, teamwork and a common culture in a firm with several hundred thousand people scattered across hundreds of locations, possibly globally. While this may be possible at the world's largest employer, Wal-Mart, banking and financial services are another matter altogether. It means a high degree of complexity, and complexity usually means increased costs.

Also in the realm of costs are conflicts of interest between the firm and its clients, as well as between clients. Regardless of size, a greater range of products, clients, and locations spell greater potential for conflicts of interest. Exploitation of these conflicts must be prevented by means of conduct guidelines and effective "Chinese walls" that limit some of the hoped-for synergies. But the costs of dealing with conflicts of interest after they occur can be horrendous, as banks' involvement in corporate financial scandals has demonstrated. Revenues may collapse as the firm's reputation takes a serious hit. Or costs may balloon as the firm scrambles to rescue its good name or deals with class-action litigation. Either way, preventing and managing conflicts of interest can and do show up on both the cost and revenue sides of the ledger in scoping out the possible effects of an M&A deal.

In short, on the cost side, the managerial lessons are don't expect too much from economies of scale on a firmwide basis, but work to exploit them in scale-sensitive businesses while aggressively pursuing operating efficiencies by shedding redundant resources as quickly as possible for an "early harvest" in the value of the transaction to shareholders. At the same time, create incentive-compatible managerial structures that help immunize the firm from the costs of complexity and exploitation of conflicts of interest, especially those creating potential franchise risks for the business.

COMPETITIVE GAINS AND LOSSES: REVENUES

In addition to cost and efficiency effects on competitive performance, M&A transactions in the financial services sector are also driven by revenue effects. Top-line gains resulting from M&A transactions can come from several sources.

The combined firm's market "footprint" tends to be greater as a result of a merger or acquisition, and this can generate disproportionate gains in revenues, for example by enabling the firm to credibly bid for larger transactions or build distribution channels to a level required by critical mass, or by extending that footprint over greater geographies or broader sets of clients. A related revenue-based benefit may be achieved if the firm is able to diversify across additional distribution channels acquired in the M&A transaction, and thereby broaden or deepen access to important market segments. Bigger firms often have more strategic options.

The most important revenue-related gain tends to be *revenue economies of scope* associated with cross-selling if the M&A transaction broadens the product range. Here the key is to examine the potential for cross-selling in each of the feasible product linkages and designing incentive-compatible reward systems to get it done. Because insufficient effort and care are often devoted to the detailed work required to extract significant revenue economies of scope, management and shareholders are frequently disappointed by the results.

In terms of top-line gains from M&A transactions, the key lessons are to identify them early, as part of the due diligence process—which itself will play an important part in defining the terms of the transaction. Once the deal is done, the revenue synergies need to be targeted at a sufficiently granular level to be exploitable in the real world, and then incentive-compatible approaches to compensation have to be carefully designed at the grass roots to make them happen. Nothing works in making cross-selling work like compensation that is transparent, fair, and reliable. In addition, absence of perceived best-in-class services will encourage clients to defect—a process made easier by modern technologies that reduce information and transactions costs. With increasingly promiscuous financial services clients, it usually pays to adopt an "open architecture" approach that extends the boundaries of the firm. Even after successfully identifying and getting to work on extracting revenue gains, doing so in a sensible way usually takes time. This pushes the top-line benefits into the future, where they are worth less to shareholders, so opportunities to take "early harvests" on the revenue side are especially valuable.

COMPETITIVE MARKET STRUCTURE

Whatever the cost and revenue gains that can be extracted from a merger or acquisition, neither are worth much if the market structure in which the firm finds itself turns out to be highly competitive. Like the dog who caught the bus, sometimes managements get what they wish for but may not in the end enjoy the fruits of all their efforts. In highly competitive markets, even the most promising cost and revenue gains tend to be eroded before long. This is how competitive markets are supposed to work, after all. The consequence is that the results of management's exertions end up benefitting mainly clients, with very little left over for shareholders in terms of returns on invested capital. So it is important from the outset to identify the firm's sources of sustainable competitive advantage and align them with the target markets where this competitive advantage can be brought to bear in a way that provides significant margins and resistance to profit-erosion. This can involve sustainable product differentiation, first-mover advantages, massive and "lumpy" capital investments, dominant positions in highly concentrated markets, regulatory barriers to competition, and a host of other factors. People usually do better owning shares in Microsoft than growing wheat. The evidence that M&A transactions which focus financial services activities do better than transactions which disperse activities is hardly surprising. So astute assessment of the future competitive structures of target markets is a prerequisite for shareholder-value gains in mergers or acquisitions.

DOING IT RIGHT

Even if they are well-targeted in terms of cost and revenue gains, successes and failures in financial services M&A transactions depend heavily on the effectiveness of post-merger integration.

It is important to be absolutely clear what the merger or acquisition is about. Are the incremental resources to be absorbed, are they to be preserved pretty much intact and perhaps leveraged into the acquirer's operating platform, or are they destined to complement and fill in existing resources, markets, or clients? As in other industries, M&A transactions represent one tool in corporate development, growth, and profitability, and a great deal of value can be destroyed if this tool is abused or misused. The integration process has to be driven by the underlying transaction rationale.

How people react to the transaction, before and after the fact, is perhaps the most important issue. Those who will be asked to leave should know it as quickly as possible after the announcement, receive clear severance terms, and be able to get on with their lives. Those who will be asked to stay should be equally clear about the incentives, functions, reporting lines, and related dimensions of the professional environment. They should end up thinking of the transaction as an important and rewarding professional opportunity that doesn't come along too frequently in life. They should want to "get with the program" with energy and imagination. Some of the most visible disasters in the history of financial services merger integration can be ascribed to people problems, sometimes with the result that the combined firm is worth little more than the acquirer was worth prior to the transactions. And it is useful to keep in mind that competitors are always circling, eager to pick up first-rate talent that is mauled in the merger process.

Information technology integration in the financial services sector is unusually important—and mistakes tend to be unusually damaging—because of the key role of information and transactions processing. IT issues need to be brought into the M&A planning early in the process, including the due diligence process, and driven by the underlying strategy. Critical issues include misalignments in IT configurations, choice of dominance of IT platforms and technical architectures, organizational infrastructure and leadership, and the costs of IT integration. Failure to deal with these issues as an integral part of the merger process has led to more than their share of value destruction—particularly in the case of client-facing IT dimensions. And IT integration is never cheap, as it involves capital and operating outlays that come soon after the completion of deals, so its earnings impact will be felt early in the game.

Culture can cut several ways in merger situations. On the one hand, a cohesive culture can be an asset for an acquirer by making clear what behavioral norms and working conditions will prevail in the combined firm. Those who are unlikely to do well under those norms can be more easily filtered out, which may help limit problems down the road. And clarity about the way things are done helps those who remain to coalesce and to move ahead. On the other hand, a powerful and exclusive culture on the side of the acquirer, as against a looser and more receptive one, may make it more difficult to achieve easy buy-in on the part of the acquired team—especially if it, too, had a strong culture. This issue may be especially problematic if the acquired resources are critical for future competitive success and, for all intents and purposes, requires what is in effect a "reverse takeover."

Branding is another key aspect of merger integration. A decision has to be made at some point what the branding strategy is to be. This itself is driven by the financial services and markets that form the activity portfolio of the combined firm, which may push the decision either toward multiple sub-brands or toward brand uniformity. Other issues include the equity already embedded in the legacy brands, the need for the appearance of uniformity and seamlessness across client-segments and geographies, and the potential for conflicts of interest that may arise in the minds of clients when confronted by a single brand covering highly diverse activities. Timing also important. Re-branding being delayed until after the dust settles from the M&A transaction often makes a lot of sense.

Finally, there is increasing evidence that financial firms can "learn to integrate"—that codified procedures which identify things that need to get done, in what sequence of priority, and what works and what doesn't can actually help ease the integration process in subsequent acquisitions. For firms that have a successful acquisitions track record and that are most likely to grow by acquisitions in the future, such learning by doing and codification appear to explain some of the acquisitions success stories in this industry. Conversely, institutional forgetfulness, underestimating the integration problems, and playing by ear have clearly been disastrous in more than a few high-profile cases.

In short, we have emphasized a number of times the importance of strategic execution in connection with M&A transaction in financial services, and post-merger integration is at the heart of this process. No matter how well founded the overall master plan is or how well a given deal fits, integration problems have an inordinate ability to derail the best laid plans.

DOES ORGANIZATIONAL STRUCTURE MATTER?

The structural profile of the financial services firm that results from its strategic development—and the use of M&A transactions as a tool in that development—carries important lessons as well.

Depending on the applicable tax regime, multifunctional firms may be more tax-efficient than specialist firms because they carry out a greater share of transactions within the firm rather than between firms. In addition, by diversifying earnings across business streams and reducing earnings volatility, overall tax liabilities may be reduced under certain tax regimes. This may also be the case when there is a difference in the tax treatment of foreign earnings and M&A transactions have produced an international or global business profile.

The evidence shows that diversified financial firms tend to have more stable cash-flows than firms that are more narrowly defined in terms of geographies, product range, or client groups to the extent that the individual earnings streams are not perfectly correlated. The result ought to be a more stable firm, which should pay dividends in cost-of-capital considerations such as debt ratings and share prices. This attribute should also be of interest to banking and financial regulators in that it makes invocation of lender-of-last-resort facilities and taxpayer bailouts less likely. However, some of the complex multifunctional financial firms that are the result of sequential mergers and acquisitions are awfully hard to understand and regulate, and it seems unlikely that management itself fully understands and controls the risks embedded in the business—especially correlations among different types of risks.

A related issue—implicit too-big-to-fail (TBTF) guarantees through likely taxpayer-financed bailouts in the event of difficulties—can be a side benefit of M&A transactions that move a firm closer to that status, including cost of capital benefits. Still, TBTF status invariably comes with strings attached, including more intrusive regulation. And there is always the question of what lender-of-last-resort facilities are actually worth, especially in the case of very large institutions based in small countries.

An institutional profile that is international or global, which almost always involves substantial M&A activity, has to be part of a strategy that makes sense in terms of the business conducted. Retail customers could care less whether they are dealing with an international or global firm unless, as a consequence, they benefit from better products or better pricing—which is not always the case. So these are essentially multilocal businesses. At the other extreme, institutional investors and major corporate clients depend on global financial firms to provide the best ideas and seamless execution in all relevant financial markets to help them achieve their own objectives.

In the case of multilocal businesses, questions must be asked about what a foreign acquirer is bringing to the party that will make the target more competitive in its own market, how some of the resources of the target can be leveraged in the acquirer's home market or in third markets, or whether the acquisition is a pure portfolio investment. In the case of global businesses, how to weld the target into an integrated business structure, how to deal with intercultural issues, and how to bridge regulatory systems are among the key questions. So far at least, firms that bridge a wide range of clients, products, and geographies in a way that produces abnormally high sustained returns to their shareholders are few and far between.

Like firms in general, the evidence suggests that the broader the range of activities engaged in by financial services players, the more likely it is that the shares will be subject to a conglomerate discount. The reasons appear to be related to weaker internal disciplines in avoiding low net present value projects in particular parts of the business and in avoiding cross-subsidization between the constituent businesses—in addition to the fact that investors may avoid the shares because of the impossibility of "clean plays" in exposures to specific types of financial services activities. If shares of nonfinancial conglomerates tend to suffer from a conglomerate discount, there is no reason that highly diverse firms covering banking, securities, insurance, and asset management should not be similarly affected.

SOLID MANAGEMENT AND LEADERSHIP

All things considered, there is no substitute for good management in the strategic positioning and implementation process of financial services firms. That means (1) targeting markets that are large and growing and increasingly concentrated, where the firm has a shot at being one of the dominant players, and (2) knitting together those markets that extract the maximum value from scale and scope linkages that may exist. The evidence shows that the first of these is substantially more important than the second. It also means paying careful attention to operating costs and risk control, both of which allow plenty of room for excellence as well as for error—especially with regard to developing and executing an integrated approach to the management of risk. And finally, it means intense and persistent attention to product quality and innovation. What shareholders are looking for is a highly disciplined and creative approach to the internal allocation of productive resources that appears to be more efficient than external markets and is likely to deliver sustainable excess returns on share capital.

Leadership of financial firms that is driven by these core objectives will find that the use of mergers and acquisitions as a strategic tool can be very rewarding indeed—the tendency to do the right thing and to do it right in an M&A context tends to grow out of the basic way the business is run. Everything else follows from that. The objective, after all, is to deliver sustainable value to the firms' owners. If not, then what is the point? Firms whose leaders take their eyes off the ball or fall victim to hubris, which is not uncommon in strategic corporate actions such as mergers and acquisitions, usually find that the market takes rather little time to signal its response.

And what about the public interest? Policymakers should support the creation of a leaner and more creative financial system as a matter of general economic policy—one that fosters capital formation and efficiency in the use of capital as well as lower information and transaction costs. Efficiency and growth are ubiquitous public policy goals, and a high-performance financial system is a *sine qua non* for achieving them. At the same time, financial instability can do massive and long-lasting damage to the economy and society. Mergers and acquisitions in the financial services sector clearly affect both sets of objectives and invariably attract keen interest on the part of regulators, who in turn tend to respond in ways that are of material interest to the financial firms themselves.

Appendix 1
Financial Service Sector Acquisitions

Note: Transactions in excess of $500 million were completed during 1985–2002. Data: Thomson Financial Securities Data.

Appendix 1, Table 1

Financial Service Sector Acquisitions Within US, 1990-2002 Exceeding $500 million

Date Announced	Date Effective	Value of Transaction ($mil)	Target Name	Acquirer Name
02/20/85	08/30/85	508.25	Landmark Banking Corp of FL	Citizens and Southern GA Corp
06/17/85	12/05/85	1835.00	First Atlanta Corp,Atlanta,GA	Wachovia Corp,Winston-Salem,NC
02/07/86	05/30/86	1070.00	Crocker National(Midland Bk)	Wells Fargo Capital C
02/13/86	06/17/86	669.50	Life Insurance Co of Virginia	Combined International Corp
02/21/86	02/02/87	695.00	Continental Bancorp Inc, PA	Midlantic Banks Inc,Edison,NJ
03/18/86	01/29/87	674.00	Quotron Systems Inc	Citicorp
04/24/86	06/11/86	600.00	Kidder, Peabody & Co	General Electric Finl Svcs
05/01/86	01/03/89	650.00	Horizon Bancorp,Morristown,NJ	Chemical New York Corp
05/07/86	01/26/87	597.30	American Fletcher,Indianapolis	BANC ONE Corp,Columbus,Ohio
06/11/86	11/01/86	765.10	First RR & Banking,Augusta,GA	First Union Corp,Charlotte,NC
06/23/86	12/31/86	1344.00	Tenneco Inc-Insurance Lines	ICH Corp
06/30/86	02/27/87	719.00	Citizens Fidelity, Louisville	PNC Financial,Pittsburgh,PA
08/06/86	11/28/86	500.00	Goldman Sachs & Co	Sumitomo Bank Ltd
08/13/86	04/22/87	650.00	Conifer/Essex Group Inc	Bank of New England,Boston,MA
09/02/86	12/29/86	758.00	Third Natl Corp,Nashville,TN	SunTrust Banks Inc,Atlanta,GA
12/15/86	05/01/87	1190.00	Texas Commerce Bancshares,TX	Chemical New York Corp
12/16/86	06/06/87	584.00	InterFirst Corp,Dallas,Texas	RepublicBank Corp
02/24/87	08/31/87	1157.10	Rainier Bancorporation,WA	Security Pacific,Los Angeles
03/18/87	01/01/88	1250.00	Norstar Bancorp,Albany,NY	Fleet Finl Group,Providence,RI
04/01/87	10/23/92	1500.00	American General Corp	American General Corp
04/27/87	11/01/87	655.00	Commerce Union Corp,Nashville	Sovran Financial,Norfolk,VA
05/27/87	06/19/87	750.00	Smith Barney Inc	Primerica Corp
07/31/87	02/29/88	726.00	Central Bancorporation Inc	PNC Financial,Pittsburgh,PA
07/31/87	02/29/88	1316.00	Fidelcor Inc,Philadelphia,PA	First Fidelity Bancorp,NJ
08/26/87	02/29/88	884.20	Shawmut Corp,Boston,MA	Hartford National Corp, CT
09/25/87	12/30/88	1377.00	Irving Bank Corp	Bank of New York,New York,NY
09/28/87	09/28/87	700.00	Salomon Inc	Berkshire Hathaway Inc
11/23/87	04/29/88	964.30	EF Hutton Group Inc	Shearson Lehman Brothers Hldg
01/13/88	12/16/88	5200.00	Farmers Group Inc	BATUS Inc(BAT Industries PLC)
01/27/88	12/01/88	635.00	Massachusetts Indemnity & Life	AL Williams Corp(Primerica)
01/27/88	07/28/88	647.90	First Kentucky National Corp	National City,Cleveland,Ohio

238

02/16/88	12/16/88	750.00	Union Bank(Standard Chartered)	California First Bank
03/07/88	06/22/88	2800.00	Montgomery Ward-Credit Card Op	General Electric Capital Corp
04/11/88	05/31/88	685.00	Manufac Hanover Consumer Svcs	Creditthrift Financial Corp
08/26/88	12/20/88	1720.00	Primerica Corp	Commercial Credit Group Inc
09/29/88	09/29/88	575.00	Westinghouse Cr-Fixed Ast Div	US WEST Financial Services Inc
12/21/88	03/21/89	1400.00	Meritor Credit(Meritor Svgs)	Ford Motor Credit Co
03/07/89	01/29/90	851.81	Florida Nat Bks of Florida Inc	First Union Corp,Charlotte,NC
06/19/89	01/05/90	500.67	Trustcorp Inc,Toledo,Ohio	Society Corp
07/12/89	01/18/90	560.60	Equitable Bancorp,Baltimore,MD	MNC Financial Inc
07/27/89	11/07/89	3350.00	Associates First Capital Corp	Ford Motor Co
09/15/89	03/02/90	713.00	First Pennsylvania Corp	CoreStates Financial Corp,PA
09/26/89	09/01/90	2054.00	Citizens & Southern Georgia	Sovran Financial,Norfolk,VA
10/03/89	03/30/90	530.00	Phil Life,Mass Life,Wabash	HMS Acquisition Corp
11/21/89	03/29/90	777.00	Equicor(Equitable Life,HCA)	CIGNA Corp
11/24/89	03/01/90	1350.00	BarclaysAmer/Finl-Br,Portfolio	Commercial Credit Group Inc
01/29/90	02/05/90	828.00	Bank New England-Credit Card	Citicorp
03/16/90	03/16/90	676.00	First City Bancorp-Credit Card	Bank of New York,New York,NY
03/30/90	04/30/90	1193.60	Ellco Leasing Corp	General Electric Capital Corp
06/25/90	08/31/90	1122.00	International Lease Finance	American International Group
08/02/90	09/19/90	2200.00	Fireman's Fund Ins-Assets	Fund American Cos Inc
10/11/90	05/10/91	1600.00	Macy Credit,Macy Receivables	General Electric Capital Corp
01/03/91	02/28/91	568.00	Shawmut Natl Corp-Credit Card	Norwest Corp,Minneapolis,MN
05/15/91	03/16/92	1186.00	AmeriTrust Corp,Cleveland,OH	Society Corp
06/20/91	12/06/91	816.50	South Carolina National	Wachovia Corp,Winston-Salem,NC
06/25/91	12/31/91	4259.00	C&S/Sovran Corp	NCNB Corp,Charlotte,NC
07/15/91	12/31/91	2044.20	Manufacturers Hanover Corp	Chemical Banking Corp
07/31/91	10/01/91	500.00	Mutual Benefit-Grp Life Ins	AMEV Holdings Inc(AMEV NV)
08/05/91	10/02/91	755.00	Chase Manhattan Leasing Co(MI)	Associates Corp of N America
08/12/91	04/22/92	4212.70	Security Pacific,Los Angeles	BankAmerica Corp
09/12/91	05/01/92	560.60	Security Bancorp,Southgate,MI	First of Amer Bk,Kalamazoo,MI
10/28/91	06/18/92	1087.00	Manufacturers National Corp	Comerica Inc,Detroit,Michigan
10/30/91	05/04/92	655.40	Merchants National Corp	National City,Cleveland,Ohio
03/04/92	01/15/93	889.80	Puget Sound Bancorp,Tacoma,WA	KeyCorp,Albany,NY(Key Corp,OH)
03/18/92	10/15/92	883.26	INB Financial Corp	NBD Bancorp,Detroit,Michigan
03/23/92	11/30/92	725.70	Team Bancshares Inc	BANC ONE Corp,Columbus,Ohio
04/14/92	03/31/93	1186.00	Valley National Corp,Phoenix	BANC ONE Corp,Columbus,Ohio
05/18/92	12/07/92	882.60	First Florida Banks Inc	Barnett Banks,Jacksonville,FL

Date	Date	Amount	Target	Acquirer
06/02/92	06/02/92	560.00	Chrysler Capital-Diversified	General Electric Capital Corp
06/05/92	05/03/93	583.90	Key Centurion Bancshares,WV	BANC ONE Corp,Columbus,Ohio
07/17/92	10/29/93	1333.00	MNC Financial Inc	NationsBank Corp,Charlotte,NC
09/14/92	05/21/93	1453.00	Boston Co	Mellon Bank Corp,Pittsburgh,PA
09/18/92	12/30/92	722.50	Travelers Corp	Primerica Corp
09/21/92	03/01/93	934.31	Dominion Bankshares,Roanoke,VA	First Union Corp,Charlotte,NC
10/21/92	02/12/93	615.20	First City Bancorp of Texas	Texas Commerce Bancshares,TX
10/27/92	04/09/93	663.00	Pacific First Bank FSB,Seattle	Washington Mutual,Seattle,WA
11/09/92	06/01/93	513.30	Colorado National Bankshares	First Bank Sys,Minneapolis,MN
11/17/92	02/01/93	2200.00	Chrysler First Inc(Chrysler)	NationsBank Corp,Charlotte,NC
12/04/92	03/26/93	576.70	Colonial Cos Inc	UNUM Corp
01/06/93	04/15/93	750.00	GNA Corp(GE Capital Corp)	General Electric Capital Corp
01/29/93	08/11/93	591.60	National Community Banks Inc	Bank of New York,New York,NY
02/04/93	12/31/93	500.00	First Chicago Corp-Commercial	General Electric Capital Corp
03/09/93	07/30/93	1150.00	Shearson Lehman Brothers Inc	Primerica Corp
04/05/93	07/14/93	550.00	United Pacific Life Insurance	General Electric Capital Corp
09/20/93	05/31/94	819.70	Valley Bancorp,Appleton,WI	Marshall & Ilsley,Milwaukee,WI
09/22/93	12/31/93	3955.90	Travelers Corp	Primerica Corp
10/01/93	03/01/94	3923.90	KeyCorp,Albany,NY(Key Corp,OH)	Society Corp
11/03/93	08/15/94	853.20	Liberty National Bancorp	BANC ONE Corp,Columbus,Ohio
12/06/93	06/06/94	567.30	Merrill Lynch & Co Inc	Merrill Lynch & Co Inc
12/06/93	08/24/94	1848.30	Dreyfus Corp	Mellon Bank Corp,Pittsburgh,PA
01/28/94	09/01/94	2162.00	Continental Bank Corp NA	BankAmerica Corp
03/18/94	09/30/94	1100.00	First Nationwide Bank,CA	First Madison Bank,FSB
07/01/94	01/24/95	790.075	Metropolitan Financial Corp	First Bank Sys,Minneapolis,MN
07/06/94	01/13/95	533.06	Anchor Bancorp Inc,New York,NY	Dime Bancorp Inc
08/01/94	02/28/95	1348.15	Southern Natl,Winston-Salem,NC	BB&T Financial Corp
08/18/94	03/01/95	585.50	Worthen Banking,Little Rock,AR	Boatmen's Bancshares,St Louis
09/12/94	01/03/95	512.169	Gencare Health Systems	United HealthCare Corp
09/15/94	10/31/94	550.78	American Income Holdings	Torchmark Corp
10/05/94	12/16/94	669.81	Kidder Peabody & Co	PaineWebber Group Inc
11/08/94	02/01/95	500.00	Barclays Business Credit Inc	Shawmut National Corp
11/28/94	01/31/95	1170.00	Franklin Life Insurance Co	American General Corp
12/06/94	05/10/95	1110.00	Continental Corp	CNA Financial Corp(Loews Corp)
12/12/94	04/03/95	531.50	Delaware Management Holdings	Lincoln National Corp
12/12/94	04/03/95	1686.52	American Financial Corp	American Premier Underwriters
12/23/94	05/02/95	2610.00	ITT Commercial Fin(ITT Fin)	Deutsche Bank N Amer(Deutsche)

12/27/94	04/03/95	1800.00	ITT-Equip Fin,Small Bus Fin	General Electric Capital Corp
01/03/95	06/01/95	515.717	Coral Gables Fedcorp Inc	First Union Natl Bk of Florida
02/21/95	11/30/95	3865.256	Shawmut National Corp	Fleet Financial Group Inc,MA
03/08/95	10/06/95	504.00	Chemical Bank New Jersey NA	PNC Bank NA,Pittsburgh,PA
04/03/95	04/03/95	1030.00	ITT Consumer Finl-Home Equity	Transamerica Financial
04/18/95	12/29/95	648.00	First Union Corp,Charlotte,NC	First Union Corp,Charlotte,NC
05/08/95	12/27/95	1476.069	West One Bancorp,Boise,Idaho	US Bancorp,Portland,Oregon
05/15/95	09/22/95	670.00	Home Savings of America-NY	GreenPoint Svgs Bk,Flushing
05/30/95	11/01/95	569.627	FirstFed Michigan Corp	Charter One Finl,Cleveland,OH
06/19/95	01/02/96	5438.174	First Fidelity Bancorp,NJ	First Union Corp,Charlotte,NC
07/10/95	01/02/96	2871.74	Midlantic Corp	PNC Bank Corp,Pittsburgh,PA
07/12/95	12/01/95	5415.302	First Chicago Corp,Illinois	NBD Bancorp,Detroit,Michigan
07/19/95	01/02/96	695.476	Premier Bancorp,Baton Rouge,LA	BANC ONE Corp,Columbus,Ohio
08/07/95	02/16/96	710.511	FirsTier Financial Inc	First Bank Sys,Minneapolis,MN
08/10/95	10/06/95	575.00	Alexander Hamilton Life Ins	Jefferson-Pilot Corp
08/25/95	01/31/96	1179.577	Fourth Financial Corp	Boatmen's Bancshares,St Louis
08/25/95	01/02/96	2349.169	GEICO Corp(Berkshire Hathaway)	Berkshire Hathaway Inc
08/28/95	05/03/96	2098.111	Integra Financial Corp	National City,Cleveland,Ohio
08/28/95	03/31/96	10439.78	Chase Manhattan Corp	Chemical Banking Corp,New York
09/05/95	01/09/96	1619.303	Bank South Corp,Atlanta,GA	NationsBank Corp,Charlotte,NC
09/11/95	03/01/96	1143.345	Summit Bancorporation	UJB Financial Corp
09/22/95	03/01/96	508.758	Brooklyn Bancorp Inc	Republic New York Corp,NY,NY
09/28/95	04/01/96	804.52	Bank of California	Union Bank,San Francisco,CA
10/10/95	04/09/96	3427.151	Meridian Bancorp Inc	CoreStates Financial Corp,PA
10/18/95	04/01/96	10929.90	First Interstate Bancorp,CA	Wells Fargo Capital C
10/23/95	03/01/96	652.722	First National Bancorp,Georgia	Regions Financial Corp
11/14/95	12/10/96	686.00	Bank of New York,New York,NY	Bank of New York,New York,NY
11/29/95	04/01/96	4000.00	Aetna Life & Casualty-Ppty	Travelers Group Inc
11/30/95	04/29/96	655.00	First NH Banks,Manchester,NH	Citizens Financial Group,RI
12/12/95	07/29/96	2058.94	BayBanks,Boston,Massachusetts	Bank of Boston Corp,Boston,MA
12/19/95	05/03/96	3260.00	National Westminster Bancorp	Fleet Financial Group Inc,MA
12/26/95	04/03/96	960.00	Life Insurance Co of Virginia	General Electric Capital Corp
01/23/96	04/16/96	551.25	BANC ONE Corp,Columbus,Ohio	BANC ONE Corp,Columbus,Ohio
03/08/96	10/07/96	504.492	Leader Financial,Memphis,TN	Union Planters Corp,Memphis,TN
03/11/96	08/02/96	838.83	Life Partners Group Inc	Conseco Inc
04/29/96	03/27/97	1171.075	Paul Revere Corp(Textron Inc)	Provident Cos
06/12/96	07/01/96	901.00	USL Capital Corp-Vehicle Fleet	Associates First Capital Corp

06/17/96	06/17/96	3975.00	Bank of New York-AFL-CIO Union	Household International Inc
06/24/96	10/31/96	1175.00	Van Kampen/American Capital	Morgan Stanley Group Inc
06/25/96	11/01/96	805.75	Heine Securities Corp	Franklin Templeton Investments
06/28/96	10/02/96	904.55	National Re Corp	General Re Corp
06/28/96	12/23/96	1891.00	American Svgs Bk FA,Irvine,CA	Washington Mutual,Seattle,WA
07/23/96	09/16/96	500.00	Allstate Reinsurance(Allstate)	SCOR US Corp(SCOR SA)
07/29/96	01/03/97	1287.77	Cal Fed Bancorp,Los Angeles,CA	First Nationwide Bank,CA
08/02/96	11/29/96	1799.24	First Colony Corp	General Electric Capital Corp
08/06/96	09/30/96	1700.00	USL Capital-Business Equipment	Mellon Bank NA,Pittsburgh,PA
08/22/96	09/12/96	575.00	USL Capital-RE Financing Op	Bankers Trust New York Corp
08/22/96	03/03/97	620.00	First Federal S&L,Rochester,NY	Marine Midland Bk,Buffalo,NY
08/26/96	03/04/97	715.45	Capitol American Financial	Conseco Inc
08/26/96	12/17/96	868.30	American Travellers Corp	Conseco Inc
08/30/96	01/06/97	9667.10	Boatmen's Bancshares,St Louis	NationsBank Corp,Charlotte,NC
09/16/96	12/31/96	793.77	Citizens Bancorp,Laurel,MD	Crestar Finl Corp,Richmond,VA
10/28/96	04/25/97	817.351	Mark Twain Bancshares,MO	Mercantile Bancorp,St Louis,MO
11/04/96	11/04/96	887.884	Mellon Bank-50 Amer Auto Assn	PNC Bank Corp,Pittsburgh,PA
11/04/96	07/02/97	977.094	United Carolina Bancshares	Southern Natl,Winston-Salem,NC
11/12/96	08/01/97	750.00	Allstate Corp	Allstate Corp
12/11/96	02/21/97	1227.383	Alexander & Alexander Services	Aon Corp
12/16/96	05/30/97	564.025	Pioneer Financial Services	Conseco Inc
12/17/96	07/16/97	816.867	Allmerica Property & Casualty	Allmerica Financial Corp
12/23/96	07/01/97	1187.05	Roosevelt Finl Group,Missouri	Mercantile Bancorp,St Louis,MO
12/24/96	04/16/97	665.089	Home Beneficial Corp	American General Corp
12/30/96	06/02/97	529.785	Liberty Bancorp Inc,Oklahoma	BANC ONE Corp,Columbus,Ohio
01/14/97	04/01/97	561.00	Oxford Resources Corp	Barnett Banks,Jacksonville,FL
01/20/97	06/27/97	7304.26	First USA Inc	BANC ONE Corp,Columbus,Ohio
01/21/97	07/08/97	1343.378	Dauphin Deposit Corp,PA	First Maryland Bancorp,MD
02/05/97	05/31/97	10573.01	Morgan Stanley Group Inc	Dean Witter Discover & Co
02/06/97	09/03/97	1092.00	Fidelity Acceptance Corp,MN	Wells Fargo Financial Inc
02/13/97	06/17/97	2374.357	USLIFE Corp	American General Corp
02/24/97	07/01/97	545.44	Security-Connecticut Corp	ReliaStar Financial Corp
02/24/97	05/13/97	875.00	Chubb Life Ins Co of America	Jefferson-Pilot Corp
02/27/97	08/01/97	916.09	Collective Bancorp Inc,NJ	Summit Bancorp,Princeton,NJ
03/06/97	07/02/97	6847.511	Great Western Finl Corp,CA	Washington Mutual,Seattle,WA
03/07/97	07/31/97	1600.00	Security Pacific Finl Services	Commercial Credit Corp
03/12/97	03/27/97	1800.00	Johnson & Higgins	Marsh & McLennan Cos Inc

03/14/97	10/01/97	1115.791	Security Capital,Milwaukee,WI	Marshall & Ilsley,Milwaukee,WI
03/20/97	08/01/97	8928.917	US Bancorp,Portland,Oregon	First Bank Sys,Minneapolis,MN
04/07/97	09/02/97	2077.351	Alex Brown Inc	Bankers Trust New York Corp
05/05/97	09/30/97	1131.17	First Michigan Bank Corp,MI	Huntington Bancshares Inc,OH
05/15/97	09/02/97	600.00	Dillon Read & Co(UBS AG)	SBC Warburg(Swiss Bank Corp)
05/15/97	10/29/97	1074.721	First Finl,Stevens Point,WI	Associated Banc,Green Bay,WI
05/21/97	10/03/97	634.109	RCSB Finl Inc,Rochester,NY	Charter One Finl,Cleveland,OH
05/21/97	06/23/97	3960.00	Transamerica-Consumer Finance	Household International Inc
06/09/97	10/01/97	3127.137	American States Financial Corp	SafeCo Corp
06/10/97	11/03/97	544.53	Jefferson Bankshares Inc,VA	Wachovia Corp,Winston-Salem,NC
06/23/97	10/17/97	517.086	Integon Corp	General Motors Acceptance Corp
06/24/97	12/16/97	2303.44	Central Fidelity Banks Inc,VA	Wachovia Corp,Winston-Salem,NC
06/30/97	11/04/97	1081.10	Colonial Penn P&C Group	General Electric Capital Svcs
06/30/97	10/01/97	1200.00	Montgomery Securities,CA	NationsBank Corp,Charlotte,NC
07/21/97	12/01/97	3319.83	Signet Bkg Corp,Richmond,VA	First Union Corp,Charlotte,NC
07/28/97	01/02/98	1400.00	CIGNA-Indiv Life Ins & Annuity	Lincoln National Corp
07/30/97	01/15/98	900.00	American Century Cos	JP Morgan & Co Inc
08/29/97	01/09/98	14821.719	Barnett Banks,Jacksonville,FL	NationsBank Corp,Charlotte,NC
09/12/97	02/25/98	1215.031	Western National Corp	American General Corp
09/15/97	02/06/98	663.498	Great Financial Corp,Kentucky	Star Banc Corp,Cincinnati,OH
09/16/97	02/02/98	1525.489	Quick & Reilly Group Inc	Fleet Financial Group Inc,MA
09/18/97	10/16/97	759.00	Whirlpool Finl-Inventory Fin	Transamerica Distn Fin Corp
09/24/97	11/28/97	8852.113	Salomon Inc	Travelers Group Inc
10/06/97	02/17/98	902.715	Coast Savings Financial Inc,CA	HF Ahmanson & Co,Irwindale,CA
10/07/97	03/30/98	822.08	New York Bancorp,Douglaston,NY	North Fork Bancorp,Melville,NY
10/15/97	04/17/98	577.352	Pinnacle Financial Svcs Inc,MI	CNB Bancshares Inc,IN
10/20/97	06/12/98	3169.472	First Commerce,New Orleans,LA	BANC ONE Corp,Columbus,Ohio
10/27/97	04/10/98	704.883	CFX Corp,Keene,New Hampshire	Peoples Heritage Finl Group,ME
10/27/97	02/23/98	1235.00	ADVANTA Corp-Credit Card	Fleet Financial Group Inc,MA
10/28/97	04/01/98	892.971	ONBANCorp Inc,Syracuse,NY	First Empire State Corp,NY
10/29/97	02/17/98	599.28	CapMAC Holdings Inc	MBIA Inc
11/05/97	12/01/97	850.234	Oppenheimer Capital LP	PIMCO Advisors LP
11/18/97	04/28/98	17122.234	CoreStates Financial Corp,PA	First Union Corp,Charlotte,NC
12/01/97	03/31/98	7052.65	First of Amer Bk,Kalamazoo,MI	National City,Cleveland,Ohio
12/08/97	05/01/98	2647.498	Deposit Guaranty,Jackson,MS	First American Corp,Tennessee
12/15/97	05/01/98	767.823	Piper Jaffray Cos	US Bancorp,Minneapolis,MN
12/18/97	04/02/98	4571.00	AT&T Universal Card Services	Citicorp

01/05/98	06/19/98	State Savings Co,Columbus,OH	897.438	Fifth Third Bancorp,Cincinnati
01/09/98	03/30/98	Fort Wayne Natl Corp,Indiana	767.63	National City,Cleveland,Ohio
01/14/98	06/26/98	CitFed Bancorp Inc,Dayton,OH	691.644	Fifth Third Bancorp,Cincinnati
01/19/98	04/24/98	USF&G Corp	3782.188	St Paul Cos Inc
01/28/98	07/31/98	First Commercial Corp,Arkansas	2489.448	Regions Financial Corp
02/02/98	07/01/98	Firstbank of IL,Springfield,IL	669.217	Mercantile Bancorp,St Louis,MO
02/05/98	09/11/98	Golden State Bancorp Inc,CA	1354.00	First Nationwide Holdings Inc
02/23/98	06/30/98	Cowen & Co	540.00	Societe Generale Securities
02/23/98	07/01/98	Magna Group Inc,St. Louis,MO	2151.031	Union Planters Corp,Memphis,TN
02/23/98	06/30/98	Money Store Inc	2215.237	First Union Corp,Charlotte,NC
03/17/98	10/01/98	HF Ahmanson & Co,Irwindale,CA	14724.958	Washington Mutual,Seattle,WA
03/26/98	10/01/98	Sumitomo Bank of California	544.313	Zions Bancorp,Utah
04/03/98	10/01/98	Long Island Bancorp,NY	1731.895	Astoria Finl,Lake Success,NY
04/06/98	10/08/98	Citicorp	72558.18	Travelers Group Inc
04/07/98	06/30/98	Green Tree Financial Corp	7358.767	Conseco Inc
04/07/98	06/30/98	Beneficial Corp	8703.812	Household International Inc
04/10/98	08/21/98	Trans Finl,Bowling Green,KY	701.445	Star Banc Corp,Cincinnati,OH
04/13/98	10/02/98	First Chicago NBD Corp	29616.038	BANC ONE Corp,Columbus,Ohio
04/13/98	09/30/98	BankAmerica Corp	61633.403	NationsBank Corp,Charlotte,NC
04/18/98	10/16/98	SPS Transaction Svcs-Assets	896.00	Associates First Capital Corp
04/22/98	10/01/98	First Evergreen Corp,IL	565.843	Old Kent Finl Corp,Michigan
05/18/98	11/13/98	Allied Group Inc	1576.098	Nationwide Mutual Insurance Co
05/20/98	10/01/98	Aetna Inc-Domestic Individual	1000.00	Lincoln National Corp
05/21/98	10/02/98	Mid Am Inc,Bowling Green,Ohio	620.243	Citizens Bancshares Inc,OH
05/26/98	02/17/99	T R Financial Corp,NY	1077.991	Roslyn Bancorp Inc,Roslyn,NY
05/28/98	11/02/98	BancWest Corp,San Francisco,CA	951.825	First Hawaiian Inc,Honolulu,HI
05/29/98	09/01/98	Robertson Stephens & Co	800.00	BankBoston Corp,Boston,MA
06/08/98	11/02/98	Wells Fargo Capital C	34352.635	Norwest Corp,Minneapolis,MN
06/12/98	10/26/98	McDonald & Co Investments Inc	577.375	KeyCorp,Cleveland,Ohio
06/15/98	11/30/98	ALBANK Financial Corp,NY	827.84	Charter One Finl,Cleveland,OH
06/19/98	12/21/98	General Re Corp	22337.855	Berkshire Hathaway Inc
07/01/98	11/20/98	Firstar Corp,Milwaukee,WI	7217.594	Star Banc Corp,Cincinnati,OH
07/20/98	12/31/98	Crestar Finl Corp,Richmond,VA	9603.107	SunTrust Banks Inc,Atlanta,GA
07/31/98	10/29/98	Kemper Reinsurance Co	500.00	General Electric Capital Svcs
08/10/98	01/01/99	Frank Russell Co(Northwestern)	905.00	Northwestern Mutual Life Ins
08/11/98	01/06/99	Avco Financial Svcs(Textron)	3900.00	Associates First Capital Corp
08/20/98	01/01/99	SunAmerica Inc	18116.984	American International Group

08/26/98	03/08/98	538.50	MainStreet Financial Corp	BB&T Corp,Winston-Salem,NC
09/03/98	09/03/98	560.00	Chevy Chase Bank FSB-Credit	First USA Inc(BANC ONE Corp)
10/12/98	12/31/98	800.00	Colonial Pacific Leasing	General Electric Capital Corp
11/20/98	02/01/99	715.00	Sanwa Business Credit	Fleet Financial Group Inc,MA
11/23/98	06/30/99	4866.474	Provident Cos	UNUM Corp
12/10/98	08/06/99	1000.00	Prudential HealthCare-HMO,POS	Aetna Inc
12/24/98	03/29/99	638.00	PNC Bank-Visa & MasterCard	MBNA Corp
02/01/99	05/10/99	1465.00	Guardian Royal Exchange US	Liberty Mutual Insurance Co
02/08/99	07/20/99	1044.88	Executive Risk Inc	Chubb Corp
03/14/99	10/01/99	15925.201	BankBoston Corp,Boston,MA	Fleet Financial Group Inc,MA
04/26/99	10/01/99	1172.166	EVEREN Capital Corp	First Union Corp,Charlotte,NC
04/30/99	09/20/99	10640.485	Mercantile Bancorp,St Louis,MO	Firstar Corp,Milwaukee,WI
05/13/99	03/05/01	500.00	Lincoln National Corp	Lincoln National Corp
05/17/99	10/01/99	954.567	St Paul Bancorp,Chicago,IL	Charter One Finl,Cleveland,OH
05/17/99	10/29/99	3961.00	LTCB-US Loan Assets Portfolio	General Electric Capital Corp
05/19/99	11/16/99	957.965	Western Bancorp,California	US Bancorp,Minneapolis,MN
05/31/99	10/01/99	6328.176	First American Corp,Tennessee	AmSouth Bancorp,Alabama
06/01/99	01/13/00	1940.477	TeleBanc Financial Corp,VA	E*Trade Group Inc
06/02/99	05/10/00	779.003	Banknorth Group Inc,VT	Peoples Heritage Finl Group,ME
06/07/99	07/22/99	1800.00	BNY Financial Corp	General Motors Acceptance Corp
06/09/99	10/01/99	1115.50	CNA Financial-Personal Ins Op	Allstate Corp
06/16/99	10/29/99	2120.738	CNB Bancshares Inc,IN	Fifth Third Bancorp,Cincinnati
06/18/99	01/11/00	1402.571	UST Corp,Boston,MA	Citizens Financial Group,RI
07/08/99	11/02/99	914.448	American Heritage Life Invt	Allstate Corp
07/09/99	09/24/99	531.00	Hull Group Inc	Goldman Sachs Group Inc
07/09/99	10/01/99	600.00	St Paul Cos-Personal Ins Cos	Metlife Auto & Home
07/20/99	12/02/99	1100.00	First Data Investor Services	PNC Bank Corp,Pittsburgh,PA
08/16/99	03/01/00	593.685	JSB Financial Inc,Lynbrook,NY	North Fork Bancorp,Melville,NY
08/20/99	02/18/00	608.31	Triangle Bancorp,Raleigh,NC	Centura Bank Inc,NC
08/25/99	01/10/00	1200.00	General Amer Life Insurance	Metropolitan Life Insurance Co
09/28/99	12/10/99	1368.036	Hambrecht & Quist Group Inc	Chase Manhattan Corp,NY
10/04/99	12/01/99	560.00	Heller Finl-Coml Svcs	CIT Group Holdings Inc
10/19/99	03/07/00	814.006	Foremost Corp of America	Farmers Insurance Group
12/06/99	05/10/00	725.00	Underwriters RE Group Inc	Swiss Re Life & Health
12/08/99	12/20/99	765.00	Fremont Financial Corp	Finova Group Inc
12/21/99	07/17/00	1049.598	Natl Bancorp of Alaska Inc	Wells Fargo & Co,California
01/13/00	06/01/00	2612.997	US Trust Corp,New York,NY	Charles Schwab Corp

02/07/00	07/07/00	1190.488	One Valley Bancorp Inc,WV	BB&T Corp,Winston-Salem,NC
02/24/00	06/12/00	555.705	eCredit.com	Internet Capital Group Inc
02/28/00	05/31/00	580.00	Reliance Group-Reliance Surety	Travelers Property Casualty
03/07/00	06/01/00	562.134	Duff & Phelps Credit Rating Co	Fitch IBCA(FIMALAC SA)
03/20/00	07/05/00	1961.366	CCB Financial Corp,Durham,NC	National Commerce Bancorp
03/21/00	04/20/00	2449.297	Travelers Property Casualty	Citigroup Inc
03/27/00	06/27/00	1324.605	Hartford Life(ITT Hartford)	Hartford Fin Svcs Group Inc
04/10/00	10/26/00	2810.488	First Security Corp,Utah	Wells Fargo & Co,California
04/28/00	06/12/00	620.00	JC Bradford & Co	PaineWebber Group Inc
05/17/00	10/09/00	1028.347	Keystone Finl,Harrisburg,PA	M&T Bank Corp,Buffalo,New York
05/23/00	08/02/00	583.00	Fidelity Leasing Inc	Euro Amer Bank,Uniondale,NY
06/05/00	07/12/00	913.75	Herzog Heine Geduld	Merrill Lynch & Co Inc
06/15/00	07/31/00	770.00	USA Group Inc	Student Loan Marketing Assn
06/20/00	08/02/00	584.079	Justin Industries Inc	Berkshire Hathaway Inc
06/20/00	10/02/00	4000.00	Sanford C Bernstein & Co Inc	Alliance Capital Mgmt Hldg LP
06/28/00	01/04/01	950.00	Marsico Capital Management	Bank of America,San Francisco
08/15/00	09/30/00	1386.05	First Union Corp-Consumer & Co	MBNA Corp
08/18/00	11/22/00	1430.528	HSB Group Inc	American International Group
08/21/00	02/12/01	1418.613	Bank United Corp,Houston,Texas	Washington Mutual,Seattle,WA
08/30/00	11/03/00	13528.94	Donaldson Lufkin & Jenrette	Credit Suisse First Boston
09/06/00	11/30/00	30957.499	Associates First Capital Corp	Citigroup Inc
09/11/00	11/02/00	6324.50	Spear Leeds & Kellogg	Goldman Sachs Group Inc
09/13/00	12/31/00	33554.579	JP Morgan & Co Inc	Chase Manhattan Corp,NY
10/02/00	02/01/01	605.00	PNC Financial Svc Group Inc	Washington Mutual,Seattle,WA
10/02/00	03/01/01	7011.635	Summit Bancorp,Princeton,NJ	FleetBoston Financial Corp,MA
10/04/00	02/27/01	21084.873	US Bancorp,Minneapolis,MN	Firstar Corp,Milwaukee,WI
10/25/00	04/10/01	815.592	Fiduciary Trust Co Intl	Franklin Templeton Investments
11/01/00	01/30/01	1386.819	Imperial Bancorp,Inglewood,CA	Comerica Inc,Detroit,Michigan
11/20/00	04/02/01	4954.174	Old Kent Finl Corp,Michigan	Fifth Third Bancorp,Cincinnati
12/18/00	03/30/01	774.367	Morgan Keegan Inc	Regions Financial Corp
01/24/01	08/09/01	1009.328	F&M National,Winchester,VA	BB&T Corp,Winston-Salem,NC
01/25/01	04/03/01	1120.00	Fortis Financial Group	Hartford Fin Svcs Group Inc
02/12/01	07/18/01	1950.00	Euro Amer Bank,Uniondale,NY	Citigroup Inc
03/27/01	07/31/01	782.045	Richmond County Financial Corp	New York Community Bancorp Inc
03/30/01	08/01/01	2118.663	Franchise Finance Corp of Amer	General Electric Capital Corp
04/02/01	06/01/01	600.00	Fleet Mortgage Corp	Washington Mutual,Seattle,WA
04/03/01	08/30/01	23398.157	American General Corp	American International Group

Date	Amount	Company	Date	Description
04/09/01	1960.00	Wachovia Corp-Credit Card Loan	07/27/01	BANK ONE Corp,Columbus,Ohio
04/16/01	13132.151	Wachovia Corp,Winston-Salem,NC	09/04/01	First Union Corp,Charlotte,NC
05/07/01	2061.502	NOVA Corp	07/24/01	US Bancorp,Minneapolis,MN
05/30/01	1380.00	Private Capital Management LP	08/01/01	Legg Mason Inc
06/05/01	1010.00	Liberty Financial Cos-Asset	11/01/01	FleetBoston Financial Corp,MA
06/06/01	536.005	Liberty Financial Cos Inc	12/13/01	Liberty Mutual Insurance Co
06/25/01	5203.961	Dime Bancorp Inc,New York,NY	01/07/02	Washington Mutual,Seattle,WA
07/10/01	2100.00	Mellon Fin-Retail Banking Bus	12/01/01	Citizens Financial Group,RI
07/30/01	5321.532	Heller Financial Inc	10/25/01	General Electric Capital Corp
09/26/01	705.00	Huntington Bancshares Inc-FL	02/15/02	SunTrust Banks Inc,Atlanta,GA
10/03/01	603.00	Janus Capital Corp	01/02/03	Investment management services
10/08/01	650.00	Morgan Stanley-745 Seventh Ave	10/30/01	Own,op office building
10/18/01	1346.85	RightCHOICE Managed Care Inc	01/31/02	Own,operate HMOs,PPOs
10/24/01	500.00	Arch Capital Group Ltd	11/20/01	Reinsurance company
11/01/01	835.00	Fruit of the Loom Inc	04/30/02	Mnfr underwear and active wear
12/11/01	2125.00	HomeSide International Inc	03/01/02	Washington Mutual,Seattle,WA
12/14/02	5541.921	Security Capital Group Inc	05/14/02	General Electric Capital Corp
12/19/01	12213.00	Travelers Property Casualty	08/20/02	Pvd ppty,casualty ins svcs
01/09/02	580.00	Bear Stearns Cos Inc	01/08/03	Investment bank holding co
01/16/02	2870.00	Providian Master Trust	02/05/02	Special purpose finance sub
01/24/02	1200.00	DaimlerChrysler Cap-Portfolio	04/11/02	Pvd financing services
02/27/02	837.031	American Commercial Lines LLC	05/29/02	Pvd marine transp svcs
04/08/02	1360.80	Datek Online Holdings Corp	09/09/02	Pvd online brokerage svcs
04/29/02	3980.793	Trigon Healthcare Inc	07/31/02	Own,op HMO
05/21/02	5882.76	Golden State Bancorp Inc,CA	11/07/02	Savings and loan; holding co
06/06/02	531.00	Monogram Credit Services LLC	06/06/02	Pvd credit card services
06/10/02	542.85	Island ECN Inc	09/23/02	Pvd online trading svcs
06/17/02	517.00	AmeriChoice Corp	09/23/02	Own,op HMO
06/17/02	507.508	Mississippi Valley Bancshares	10/01/02	Commercial bank holding co
08/13/02	725.00	State Street Bank & Trust Co-	12/31/02	Pvd corp trust svcs
08/22/02	746.374	American Financial Holdings	02/14/03	Savings and loan holding co
08/28/02	1300.00	SR Investment Inc(National)	10/01/02	Mortgage bank
09/26/02	2879.956	Allfirst Financial Inc,MD	04/01/03	Commercial bank
11/15/02	753.973	FBR Asset Investment Corp VA	03/31/03	Real estate investment trust
12/20/02	1150.00	American Skandia Inc	05/01/03	Pvd insurance,financial svcs

Appendix 1, Table 2

Financial Service Sector Acquistions Cross-border US, 1990-2001 Exceeding $500 million

Date Announced	Date Effective	Value of Transaction ($mil)	Target Name	Target Nation	Acquirer Name
04/03/89	11/15/89	1518.986	Koito Manufacturing Co Ltd	Japan	Boone Co
11/15/93	03/15/94	1072.531	Tiphook PLC-Core Container Bus	United Kingdom	TransAmerica Corp
12/27/94	05/04/95	1400.00	Island Finance(ITT Corp)	Puerto Rico	Norwest Corp,Minneapolis,MN
07/21/95	10/16/95	821.177	Smith New Court PLC	United Kingdom	Merrill Lynch & Co Inc
10/12/95	12/13/95	1515.085	Sovac(Eurafrance)	France	General Electric Capital Corp
09/18/97	05/01/98	664.52	Whirlpool Finl-Consumer	Supranational	Transamerica Distn Fin Corp
09/22/97	01/09/98	815.182	Woodchester Investments PLC	Ireland-Rep	General Electric Capital Corp
11/19/97	01/16/98	5256.008	Mercury Asset Management Group	United Kingdom	Merrill Lynch & Co Inc
02/18/98	04/01/98	593.871	Toho Mutual-New Bus Op & Sales	United Kingdom	GE Financial Assurance
03/19/98	08/21/98	994.76	DIC Finance(Daiei Inc)	Japan	Associates First Capital Corp
05/29/98	08/28/98	503.93	Nikko Securities Co Ltd	Japan	Salomon Smith Barney Holdings
05/29/98	08/28/98	1079.85	Nikko Securities Co Ltd	Japan	Salomon Smith Barney Holdings
06/10/98	10/06/98	675.00	Banco de Investimentos Garanti	Brazil	CS First Boston
06/22/98	08/27/98	806.298	Midland Walwyn Inc	Canada	Merrill Lynch & Co Inc
08/25/98	12/01/98	2129.629	Sedgwick Group PLC	United Kingdom	Marsh & McLennan Cos Inc
01/26/99	03/05/99	6565.60	Japan Leasing Corp	Japan	General Electric Capital Corp
03/08/99	11/15/99	2690.241	Newcourt Credit Group Inc	Canada	CIT Group Holdings Inc
03/23/99	08/31/99	655.318	RBS Trust Bank Ltd(RBSTB)	United Kingdom	Bank of New York,New York,NY
06/18/99	08/31/99	1303.658	BTFund Mgmt,BT Invest Svcs	Australia	Principal Financial Group Inc
08/16/99	03/24/00	778.444	Terra Nova(Bermuda)Holdings	Bermuda	Markel Corp
12/06/99	01/17/00	570.00	Seguros Monterrey Aetna	Mexico	New York Life Insurance Co
12/20/99	03/01/00	2323.68	Toho Mutual Life	Japan	General Electric Capital Corp
01/18/00	05/01/00	2209.95	Schroders-Worldwide Investment	United Kingdom	Salomon Smith Barney Holdings
03/30/00	05/31/00	1643.262	Gartmore Investment Management	United Kingdom	Nationwide Mutual Insurance Co
04/11/00	08/01/00	7697.628	Robert Fleming Holdings Ltd	United Kingdom	Chase Manhattan Corp,NY
05/15/00	06/06/00	610.918	Bank Handlowy SA	Poland	Citigroup Inc
10/20/00	04/03/01	1270.136	Kyoei Life Insurance Co	Japan	Prudential Insurance Co
02/23/01	04/20/01	517.44	Chiyoda Mutual Life Insurance	Japan	American International Group
05/17/01	08/06/01	12821.001	Banacci	Mexico	Citigroup Inc
06/22/01	04/08/02	522.44	National Mutual Life Assurance	United Kingdom	General Electric Capital Corp
05/27/02	06/20/02	962.00	Aseguradora Hidalgo SA	Mexico	Metlife
11/04/02	01/31/03	1500.09	Deutsche Bank-Securities Div	Germany	State Street Corp,Boston,MA
12/11/02	03/05/03	1600.00	Grupo Financiero Santander	Mexico	Bank of America Corp

Appendix 1, Table 3

Financial Service Sector Acquistions Within Europe, 1990-2002 Exceeding $500 million

Date Announced	Date Effective	Value of Transaction ($mil)	Target Name	Target Nation	Acquirer Name	Acquirer Nation
08/18/86	08/18/86	520.90	Fondiaria Assicurazioni SpA	Italy	Iniziativa META(Montedison)	France
10/19/86	12/31/88	2107.375	Abbey Life Group PLC(ITT Corp)	United Kingdom	Lloyds Bank PLC	United Kingdom
10/31/86	01/30/87	980.00	Bank fur Gemeinwirtschaft AG	Germany	Aachener und Muenchener	Germany
12/03/86	12/03/86	603.00	Banca d'America e d'Italia	Italy	Deutsche Bank AG	Germany
07/16/87	09/30/87	855.683	Mercantile House Holdings PLC	United Kingdom	British & Commonwealth Hldgs	United Kingdom
09/11/87	12/31/87	749.918	Equity & Law Life Assurance	United Kingdom	Cie du Midi UK(Cie du Midi)	United Kingdom
10/02/87	12/31/87	1261.568	Hill Samuel Group PLC	United Kingdom	TSB Group PLC	United Kingdom
01/22/88	09/30/88	3250.00	Banco de Vizcaya	Spain	Banco de Bilbao	Spain
11/25/88	12/30/88	532.62	Banco Urquijo Union SA	Spain	Grupo March	Spain
01/11/89	12/31/89	569.52	Banque Dumenil Leble SA	France	CERUS SA	France
02/09/89	10/04/89	911.165	Postbank NV(Netherlands)	Netherlands	Nederlandsche Middenstandsbank	Netherlands
03/15/89	12/29/89	955.50	CREDIOP	Italy	Istituto Bancario San Paolo di	Italy
05/24/89	01/31/90	523.26	Banco di Santo Spirito SpA	Italy	Cassa di Risparmio di Roma	Italy
07/27/89	12/31/89	1989.689	Colonia Versicherung AG	Germany	Cie Financiere Groupe Victoire	France
10/02/89	10/03/89	1019.85	Via-Rhin & Moselle	France	Allianz Versicherungs-AG	Germany
10/26/89	10/30/89	830.44	Thomson-CSF Finance SA	France	Credit Lyonnais SA(France)	France
11/27/89	03/30/90	1482.475	Morgan Grenfell Group PLC	United Kingdom	Deutsche Bank AG	Germany
12/01/89	12/31/89	2736.00	Fondiaria Assicurazioni SpA	Italy	GAIC International SA	Luxembourg
12/07/89	06/06/90	881.44	Nordbanken(Sweden)	Sweden	Post-Och Kreditbanken PKbanken	Sweden
12/18/89	03/29/90	2445.12	Cie Financiere Groupe Victoire	France	UAP	France
12/28/89	03/02/90	1000.835	TDB American Express	Switzerland	Cie Banque & d'Investissements	Switzerland
02/12/90	02/12/90	579.006	Girobank-Leasing Operations	United Kingdom	Norwich Union Life Ins Society	United Kingdom
03/26/90	08/29/90	2414.132	ABN NV	Netherlands	AMRO	Netherlands
04/02/90	12/14/90	2269.83	Groupe Assurance Generale-Ops	Belgium	AMEV NV-Operations	Netherlands
05/15/90	09/07/90	991.87	Banque Arabe et Internationale	France	BNP(France)	France
06/06/90	01/25/91	522.92	Uni Forsikring	Norway	Storebrand ASA	Norway
06/06/90	06/06/90	1229.34	Banco Central SA	Spain	UAP	France
09/13/90	09/27/90	554.515	Irish Life Assurance PLC	Ireland-Rep	Irish Life PLC	Ireland-Rep
09/24/90	09/28/90	804.54	Gota AB(Proventus AB)	Sweden	Foersaekringsbolaget SPP	Sweden
09/29/90	09/29/90	568.82	Statsanstalten Livsforsikring	Denmark	Baltica Holding A/S	Denmark
10/22/90	06/25/91	2083.23	Banca di Roma SpA (IRI)	Italy	SIPAB(Cassa di Risparmio)	Italy
10/22/90	02/28/91	2425.50	Banco di Santo Spirito SpA	Italy	Cassa di Risparmio di Roma	Italy
11/05/90	03/04/91	7457.50	NMB Postbank Groep NV	Netherlands	Nationale-Nederlanden NV	Netherlands
01/16/91	10/07/91	1201.428	Oesterreichische Laenderbank	Austria	Zentralsparkasse und Banken	Austria
05/03/91	09/07/91	1100.001	Banco de Credito Industrial	Spain	EXTEBANK(Spain)	Spain
05/10/91	12/31/91	555.544	La Union y El Fenix Espanol	Spain	Corporacion BV(Banco Espanol)	Netherlands

249

07/17/91	07/17/91	3291.705	Banca di Roma(SIPAB)	Italy	Cassa di Risparmio di Roma	Italy
10/01/91	10/01/91	1684.20	CREDIOP	Italy	Istituto Bancario San Paolo di	Italy
12/23/91	01/08/92	680.015	Aachener und Muenchener	Germany	AGF(France)	France
12/31/91	12/31/91	711.48	Statsanstalten	Denmark	Baltica Holding A/S	Denmark
01/22/92	12/31/91	888.352	Bank fur Gemeinwirtschaft AG	Germany	Credit Lyonnais SA(France)	France
01/31/92	01/31/92	726.579	Banco Vitalicio de Seguros	Spain	Central Hispano-Generali Grupo	Spain
03/17/92	11/13/92	5708.381	Midland Bank PLC	United Kingdom	HSBC Holdings PLC(HSBC)	United Kingdom
01/06/93	04/01/93	1101.096	Swiss Volksbank	Switzerland	CS Holding AG	Switzerland
05/26/93	07/08/99	7609.582	Credit Lyonnais SA(France)	France	Investors	France
05/28/93	09/30/93	1072.002	ASLK-CGER Insurance,ASLK-CGER	Belgium	Fortis International NV	Netherlands
10/08/93	12/31/93	3035.179	Vinci BV(UAP/France)	Netherlands	UAP	France
11/12/93	01/04/94	596.997	Bank Leu Ltd(CS Holding AG)	Switzerland	CS Holding AG	Switzerland
01/28/94	08/01/94	2287.107	Banesto	Spain	Banco de Santander SA	Spain
02/04/94	02/04/94	1304.844	CIBC Mortgages PLC	United Kingdom	Abbey National PLC	United Kingdom
04/21/94	08/01/95	2871.90	Cheltenham & Gloucester Bldg	United Kingdom	Lloyds Bank PLC	United Kingdom
06/10/94	10/06/94	2097.753	Cie Financiere Groupe Victoire	France	Commercial Union PLC	United Kingdom
08/22/94	12/01/94	646.60	Bankgesellschaft Berlin AG	Germany	NORD/LB	Germany
09/20/94	11/01/94	548.392	New Bank of Argovie	Switzerland	CS Holding AG	Switzerland
09/30/94	02/28/95	1786.45	Elvia Schweizerische	Switzerland	Riunione Adriatica di Securita	Italy
09/30/94	01/19/95	2717.053	Vereinte/Magdeberger	Germany	Allianz AG Holding	Germany
10/26/94	02/03/95	2354.352	Gruppo Bancario Credito Romagn	Italy	Credito Italiano SpA	Italy
02/09/95	04/01/95	827.098	KOP	Finland	Unitas Oy	Finland
03/03/95	03/09/95	1074.15	Barings PLC-Assets	United Kingdom	Internationale Nederlanden	Netherlands
04/21/95	08/05/96	2151.225	Natl & Provincial Bldg Society	United Kingdom	Abbey National PLC	United Kingdom
04/27/95	12/22/95	731.085	Credit Lyonnais Bank Nederland	Netherlands	Generale de Banque SA	Belgium
05/02/95	07/03/95	3159.312	SG Warburg Grp PLC-Inv Bkg Arm	United Kingdom	Schweizerischer Bankverein	Switzerland
05/23/95	05/24/95	1012.32	Baltica Forsikring A/S	Denmark	Tryg Forsikring A/S	Denmark
05/23/95	08/31/95	1207.68	Danica(Baltica Holding A/S)	Denmark	Den Danske Bank AS	Denmark
06/26/95	08/23/95	1554.443	Kleinwort Benson Group PLC	United Kingdom	Dresdner Bank AG	Germany
07/21/95	08/31/95	840.249	Sun Life Hldgs(TransAtlantic)	United Kingdom	UAP	France
09/15/95	09/29/95	961.408	Schweizerische Lebensversicher	Switzerland	Union Bank of Switzerland	Switzerland
10/09/95	12/28/95	15315.612	Lloyds Bank PLC	United Kingdom	TSB Group PLC	United Kingdom
12/13/95	01/29/96	670.992	BFCE	France	Credit National	France
12/21/95	12/21/95	501.02	Scottish Equitable PLC	United Kingdom	Aegon NV	Netherlands
12/21/95	04/10/96	527.51	Indosuez UK Asset Management	United Kingdom	National Westminster Bank PLC	United Kingdom
02/19/96	11/27/96	3069.845	Credit Communal de Belgique SA	Belgium	Credit Local de France SA	France
03/14/96	03/22/96	539.414	Finansbanken ASA(Sparebanken)	Norway	Industri og Skipsbanken	Norway
03/22/96	12/31/96	1228.40	Clerical Med & Gen Life Assur	United Kingdom	Halifax Building Society	United Kingdom
03/25/96	08/29/97	904.74	Bristol & West Bldg Society	United Kingdom	Bank of Ireland	Ireland-Rep
04/15/96	04/19/96	504.562	Bracehold Ltd(Banque Paribas)	United Kingdom	Halifax Loans(Halifax Bldg)	United Kingdom
04/29/96	05/02/96	2289.30	Banque Indosuez(Cie de Suez)	France	Credit Agricole	France
05/03/96	07/19/96	3807.431	Royal Insurance Holdings PLC	United Kingdom	Sun Alliance Group PLC	United Kingdom

Date	Date	Value	Company	Country	Company	Country
08/08/96	11/15/96	1207.97	United Friendly Group PLC	United Kingdom	Refuge Group PLC	United Kingdom
08/26/96	09/24/96	897.604	Banco de Fomento e Exterior SA	Portugal	Banco Portugues de Investiment	Portugal
08/27/96	12/06/96	2721.075	Mercantile and General Reinsur	United Kingdom	Swiss Reinsurance Co	Switzerland
09/23/96	12/11/96	2588.865	Lloyds Abbey Life PLC	United Kingdom	Lloyds TSB Group PLC	United Kingdom
10/04/96	03/06/97	1436.00	MeesPierson NV(ABN-AMRO Hldg)	Netherlands	Fortis AG	Belgium
11/12/96	01/15/97	10605.412	UAP	France	Axa SA	France
12/12/96	02/17/97	3344.179	Stadshypotek	Sweden	Svenska Handelsbanken AB	Sweden
01/14/97	04/18/97	539.50	Societe Anonyme Francaise de	France	Swiss Reinsurance Co	Switzerland
01/14/97	03/11/97	1537.111	Creditanstalt-Bankverein AG	Austria	Bank Austria AG	Austria
02/18/97	05/30/97	1348.091	Foreningsbanken	Sweden	Sparbanken Sverige AB	Sweden
03/05/97	03/20/97	691.254	GiroCredit Bank AG	Austria	Erste Oesterreichische	Austria
03/25/97	09/30/97	3918.706	Scottish Amicable Life	United Kingdom	Prudential PLC	United Kingdom
05/20/97	01/02/98	3919.50	Cassa di Risparmio delle Provi	Italy	Banco Ambrosiano Veneto SpA	Italy
07/01/97	11/10/97	769.77	Hamburgische Landesbank	Germany	Landesbank Schleswig-Holstein	Germany
07/02/97	08/09/97	1156.095	Axa Equity and Law Life,Axa	United Kingdom	Sun Life and Provincial	United Kingdom
07/03/97	01/28/98	4061.94	Hamburg Mannheimer Versicher	Germany	Victoria Holding AG	Germany
07/21/97	09/10/97	12133.604	Bayerische Hypotheken	Germany	Bayerische Vereinsbank AG	Germany
07/28/97	01/03/97	1218.38	Credito Bergamasco	Italy	Banca Popolare di Verona	Italy
08/11/97	12/15/97	9661.743	Winterthur Schweizerische	Switzerland	Credit Suisse Group	Switzerland
08/27/97	10/31/97	541.016	Creditanstalt-Bankverein AG	Austria	Bank Austria AG	Austria
09/04/97	09/10/97	560.00	Banco di Sicilia SpA	Italy	Mediocredito Centrale	Italy
10/02/97	12/12/97	2204.16	Trygg-Hansa AB	Sweden	Skandinaviska Enskilda Banken	Sweden
10/13/97	04/01/98	4292.00	Merita Oy	Finland	Nordbanken(Venantius/Sweden)	Sweden
10/13/97	09/07/98	18354.59	BAT Industries PLC-Financial	United Kingdom	Zurich Versicherungs GmbH	Switzerland
11/10/97	12/19/97	2101.20	Athena Assurances	France	AGF	France
11/11/97	12/19/97	4515.978	Banque Bruxelles Lambert SA	Belgium	ING Groep NV	Netherlands
11/14/97	11/14/97	584.782	CGER-Banque(ALSK-CGER Banque)	Belgium	Fortis International NV	Netherlands
11/14/97	01/12/98	585.621	ASLK-CGER Banque	Belgium	Fortis International NV	Netherlands
11/17/97	05/12/98	5118.034	AGF	France	Allianz AG	Germany
11/25/97	01/16/98	1897.721	Cetelem SA	France	Cie Financiere de Paribas SA	France
11/25/97	05/12/98	2447.63	Cie Bancaire SA	France	Cie Financiere de Paribas SA	France
12/08/97	06/29/98	23008.673	Schweizerischer Bankverein	Switzerland	Union Bank of Switzerland	Switzerland
12/17/97	12/19/97	673.69	GRS Holding Co Ltd	United Kingdom	Royal Bank of Scotland Group	United Kingdom
12/17/97	02/24/98	718.272	PPP Healthcare Group PLC	United Kingdom	Guardian Royal Exchange PLC	United Kingdom
12/19/97	02/27/98	501.00	Hambros PLC-Banking Group	United Kingdom	Societe Generale SA	France
12/22/97	07/20/98	736.56	GPA Vie(Athena Assurances)	France	Assicurazioni Generali SpA	Italy
12/22/97	07/21/98	758.026	Royal Nederland Verzekeringsgr	Netherlands	AGF(Allianz AG)	France
07/09/98	07/09/98	5075.062	Aachener und Muenchener	Germany	Assicurazioni Generali SpA	Italy
01/30/98	07/09/98	2215.992	ABB Verzekeringen NV	Belgium	Almanij NV	Belgium
01/30/98	06/04/98	5048.31	CERA	Belgium	Almanij NV	Belgium
02/11/98	06/18/98	744.306	Banco Totta e Acores SA	Portugal	Banco Pinto & Sotto Mayor SA	Portugal
02/19/98	04/06/98	3849.773	Banesto	Spain	Banco de Santander SA	Spain

251

02/25/98	06/02/98	11152.507	General Accident PLC	United Kingdom	Commercial Union PLC	United Kingdom
03/09/98	04/19/99	1228.50	Birmingham Midshires Bldg Scty	United Kingdom	Halifax PLC	United Kingdom
03/17/98	06/11/98	7654.953	Almanij-Banking and Insurance	Belgium	Kredietbank NV	Belgium
03/23/98	06/26/98	817.65	Landesbank Berlin	Germany	Bankgesellschaft Berlin AG	Germany
03/25/98	05/15/98	590.671	Natexis SA	France	Caisse Centrale Banques Popula	France
03/26/98	06/30/98	1278.182	Parfinance SA	France	Imetal SA(Parfinance)	France
04/14/98	08/01/98	1515.24	Banque Sofinco(Suez Lyonnaise)	France	Credit Agricole	France
04/15/98	06/17/98	2217.066	Cie Financiere de Credit(GAN)	France	Credit Mutuel SA	France
04/15/98	10/15/98	10959.00	Unicredito SpA	Italy	Credito Italiano SpA	Italy
04/27/98	11/03/98	9492.386	Istituto Mobiliare Italiano	Italy	Istituto Bancario San Paolo di	Italy
05/05/98	07/28/98	3137.838	Royale Belge SA	Belgium	AXA-UAP	France
05/18/98	06/29/98	12298.535	Generale de Banque SA	Belgium	Fortis AG	Belgium
06/11/98	07/31/98	747.46	Banca Popolare Friuladria	Italy	Banca Intesa SpA	Italy
06/11/98	01/31/99	1690.972	Cassa di Risparmio di Parma e	Italy	Banca Intesa SpA	Italy
06/11/98	11/02/98	2040.26	BG Bank	Denmark	Realkredit Danmark	Denmark
06/26/98	11/27/98	1290.30	Banca della Svizzera Italiana	Switzerland	Assicurazioni Generali SpA	Italy
06/29/98	12/11/98	521.44	Banco de Credito Local de SP	Spain	Dexia Banco Local SA	Spain
06/29/98	07/27/98	732.062	Generale de Banque SA	Belgium	Fortis AG	Belgium
07/01/98	07/02/98	2830.725	Centrale Gan(France)	France	Groupama SA(Groupe des)	France
07/06/98	07/28/98	912.857	Axa Belgium(Axa SA)	Belgium	Royale Belge SA	Belgium
07/08/98	02/11/99	593.812	Credit Lyonnais Belgium	Belgium	Deutsche Bank AG	Germany
08/06/98	12/28/99	540.80	Cassa di Risparmio di Trento e	Italy	Credito Italiano SpA	Italy
08/18/98	11/27/98	1203.72	London & Manchester Group PLC	United Kingdom	FP Business Holdings PLC	United Kingdom
09/10/98	02/19/99	1873.847	Banca Agricola Mantovana	Italy	Monte dei Paschi di Siena	Italy
09/14/98	09/14/98	1473.50	BHF Bank	Germany	ING Groep NV	Netherlands
09/23/98	10/02/98	796.129	National Mortgage Bank Greece	Greece	National Bank of Greece	Greece
09/23/98	12/31/98	1730.646	Banca San Paolo di Brescia	Italy	Credito Agrario Bresciano SpA	Italy
10/07/98	10/31/98	601.045	Bank Przemyslowo-Handlowy SA	Poland	Bayerische Vereinsbank AG	Germany
10/07/98	02/12/99	1522.835	ASLK-CGER Banque	Belgium	Fortis International NV	Netherlands
10/27/98	11/16/98	524.223	London & Edinburgh Ins	United Kingdom	Norwich Union PLC	United Kingdom
10/27/98	01/22/99	645.541	An-Hyp NV	Belgium	Royale Belge SA	Belgium
11/03/98	06/09/99	1298.419	Cassa di Risparmio di Reggio	Italy	Banca Popolare di Brescia	Italy
11/04/98	09/09/99	2076.687	Wuerttembergische AG Versicher	Germany	Wuestenrot Beteiligungs GmbH	Germany
11/12/98	05/07/99	779.305	Fokus Bank A/S	Norway	Den Danske Bank AS	Denmark
12/09/98	05/14/99	2733.128	Irish Life PLC	Ireland-Rep	Irish Permanent PLC	Ireland-Rep
01/15/99	04/15/99	11320.759	Banco Central Hispanoamericano	Spain	Banco de Santander SA	Spain
02/01/99	05/10/99	962.986	Albingia Versicheruns-AG	Germany	AXA Colonia Konzern AG	Germany
02/01/99	07/14/99	5691.555	Guardian Royal Exchange PLC	United Kingdom	Sun Life and Provincial	United Kingdom
02/22/99	03/24/99	943.769	Banca del Gottardo	Switzerland	Schweizerische Lebensversicher	Switzerland
02/22/99	12/21/99	3847.346	Storebrand-Non-Life Operations	Norway	Skandia Foersakrings-Non-Life	Sweden
02/24/99	07/29/99	542.687	Lloyd Continental	France	Schweizerische Lebensversicher	Switzerland
03/05/99	06/30/99	754.65	Banca Nazionale dell' Ag SpA	Italy	Banca Antoniana Popolare	Italy

Date	Date	Amount	Target	Country	Acquirer	Country
03/09/99	08/06/99	13200.552	Paribas SA	France	BNP	France
03/10/99	08/13/99	1214.119	Tryg-Baltica Forsikring	Denmark	Unidanmark A/S	Denmark
03/11/99	05/28/99	2986.997	M&G Group PLC	United Kingdom	Prudential PLC	United Kingdom
03/23/99	12/01/99	579.143	Postbanken(Norway)	Norway	Den Norske Banken ASA	Norway
03/29/99	04/19/99	898.688	Ionian Bank	Greece	Alpha Credit Bank	Greece
04/14/99	06/18/99	942.711	Arnhemsche Maatschappij tot	Netherlands	ING Bank NV(ING Groep NV)	Netherlands
04/28/99	06/11/99	588.237	Banca del Gottardo(Swiss Life)	Switzerland	Schweizerische Lebensversicher	Switzerland
05/10/99	12/31/99	2590.963	Safra Republic Holdings SA	Luxembourg	HSBC Holdings PLC(HSBC)	United Kingdom
05/29/99	10/12/99	3856.288	Casse Venete	Italy	Caer	Italy
05/31/99	06/25/99	1110.103	Ceskoslovenska Obchodni Banka	Czech Republic	KBC Bancassurance Holding NV	Belgium
05/31/99	12/02/99	12790.632	Banca Commerciale Italiana SpA	Italy	Banca Intesa SpA	Italy
06/02/99	09/02/99	563.248	Banca Nazionale dell' Ag SpA	Italy	Banca Antoniana Popolare	Italy
06/07/99	06/01/99	1555.568	Cia de Seguros Mundial	Portugal	Banco Santander Central Hispan	Spain
06/09/99	08/04/99	2104.569	Ergobank SA	Greece	EFG Eurobank SA	Greece
06/21/99	10/08/99	509.55	Tryg-Hansa Forsakrings AB	Sweden	Codan Forsikring AS	Denmark
06/23/99	03/03/00	11119.50	Scottish Widows Fund & Life	United Kingdom	Lloyds TSB Group PLC	United Kingdom
07/12/99	08/06/99	718.908	Credit Foncier de France	France	Caisses d'Epargne	France
08/12/99	10/07/99	1220.548	Guardian RE-UK Life,Pensions	United Kingdom	Aegon UK(AEGON NV)	United Kingdom
08/13/99	09/27/99	2337.671	BHF Bank	Germany	ING Groep NV	Netherlands
09/09/99	12/31/99	818.759	CNCE	France	CDC	France
09/14/99	12/27/99	833.60	Banca del Salento	Italy	Monte dei Paschi di Siena	Italy
09/14/99	01/13/00	10179.615	INA	Italy	Assicurazioni Generali SpA	Italy
09/19/99	11/08/99	6131.13	Dexia France	France	Dexia Belgium	Belgium
09/20/99	03/31/01	2780.131	Christiania Bank	Norway	MeritaNordbanken(Nordbanken)	Finland
09/20/99	01/24/00	4824.591	Merita Oy	Finland	Nordbanken Holding AB	Sweden
09/20/99	10/21/99	6172.173	Paribas SA (BNP)	France	BNP	France
10/13/99	12/31/00	1549.421	Leonia Bank PLC	Finland	Vakuutusosakeyhtio Sampo	Finland
10/14/99	10/14/99	556.00	EFIBANCA	Italy	Banca Popolare di Lodi SCARL	Italy
10/19/99	01/28/00	11377.206	Argentaria Caja Postal y Banco	Spain	Banco Bilbao Vizcaya SA	Spain
10/22/99	10/22/99	821.296	Invensys-Paper Tech Group	United Kingdom	Apax Partners & Co Ltd	United Kingdom
10/22/99	01/04/00	1703.114	Bank fur Gemeinwirtschaft AG	Germany	Skandinaviska Enskilda Banken	Sweden
10/26/99	08/03/00	527.911	Ceska Sporitelna Savings Bank	Czech Republic	Erste Bank Der Oesterreichisch	Austria
10/29/99	02/01/00	695.59	Paribas SA (BNP)	France	BNP	France
11/10/99	04/25/00	721.145	Ionian Bank	Greece	Alpha Credit Bank	Greece
11/11/99	06/01/00	1307.504	Cia de Seguros Mundial	Portugal	Caixa Geral de Depositos SA	Portugal
11/12/99	04/07/00	1715.776	Banco Totta e Acores SA	Portugal	Banco Santander Central Hispan	Spain
11/12/99	03/13/00	38524.645	National Westminster Bank PLC	United Kingdom	Royal Bank of Scotland Group	United Kingdom
11/29/99	12/03/99	2052.74	Mediocredito Centrale	Italy	Banca di Roma(SIPAB)	Italy
12/03/99	06/16/00	713.46	Casse del Tirreno SpA	Italy	Banca Popolare di Lodi SCARL	Italy
12/04/99	04/14/00	641.58	Vesta Skadeforsikring,Vesta	Norway	Tryg-Baltica Forsikring	Denmark
12/09/99	12/10/99	725.014	Banco Bilbao Vizcaya SA	Spain	Unicredito Italiano	Italy
12/10/99	05/25/00	1409.996	Banca Regionale Europea	Italy	Banca Lombarda SpA	Italy

Date	Date	Value	Target	Country	Acquirer	Country
12/20/99	06/16/00	574.924	Xiosbank	Greece	Piraeus Bank Group	Greece
12/20/99	06/16/00	705.636	Macedonia-Thrace Bank(Greece)	Greece	Piraeus Bank Group	Greece
01/20/00	01/20/00	505.979	Banque Sofinco(Credit Agricol)	France	Credit Agricole	France
01/21/00	09/07/00	1595.848	Ergobank SA	Greece	EFG Eurobank SA	Greece
01/28/00	03/10/00	1628.702	Banque Generale du Luxembourg	Luxembourg	Fortis(NL) NV	Netherlands
02/21/00	05/30/00	11858.325	Norwich Union PLC	United Kingdom	CGU PLC	United Kingdom
02/22/00	05/05/00	2462.569	United Assurance Group	United Kingdom	Royal London Mutual Insurance	United Kingdom
03/06/00	04/20/00	700.599	UAF(Credit Lyonnais SA)	France	Credit Lyonnais SA	France
03/06/00	06/02/00	4425.782	Unidanmark A/S	Denmark	MeritaNordbanken(Nordbanken)	Finland
03/14/00	08/02/00	867.088	Labouchere NV(Aegon NV)	Netherlands	Dexia Belgium	Belgium
03/31/00	06/19/00	1838.804	Banco Pinto & Sotto Mayor SA	Portugal	Banco Comercial Portugues SA	Portugal
03/31/00	06/19/00	2175.538	Banco Pinto & Sotto Mayor SA	Portugal	Banco Comercial Portugues SA	Portugal
04/01/00	07/18/00	11099.996	Credit Commercial de France	France	HSBC Holdings PLC(HSBC)	United Kingdom
04/20/00	06/01/00	1177.819	Cia de Seguros Mundial	Portugal	Caixa Geral de Depositos SA	Portugal
05/02/00	06/15/00	517.688	Colonial-UK Life Ins & Pens	United Kingdom	Winterthur Insurance Co	Switzerland
05/02/00	07/10/00	3535.148	Sun Life and Provincial	United Kingdom	AXA	France
06/21/00	10/31/00	2037.977	Banco di Napoli Holding SpA	Italy	San Paolo-IMI SpA	Italy
06/26/00	12/01/00	2347.888	Entrium Direct Bankers AG	Germany	Bipop-Carire	Italy
07/17/00	12/05/00	900.30	Royal Scot Assce,NatWest Life	United Kingdom	CGNU PLC	United Kingdom
07/22/00	02/01/01	7317.012	Bank Austria AG	Austria	HypoVereinsbank AG	Germany
08/11/00	10/25/00	7962.505	Woolwich PLC	United Kingdom	Barclays PLC	United Kingdom
08/17/00	12/01/00	589.131	Bayerische Vita	Italy	Ergo Versicherungsgruppe AG	Germany
08/17/00	08/19/00	1170.066	Oesterreichische Postsparkasse	Austria	BAWAG	Austria
09/01/00	09/01/00	914.856	Chartered Trust,ACL Autolease	United Kingdom	Lloyds UDT(Lloyds TSB Group)	United Kingdom
09/07/00	08/01/01	2589.12	Scottish Provident Institution	United Kingdom	Abbey National PLC	United Kingdom
09/13/00	12/06/00	623.178	Self Trade	France	Direkt Anlage Bank AG	Germany
09/20/00	01/20/01	570.67	Banco Herrero SA	Spain	Banc Sabadell SA	Spain
09/21/00	12/22/00	553.467	Zwolsche Algemeene NV	Netherlands	AGF(Allianz AG)	France
10/02/00	07/01/01	1614.03	Scottish Life Assurance Co	United Kingdom	Royal London Mutual Insurance	United Kingdom
10/02/00	03/28/01	3079.528	RealDanmark A/S	Denmark	Danske Bank A/S	Denmark
10/09/00	12/19/00	3689.074	ASR Verzekeringsgroep	Netherlands	Fortis(NL) NV	Netherlands
10/11/00	05/01/01	3144.305	Banca Commerciale Italiana SpA	Italy	Banca Intesa SpA	Italy
10/19/00	03/02/01	1513.049	Perpetual PLC	United Kingdom	Amvescap PLC	United Kingdom
11/21/00	06/29/01	1003.11	Banca Carime SpA(Banca Intesa)	Italy	Banca Popolare Commercio e	Italy
12/20/00	06/26/01	600.60	Banca di Legnano(Banca Comm)	Italy	Banca Popolare di Milano	Italy
12/20/00	02/12/01	728.46	SPP Livforsakring AB	Sweden	Svenska Handelsbanken AB	Sweden
12/22/00	12/22/00	609.574	Foreign & Colonial Mgmt Ltd	United Kingdom	Eureko BV(Topdanmark,6 others)	Netherlands
01/10/01	01/10/01	1639.716	Bankgesellschaft Berlin AG	Germany	Berlin	Germany
02/05/01	03/01/01	1468.40	Equitable Life Assurance Soc	United Kingdom	Halifax Group PLC	United Kingdom
02/06/01	05/18/01	878.178	Deutsche Bank-Leasing & Fleet	Germany	Societe Generale SA	France
02/13/01	08/16/01	5271.012	GZ Bank AG	Germany	DG Bank	Germany
03/13/01	07/03/01	3040.416	Artesia Banking Corp NV/SA	Belgium	Dexia Belgium	Belgium

03/22/01	07/23/01	781.19	Perstorp AB	Sweden	Sydsvenska Kemi AB	Sweden
04/01/01	07/23/01	2187.021	Allianz Lebensversicherungs AG	Germany	Allianz AG	Germany
04/01/01	07/19/01	3392.677	Ergo Versicherungsgruppe AG	Germany	Muenchener Rueckversicherungs	Germany
04/01/01	07/20/01	19655.942	Dresdner Bank AG	Germany	Allianz AG	Germany
04/06/01	04/06/01	529.221	People's Bank-UK Credit Card	United Kingdom	Citibank International PLC	United Kingdom
04/06/01	04/06/01	918.557	Calve-Delft Bel Mij	Netherlands	Fortis(NL)NV	Netherlands
04/12/01	04/11/02	1067.416	VHDB,DB Vida,DB Vita	Germany	Zurich Financial Services Grp	Switzerland
04/24/01	10/04/01	652.335	PZU(Poland)	Poland	Eureko BV	Netherlands
05/04/01	09/10/01	14904.444	Bank of Scotland PLC	United Kingdom	Halifax Group PLC	United Kingdom
05/09/01	05/31/01	553.003	Deutsche Bank-Trianon Bldg	Germany	DGZ-DekaBank	Germany
05/21/01	01/03/02	792.879	Sampo-Ppty & Casulty Insurance	Finland	If P&C Insurance Ltd	Sweden
05/22/01	7/21/2001	921.393	Kempen and Co NV	Netherlands	Dexia Belgium	Belgium
05/29/01	07/26/01	840.148	Interamerican SA	Greece	Eureko BV(Topdanmark,6 others)	Netherlands
06/25/01	05/16/02	876.67	AKB Privat & Handelsbank AG	Germany	Banco Santander Central Hispan	Spain
06/25/01	01/01/02	2998.039	CNCE-Banking Assets	France	CDC-Banking Assets	France
06/28/01	10/05/01	1019.995	Komercni Banka AS	Czech Republic	Societe Generale SA	France
09/13/01	11/01/01	1042.36	CIC(Credit Mutuel SA)	France	Credit Mutuel SA	France
09/27/01	12/17/01	12469.946	Fortis(NL)NV	Netherlands	Fortis (B)	Belgium
10/10/01	12/15/01	570.455	Caisse Reg-National Subsids	France	Credit Agricole	France
10/10/01	12/14/01	1794.793	Caisses Regionales	France	Credit Agricole	France
10/16/01	10/16/01	772.14	Cora(Grands Magasins B)	France	Deutsche Bank AG	Germany
10/17/01	06/01/02	5323.57	Cardine Banca SpA	Italy	San Paolo-IMI SpA	Italy
10/24/01	04/14/02	557.096	Banca Popolare di Crema	Italy	ICCRI-Banca Federale Europea	Italy
10/29/01	01/08/02	806.526	London Intl Fin Fut & Opt Exch	United Kingdom	Euronext NV	Netherlands
10/30/01	08/13/02	2084.402	Eurohypo AG(Deutsche Bank AG)	Germany	Deutsche Hypothekenbank	Germany
10/30/01	01/02/02	1552.294	Moeara Enim Petroleum Mij	Netherlands	Fortis(NL)NV	Netherlands
10/30/01	08/13/02	1831.939	Rheinische Hypothekenbank AG	Germany	Deutsche Hypothekenbank	Germany
10/31/01	03/20/02	798.674	Hellenic Indl Development Bank	Greece	Piraeus Bank Group	Greece
11/02/01	01/04/02	516.051	Prudential PLC-UK General Bus	United Kingdom	Winterthur Schweizerische	Switzerland
11/14/01	06/01/02	1777.516	Banca Popolare di Novara Scarl	Italy	Banca Popolare di Verona	Italy
12/14/01	07/01/02	4580.73	Rolo Banca 1473(Credito Itali)	Italy	Unicredito Italiano	Italy
12/18/01	12/18/01	1035.297	Gucci Group NV	Netherlands	Credit Lyonnais SA	France
12/21/01	12/21/01	1039.568	Baloise Holding AG	Switzerland	Strategic Money Management Co	Netherlands
02/01/02	07/11/02	1507.625	Cedel International SA	Luxembourg	Deutsche Boerse AG	Germany
02/05/02	02/13/02	704.41	Fondiaria Assicurazioni SpA	Italy	Investor Group	Italy
03/03/02	07/01/02	1567.742	Bipop-Carire-Traditional Ops	Italy	Banca di Roma	Italy
03/14/02	07/01/02	2092.70	Banca Di Roma-Asset Management	Italy	Bipop-Carire	Italy
03/22/02	05/14/02	646.411	Ceska Sporitelna Savings Bank	Czech Republic	Anteilsverwaltung	Austria
05/14/02	11/01/02	1633.052	ICCRI-Banca Federale Europea	Italy	Investimenti Immobiliari	Italy
05/14/02	07/31/02	507.548	Sanpaolo Invest(San Paolo-IMI)	Italy	Banca Fideuram(IMI)	Italy
05/23/02	05/13/02	832.42	RMF Investment Group	Switzerland	Man Group PLC	United Kingdom
05/30/02	12/29/02	1663.664	SAI	Italy	Fondiaria Assicurazioni SpA	Italy

255

06/19/02	09/30/02	732.354	Nordea-Insurance Business	Sweden	Tryg i Danmark smba	Denmark
08/06/02	08/06/02	679.14	Ceska Sporitelna Savings Bank	Czech Republic	Erste Bank Der Oesterreichisch	Austria
09/10/02	09/10/02	516.805	Fondiaria Assicurazioni SpA	Italy	SAI	Italy
09/10/02	01/10/03	694.493	Riunione Adriatica di Securita	Italy	Riunione Adriatica di Securita	Italy
10/16/02	12/16/02	504.147	Guinness Peat Group PLC	United Kingdom	Brunel Holdings PLC	United Kingdom
10/22/02	03/31/03	775.895	Seguros E Pensoes Group	Portugal	Banco Comercial Portugues SA	Portugal
10/23/02	12/20/02	1217.00	Vivendi Publishing-europe	France	Natexis Banques Populaires	France
10/25/02	12/23/02	848.318	FACET(Finaref/PPR)	France	BNP Paribas SA	France
10/30/02	02/26/03	1514.436	Finaref	France	Credit Agricole SA	France
11/01/02	12/05/02	624.867	Hirslanden Holding AG	Switzerland	BC Partners	United Kingdom
11/25/02	11/25/02	2202.86	Credit Lyonnais SA	France	BNP Paribas SA	France
12/02/02	12/02/02	926.646	Credit Lyonnais SA	France	BNP Paribas SA	France
12/04/02	12/30/02	797.20	Capitalia SpA-Branches(135)	Italy	Investor Group	Italy
12/09/02	12/09/02	654.728	Credit Lyonnais SA	France	Credit Agricole SA	France

Appendix 1, Table 4

Financial Service Sector Acquistions Cross-border Europe, 1990-2002 Exceeding $500 Million

Date Announced	Date Effective	Target Name	Target Nation	Acquirer Name	Value of Transaction ($mil)	Acquirer Nation
04/02/85	09/16/85	Fred S James & Co Inc	United States	Sedgwick Group PLC	660.00	United Kingdom
09/18/86	12/03/86	Jackson National Life Ins Inc	United States	Prudential PLC	606.00	United Kingdom
08/05/87	02/01/88	First Jersey National Corp	United States	National Westminster Bank PLC	770.60	United Kingdom
05/10/88	12/22/88	First Boston Inc	United States	Credit Suisse First Boston	1100.00	Switzerland
06/20/88	12/29/88	NZI Corp Ltd	New Zealand	General Accident Fire & Life	738.245	United Kingdom
02/17/89	05/11/89	Maryland Casualty Co	United States	Zurich Versicherungs GmbH	740.00	Switzerland
03/12/90	04/30/90	General Casualty Cos	United States	Winterthur Schweizerische	630.00	Switzerland
06/04/90	10/08/90	Corroon & Black Corp	United States	Willis Faber PLC	837.00	United Kingdom
08/02/90	01/02/91	Fireman's Fund Insurance Co	United States	Allianz AG Holding	3100.00	Germany
10/01/90	02/13/91	Home Insurance Co(AmBase Corp)	United States	TVH Acquisition Corp	940.00	Sweden
05/09/91	07/18/91	Equitable Life Assurance	United States	Axa Midi Assurances SA	1000.00	France
08/07/91	03/03/92	Executive Life Ins-Junk Bond	United States	Altus Finance SA	3250.00	France
02/24/92	01/04/93	First Interstate Bank-Corp	Hong Kong	Standard Chartered PLC	899.659	United Kingdom
07/06/93	06/01/94	Cragin Financial Corp	United States	ABN-AMRO Holding NV	501.60	Netherlands
08/31/94	04/26/95	Brinson Partners Inc	United States	Schweizerischer Bankverein	750.00	Switzerland
01/19/95	09/18/95	Natl Mutual Life Assn of AU	Australia	Axa SA	817.128	France
09/20/95	12/01/95	Bank of Western Australia	Australia	Bank of Scotland PLC	680.40	United Kingdom
06/11/96	10/10/96	Greenwich Capital Markets Inc	United States	National Westminster Bank PLC	590.00	United Kingdom
08/14/96	11/25/96	American Re Corp	United States	Muenchener Rueckversicherungs	3967.84	Germany
11/04/96	02/28/97	AIM Management Group Inc	United States	Invesco PLC	1598.717	United Kingdom
11/22/96	05/01/97	Standard Fed Bancorp,Troy,MI	United States	ABN-AMRO Holding NV	1971.138	Netherlands
12/27/96	06/11/97	Providan Corp-Insurance	United States	Aegon NV	3503.77	Netherlands
02/05/97	09/12/97	Banco Multiplic-Consumer & Cor	Brazil	Lloyds TSB Group PLC	600.024	United Kingdom
05/27/97	08/22/97	Banco Rio de la Plata SA	Argentina	Banco de Santander SA	594.00	Spain
05/30/97	08/12/97	Roberts SA de Inversiones	Argentina	HSBC Holdings PLC(HSBC)	688.002	United Kingdom
06/27/97	12/31/97	Scudder Stevens & Clark Inc	United States	Zurich Versicherungs GmbH	1667.00	Switzerland
07/08/97	10/24/97	Equitable of Iowa Cos	United States	ING Groep NV	2626.389	Netherlands
08/28/97	10/08/97	Furman Selz LLC	United States	ING Barings(ING Groep NV)	600.00	United Kingdom
10/20/97	12/31/97	Canadian General Insurance Grp	Canada	General Accident PLC	532.688	United Kingdom
01/29/98	06/01/98	Chancellor LGT Asset Mgmt	United States	Amvescap PLC	1300.00	United Kingdom
03/09/98	08/31/98	John Alden Financial Corp	United States	Fortis BV(Fortis AG,AMEV)	583.113	Netherlands
04/29/98	10/07/98	Banco Excel Economico SA	Brazil	Banco Bilbao Vizcaya SA	878.038	Spain
05/07/98	05/07/98	Weiss Peck & Greer	United States	Robeco NV	575.00	Netherlands
05/29/98	09/01/98	Netherlands Insurance Co	United States	Guardian Royal Exchange PLC	775.00	United Kingdom
07/08/98	11/05/98	Banco Real SA	Brazil	ABN-AMRO Holding NV	2100.00	Netherlands
07/24/98	10/27/98	Constitution Re(Exor America)	United States	Gerling Konzern Versicherungs	700.00	Germany

257

Date	Date	Amount	Target	Target Country	Acquirer	Acquirer Country
07/27/98	11/30/98	1794.749	Life Re Corp	United States	Swiss Reinsurance Co	Switzerland
08/14/98	09/04/98	762.50	Citizens Financial Group,RI	United States	Royal Bank of Scotland Group	United Kingdom
08/16/98	01/01/99	500.00	Clarendon Insurance Group	United States	Hannover Rueckversicherungs	Germany
11/30/98	06/04/99	9082.072	Bankers Trust New York Corp	United States	Deutsche Bank AG	Germany
12/10/98	05/20/99	1300.00	Bank America-Asian Retail	Taiwan	ABN-AMRO Holding NV	Netherlands
02/01/99	05/10/99	1596.607	Guardian Royal Exchange O/Seas	Multi-National	AXA	France
02/15/99	07/06/99	650.00	Warburg Pincus Asset Mgmt	United States	Credit Suisse Asset Management	Switzerland
02/18/99	07/21/99	10790.68	TransAmerica Corp	United States	Aegon NV	Netherlands
03/08/99	08/18/99	2823.509	American Bankers Ins Group Inc	United States	Fortis AG	Belgium
04/13/99	05/03/99	600.00	O'Higgins Central Hispano	Chile	Banco de Santander SA	Spain
05/10/99	12/31/99	7702.864	Republic New York Corp,NY,NY	United States	HSBC Holdings PLC(HSBC)	United Kingdom
05/17/99	04/16/02	657.236	Banco Santiago	Chile	Banco Santander Central Hispan	Spain
06/03/99	08/06/99	847.077	Keppel TatLee Bank Ltd	Singapore	Allied Irish Banks PLC	Ireland-Rep
07/12/99	11/16/99	1390.578	Orion Capital Corp	Bermuda	Royal & Sun Alliance Insurance	United Kingdom
09/14/99	12/17/99	675.00	Global Asset Management GAM	Bermuda	UBS AG	Switzerland
10/06/99	05/05/00	1930.242	PIMCO Advisors Holdings LP	United States	Allianz AG	Germany
10/29/99	05/05/00	1127.733	PIMCO Advisors LP	United States	Allianz AG	Germany
11/29/99	03/31/00	1954.40	Nippon Dantai Life Insurance	Japan	AXA	France
01/03/00	01/19/00	834.998	Banco Meridional Do Brasil SA	Brazil	Banco Santander Central Hispan	Spain
01/20/00	01/20/00	1000.00	Banco Bozano Simonsen SA	Brazil	Banco Santander Central Hispan	Spain
02/10/00	07/20/00	675.421	Banco Rio de la Plata SA	Argentina	Banco Santander Central Hispan	Spain
02/15/00	04/13/00	555.00	Valores Consolidados(Savia SA)	Mexico	ING Groep NV	Netherlands
03/10/00	03/30/00	529.00	Patagon.Com	United States	Banco Santander Central Hispan	Spain
03/14/00	07/05/00	2548.567	Finl Security Assurance Hldgs	United States	Dexia Belgium	Belgium
03/15/00	07/05/00	620.40	White Mountains Holdings	United States	Dexia Belgium	Belgium
04/19/00	07/31/00	1339.859	ANZ Grindlays Bank Ltd	Australia	Standard Chartered PLC	United Kingdom
04/28/00	09/02/00	5973.846	ReliaStar Financial Corp	United States	ING Groep NV	Netherlands
05/08/00	05/24/00	1542.645	Grupo Financiero Serfin SA de	Mexico	Banco Santander Central Hispan	Spain
05/09/00	08/01/00	1750.743	Trimark Financial Corp	Canada	Amvescap PLC	United Kingdom
05/15/00	10/25/00	1228.615	Pioneer Group Inc	United States	Unicredito Italiano	Italy
06/12/00	08/28/00	1954.00	Grupo Financiero Bancomer SA	Mexico	Banco Bilbao Viz Argent(BBVA)	Spain
06/16/00	10/30/00	2185.846	NVEST LP	United States	CDC Asset Management Europe	France
07/12/00	11/03/00	16542.565	PaineWebber Group Inc	United States	UBS AG	Switzerland
07/20/00	12/13/00	7632.665	Aetna-Finl Svcs & Int'l Bus	United States	ING Groep NV	Netherlands
09/01/00	10/31/00	1319.947	Chase Manhattan-HK Banking	Hong Kong	Standard Chartered PLC	United Kingdom
09/18/00	01/05/01	1255.00	Wasserstein Perella Group Inc	United States	Dresdner Bank AG	Germany
10/12/00	12/01/00	898.645	National Discount Brokers	United States	Deutsche Bank AG	Germany
10/18/00	02/01/01	825.00	Alleghany Asset Management Inc	United States	ABN-AMRO Holding NV	Netherlands
10/18/00	02/14/01	2220.00	Nicholas-Applegate Capt Mgmt	United States	Allianz AG	Germany
11/20/00	11/28/00	4742.453	Banco do Estado de Sao Paulo	Brazil	Banco Santander Central Hispan	Spain
11/23/00	04/02/01	2750.00	Michigan National Corp	United States	ABN-AMRO Holding NV	Netherlands
02/15/01	02/16/01	536.015	Caixa Seguros SA	Brazil	CNP Assurances	France

03/08/01	06/18/01	1600.00	JC Penney Co-Direct Marketing	United States	Aegon NV	Netherlands
04/11/01	07/09/01	886.073	TCW Group Inc	United States	Societe Generale SA	France
04/26/01	09/28/01	635.00	Fidelity & Guaranty Life	United States	Old Mutual PLC	United Kingdom
05/07/01	12/20/01	2480.381	BancWest Corp,Honolulu,HI	United States	BNP Paribas SA	France
06/04/01	06/22/01	791.00	Seguros Comercial America SA	Mexico	ING Groep NV	Netherlands
07/30/01	12/07/01	2000.00	Lincoln Re(Lincoln National)	United States	Swiss Reinsurance Co	Switzerland
09/24/01	04/08/02	2500.00	Zurich Scudder Investments Inc	United States	Deutsche Bank AG	Germany
12/10/01	03/15/02	2400.00	United California Bank,LA,CA	United States	BNP Paribas SA	France
07/23/02	11/25/02	600.00	Ping An Insurance Co Ltd	China	HSBC Ins Hldgs Ltd	United Kingdom
08/21/02	11/25/02	1134.703	Grupo Financiero Bital SA	Mexico	HSBC Holdings PLC(HSBC)	United Kingdom
11/14/02	03/28/03	15294.063	Household International Inc	United States	HSBC Holdings PLC(HSBC)	United Kingdom

Appendix 1, Table 5

Financial Services Sector Acquisitions Within Latin America, 1990-2001 Exceeding $500 million

Date Announced	Date Effective	Value of Transaction ($mil)	Target Name	Target Nation	Acquirer Name	Acquirer Nation
02/28/92	03/06/92	615.00	Banco Mexicano Somex SNC	Mexico	InverMexico SA de CV	Mexico
09/17/93	09/20/93	583.002	Aseguradora Mexicana(Mexico)	Mexico	Grupo Financiero Mexival	Mexico
09/19/95	01/13/97	973.219	Banco O'Higgins	Chile	Banco Santiago	Chile
11/17/95	11/17/95	1040.10	Banco Nacional SA	Brazil	Uniao de Bancos Brasileiros SA	Brazil
04/10/96	07/01/96	880.685	Banco Santander Chile	Chile	Banco Osorno y la Union	Chile
05/09/97	05/30/97	594.00	Banco de Credito Argentino SA	Argentina	Banco Frances del Rio de la	Argentina
11/04/98	11/04/98	756.27	Banco Pontual	Brazil	Banco de Credito Nacional SA	Brazil
04/28/00	10/02/00	517.746	Boavista Inter-Atlantico	Brazil	Banco Bradesco SA	Brazil
06/12/00	07/18/00	544.862	Casa de Bolsa BBV Probursa SA	Mexico	Grupo Financiero Bancomer SA	Mexico
07/04/00	09/29/00	593.872	Banco Bandeirantes SA(Caixa)	Brazil	Unibanco Holdings SA	Brazil
10/17/00	10/17/00	868.40	Banco do Estado do Parana SA	Brazil	Banco Itau SA(Itau)	Brazil
08/08/01	01/01/02	942.889	Banco De A Edwards SA	Chile	Banco de Chile(Sociedad)	Chile
01/14/02	03/25/02	541.972	Banco Mercantil Sao Paulo	Brazil	Banco Bradesco SA	Brazil
01/18/02	02/26/02	1240.00	Afore Banamex Aegon	Mexico	Grupo Financiero Banamex SA	Mexico
04/17/02	08/01/02	1678.241	Banco Santander Chile SA	Chile	Banco Santiago	Chile
11/07/02	02/26/03	875.876	Banco BBA Creditanstalt SA	Brazil	Banco Itau SA(Itau)	Brazil

For Latin America Cross-border see Appendix 1, Tables 2 (US Cross-border) and 4 (Europe Cross-border).

Appendix 1, Table 6

Financial Services Sector Acquisitions Within Asia, 1990-2002 Exceeding $500 million

Date Announced	Date Effective	Value of Transaction ($mil)	Target Name	Target Nation	Acquirer Name	Acquirer Nation
02/24/95	04/22/96	512.98	United Malayan Banking Corp	Malaysia	Sime Darby Bhd	Malaysia
05/19/95	04/03/96	1033.824	Malaysia National Insurance	Malaysia	Timah Langat(Permodalan Nasio)	Malaysia
06/20/96	10/07/96	908.599	CityTrust Banking Corp	Philippines	Bank of Philippine Islands	Philippines
10/04/96	10/04/96	600.00	China Financial Trust	China	Guangdong Development Bank	China
07/24/98	08/06/98	933.28	Post Office Savings Bank	Singapore	DBS Bank	Singapore
10/21/99	04/10/00	1216.031	Far East Bank & Trust Co	Philippines	Bank of Philippine Islands	Philippines
06/26/00	11/09/00	1423.254	Public Bank-Commercial Banking	Malaysia	Hock Hua Bank Bhd	Malaysia
11/20/00	02/06/01	559.978	FPB Bank Holding Co Ltd	Hong Kong	Bank of East Asia Ltd	Hong Kong
12/22/00	11/01/01	2172.928	H&CB	South Korea	Kookmin Bank	South Korea
04/11/01	09/03/01	5679.702	Dao Heng Bank Group(Guoco)	Hong Kong	DBS Group Holdings Ltd	Singapore
04/11/01	01/10/03	1964.934	DBS Diamond Holdings Ltd	Hong Kong	DBS Bank	Singapore
05/09/01	05/09/01	524.40	ANZ Banking Group Ltd	Australia	ANZ Banking Group Ltd	Australia
06/12/01	09/24/01	3753.906	Keppel Capital Holdings Ltd	Singapore	Oversea-Chinese Banking Corp	Singapore
06/15/01	09/29/01	737.10	AMP General Insurance Ltd	Australia	Suncorp-Metway Ltd	Australia
06/29/01	09/24/01	5463.908	Overseas Union Bank Ltd	Singapore	UOB	Singapore
07/27/01	12/23/02	538.303	EON Bank Bhd(Edaran Otomobil)	Malaysia	Kedah Cement Holdings Bhd	Malaysia
09/08/01	11/26/01	685.87	Guoco Group Ltd	Hong Kong	Guoco Group Ltd	Hong Kong
09/12/01	01/17/02	538.44	HKCB(CH Resources(Hldgs)Ltd)	Hong Kong	CITIC Ka Wah Bank Ltd	Hong Kong
09/12/01	12/19/01	967.497	Fubon Comercial Bank Co Ltd	Taiwan	Fubon Insurance Co Ltd	Taiwan
09/12/01	12/19/01	1027.31	Fubon Securities Co Ltd	Taiwan	Fubon Insurance Co Ltd	Taiwan
09/12/01	01/17/02	538.44	HKCB(CH Resources(Hldgs)Ltd)	Hong Kong	CITIC Ka Wah Bank Ltd	Hong Kong
10/24/01	03/30/02	796.218	ICICI Ltd	India	ICICI Banking Corp	India
03/14/02	03/28/02	534.184	BCA	Indonesia	Investor Group	Indonesia
04/10/02	05/01/02	708.621	ANZ-Funds & Insurance	Australia	ING-Funds & Insurance	Australia
05/02/02	05/31/02	918.897	AGC(Westpac Banking Corp)	Australia	GE Capital Finance Australia	Australia
05/07/02	12/30/02	2113.787	ICBC	Taiwan	CTB Financial Hldg Co	Taiwan
08/07/02	12/23/02	2346.522	Taipei Bank	Taiwan	Fubon Financial Holding Co Ltd	Taiwan
08/12/02	12/18/02	2932.538	UWCCB	Taiwan	Cathay Financial Hldg Co Ltd	Taiwan
08/19/02	12/01/02	952.848	Seoul Bank,Seoul,SK(SK)	South Korea	Hana Bank,Seoul,South Korea	South Korea
08/22/02	10/31/02	571.83	BT Financial Group-Cert Bus	Australia	Westpac Banking Corp	Australia
10/18/02	01/02/03	1021.549	CGU Ins AU Ltd,NZ Ins Co Ltd	Australia	Insurance Australia Group Ltd	Australia
11/07/02	11/07/02	748.512	ICBC	Taiwan	Investor Group	Taiwan

261

Appendix 1, Table 7

Financial Services Sector Acquisitions Cross-border Asia, 1990-2002 Exceeding $500 million

Date Announced	Date Effective	Value of Transaction ($mil)	Target Name	Target Nation	Acquirer Name	Acquirer Nation
07/15/87	12/15/87	752.00	Marine Midland Banks Inc	United States	HSBC Hong Kong(HSBC Hldg PLC)	Hong Kong
11/13/87	12/31/87	673.703	Midland Bank PLC	United Kingdom	HSBC Hong Kong(HSBC Hldg PLC)	Hong Kong
03/26/97	04/01/97	999.802	Banco Bamerindus do Brasil	Brazil	HSBC Hong Kong(HSBC Hldg PLC)	Hong Kong

For Asia Cross-border see also Appendix 1, Tables 2 (US Cross-border) and 4 (Europe Cross-border).

APPENDIX 2
Case Studies

Appendix 2, Table 1

Case Study – CIBC [Commercial Imperial Bank of Canada] & Wood Gundy

Company & transactional overview

	CIBC	Wood Gundy
Company Background	Large Canadian commercial bank, in a market underpinned by long-standing relationships with institutional clients.	• Large Canadian investment bank, but in serious financial difficulty when acquired. • Serious talent drain problem prior to acquisition. • Four years after purchase [1992], it had lost 1/3 of its market share [underwriting] while market had grown by 70%.
Cultural and other company characteristics	• Staid corporate banking culture • Hierarchical • Process-driven	• Stodgy • Deal-driven • Performance based compensation [bonus]
Leadership characteristics	Al Flood, CEO, had risen through the CIBC ranks ["a lifer"], but with strong vision of "universal banking." Cautious in nature.	Senior team nearing retirement
Transaction date	1988	
Transaction type [A]	Acquirer	Acquired
Transaction justification/ Integration goals	Domain extension ["universal banking"], convergence of commercial and investment banking to leverage client relationships.	
Integration approach	Symbiotic	

Integration issues and actions:

Integration issues	Challenges/Decisions/Actions
Leadership	By 1990, senior CIBC managers took over key positions from retiring WG senior executives [CEO, President].

Human Resources	• No apparent terminations, replacement of WG staff by CIBC personnel through attrition.
	• **Compensation:** alignment of compensation between corporate bankers [CIBC staff] brought into WG with that of investment bankers was very slow, as CIBC leadership was extremely wary of bringing too drastic change to WG. **Eventually, this imbalance was addressed by setting up a single bonus pool for both types of bankers, which apparently led to the disappearance of turf battles between both sides.** This bonus pool system had the following characteristics:
	  ✓ **Funding:** determined as a function of revenues earned by the unit and management perception on how large it should be [partly based on assessing bonuses paid by competitors].
	  ✓ **Distribution:** bonus size was based on the assessed "value brought to the organization" by an individual, a subjective notion decided by a team of each of the senior managers of the CIBC divisions. These managers then set the bonus for each of the top 50-100 people from both corporate and investment banking, aiming to maintain equity between the two units. Unit managers were then responsible for distributing their allocated bonuses to their staff in an equitable manner.

Bridging the cultural gap	• Initially, the two cultures clashed, seriously undermining morale. The investment bankers considered the corporate bankers "slow and stupid," while the corporate bankers viewed the investment bankers as "sleazy and greedy." • Uncertainty about CIBC's "universal banking" strategy demoralized WG's investment bankers, as communication efforts by CIBC top management were too limited in breadth [eg. not enough communication vehicles]. • In time, the realignment of compensation policies and the introduction of the RM system helped bridge the cultural gap by shifting the focus away from "investment bankers" vs. "corporate bankers."

Integration issues	Challenges/Decisions/Actions
Integration level implemented	• High, all organizational functions, procedures, policies of WG eventually aligned with those of CIBC.
Integration speed/timeliness	• Faster move on: ✓ Integrating WG money market activities within CIBC's treasury functions [1989] ✓ Integrating CIBC and WG trading rooms [1992] • Slower-move on: ✓ Integrating corporate lending and underwriting activities [1994] **Note:** it appears that CIBC moved faster in its integration process than its rival competitors, which had also bought investment banks.
Integration steps	• Prior to accelerating integration in 1992, CIBC stabilized operations of WG [1988-1992] by devoting financial and management resources. • Put operations side-by side by placing both WG and corporate lending under one combined group senior manager. • No clear evidence of an Interface Management [IM] team, as much of the initial integration planning and subsequent implementation was made by the combined group senior manager [spent 50% of his time at addressing integration issues]. • A "change" team was formed including both corporate and investment banking senior managers to identify/manage specific change initiatives [e.g. building or acquiring new product capabilities and finding new customers]. This, however, led to serious turf-battles between both sides, each accusing the other of trying to "poach" new products and/or customers. • Management recognized that to make the "integrated financial services" strategy work, it had to minimize turf battles between corporate and investment bankers. This was accomplished by building a client-focused team [of both corporate and investment bankers] around individuals ["relationship managers"] having high level relationships with either existing or target senior client management. These relationship managers [RMs] were deliberately not given budgetary responsibilities, and were therefore not seen as a threat by the corporate and investment banking units. The RMs knew best the client, who perceived them as an ombudsmen within the firm, bringing them to the various product specialists [ranging from project financing to "plain vanilla loans"].
Integration capabilities	Evidence not found.

Scorecard:

Impact area	Score [+, -, M]	Actual outcome
Client retention/extension	+	By 1998, CIBC had become one of the largest advisors in Canada. Between 1998 and 1999, it had advised 10 of the 25 largest transactions in Canada, while no other institution Canadian or foreign showed up more than five times.
Geographic presence in major markets	+	Became the only Canadian bank with a considerable US presence [thanks in part to the Oppenheimer acquisition]. Secured key role in several large cross-border transactions with the US including clients such as AT&T.
Employee retention	-	During integration, there was a 60% turnover of the 5,000 staff in corporate banking
IT disruptions	N/A	
Leveraging of distribution channel	+	Able to successfully bundle loans, equity, and investment banking services.
Product coverage	+	Able to widen product coverage through either "in-house" development efforts or acquiring specialist firms [e.g. fixed income sales & trading]
Cross-selling	N/A	
Leveraging of knowledge	?	

M = mitigated

Source: Raynor, M., 1999. "CIBC, Corporate and Investment Banking." Case studies A, B, C. (Cambridge, Mass.: Harvard Business School).

Case Study – Banco Santander & Banco Central Hispano

Company & transactional overview

	Banco Santander	Banco Central Hispano
Company Background	• Family-run Spanish bank since mid-1800s, with the Botín family still owning a 5% share in 1999. Had considerable investment banking activities, and developed a strong presence in Latin America [Chile, Mexico, Brazil] through a host of acquisitions. Its Chilean bank, Banco Osorno y la Union, had for a long time been that country's largest bank. • Had recently bought Banesto, a Spanish bank with a strong retail presence, but preserved its brand name.	• Product of merger of Banco Central and Banco Hispano Americano [1992]. • Corcostegui becomes CEO in 1994 to turn around the troubled bank. Streamlines back offices and cuts staff by one-third.
Cultural characteristics	• Loose, informal, revolving around CEO, E. Botín. • Anglo-Saxon model: focus on shareholder value, bottom-line oriented, aggressive selling.	• Conservative, staid, slow-moving • German model: large industrial holdings, some unprofitable lending [values customer relationships].
Leadership characteristics	• Botín [CEO]: more autocratic, deal-maker, risk-taker, listened to advice but made most decisions himself on loans, acquisitions, therefore decision-making was rapid. • Dominant personality but recognized the need to attract talent. • Resistance to change? The perception was yes, that he was going to appoint his daughter, Ana [head of IB] as his successor.	• Corcostegui [CEO]: perceived as more thoughtful, detail-oriented and a consensus builder. Had managed the integration of Banco Bilbao and Banco Vizcaya, but eventually left as he lost the chairmanship to Ybarra. • May have had a more conservative image, but was open to innovations [internet initiatives]. Had a good rapport with institutional investors.
Transaction date	1999	
Transaction type	Merger of equals	
Transaction justification/integration goals	• Domain strengthening [consolidation] • Dilute the role of Latin American operations [which was representing 30% of overall banking activities in 1999. • New talent: E. Botín realized the importance of bringing in new managers. Senior management was thin at Santander, as few bankers appreciated working for Botín.	• Domain strengthening [consolidation]
Integration approach	Symbiotic	

Integration issues and actions:

Integration issues	Challenges/Decisions/Actions
Leadership	▪ Leadership structure, appointments decided prior to merger announcement. ▪ Middle-management appointments announced shortly after the merger. ▪ Senior executive team [G4]: Botín & Amusategui [BCH] as co-Chairmen; Inciarte [BS] as vice-Chairman; and Corcóstegui as CEO. Both sides learned from the BBV [Banco Bilbao Vizcaya] fiasco, in which the 2 co-CEOs did not agree and the Spanish government intervened to name a successor. Employee disruption related problems lasted for years. ▪ **Putting interests of the bank before that of his family [Botín]:** did not support his daughter, who had been offered to manage global wholesale banking, actually a demotion since she had also been running Latin American operations. Botín kept the deal secret from her. She subsequently resigned, as BCH bankers considered her a threat. ▪ **Working chemistry:** strong prior relationship between Botín and Corcóstegui; Corcóstegui's low-key, consensus-building approach reduced tensions. Complementary personality fit ["we see everything the same way"]. ▪ **Roles were well-defined:** Botín focused on deal-making, Corcóstegui on operations. [there was a wide range of issues to deal with: acquisition of Credito Predial Portugues that included a fight with the Portuguese government, winning of the auction of Banco Serfín in Mexico. ▪ **Frequent interactions:** met daily for hours to work out strategy and discuss results.
Human Resources	?
Integration level implemented	▪ High level for back-office [operations] functions, and IT platform in order to concentrate on cost-savings. ▪ High level on physical facilities [branches], by planning to close 450 branches in 2000 and another 450 in 3001. ▪ Low level for retail brands by adopting a multibranded strategy [keep Santander, Banesto and BCH retail brands separate]. If the branch of their original retail brand were closed, customers were to be redirected to the closest branch remaining open in the area even if this branch was operated under one of the other brand names.
Integration speed/timeliness	▪ The decision regarding the conversion of the IT platform was made quickly within a few months of the merger announcement.
IT conversion	▪ The IT platform of BCH was chosen over that of Santander, as the cost of merging the two platforms was estimated to be too high.
Integration steps	
Integration capabilities	Not evident.

Scorecard:

Impact area	Score [+/-]	Actual outcome
Client retention/extension	+	Loss of only 1.6% of retail customer base in 1999-2000 due to adoption of multi-brand strategy. The lower post-merger customer visibility in its investment banking activities was explained by BSCH's deliberate strategy to lower its risk profile.
Geographic presence in major market	+	Smooth integration process, allowed merged BSCH to expand its market presence through external growth, by acquiring in 2000 Bozano Simonsen [Brazil], Credito Predial Portugues [Portugal] and Banco Serfin [Mexico], launching an internet initiative [Patagon.com].
Employee retention	?	
IT disruptions	+	Given the high retail client retention rate in Spain, IT disruptions must have been relatively minor.
Leveraging of distribution channel	?	
Cross-selling	?	
Product/brand coverage	+	Its multi-brand strategy of keeping all three retail brands in Spain [Santander, BCH and Banesto] seemed to have maintained BSCH's overall brand coverage and avoid retail market share losses.
Leveraging of knowledge	?	

Sources:
Caplen, B., June 2000. "Merger Lessons from Spain." *Euromoney*, 374, 63.
Davis, S. 2000. *Bank Mergers, Lessons for the Future.* London: Mac Millan Press Ltd.
Institutional Investor. January 1998. "Bargain hunting, Santander style." 23 (1), 36.
Pearson, M., 1998. *Mergers and Acquisitions in Financial Services: A Global Analysis of M&A Corporate Strategy in the 1990s.* Dublin: Lafferty Group.
Popper, M., February 1999. "Angel Corcostegui, the Merger Master." *Institutional Investor*, 24 (2), 8.
Stewart, J., January 1995. "In Search of Spanish Synergy." *Euromoney*, 309, 42.
Tamzin, B., Bleakley, F., March 1999. "Botin's Sudden Exit." *Institutional Investor*, 24, 11.

Appendix 2, Table 3

Case Study — Banc One [Acquisitions through the early 1990s]

Company & transactional overview:

	Banc One	Acquired firms
Company Background	• US Bank holding group, that incorporated acquired "affiliate" banks into a decentralized "uncommon partnership", through which the Banc One franchise name, its corporate values and operating principles were transferred to the acquired firm. In return, Banc One aimed to transfer from the acquired firm product & concept innovations [best practices] back to the parent and its other affiliates. • Focused mostly on retail and small-size wholesale market [no loans made over USD 50 million]. • Was one of the most profitable US banks until the mid-1990s, averaging an ROE of 17% for the 1983-1993 decade. • Merged with First Chicago NBD in 1998 • Long-time Chairman John Mc Coy resigned in 1999.	Apart from M Corp., a large failed Texas bank acquired in 1989, most acquired firms were "average banks" in healthy financial condition.
Cultural characteristics	• People-oriented ["banking is people"] • Customer-oriented	
Leadership characteristics	• Decentralized structure [each affiliate bank has its own CEO, reporting to the Banc Corp. CEO] • Overall leadership centered around the Banc Corp. CEO, John Mc Coy	
Transaction date	Mid-1960s through mid-1990s	
Transaction type	All acquisitions [137 different banks]	
Transaction justification/integration goals	Domain extension [gaining presence in new geographical markets], domain exploration [leveraging knowledge/best practice] from acquired firms	
Integration approach	Preservation [until the early 1990s]	

Integration:

Integration issues	Challenges/Decisions/Actions
Leadership	• Banc One almost always kept the CEO and senior management of acquired firm in place • Decision-making relying on Mc Coy's charisma, as he had to manage 80 or more "affiliate" bank chiefs.

Human Resources	• Few restructurings, since HR decisions were left to the acquired firm
	• Motivating people:
	  ➢ Compensation: base-salaries usually not realigned [decision left to local management]; senior managers of all "affiliates" received a performance-based bonus
	  ➢ Friendly competition: since "affiliates" did not compete in the same regional markets, Banc One encouraged friendly competition throughout the group, using a uniform measure of financial performance [MICS]. This policy was aimed at motivating staff at all levels in acquired "affiliates."

Bridging the cultural gap	• Through its many acquisitions of small banks, senior Banc One management feared the lack of a cohesive culture and therefore was strongly committed to developing and maintaining a Banc One identity, the "glue that would hold together its federation."
	• Banc One centered its cultural identity around the following behavior characteristics that it strongly encouraged:
	  ➢ Financial performance: at all levels throughout the organization, financial performance was strongly encouraged.
	  ➢ Quality of service: quality of customer service had become the mantra of senior management, encouraged through issued statements of common identity ["9,000 people who care"].
	  ➢ Integrity: all middle and senior management of acquired firms had to sign a comprehensive "code of ethics."
	• Communication vehicles: Banc One culture was disseminated through:
	  ➢ Company songs: these were encouraged to be sung at company events ["There is no solution to dilution, M Bank's pain is Banc One's gain."]
	  ➢ Banc One College: used to transfer corporate values and operating standards to staff of "affiliates."
	  ➢ Awards: "Blue One" award given to staff with the highest profitability and best customer service

Integration issues	Challenges/Decisions/Actions
Integration level implemented	- **High level of integration**: R&D functions, operating procedures, financial reporting [MICS] accounting and auditing systems. - **Uneven level of integration**: IT & data-processing functions and systems due to the slowness in conversion. - **Low level of integration**: many back-office functions [there were still 92 check-processing and 23 telephone banking centers customer centers in the mid-1990s], front-office functions [sales, administration], HR policies, product range. Local bank managers were setting own certificate of deposit rates and handling their own product marketing.
Integration speed/timeliness	- **Financial reporting [MICS] and accounting systems**: fast, around 3-4 months after acquisition date. - **IT systems conversion**: process took usually about 11 months, sometimes longer. Slowness was due in large part to decentralized decision making regarding technology issues, as the acquired bank was usually heavily involved in the IT integration process.
IT conversion	- Until the mid-1990s, Banc One integrated the IT platforms of its "affiliates" with each other by keeping the original platforms in place and connecting ["patching"] them through an interface solution.
Integration steps	- **Inter-face management [IM]**: role played by the "affiliation manager." The affiliation manager worked with "affiliates" during the pre and post acquisition ["affiliation"] process. Named the conversion director from Banc One Services Corp. responsible for systems conversion. Explained the Banc One approach ["uncommon partnership"] to affiliate, helped coordinate and distribute Banc One policy manuals [corporate policy, accounting policy...] to affiliate management. Worked on an ongoing basis to explain integration guidelines. - **Establishing controls**: by requiring acquired "affiliates" to adopt Banc One's financial control system [MICS] that provided a standard measure of performance within the entire group. MICS became the "bible" of Banc One managers, as everyone was measured in the same way. - **Nurturing and practical support**: Banc One helped improve capabilities of existing management by providing general management skills and operating procedures. Moreover, "affiliates" had access to Banc One's R&D resources, shared data-processing [for a fee], product suggestions, in order to focus more on customers and not get bogged down in administrative detail. - **Accumulating business learning**: Banc One leveraged knowledge [transfer of best practices] from its "affiliates" through continuing education at Banc One College, the executive network and by fostering an atmosphere of informality and openness.
Integration capabilities	**Extensive knowledge codification**: a conversion management guide helped the affiliation manager, the conversion director, and "affiliate" management plan to implement integration. Listed the major tasks to be completed with a specific time-line for each one. Integration process was split into 3 phases: evaluation [pre-acquisition], conversion [to last 250 days after acquisition announcement date], and review.

Scorecard:

Impact area	Score [+/-]	Actual outcome
Client retention/extension	+	Extended its retail customer base throughout its geographic markets due to a generally good quality of service.
Geographic presence in major market	+	Gained a strong presence in retail/small-size wholesale markets throughout the mid-west and Texas [14 states]
Employee retention/replacement	+	Since HR responsibilities were left to acquired "affiliates," there were few restructurings. In the short-run, this was probably an advantage, as it minimized employee disruptions. However, in the long-run this policy tended to bloat the staff size of the "affiliates', as most local managers were reluctant to make job-cuts.
IT/DP problems	?	
Economies of scale achieved	-	■ The negative aspects of the "uncommon partnership" due to the greater autonomy of local management [greater bureaucracy, lack of standardization, duplication...] were started to be felt by 1994. By the mid to late 1990s, Banc One had become one of the less cost efficient US banks [efficiency ratio of 62% in 1998, ranked 7th out of the 10 largest US banks]. ■ A move toward consolidation ["the national partnership"] was underway starting in 1994-1995 to bring costs in line by: curtailing the authority of the "affiliate" bank chiefs; trimming 10% of the work force [5,500 job cuts]; integrating back-office functions telephone banking centers and check-clearing centers], and achieving IT commonality [replacing the "patched IT network" with a common platform].
Leveraging of distribution channel	?	It should be mentioned that Banc One extensively used its retail branch network as a distribution channel for its large credit card business [First USA], which it acquired in 1997.
Cross-selling	N/A	
Product/brand coverage	-	Due to a lack of standardization, there was a proliferation of retail financial products [65 different ones by 1993]. These were reduced to a total of 10.
Leveraging knowledge	+	Was successful [although hard to measure]

Sources:

Banking Management. April 1993. "The Electronic Bank Budget." 69 (4), 21.
Burger, K., April 1990. "Banc One Corp. Profit through Paradox." *Bank Systems and Technology*. 27 (4), 34.
Cahill, J., August 3, 1998. "Doubts Grow Over Banc One's Skill with Cost Scalpel – Firm Lags on Current Program of Cuts as First Chicago Merger Looms." *The Wall Street Journal*.
Davis, S. 2000. *Bank Mergers; Lessons for the Future*. London: Mac Millan Press Ltd.
Murray, M., March 10, 1998. "After Long Overhaul, Banc One Now Faces Pressure to Perform – Mc Coy Drops Old System of Autonomous Banks, Turns to Centralization –John Boy and John God." *The Wall Street Journal*.
Myers, P., 1989. "Banc One Corporation, 1989." *Case study*. Harvard Business School.
Spiegel, J., Gart, A., Gart, S., 1996. *Banking Redefined*. London, Singapore and Chicago: Irwin Professional Publishing.
Uyterhoven, U., 1993. "Banc One Corporation, 1993." *Case study*. Harvard Business School.

271

Appendix 2, Table 4
Case Study - Deutsche Bank and Bankers Trust

Company & transactional overview

	Deutsche Bank [DB]	Bankers Trust [BT]
Company Background	• Global German-based bank with commercial and investment banking activities. • Retail banking presence weak in Germany [5-6% of market share], but with extensive networks in Spain and Italy. • Decided to concentrate its strategic development on expanding its global investment banking presence as well as fund management. • Had started to build its investment banking capabilities with the acquisition of UK investment banking firm Morgan-Grenfell in 1989. DB had first given Morgan Grenfell much autonomy, but had fully integrated the firm following several trading scandals in the mid-1990s. However, DB had not been very successful in building up its investment banking business, despite hiring high-profile bankers from US firms. Since its acquisition of Morgan Grenfell, DB had spent as much as USD 3 billion to become a top investment bank. DB had spent a further USD 1.5 billion to foster cooperation between its investment bankers and commercial bankers. However, many investment bankers had left due to constant reorganizations.	• **US investment bank with a core focus on derivatives:** BT had originally been a commercial bank transforming itself into an investment bank as early as 1978 by underwriting commercial paper. Had since moved into derivatives, which had become its core business by the mid-1980s. • **Had a tarnished reputation:** was in 1996 still seriously weakened due to the collapse of its derivatives business following large customer losses [ex: Procter & Gamble] in 1994. Frank Newman was appointed CEO in 1996 to turn around BT, in part by curbing its aggressive culture and shifting the focus away from derivatives. • **Recent diversification:** Had recently gained a reasonable presence in junk bonds and asset management. Had bought Alex Brown Inc. in 1997 to move into equity underwriting. Alex Brown had specialized in some high-tech IPOs [eg. Amazon]. BT and Alex Brown Inc. were combined into 2 divisions: BT Alex Brown [investment banking arm] and the Private Client Services Group [retail arm]. • However, BT was not very competitive even in its less volatile markets [asset management and global custody], and still relatively weak in M&A advisory.
Cultural characteristics	• Stolid, hierarchical. • More of a commercial banking culture. • German. • Had a poor reputation of bringing in outside [foreign] investment bankers and keeping them ["no one wanted to work for DB"].	• Risk-taking, aggressive, market driven. • American

Leadership characteristics	• **Rolf Breuer:** CEO of DB. Spent his entire career at DB, and had been Chairman for 1.5 years.
	  ✓ Came from the securities-trading side of the business, unlike his predecessors at DB who had come from commercial banking.
	  ✓ Fluent in English and French, unlike many of his counterparts in German banking.
	• Senior management composition was heavily weighted towards Germans [especially, the management board or Vorstand]
		• **Frank Newman:** CEO of BT since 1996.
		  ✓ Had been US Treasury undersecretary in the Clinton administration.
		  ✓ Previously, had been the CFO of Wells Fargo and Bank of America, where he had in the late 1980s acquired significant experience in managing around large and troubled banks.
		  ✓ However, was not very popular with BT staff, who felt that he had seriously impaired BT's risk-taking culture without substituting much else.
		• Short on senior management

Transaction date	Late 1998 – early 1999	
Transaction type	Acquirer	Acquired
Transaction justification/integration goals	Domain extension. DB wanted to build a presence in the US and expand its capital market and investment banking business. BT was bought because DB had been unable to build an investment banking capability.	
Integration approach	Absorption	

272

Integration issues and actions:

Integration issues	Challenges/Decisions/Actions
Leadership	• **Leadership structure:** ✓ Originally, Frank Newman [BT CEO] was to remain as co-head of investment and corporate banking, sharing the responsibilities with Ackerman [a DB senior vice-president and a Vorstand {board} member]. Initially, Newman was also offered a seat on the DB Vorstand. ✓ However, Newman resigned in mid-1999 as Vorstand members had doubts about how he would relate to younger members and feared the swelling of its membership. It seems that many BT and DB staffers were not sorry to see Newman depart, as he had never been very popular. • **Communication:** ✓ **Failure to communicate a commitment to US operations:** many BT employees remained unconvinced that DB had a coherent strategy. Worse, there was a general misunderstanding at BT that DB had a "Europe first policy" and "had given up on the US market_," a perception that was picked up by enough BT clients. Furthermore, this situation contributed to the loss of some key talent at BT [see below] and made recruitment in the US more difficult.
Human Resources	• **HR replacement:** ✓ **Extent of HR replacement:** about 5,500 layoffs were announced for the New York and London offices due to overlapping operations [to provide cost-savings of USD 600 million]. ✓ **Selection process:** used a system of "meritocracy," through which the best talented individuals of both companies would be retained in the combined firm. ✓ **Poor communication:** although the selection process was fairly transparent, communication efforts appeared insufficient. Some DB and BT investment bankers complained that they had read about the job-cut details first in the press before DB management had actually informed them. • **HR retention:** ✓ **A retention policy biased toward BT senior management:** prior to completion of the merger, BT managers who agreed not to leave were given large financial incentives in order to buy DB more time for deciding which personnel to keep. A retention pool of USD 400 million was set-aside for this purpose. However, many BT staffers resented the bias of the retention package towards senior managers, as Frank Newman and Richard Daniel [BT's number two executive] received packages worth USD 100 million and USD 25 million respectively. Enough BT employees were resentful feeling that BT senior management failed in raising their compensation package with the new firm leading to disillusionnement and loss in morale. ✓ **Trying to stem departures:** aware of the loss in employee morale and the fact that other firms were attempting to poach BT staff, DB resorted to generous compensation inducements for retaining personnel. DB could not afford another disaster such as when its top technology banker [Quattrone] had walked out with his 100-member team in 1998. DB promised to pay BT managers a portion of the 1999 bonuses in mid-July 1999 after the merger completion. However, as soon as these bonuses were paid out, the exodus continued. DB was falling into a trap, in which certain BT employees were considering offers from competing firms for the sole purpose of extracting higher compensation and greater guarantees from DB ["Essentially employees are holding Deutsche Bank up"].
Bridging the cultural gap	• The two main cultural conflicts undermining BT employee morale were: ✓ BT's entrepreneurial and free-wheeling spirit vs. DB's quest for organizational control and commercial banking mentality [more of an issue] ✓ BT's Anglo-Saxon culture vs. DB's German culture [less of an issue]. • **Communication:** communication efforts to bridge the cultural gap lacked consistency and were insufficient ✓ Some senior DB officials did officially support the need for an entrepreneurial spirit within the bank, while others [Breuer] strongly stated after the BT merger that he intended to place tight controls on BT and fully integrate it into German operations ["we don't believe in autonomy"]. ✓ Although DB did try to dispel notions that Germans were running the bank by stressing that 3 out of 5 of DB's foreign business units were managed by non-Germans, yet some stories gained wide circulation among BT staff [a senior DB manager telling his US colleague: "when thinking of our perspective, just remember the order of letters in the alphabet: Frankfurt, London, New York"].
Integration level implemented	■ High level of integration [full absorption]
Integration speed/timeliness	?
IT/technology conversion	• IT decisions between DB and BT were made on a case-by-case basis. Some particular systems were discarded, others kept with the hope that they could be later combined. • Risk management presented another integration challenge. DB had previously tried to install a global risk management system across their operations, but had failed due to internal conflicts over methodology and technology. Prior to the merger, BT had developed yet another risk management system using other technology.
Integration steps	• **Strengthening [weakening] the organization:** with the aim of bolstering BT by deepening its staff and management, DB brought in outsiders mostly from Merrill Lynch in the hope that they would bring their business relationships with them. Ironically, these individuals were recruited into BT's bond business, which was probably one of its strongest units. Instead of strengthening BT, this situation caused considerable internal conflict and soon veterans from BT's bond business began to leave.
Integration capabilities	Not evident.

273

Scorecard:

Impact area	Score [+/-]	Actual outcome
Client retention/extension	?	
Geographic presence in major market	?	By 2000, still lagged behind J.P. Morgan Chase and Goldman Sachs. Ranked 6th in global debt and underwriting, 13th in global M&A. In the US IPO market, had moved to 6th from 9th position in 1999.
Employee retention	-	A year after the merger [summer 2000], DB was still losing senior managers and their teams to other banks.
IT disruptions	?	
Economies of scale achieved	?	
Leveraging of distribution channel	?	
Cross-selling	?	
Product/brand coverage	?	
Leveraging of knowledge	?	

Sources:

Copulsky, E. December 21, 1998. "BT Dangles a Golden Carrot to Get Bankers to Stay: Also Tweaks Change-of-Control Packages for Managing Directors." *The Investment Dealers' Digest.*
Copulsky, E. May 31, 1999. "July 4 Means Real Independence for BT Staff." *The Investment Dealers' Digest.*
Copulsky, E. September 6, 1999. "Deutsche' Latest Stand." *The Investment Dealers' Digest*
Currie, A. March 2000. "Tribal Warfare in North America." *Euromoney*, 371, 1-36.
Davis, S. 2000. *Bank Mergers, Lessons for the Future.* London: Mac Millan Press Ltd.
The Economist. November 28, 1998. "The Battle of the Bulge Bracket," 349, 73-74.
The Economist. July 3, 1999. "Finance and Economics: Frank Exchange," 352, 65-66.
Feinberg, P. August 7, 2000. "Opinions Differ on Deutsche's Progress." *Pensions and Investments*, 28 (16), 3.
Grygo, E. April 24, 2000. "Merger-Happy Deutsche Bank Keeps It Busy at the Front Line of Planning." *Infoworld*, 22 (17), 44.
Guyon, J. January 11, 1999. "Why Deutsche Is Banking on BT." *Fortune*, 39 (1), 90.
Helland, E. February 1999. "Why Deutsche Technology May Stunt Bankers Trust Integration." *Wall Street & Technology*, 17 (2), 38-40.
Lee, P. May 1997. "Newman's Vision Thing." *Euromoney*, 337, 34-35.
Marshall, J. February 1999. "Bankers to Compete with Morgan Grenfell." *Global Investor*, 119, 5.
Marshall, J. January 1999. "The Biggest Yet." *US Banker*, 109 (1), 12.
Pearson, M. 1998. *Mergers and Acquisitions in Financial Services: A Global Analysis of M&A Corporate Strategy in the 1990s.* Dublin: the Lafferty Group.
Peterson, T., Silverman, G. December 7, 1998. " Is Deutsche Bank 'Out of Its Depth'?" *Business Week*, 3607, 126.
Rhoades, C. November 25, 1998. " Deutsche Bank's Breuer Faces Challenge of Bridging Culture Gap." *The Asian Wall Street Journal*, p. 26.
Shearlock, P. January 1999. "Deutsche's Gamble." *The Banker*, 149 (875), 16-17.
Tunick, B. February 26. "Lagging Rivals, but Striving, Deutsche Ousts BT Executives." *The Investment Dealer's Digest*, pp. 6-7.

Appendix2, Table 5

Case Study – NationsBank [Bank of America] and Montgomery Securities

Company & transactional overview

	NationsBank [Bank of America]	Montgomery Securities
Company Background	■ Originally called NCNB [North Carolina National Bank]. Managed by fast-charging CEO, Hugh Mc Coll. Acquired, from 1983 through the mid 1990s, more than 50 banks throughout the US south and southwest. Changed its name to NationsBank in 1991. Merged in 1998 with Bank of America and adopted its name. The newly combined BofA became at the time the largest US financial services firm after Citigroup with USD 614 billion in assets. Hugh Mc Coll became CEO of the new bank, while David Coulter, the former CEO of the old BofA became President and designated successor. However, Coulter was forced to resign two weeks into the merger [October 1998] due to a large write-down of a hedge-fund loan that he had arranged. Other senior executives from the old BofA resigned in the following months. ■ **Growth strategy:** For years, NationsBank's growth strategy was based on building scale in retail and commercial banking quickly [average asset growth p.a. of 25% between 1983 and 1995] by expanding its geographical presence or consolidating its existing position in certain states. The Bank of America deal was to provide NationsBank with a key opening on the US west coast, allowing the combined entity to become the first true coast-to-coast US bank with an extensive network serving 30 million households and 2 million businesses. Although aiming to derive large-scale economies by consolidating its operations with BofA, NationsBank was also hoping to grow revenue by better leveraging BofA's large retail distribution channel. ■ **Building capital markets capabilities:** As H. McColl aimed to develop NationsBank as a financial services firm, he gradually started growing its capital markets business. His 1994 acquisition of derivatives firm Chicago Research and Trading [CRT] was the cornerstone of this effort. By 1997, NationsBank had built important capabilities in fixed-income trading and research with the largest trading-floor outside of NY. Despite subsequently spending large sums to attract outside talent, NationsBank's investment banking arm [NationsBank Capital Markets Inc.,] had not been successful in becoming a major capital markets player especially in underwriting and M&A advisory areas. The acquisition of a full-fledged investment bank therefore seemed the best solution. In fact, future merger partner BofA had come to the same decision by acquiring in 1997 Robertson Stephens, the investment banking rival of Montgomery Securities. ■ **Moving towards "universal banking:"** NationsBank planned to leverage its key corporate banking customer network by integrating investment and corporate banking activities to provide a "one stop shop" ["universal banking"] to its customers. This same strategy was still pursued after the BofA merger. ■ **Integration approach/track-record:** NationsBank appeared to have successfully integrated its acquisitions up until the Barnett Banks transaction in 1997. NationsBank's integration approach was usually based on quickly and completely absorbing the acquired firm into its fold, and by imposing its aggressive culture. The bank also tended to deeply slash costs especially in its "in market" acquisitions. NationsBank had developed an "in house" acquisition competence by creating early-on a full-time integration unit with a large staff [50 individuals] and extensively codifying prior acquisition knowledge [conversion manuals, project management software...]. Realizing the important cultural differences between the two firms, NationsBank's integration of derivatives firm CRT was slow and gradual, and appeared successful. However, NationsBank showed strains with its integration of Barnett Banks and especially of BofA. With Barnett Banks, a botched systems conversion and degradation in customer service due to deep employee cuts [55% of the cost base had been slashed] had triggered significant customer withdrawals. The complete integration of BofA was daunting due to its very large size.	■ Firm tracing its roots back to 1969, when founded by Sanford Robertson. Thomas Weisel became a partner in 1978, shifting the focus of the firm from corporate finance to trading. After bitter disagreements with Weisel, Robertson left to start his own firm [Robertson Stephens]. Weisel changed the name of the firm to Montgomery Securities. Strength in: ✓ Equity sales and trading [OTC] ✓ Corporate finance: ranked 10th largest US underwriter for IPOs in 1997; M&A advisory; strong focus on high-tech clients [e.g. Yahoo!]. ✓ Growing high-yield bond business [based in NY]
Cultural characteristics	■ Aggressive but team oriented. • Bureaucratic/centralized organization. • Many southerners, especially in senior management positions. • Bottom-line-oriented [any employee who identified cost-savings, received a check for 10% of the amount saved].	■ Aggressive "trading mentality" ["West coast Salomon Brothers"]. ■ Entrepreneurial, dynamic.
Leadership characteristics	■ **Hugh Mc Coll:** combative ex-Marine [hand grenade on desk]; uncomfortable with subordinates challenging his opinions [talented senior managers picked up in acquisitions usually did not last long]; had a tight clamp on managerial decision making and autonomy.	■ **Thomas Weisel:** former nationally ranked speed skating champion, trader.
Transaction date	July 1997	
Transaction type	Acquiring	Acquired
Transaction justification/Integr. goals	Market extension: to acquire strong investment banking capabilities that it could not develop internally, especially in corporate finance.	
Integration	Absorption	

Integration issues and actions:

Integration issues	Challenges/Decisions/Actions
Leadership	• **Originally defined leadership structure and area responsibilities:** after acquisition in mid 1997, Thomas Weisel becomes CEO of the rechristened NationsBanc Montgomery Securities [NMS], becoming the main investment-banking arm of NationsBank. Mc Coll seemed to indicate to Weisel that he wanted a "reverse take-over" by NMS of NationsBank's capital markets activities ["you know we haven't been able to get it right, we want you to take over and drive the bus"].
	• **Misalignment of vision and strategy:** clear differences soon emerged between Weisel and NationsBank senior management regarding the direction to take NMS. Weisel preferred that NMS remain largely focused on the high-tech sector, whereas NationsBank wanted to redirect NMS towards its larger size customer base in sectors in which it had a strong presence [oil, food & beverage, retail...]. Furthermore, Weisel did not seem to particularly agree with NationsBank/BofA's "universal banking" approach, which he described as "selling a suite of banking products."
	Turf battles: originally, NationsBank agreed that Weisel and NMS would continue running its own businesses, including its lucrative high-yield bond business. However, the situation changed after the BofA merger [April 1998] that took place 8-9 months after the acquisition of Montgomery Securities. The senior management of the new BofA decided to merge the bond businesses of all three firms [NationsBank, BofA, and NMS] together, which would be managed by former NationsBank Capital Markets Inc. out of Charlotte. In addition, NMS was stripped of its private equity activities that were transferred to former NationsBank capital markets executives.
	Weisel's clash with Mc Coll and departure: after a sharp conversation with H. Mc Coll ["Tom, don't you understand that you have been bought?"], Weisel leaves NMS in September 1998 due to the differences in vision/strategy for the firm and the bitter turf battles described above. He founds a new investment-banking firm, Thomas Weisel LLC, focusing on corporate finance products and services for emerging growth companies.
	Succession and senior management turnover: Lewis Coleman, CFO of the old BofA, is named as successor CEO to Weisel. However, key senior executives from NMS [including 31 of its 68 partners], as well as many staffers, defect to Weisel at his new firm. To fill the gaps in senior management, senior investment bankers from outside firms are recruited by providing high compensation packages. NMS is renamed Banc of America Securities [BAS] seven months later [May 1998].
Human Resources	• **Original recruitment and retention efforts:** in early 1998, NMS set up a USD 600 million private equity fund with co-investment features in order to attract and retain talented individuals [selected employees would be invited to participate as co-investors]. However, the control of the fund was turned over to NationsBank's former capital markets operations in the summer of 1998.
	• **Massive employee defections:** between Weisel's departure in September 1998 and early 1999, NMS lost 20% of its investment banking professionals [about 160 individuals including 31 partners] to Weisel's new firm. Most of the departures were due to a strong loyalty to Weisel and a shared feeling of uncertainty/distrust about BofA's future intentions prevailing at the time within NMS. The atmosphere for those remaining at NMS was further strained by incidents of departing bankers having their bonuses temporarily taken away by NationsBank/BofA [dubbed "an administrative error" by NationsBank] and legal conflicts between the firm and some key former NMS officials who had defected to Weisel's firm. NationsBank/BofA had taken 10 former employees to court claiming that they had violated confidentiality and non-competition agreements. These large defections were expensive, as NationsBank/BofA was forced to accelerate the payout to departing/former MS partners originally planned over three years [cost of USD 460 million].
Bridging the cultural gap	• **A feeling of cultural takeover:** Little effort seems to have been made to narrow the gap between NMS's entrepreneurial/trading environment and NationsBank's centralized/corporate banking culture. In fact, it seems that many NMS employees felt to have been the victims of an aggressive cultural takeover by NationsBank. They resented certain actions taken early on by the parent [objections to NMS' extensive art-work in their offices, scrapping of their long-held slogan "Power of Growth"] and believed that these were indicators of far worse things to come.
Integration level implemented	High level of integration achieved, with all NMS activities eventually integrated into NationsBank/BofA capital markets operations. The old Montgomery Securities brand name only survived in the form of the "Montgomery equities sales and trading division" within Bank of America Securities. However, NationsBank/BofA may have integrated NMS to a greater extent than originally planned due to the accelerated erosion of the NMS franchise.
Integration speed/timeliness	
Integration steps	• Was there an Interface Management established by NationsBank for this particular integration? • What powers and responsibilities did NationsBank assign to the IM?
Integration capabilities	Not evident in this situation

276

Scorecard:

Impact area	Score [+/-]	Actual outcome
Client retention/extension	?	• Lost key clients to Weisel [Oracle, Cisco, Yahoo!, Mirage Resorts].
Presence in major market	?	• US ranking in IPO underwriting: 15th [2000]. • US ranking in M&As: 13th [2000] ahead of 14th ranked Weisel LLC. • US ranking in high-yield bond origination:
Employee retention	-	• Lost more than 20% of investment banking professionals [including nearly half of the Montgomery partners].
IT disruptions	?	
Leveraging of distribution channel	?	
Cross-selling	?	
Product/brand coverage	?	
Leveraging of knowledge	?	

Sources:

The Economist, January 27, 2001. "Deal Making Done." 358 (8206), 71–72.
Bransten, L. January 19, 1999. "Montgomery Securities Founder Starts Rival Investment Bank Aimed at Giants." *The Wall Street Journal*.
Brooks, R. September 18, 1998. "NationsBank Unit's Founder Weisel Is Expected to Leave after Turf Battle." *The Wall Street Journal*.
Celarier, M. February 1998. "US Banks Dare to Cross Cultures." *Euromoney*, 346, 46–49.
Celarier, M. May 1998. " A Bad Case of Sibling Rivalry." *Euromoney*, 349, 33.
Copulsky, E. August 31, 1998. "Investment Banking Scorecard." *The Investment Dealer's Digest*, p. 9.
Copulsky, E. September 28, 1998. "Weisel Leaves NationsBank to Start His Own Boutique: New San Francisco Firm Will Combine Advisory and Merchant Banking." *The Investment Dealer's Digest*, p. 1.
Copulsky, E. May 17, 1999. "Montgomery Name Disappears, as Bank of America Securities Debuts." *The Investment Dealer's Digest*, pp. 11–12.
Currie, A. November 1999. "When Cutting Costs Is Not Enough." *Euromoney*. 59.
Davis, S. 2000. *Bank Mergers, Lessons for the Future*. London: Mac Millan Press Ltd.
Eade, P. January 1996. "Jack of All Trades." *Euromoney*. p. 47.
Horowitz, J. April 6, 1998. "NationsBank Sees Rosenfeld's Fund as Recruiting Pool." *The Investment Dealer's Digest*, 64 (14), 5–6.
Horowitz, J. Jan 12 1998. "Montgomery Explodes with Expansion Plans." *The Investment Dealer's Digest*, 64 (2), 5–6.
King, R. T., Swisher, K. April 14, 1998. "Banks Bulking Up: What Happens Next—Citigroup, Bank America's Goals Differ—Bank America Deal to Join Bitter Rivals. *The Wall Street Journal*.
Mc Murray, S. October 1994. "The Culture Catch at CRT." *Institutional Investor*, 28 (10), 206.
Mc Reynolds, R. October 1999. "Robbie's on a Roll." *US Banker*, 109 (10), 35–37.
Pearson, M. 1998. *Mergers and Acquisitions in Financial Services: A Global Analysis of M&A Corporate Strategy in the 1990s*. Dublin: the Lafferty Group.
Raghavan, A., Brooks, R. September 22, 1998. "Weisel's Quitting NationsBank Prompts a 'What Went Wrong?'" *The Wall Street Journal*.
Schack, J. February 21. "Best-Laid Plans." *Institutional Investor*, 35 (2), 60–68.
Sherer, P., Mollenkamp, C. February 16, 2000. "Deals and Dealmakers: Bank of America Aspires to Be a Big Investment Banker." *The Wall Street Journal*.
Smalhout, J. February 2000. "Lessons of Mc Coll's Long March." *Euromoney*, p. 117.
The Wall Street Journal, September 23, 1998. "NationsBank Names Lewis Coleman CEO of Montgomery Unit."
Zuckerman, G., Brooks, R. April 30, 1999. "Investment Banking Indigestion: A Recipe." *The Wall Street Journal*.

Appendix 2, Table 6
Case Study – The GE Capital Approach to Integration

GE Capital Overview

Company Background	• Subsidiary of GE • Financial services conglomerate with 27 separate business units, including 50,000 employees worldwide. • Businesses range from credit-card services, to commercial real estate financing to transportation equipment leasing financing.
Acquisitions and growth strategy	• Acquisitions are an important part of growth strategy. Each EVP [executive vice president], responsible for managing one or more business units, has a business development officer focusing on finding, analysing and negotiating acquisitions.
Transaction type	All acquisitions
Transaction justification/integration goals	• **Domain strengthening**: consolidating an acquisition into a GE business line [ex: Chase Manhattan's leasing business into GE's Capital Vendor Services]. • **Domain exploration**: acquisition turned into a new business line [ex: Travelers' Mortgage Services becoming its own business unit]. • **Hybrid**: parts of an acquisition are consolidated into an existing GE Capital business unit, other parts are kept as stand-alone operations and becoming their own business line.
Integration approaches	Mostly absorption, some preservation

Views on integration	• Acquisition integration seen as a competitive advantage
	• Acquisition integration seen as a replicable process
	• **Importance of integration planning**: earlier is better, during the pre-announcement phase. Integration planning starts in the due diligence phase. Due diligence managers constantly report in. This fosters better decisions as to whether the deal should be closed at all.
	• **A pathfinder model for integration**: has built an acquisition model through GE workshops, which it has applied successfully to different acquisitions. The model is divided into four "action" stages, each of which is divided into two or three sub-processes:
	  ✓ **Pre-acquisition** [due diligence, negotiation and announcement, closure]
	  ✓ **Foundation building** [launch, acquisition integration work-out, strategy formulation]
	  ✓ **Rapid-integration** [implementation, course assessment and readjustment]
	  ✓ **Assimilation** [long-term plan evaluation and assessment, capitalizing on success]

Development of integration capabilities	• Has engaged hundreds of staff in making acquisitions a core competence with specific workout teams to map out the transaction process and identify key issues in integration. • Created in 1992 a "change acceleration" methodology that identifies best integration practices and develops a set of model approaches. • Has sponsored conferences to refine practices, share tools and discuss case studies of past integrations and those in progress. These lessons are on-line to all GE Capital business leaders over the intranet. Other tools: 100 day-plans, functional integration checklists, consulting resources. These tools are kept up to date and corporate HR is in charge of disseminating them.

The GE Capital Integration Process

	Actions	Outcomes
PRE-ACQUISITION		
Assessing the cultural and business practice gap	• At pre-merger stage during due diligence, identify cultural/business practice differences and assess whether they are bridgeable [even though financials may be excellent]	• Decide whether or not to pursue the acquisition evaluation process
Interface management	• Select the integration manager [head of the interface management team]	
Assess leadership and management of acquired firm	• Evaluate the strengths and weaknesses of the senior and mid-management of the acquired firm	• Decide if and what management changes will be necessary
Bridging the cultural gap	• Develop a communication strategy including the following considerations: ➤ **Audiences:** senior managers from both firms, IM manager and team, other employees of acquired firm and GE, clients and community. ➤ **Timing:** the timing of communication for each audience may be different [before announcement, at time of closure, 2 months later]. ➤ **Mode:** newsletters, videos, memos, town meetings, management visits. ➤ **Message:** transparency is emphasized ["information is not hidden from employees"]. Avoid saying: It will be business as usual." and "it's a merger of equals" if it is not.	• The more that people know what is happening, the more they will be amenable to change and overcome cultural differences.
FOUNDATION BUILDING		
Interface management	• Introduce integration manager to acquired firm staff. • **Recognized role of integration manager as full-time.** The role evolved over time, emerged especially with Gelco acquisition [leasing company], as its acquisition went smoothly However, the critical role of IM was not recognized until several acquisitions later. • **Use two IM types:** high-potential individual [are less-seasoned and focus on straightforward acquisitions] and seasoned-hand [know GE Cap and have good mgmt. Skills, focus on more complex ones]. Usually, pick the ones that have been on the due diligence team, are the most effective]. • **IM manager responsibilities:** responsible for creating and delivering integration plan. *Gate-keeper* [screening information requests from the parent], *Facilitates/manages integration process* [works with acquired company to make its practices more consistent with those of GE, add new functions such as quality improvement/risk management], help acquired firm [explain GE culture, business customs, changes in roles/responsibilities], explains the acquired company culture and practices to GE executives. • **IM manager manages the "connective tissue" between both firms;** defuses potential conflicts [e.g., introduction of the integrity policy in European acquisition, where he used a more sensitive, softer tack by using a more constructive approach by using acquired firm's own managers rather than GE's. • **IM manager responsibilities do not include:** P&L as it would reduce the accountability of managers of acquiring firm and acquired company.	
HR retention/replacement	• **Selection process:** use transparency and fairness. Show respect for those who have been terminated. • **Speed in communicating and executing layoffs:** GE delayed the restructuring [personnel reduction] for a year or more in order to avoid employee disruptions.	• **Builds credibility:** Powerful way of helping those that remain to develop positive feeling about their new employer.
Re-engage the acquired firm/bridging the cultural gap	• **Prepare and implement 100-day integration plan:** is a blueprint of the actions needed to integrate the company into GE Capital [ex: what functions to integrate, steps for financial compliance, compensation/benefit realignment]. Involves GE Capital business manager, IM manager and managers of acquired firm. Acquired firm managers present the positive aspects of their company, product and plans, and asked to identify areas of synergies and of possible improvement and strengths [eg. areas where best practice can be imported or exported]. GE Capital executives present policies, standards and practices of the company [what needs to be incorporated into the company]. • **Communication:** disseminate the 100 day integration plan	• Cultural differences are discussed in a constructive way, each side learns about each other's culture. • Re-engages acquired company management by providing a time-line, challenges and new sense of purpose.
Strengthening the firm and establishing control	• Commit sufficient resources, introduce systems of control & assign accountability	

RAPID INTEGRATION		
Accelerating integration/bridging the cultural gap	• **Confronting cultural differences head-on through "cultural workout sessions"** [especially for non-US acquisitions]: involves a cross-cultural analysis over 3 day period with consulting firms at the close of the 100 day integration plan period. Focuses on identifying cultural differences and convergences between firms, discussing their implications for doing business [how to go to market, differentiation in authority concepts]; re-orient the debate to the future [where do they want to take the company for the next 6 months, resulting in a new business plan outline].	• **Work-out session:** brings together in a concrete plan the goals established as part of the original M/A justification and dreams/aspirations of new management team to be used after the 100-day period [building on the 100-day integration plan]. A very effective way to bridge the cultural gap.
Assessment and adjustment	• **Audit the course of the integration process** • **With feedback, modify course of integration if necessary**	• Will help to address the challenge of determinism [lack of flexibility in adjusting to new situations]
ASSIMILATION		
Bridging the cultural gap	• **Continuing-education:** through Capital University • **Long-term management exchange:** non-US middle managers learn about US and GE Capital culture by being assigned to GE Capital business units in the US.	• Narrowing the cultural gap through immersion
Further codifying integration knowledge	• **Continue developing integration tools, practices and processes**	

Source: Ashkenas, R.N., DeMonaco, L.J., Francis, S.C. January-February 1998. "Making the Deal Real: How GE Capital Integrates Acquisitions." *Harvard Business Review.*

References

Akhavein, J. D., Berger, A. N., and Humphrey, D. B. 1997. "The Effects of Mega-mergers on Efficiency and Prices: Evidence from a Bank Profit Function." *Review of Industrial Organization,* 12.

Amihud, Y., de Long, G., and Saunders, A. 2002. "The Effects of Cross-Border Mergers on Bank Risk and Value." *Journal of International Money and Finance.* Forthcoming.

Amihud, Y., and Lev, B. 1981. "Risk Reduction as a Managerial Motive for Conglomerate Mergers." *Bell Journal of Economics,* March.

Ashkenas, R., DeMonaco, L. J., and Francis, S. C. 1998. "Making the Dean: How GE Capital Integrates Acquisitions." *Harvard Business Review,* January–February.

Bank Director. 2002. "Caveat Acquirer—Beware of Customer Runoff." January.

Bank for International Settlements. 1999. *Report on Consolidation in the Financial Sector.* Basle: BIS, 136.

Beatty, R., Santomero, A., and Smirlock, M. 1987. "Bank Merger Premiums: Analysis and Evidence." *New York University Salomon Center for the Study of Financial Institutions Monograph Series on Economics and Finance,* 3.

Berger, A. N., Demsetz, R. S., and Strahan, P. E. 1998. *The Consolidation of the Financial Services Industry: Causes, Consequences, and Implications for the Future.* New York: Federal Reserve Bank of New York.

Berger, A. N. and DeYoung, R. 2001. "The Effects of Geographic Expansion on Bank Efficiency." Working paper, Board of Governors of the Federal Reserve System, Washington, D.C.

Berger, A. N., DeYoung, R., Genay, H., and Udell, G. F. 2000. "Globalization of Financial Institutions: Evidence from Cross-Border Banking Performance," *Brookings-Wharton Papers on Financial Services,* 3.

Berger, A. N., Hancock, D., and Humphrey, D. B. 1993. "Bank Efficiency Derived from the Profit Function." *Journal of Banking and Finance,* April.

Berger, A. N., and Hannan, T. H. 1996. "Using Measures of Firm Efficiency to Distinguish Among Alternative Explanations of the Structure-Performance Relationship." *Managerial Finance.*

Berger, A. N., and Humphrey, D. B. 1992a. "Measurement and Efficiency Issues in Commercial Banking." In *Output Measurement in the Service Sector*, Zvi Griliches, ed. Chicago, IL: University of Chicago Press.

Berger, A. N., and Humphrey, D. B. 1992b. "Megamergers in Banking and the Use of Cost Efficiency as an Antitrust Defense," *The Antitrust Bulletin*, 37.

Berger, A. N., and Humphrey, D. B. 1993. "Bank Scale Economies, Mergers, Concentration, and Efficiency: The U.S. Experience." *Revue d'Economies Financiere*, 27.

Berger, A. N., Hunter, W. C., and Timme, S. J. 1993. "The Efficiency of Financial Institutions: A Review of Research Past, Present and Future." *Journal of Banking and Finance*, April.

Berger, A. N., and Mester, L. 1997. "Inside the Black Box: What Explains Differences in the Efficiencies of Financial Institutions?" *Journal of Banking and Finance* 21.

Berger, P. G., and Ofek, E. 1995. "Diversification's Effect on Firm Value," *Journal of Financial Economics*, 37.

Billet, M. 1996. "Targeting Capital Structure: The Relationship Between Risky Debt and the Firm's Likelihood of Being Acquired." *Journal of Business*, 69.

Bohl, D. L. (Ed.). 1989. *Tying the Corporate Knot: An American Management Association Research Report on the Effects of Mergers and Acquisitions*. New York: American Management Association.

Boyd, J., and Graham, S. 1991. "Investigating the Bank Consolidation Trend." Federal Reserve Bank of Minneapolis *Quarterly Review*, 15, Spring.

Bozman, J. S. 1989. "Merging Without Purging." *Computerworld*, 23 (18).

Brewer, E., Jackson, W., Jagtiani, J., and Nguyen, T. 2001. "The Price of Bank Mergers in the 1990s." Federal Reserve Bank of Chicago *Economic Perspectives*, 30.

Brown, S. J., and Warner, J. B. 1985. "Using Daily Stock Returns: The Case of Event Studies." *Journal of Financial Economics*, 14.

Buch, C. 2002. "Information or Regulation: What Is Driving the International Activities of Commercial Banks?" *Journal of Money, Credit and Banking*, 23.

Buch, C., and de Long, G. 2001. "International Bank Mergers: What's Luring the Rare Animal?" Working paper, Kiel Institute of World Economics, Kiel, Germany.

Buck-Lew, M., Wardle, C. E., and Pliskin, N. 1992. "Accounting for Information Technology in Corporate Acquisitions." *Information and Management*, 22.

Buono, A. F., and Bowditch, J. L. 1989. *The Human Side of Mergers and Acquisitions*. San Francisco: Jossey-Bass.

Caldwell, B., and Medina, D. 1990. "After the Merger," *Information Week*, January 15.

Caplen, B. 2000. "Merger Lessons from Spain." *Euromoney*, June.

Chandler, A. D. 1962. *Strategy and Structure: Chapters in the History of the Industrial Enterprise*. Cambridge, Mass.: MIT Press.

Clark, J. 1988. "Economies of Scale and Scope at Depository Financial Institutions: A Review of the Literature." *Economic Review*, Federal Reserve Bank of Kansas City.

Cornett, M., and Tehranian, H. 1992. "Changes in Corporate Performance Associated with Bank Acquisitions." *Journal of Financial Economics*, 31.

Cornett, M., Hovakimian, G., Palia, D., and Tehranian, H. 1998. "The Impact of the Manager-Shareholder Conflict on Acquiring Bank Returns." Working paper, Boston College, Boston, Mass.

Crossan, M. M., and Inkpen, A. C. 1992. "Believing Is Seeing: An Exploration of the Organizational Learning Concept and the Evidence from the Case of Joint Venture Learning." Working paper, University of Western Ontario Business School.

Cumming, C., and Hirtle, B. J. 2001. "The Challenges of Risk Management in Diversified Financial Companies." *Federal Reserve Bank of New York, Economic Policy Review*, 7 (1).

Cummins, J. D., and Zi, H. 1998. "Comparisons of Frontier Efficiency Levels." *Journal of Productivity Analysis*, June.

Cybo-Ottone, A., and Murgia, M. 1997. "Mergers and Acquisitions in European Banking Markets," Working paper, Associazione Bancaria Italiana and Università Degli Studi di Pavia, Italy.

Datta, D. K. 1991. "Organizational Fit and Acquisition Performance: Effects of Post-Acquisition Integration." *Strategic Management Journal*, 12.

Davis, S. I. 2000. *Bank Mergers: Lessons for the Future*. New York: St. Martin's Press. 1993.

De Long, G. 1993. "The Influence of Foreign Banking on Foreign Direct Investment: Association and Causality." Mimeo, Baruch College, New York.

De Long, G. 2001a. "Focusing Versus Diversifying Bank Mergers: Analysis of Market Reaction and Long-term Performance." Working paper, Baruch College, New York.

De Long, G. 2001b. "Stockholder Gains from Focusing Versus Diversifying Bank Mergers." *Journal of Financial Economics*, 59.

De Long, G., Smith, R. C., and Walter. I. 2001. *M&A Database: Financial Services*. New York University Salomon Center, New York.

Demsetz, R. S., Saidenberg, M. R., and Strahan, P. E. "Banks with Something to Lose: The Disciplinary Role of Franchise Value." *Federal Reserve Bank of New York Policy Review*, October 1996.

Dermine, J., and Hillion, P. (Eds.). 1999. *European Capital Markets With a Single Currency*. Oxford: Oxford University Press.

Deutsche Bank AG. 1998. "Investment Banking and Commercial Banking: Can They Be Combined Under One Roof?" Paper presented at the 95th Session of the Institut International d'Etudes Bancaires, Naples, Italy, 16–17 October.

Economides, N. 1996. "The Economics of Networks." *International Journal of Industrial Organization*, 14 (6).

Economist. 1999. "Pretenders to the Crown." April 15.

Enz, C. A. 1988. "The Role of Value Congruity in Inter-Organizational Power." *Administrative Science Quarterly*, 33.

Fiderio, J. 1989. "What IS Puts Together, Business Deals Can Sunder." *Computerworld*, 23 (17).

Giddy, I. 1984. "Is Equity Underwriting Risky for Commercial Bank Affiliates?" In *Deregulating Wall Street: Commercial Bank Penetration of the Corporate Securities Market*, Ingo Walter, ed. New York: John Wiley & Sons.

Goldberg, L. G., Hanweck, G. A., Keenan, M., and Young, A. 1991. "Economies of Scale and Scope in the Securities Industry." *Journal of Banking and Finance* 15.

Gray, J., and Gray, H. P. 1981. "The Multinational Banks: A Financial MNC?" *Journal of Banking and Finance*, 5.

Green, S. "Merging Technologies." 1997. *Mortgage Finance Gazette*. April 15.

Grubel, H. 1977. "A Theory of Multinational Banking." *Banca Nazionale del Lavoro*.

Gutek, B. A. 1978. "On Accuracy of Retrospective Attitudinal Data." *Public Opinion Quarterly*, 42.

Hamel, G., Prahalad, C. K., and Doz, Y. L. 1989. "Collaborate with Your Competitors and Win, *Harvard Business Review*, January/February.

Haspeslagh, P., and Jemison, D. 1991. *Managing Acquisitions*. New York: Free Press.

Henderson, J., and Venkatraman, N. 1992. "Strategic Alignment: A Model for Organizational Transformation Through Information Technology." In T. Kochon and M. Unseem (Eds.), *Transformation Organisations*. New York: Oxford University Press.

Hoffmann, T. 1999. "Fleet Aims to Dodge Merger Potholes: Analysts Believe Bank Will Avoid Missteps That Have Plagued Banc One, First Union." *Computerworld*, December 13.

Houston, J., James, C., and Ryngaert, M. 1999. "Where Do Merger Gains Come From? Bank Mergers From the Perspective of Insiders and Outsiders." Working paper, University of Florida, Gainesville, Fla.

Houston, J., and Ryngaert, M. 1994. "The Overall Gains from Large Bank Mergers." *Journal of Banking and Finance*, 18.

Israel, R. 1991. "Capital Structure and the Market for Corporate Control: The Defensive Role of Debt Financing." *Journal of Finance*, 46.

James, C. 1991. "The Losses Realized in Bank Failures." *Journal of Finance*, 46.

James, C., and Weir, P. 1987. "Returns to Acquirers and Competition in the Acquisition Market: The Case of Banking." *Journal of Political Economy*, 95.

Jensen, M. 1986. "Agency Costs of Free Cash Flow, Corporate Finance, and Takeovers." *American Economic Review*, 76.

Jensen, M., and Ruback, R. 1983. "The Market for Corporate Control: The Scientific Evidence," *Journal of Financial Economics*, 11.

John, K., and Ofek, E. 1995. "Asset Sales and Increase in Focus." *Journal of Financial Economics*, 37.

Johnson, M. 1989. "Compatible Information Systems: A Key to Merger Success," *Healthcare Financial Management*, 43 (6).

Johnston, K. D. and Zetton, P. W. 1996. "Integrating Information Technology Divisions in a Bank Merger—Fit, Compatibility and Models of Change." *Journal of Strategic Information Systems*, 5.

Kane, E. J. 1987. "Competitive Financial Reregulation: An International Perspective." In R. Portes and A. Swoboda (Eds.), *Threats to International Financial Stability*. Cambridge: Cambridge University Press.

Kane, E. J. 2000. "Incentives for Banking Megamergers: What Motives Might Regulators Infer from Event-Study Evidence?" *Journal of Money, Credit, and Banking*, 32.

Kitching, J. 1967. "Why Do Mergers Miscarry?" *Harvard Business Review*, 45 (6).

Kroszner, R., and Rajan, R. 1994. "Is the Glass-Steagall Act Justified? A Study of the U.S. Experience with Universal Banking Before 1933." *American Economic Review*, 84.

Lamfalussy Committee. 2001. Final Report of the Wise Men on the Regulation of European Securities Markets. Brussels: Commission of the European Union.

Lang, G., and Wetzel, P. 1998. "Technology and Cost Efficiency in Universal Banking: A Thick Frontier Approach." *Journal of Productivity Analysis*, 10.

Lewis, M. 1990. In "Banking as Insurance." *The Future of Financial Services and Systems*, Edward P.M. Gardener (Ed). New York: St. Martin's Press.

Linder, J. 1989. *Integrating Organizations Where Information Technology Matters*, DBA Thesis, Graduate School of Business Administration, Harvard University, Boston.

Linder, J., and Crane, D. 1992. "Bank Mergers: Integration and Profitability." *Journal of Financial Services Research*, 7.

Llewellyn, D. T. 1996. "Universal Banking and the Public Interest: A British Perspective." In Anthony Saunders and Ingo Walter (Eds.), *Universal Banking: Financial System Design Reconsidered*. Chicago: Irwin.

Lown, C. S., Osler, C. L., Strahan, P. E., and Sufi, A. 2000. "The Changing Landscape of the Financial Services Industry: What Lies Ahead?" *Federal Reserve Bank of New York Economic Policy Review*, October.

Lubatkin, M. 1987. "Merger Strategies and Stockholder Value." *Strategic Management Journal*, 8.

McCartney, L., and Kelly, J. 1984. "Getting Away with Merger: What Looks to Investment Bankers Like a Heavenly Marriage Can Be Hell in the Computer Room." *Datamation*, 30 (20).

Miller, M., and Modigliani, F. 1961. "The Cost of Capital, Corporation Finance and the Theory of Investment." *Journal of Finance*, 48.

Mitchell, K., and Onvural, N. 1995. "Economies of Scale and Scope at Large Commercial Banks: Evidence from the Fourier Flexible Functional Form." Working paper, North Carolina State University, NC.

Nairn, G. 1999. "Global Merger Wave Poses Big Challenges for Rival IT." *Financial Times Information Technology*, May 5.

Nonaka, I. 1994. "A Dynamic Theory of Organizational Knowledge Creation." *Organization Science* (5).

O'Hara, M., and Shaw, W. 1990. "Deposit Insurance and Wealth Effects: The Value of Being 'Too Big to Fail.' " *Journal of Finance*, 45.

Penrose, E. 1959. *The Theory of the Growth of the Firm*. Oxford: Basil Blackwell.

Penzel. H.-G., and Pietig, C. 2000. *MergerGuide—Handbuch für die Integration von Banken*. Wiesbaden: Gabler Verlag.

Pilloff, S. 1996. "Performance Changes and Shareholder Wealth Creation Associated with Mergers of Publicly Traded Banking Institutions." *Journal of Money, Credit, and Banking*, 28.

Pilloff, S., and Santomero, A. 1997. "The Value Effects of Bank Mergers and Acquisitions." The Wharton School Center for Financial Institutions. Working papers 97–107.

Pliskin, N., Romm, T., Lee, A. S., and Weber, Y. 1993. "Presumed Versus Actual Organizational Culture: Managerial Implications for Implementation of Information Systems." *The Computer Journal*, 36 (2).

Porter, M. E. 1987. "From Competitive Advantage to Corporate Strategy." *Harvard Business Review*, 5.

Puri, M. 1996. "Commercial Banks in Investment Banking: Conflict of Interest or Certification Role?" *Journal of Financial Economics*, 40.

Rau, R. P. 2000. "Investment Bank Market Share, Contingent Fee Payments, and the Performance of Acquiring Firms." *Journal of Financial Economics*, 56.

Rentch, J. R. 1990. "Climate and Culture: Interaction and Qualitative Differences in Organizational Meanings." *Journal of Applied Psychology*, 75 (6).

Romm, T., Pliskin, N., Weber, Y., and Lee, A. S. 1991. "Identifying Organizational Culture Clash in MIS Implementation: When Is It Worth the Effort?" *Information and Management*, 21.

Santomero, A. 1995. "Financial Risk Management: The Whys and Hows." *Financial Markets, Institutions, and Instruments*, 4.

Santomero, A., and Chung, E. J. 1992. "Evidence in Support of Broader Bank Powers." *Financial Markets, Institutions, and Instruments*, 1.

Saunders, A., and Cornett, M. 2002. *Financial Institutions Management*, Fourth Edition. New York: McGraw Hill/ Irwin.

Saunders, A., and Wilson, B. 1999. "The Impact of Consolidation and Safety-Net Support on Canadian, US and UK Banks, 1893–1992." *Journal of Banking and Finance*, 23.

Saunders, A., and Walter, I. 1994. *Universal Banking in the United States*. New York: Oxford University Press.

Saunders, A., and Walter, I. (Eds.). 1995. *Universal Banking*. Burr Ridge, Ill.: Irwin Professional.

Savage, D. T. 1993. "Interstate Banking: A Status Report." *Federal Reserve Bulletin* 73, December.

Siems, T. F. 1996. "Bank Mergers and Shareholder Value: Evidence from 1995's Megamerger Deals." *Federal Reserve Bank of Dallas Financial Industry Studies*, August.

Silverstein, S., and Vrana, D. 1998. "After Back-Slapping Wanes, Mega-Mergers Often Fail." *Los Angeles Times*, April 19.

Smith, C., and Stultz, R. 1985. "The Determinants of Firms' Hedging Policies." *Journal of Financial and Quantitative Analysis*, 20.

Smith, R. C., and Walter, I. 1995. "JP Morgan and Banco Espanol de Credito: Teaching Note." *Case Studies in Finance and Economics*, C53. New York: New York University Salomon Center.

Smith, R. C. and Walter, I. 1997. *Street Smarts: Linking Professional Conduct and Shareholder Value in the Securities Industry*. Boston: Harvard Business School Press.

Smith, R. C., and Walter, I. 2003. *Global Banking*. Second Edition. New York: Oxford University Press.

Srinivasan, A., Saunders, A., and Walter, I. 2001. "Price Formation in the OTC Corporate Bond Markets: A Field Study of the Inter-Dealer Market," *Journal of Economics and Business*, Fall.

Stefanadis, C. 2002. "Specialist Securities Firms in the Gramm-Leach-Bliley Era. Federal Reserve Bank of New York. Working Paper.

Strassmann, P. 2001. A Deal Gone Bad? *Computerworld*, May 7.

Stylianou, A. C., Jeffries, C. J., and Robbins, S. S. 1996. "Corporate Mergers and the Problem of IS Integration." *Information & Management* 31.

Tamzin, B., and Bleakley, F. 1999. "Botins's Sudden Exit," Institutional Investigator, 24 (11).

Trautwein, F. 1990. "Merger Motives and Merger Prescriptions." *Strategic Management Journal*, 11.

Vander Vennet, R. 1998. "Causes and Consequences of EU Bank Takeovers." In *the Changing European Landscape*, Sylvester Eijffinger, Kees Koedijk, Marco Pagano, and Richard Portes, eds. (Centre for Economic Policy Research: Brussels, Belgium).

Verweire, K., and Ven den Berghe, L. 2002. "The Performance Consequences of Diversification in the Financial Services Industry: The Case of Financial Conglomerates in Belguim and the Netherlands." Working paper, Vlerick Leuven Gent Management School.

Walter, I. 1988. *Global Competition in Financial Services.* Cambridge: Ballinger-Harper & Row.

Walter, I. 1990. *The Secret Money Market.* New York: Harper Business.

Walter, I. 1993a. *The Battle of the Systems: Control of Enterprises in the Global Economy.* Kiel: Kieler Studien Nr. 122, Institut für Weltwirtschaft.

Walter, I. 1993b. *High-Performance Financial Systems.* Singapore: Institute for Southeast Asian Studies.

Walter, I., and Itiraki, T. (Eds.). 1993. *Restructuring Japan's Financial Markets.* Homewood, Ill.: Business One Irwin.

Walter, I., and Smith, R. C. 2000. *High Finance in the Euro-zone.* London: Financial Times-Prentice Hall.

Watkins, T. 1992. "Information Systems: The UK Retail Financial Services Sector in Information Systems for Strategic Advantage." *Marketing Intelligence and Planning,* 10 (6).

Weber, Y., and Pliskin, N. 1996. "The Effect of Information System Integration and Organization Culture on a Firm's Effectiveness." *Information and Management,* 30.

Weber, Y., and Schweiger, D. M. 1992. "Top Management Culture Conflict in Mergers and Acquisitions: A Lesson from Anthropology." *International Journal of Conflict Management,* 3 (4).

Yu, L. 2001. "On the Wealth and Risk Effects of the Glass-Steagall Overhaul: Evidence from the Stock Market." Working paper, New York University.

Zollo, M. 1998. *Knowledge Codification, Process Routinization, and the Creation of Organizational Capabilities: Post Acquistion Management in the United States Banking Industry.* Doctoral Dissertation. The Wharton School, University of Pennsylvania.

Zollo, M. 2000. "Can Firms Learn to Acquire? Do Markets Notice?" Working paper, The Wharton School, University of Pennsylvania.

Zollo, M., and Singh, H. 1999. "Learning to Acquire: Knowledge Codification, Process Routinization and Post-Acquisition Integration Strategies." Working paper of the Wharton Financial Institution Center, presented at the Annual Meeting of the Academy of Management in Boston.

Suggested Readings

Accenture, 2000. "Long-term Performance of Financial Services Mergers." Working paper. New York. Accenture, 2001.

Adkisson, J. A., and Fraser, D. R. 1990. "The Effect of Geographical Deregulation on Bank Acquisition Premium." *Journal of Financial Services Research*, 4.

Akhavein, J., Allen, D., Berger, N., and Humphrey, D. B. 1997. "The Effects of Megamergers on Efficiency and Prices: Evidence from a Bank Profit Function." *Review of Industrial Organization*, 12.

Allen, L., and Cebenoyan, A. S. 1991. "Bank Acquisitions and Ownership Structure: Theory and Evidence." *Journal of Banking and Finance*, 15.

Allen, L., Jagtiani, J., and Saunders, A. 2000. "The Role of Financial Advisors in Mergers and Acquisition." Federal Reserve Banking of Chicago, Working paper, *Emerging Issues Series* # S&R-2000-1R.

Amel, D. 1988. "State Laws Affecting Commercial Bank Branching, Multibank Holding Company Expansion, and Interstate Banking." Board of Governors of the Federal Reserve System, Washington, D.C.

Amihud, Y., and Lev, B. 1981. "Risk Reduction as a Managerial Motive for Conglomerate Mergers." *Bell Journal of Economics*, March, 605–617.

Amit, R., and Livnat, J. 1988. "Diversification Strategies, Business Cycles and Economic Performance." *Strategic Management Journal*, 9.

Bank for International Settlements. 1999. *Report on Consolidation in the Financial Sector*. Basle: BIS, 136.

Baradwaj, B., Fraser, D., and Furtado, E. 1990. "Hostile Bank Takeover Offers." *Journal of Banking and Finance*, 14.

Barth, J. R., Brumbaugh, R. D., Jr., and Wilcox, J. A. 2000. "The Repeal of Glass-Steagall and the Advent of Broad Banking." *Journal of Economic Perspectives*, 14.

Beatty, R., Santomero, A., and Smirlock, M. 1987. "Bank Merger Premiums: Analysis and Evidence." *New York University Salomon Center for the Study of Financial Institutions Monograph Series on Economics and Finance*, 3.

Benston, G. J., Hunter, W. C., and Wall, L. D. 1995. "Motivations for Bank Mergers and Acquisitions: Enhancing the Deposit Insurance Put Option versus Earnings Diversification." *Journal of Money, Credit, and Banking*, 27.

Berger, A. N., Demsetz, R. S., and Strahan, P. E. 1998. *The Consolidation of the Financial Services Industry: Causes, Consequences, and Implications for the Future.* New York: Federal Reserve Bank of New York.

Berger, A. N., and DeYoung, R. 2001. "The Effects of Geographic Expansion on Bank Efficiency." Working paper, Board of Governors of the Federal Reserve System, Washington, D.C.

Berger, A. N., DeYoung, R., Genay, H., and Udell, G. F. 2000. "Globalization of Financial Institutions: Evidence from Cross-Border Banking Performance." *Brookings-Wharton Papers on Financial Services,* 3.

Berger, A. N., Hancock, D., and Humphrey, D. B. 1993. "Bank Efficiency Derived from the Profit Function." *Journal of Banking and Finance,* April, 317–347.

Berger, A. N., and Hannan, T. H. 1987. "The Price-Concentration Relationship in Banking." *Review of Economics and Statistics,* 71.

Berger, A. N., and Hannan, T. H. 1996. "Using Measures of Firm Efficiency to Distinguish Among Alternative Explanations of the Structure-Performance Relationship." *Managerial Finance.*

Berger, A. N., and Humphrey, D. B. 1992a. "Measurement and Efficiency Issues in Commercial Banking." In *Output Measurement in the Service Sector,* Zvi Griliches, ed. Chicago: University of Chicago Press.

Berger, A. N., and Humphrey, D. B. 1992b. "Megamergers in Banking and the Use of Cost Efficiency as an Antitrust Defense." *The Antitrust Bulletin,* 37, 541–600.

Berger, A. N., and Humphrey, D. B. 1993. "Bank Scale Economies, Mergers, Concentration, and Efficiency: The U.S. Experience." *Revue d'Economie Financière,* 27.

Berger, A. N., Hunter, W. C., and Timme, S. J. 1993. "The Efficiency of Financial Institutions: A Review of Research Past, Present and Future." *Journal of Banking and Finance,* April.

Berger, A. N., and Mester, L. 1997. "Inside the Black Box: What Explains Differences in the Efficiencies of Financial Institutions?" *Journal of Banking and Finance,* 21.

Berger, P. G., and Ofek, E. 1996. "Bustup Takeovers of Value-Destroying Diversified Firms." *Journal of Finance,* 51 (4).

Berger, P. G., and Ofek, E. 1995. "Diversification's Effect on Firm Value." *Journal of Financial Economics,* 37.

Boot, W. A., and Thakor, A. V. 1997. "Banking Scope and Financial Innovation." *Review of Financial Studies,* 10.

Bowers, H. M., and Miller, R. 1990. "Choice of Investment Banker and Shareholders Wealth of Firms Involved in Acquisitions." *Financial Management,* 19.

Boyd, J., and Graham, S. 1991. "Investigating the Bank Consolidation Trend." Federal Reserve Bank of Minneapolis, *Quarterly Review.*

Boyd, J., Graham, S., and Hewitt, R. S. 1993. "Bank Holding Company Mergers with Non-bank Financial Firms: Effects on the Risk of Failure." *Journal of Financial Economics,* 17.

Bradley, M., Desai, N., and Han Kim, E. 1988. "Synergistic Gains from Corporate Acquisitions and the Division Between the Stock Holders of Target and Acquiring Firms." *Journal of Financial Economics,* 21.

Brewer, E., Jackson, W., Jagtiani, J., and Nguyen, T. 2000. "The Price of Bank Mergers in the 1990s." Federal Reserve Bank of Chicago, *Economic Perspectives,* 30.

Brickley, J., and James, C. 1987. "The Takeover Market, Corporate Board Composition, and Ownership Structure: The Case of Banking." *Journal of Law and Economics*, 30.

Buch, C. 2001. "Information or Regulation: What Is Driving the International Activities of Commercial Banks?" *Journal of Money, Credit, and Banking*, 23.

Buch, C., and De Long, G. 2001. "International Bank Mergers: What's Luring the Rare Animal?" Working paper, Kiel Institute of World Economics, Kiel, Germany.

Buono, A. F., and Bowditch, J. L. 1989. *The Human Side of Mergers and Acquisitions.* San Francisco: Jossey-Bass.

Caplen, B. 2000. "Merger Lessons from Spain." *Euromoney*, June.

Cetorelli, N. 1999. "Competitive Analysis in Banking: Appraisal of the Methodologies." Federal Reserve Bank of Chicago, *Economic Perspectives*, 23 (First Quarter).

Chang, S. J. 1996. "An Evolutionary Perspective on Diversification and Corporate Restructuring: Entry, Exit, and Economic Performance during 1981–89." *Strategic Management Journal*, 17 (8).

Chatterjee, S. 1986. "Types of Synergy and Economic Value: The Impact of Acquisitions on Merging and Rival Firms." *Strategic Management Journal*, 7 (2).

Chatterjee, S., and Lubatkin, M. H. 1990. "Corporate Mergers, Stockholder Diversification and Changes in Systematic Risk." *Strategic Management Journal*, 11.

Cheng, D., Gup, B., and Wall, L. 1989. "Financial Determinants of Bank Takeovers." *Journal of Money, Credit and Banking*, 21 (4).

Clark, J. 1988. "Economies of Scale and Scope at Depository Financial Institutions: A Review of the Literature." *Economic Review*, Federal Reserve Bank of Kansas City, June.

Cornett, M. M., and Sankar, D. 1991. "Common Stock Returns in Corporate Takeover Bids: Evidence from Interstate Bank Mergers." *Journal of Banking and Finance*, 15.

Cornett, M. M. 1991. "Medium of Payment in Corporate Acquisitions: Evidence from Interstate Bank Mergers." *Journal of Money, Credit and Banking*, 23.

Cornett, M. M., and Tehranian, H. 1992. "Changes in Corporate Performance Associated with Bank Acquisitions." *Journal of Financial Economics*, 31.

Cornett, M. M., Hovakimian, G., Palia, D., and Tehranian, H. 1998. "The Impact of the Manager-Shareholder Conflict on Acquiring Bank Returns." Working paper, Boston College.

Cotter, J., Shivdasani, A., and Zenner, M. 1997. "Do Independent Directors Enhance Target Shareholder Wealth During Tender Offers?" *Journal of Financial Economics*, 43.

Crossan, M. M., and Inkpen, A. C. 1992. "Believing Is Seeing: An Exploration of the Organizational Learning Concept and the Evidence from the Case of Joint Venture Learning." Working paper, University of Western Ontario Business School.

Cummins, J. D., and Zi, H. 1998. "Comparisons of Frontier Efficiency Levels." *Journal of Productivity Analysis*, June.

Cybo-Ottone, A., and Murgia, M. 1997. "Mergers and Acquisitions in European Banking Markets," Working paper, Associazione Bancaria Italiana and Università Degli Studi di Pavia, Italy.

Datta, D. K. 1991. "Organizational Fit and Acquisition Performance: Effects of Post-Acquisition Integration." *Strategic Management Journal*, 12.

Datta, D. K., and Grant, J. H. 1990. "Relationship Between Type of Acquisition, the Autonomy Given to the Acquired Firm, and Acquisition Success: An Empirical Analysis." *Journal of Management*, 16 (1).

Datta, D. K., Rajagopalan, N., and Rasheed, A. M. A. 1991. "Diversification and Performance: Critical Review and Future Directions." *Journal of Management Studies*, 28 (5).

Davis, P. S., Robinson, R. B., Pearce, J. A., and Park, S. H. 1992. "Business Unit Relatedness and Performance: A Look at the Pulp and Paper Industry." *Strategic Management Journal*, 13.

Davis, R., and Duhaime, I. M. 1952. "Diversification, Vertical Integration, and Industry Analysis: New Perspectives and Measurement." *Strategic Management Journal*, 13 (5).

Davis, S. I. 2000. *Bank Mergers: Lessons for the Future.* New York: St. Martin's Press.

De Long, G. 1993. "The Influence of Foreign Banking on Foreign Direct Investment: Association and Causality." Mimeo, Baruch College, New York.

De Long, G. 2001. "Focusing versus Diversifying Bank Mergers: Analysis of Market Reaction and Long-term Performance." Working paper, Baruch College, New York.

De Long, G. 2001. "Stockholder Gains from Focusing versus Diversifying Bank Mergers." *Journal of Financial Economics*, 59.

De Long, G., Smith, R. C., and Walter, I. 2001. *M&A Database: Financial Services.* New York University Salomon Center.

Demsetz, R. S., Saidenberg, M. R., and Strahan, P. E. 1996. "Banks with Something to Lose: The Disciplinary Role of Franchise Value." *Federal Reserve Bank of New York Policy Review*, October.

Desai, A., and Stover, R. D. 1985. "Bank Holding Company Acquisitions, Stockholder Returns, and Regulatory Uncertainty." *The Journal of Financial Research*, 8.

Dess, G. G., Ireland, R. D., and Hitt, M. A. 1990. "Industry Effects and Strategic Management Research." *Journal of Management*, 16.

Dess, G. Gupta, G. A., Hennart, J. F., and Hill, C. W. L. 1995. "Conducting and Integrating Strategy Research at the International, Corporate, and Business Level: Issues and Directions." *Journal of Management*, 21 (3).

DeYoung, R. 1999. "Mergers and the Changing Landscape of Commercial Banking." Federal Reserve Bank of Chicago, *Chicago Fedletter*, 45.

Deutsche Bank AG. 1998. "Investment Banking and Commercial Banking: Can They Be Combined Under One Roof?" Paper presented at the 95th Session of the Institut International d'Etudes Bancaires, Naples, Italy, October 16–17.

Dubofsky, P., and Varadarajan, P. 1987. "Diversification and Measures of Performance: Additional Empirical Evidence." *Academy of Management Journal*, 30 (3).

Dubofsky, D. A., and Fraser, D. R. 1989. "The Differential Impact of Two Significant Court Decisions Concerning Banking Consolidation." *Journal of Banking and Finance*, 13.

Eckbo, B. Espen, and Langohr, H. 1989. "Information Disclosure, Measure of Payment, and Takeover Premiums: Public and Private Tender Offers in France." *Journal of Financial Economics*, 24.

Fama, E. 1980. "Agency Problems and the Theory of the Firm." *Journal of Political Economy*, 88.

Fama, E., and Jensen, M. 1983. "Separation of Ownership and Control." *Journal of Law and Economics*, 26.

Fiegenbaum, A., and Thomas, H. 1990. "Strategic Groups and Performance: The US Insurance Industry, 1970–84." *Strategic Management Journal*, 11 (3).

Flanagan, D. J. 1996. "Announcements of Purely Related and Purely Unrelated Mergers and Shareholder Returns: Reconciling the Relatedness Paradox." *Journal of Management*, 22 (6).

Fraser, D. R., and Kolari, J. W. 1998. "Pricing Small Bank Acquisitions." *Journal of Retail Banking*, 10.

Frider, L. A. 1988. "The Interstate Banking Landscape: Legislative Policies and Rationale." *Contemporary Policy Issues*, 6.

Geringer, J. M., Tallman, S., and Olsen, D. M. 2000. "Product and International Diversification among Japanese Multinational Firms." *Strategic Management Journal*, 21 (1).

Giddy, I. 1986. "Is Equity Underwriting Risky for Commercial Bank Affiliates?" In Ingo Walter (ed.), *Deregulating Wall Street: Commercial Bank Penetration of the Corporate Securities Market*. New York: John Wiley & Sons.

Gnehm, A., and Thalmann, C. 1989. "Conflicts of Interest in Financial Operations: Problems of Regulation in the National and International Context." Working paper, Swiss Bank Corporation, Basel.

Goldberg, L. G., Hanweck, G. A., Keenan, M., and Young, A. 1991. "Economies of Scale and Scope in the Securities Industry." *Journal of Banking and Finance*, 15.

Govindarajan, V., and Fisher, J. 1990. "Strategy, Control Systems, and Resource Sharing: Effects on Business-Unit Performance." *Academy of Management Journal*, 33 (2).

Grant, R. M., and Jammine, A. P. 1988. "Performance Differences Between the Wrigley/Rumelt Strategic Categories." *Strategic Management Journal*, 9.

Grant, R. M., Jammine, A. P., and Thomas, H. 1988. "Diversity, Diversification, and Profitability among British Manufacturing Companies." *Academy of Management Journal*, 31.

Gray, J., and Gray, H. P. 1981. "The Multinational Banks: A Financial MNC?" *Journal of Banking and Finance*, 5.

Grubel, H. 1977. "A Theory of Multinational Banking." *Banca Nazionale del Lavoro*, August.

Gupta, A. K., and Govindarajan, V. 1986. "Resource Sharing Among SBUs: Strategic Antecedents and Administrative Implications." *Academy of Management Journal*, 29 (4).

Hall, E. H., and St. John, C. H. 1994. "A Methodological Note on Diversity Measurement." *Strategic Management Journal*, 15 (2).

Hamel, G., Prahalad, C. K., and Doz, Y. L. 1989. "Collaborate With Your Competitors and Win." *Harvard Business Review*, January/February.

Harrison, J. S., Hall, E. H., and Nargundkar, R. 1993. "Resource Allocation as an Outcropping of Strategic Consistency: Performance Implications." *Academy of Management Journal*, 36 (5).

Haspeslagh, P., and Jemison, D. 1991. *Managing Acquisitions*. New York: Free Press.

Healy, P. M., Palepu, K., and Ruback, R. S. 1991. "Does Corporate Performance Improve After Mergers?" *Journal of Financial Economics*, 31.

Herring, R. J., and Santomero, A. M. 1990. "The Corporate Structure of Financial Conglomerates." *Journal of Financial Services Research*, September.

Hill, C. W. L., and Hansen, G. S. 1991. "A Longitudinal Study of the Cause and Consequences of Changes in Diversification in the U.S. Pharmaceutical Industry 1977–86." *Strategic Management Journal*, 12 (3).

Hill, C. W. L., Hitt, M. A., and Hoskisson, R. E. 1992. "Cooperative Versus Competitive Structures in Related and Unrelated Diversified Firms." *Organization Science*, 3 (4).

Hill, C. W. L., and Snell, S. A. 1998. "External Control, Corporate Strategy, and Firm Performance in Research-Intensive Industries." *Strategic Management Journal*, 9 (6).

Holder, C. L. 1993. "Competitive Considerations in Bank Mergers and Acquisitions: Economic Theory, Legal Foundation, and the Fed." Federal Reserve Bank of Atlanta, *Economic Review*, 78.

Hoskisson, R. E., Hitt, M. A., Johnson, R. A., and Moesel, D. D. 1993. "Construct Validity of an Objective (Entropy) Categorial Measure of Diversification Strategy." *Strategic Management Journal*, 14 (3).

Houston, J., James, C., and Ryngaert, M. 1999. "Where Do Merger Gains Come From? Bank Mergers From the Perspective of Insiders and Outsiders." Working paper, University of Florida.

Houston, J., and Ryngaert, M. 1994. "The Overall Gains from Large Bank Mergers." *Journal of Banking and Finance*, 18.

Hunter, W. C., and Walker, M. B. 1990. "An Empirical Explanation of Investment Banking Merger Fee Contracts." *Southern Economic Journal*, 56.

Hunter, W. C., and Wall, L. 1989. "Bank Mergers Motivations: A Review of the Evidence and Examination of Key Target Bank Characteristics." Federal Reserve Bank of Atlanta, *Economic Review*, 74.

Israel, R. 1989. "Capital Structure and the Market for Corporate Control: The Defensive Role of Debt Financing." *Journal of Finance*, 66.

Jackson, W. E., III. 1992. "Is the Market Well Defined in Bank Merger and Acquisition Analysis?" *The Review of Economics and Statistics*, 74.

James, C. 1991. "The Losses Realized in Bank Failures." *Journal of Finance*, 46.

James, C., and Weir, P. 1987. "Returns to Acquirers and Competition in the Acquisition Market: The Case of Banking." *Journal of Political Economy*, 95.

Jensen, M. 1986. "Agency Costs of Free Cash Flow, Corporate Finance, and Takeovers." *American Economic Review*, 76.

Jensen, M., and Ruback, R. 1983. "The Market for Corporate Control: The Scientific Evidence." *Journal of Financial Economics*, 11.

John, K., and Ofek, E. 1995. "Asset Sales and Increase in Focus." *Journal of Financial Economics*, 37.

Johnson, G., and Thomas, H. 1987. "The Industry Context of Strategy, Structure and Performance: The UK Brewing Industry." *Strategic Management Journal*, 8 (4).

Kane, E. 2000. "Incentives for Banking Megamergers: What Motives Might Regulators Infer from Event-Study Evidence?" *Journal of Money, Credit, and Banking*, 32.

Kane, E. J. 1998. "Megabank Mergers and the Too-Big-To-Fail Doctrine: Some Preliminary Results." Working paper, Boston College.

Keats, B. W. 1990. "Diversification and Business Economic Performance Revisited: Issues of Measurement and Causality." *Journal of Management*, 16 (1).

Kitching, J. 1967. "Why Do Mergers Miscarry?" *Harvard Business Review*, 45 (6).

Kroszner, R., and Rajan, R. 1994. "Is the Glass-Steagall Act Justified? A Study of the U.S. Experience with Universal Banking Before 1933." *American Economic Review*, 84.

Kwan, S.. 1998. "Securities Activities by Commercial Banking Firms' Section 20 Subsidiaries: Risk, Return, and Diversification Benefits." Working paper, Federal Reserve Bank of San Francisco.

Kwast, M. L., Starr-McCluer, M., and Wolken, J. 1997. "Market Definition and the Analysis of Antitrust in Banking." *Antitrust Bulletin*, 42.

Lamont, B. T., and Anderson, C. R. 1985. "Mode of Corporate Diversification and Economic Performance." *Academy of Management Journal*, 28 (4).

Lang, G., and Wetzel, P. 1998. "Technology and Cost Efficiency in Universal Banking: A Thick Frontier Approach," *Journal of Productivity Analysis*, 10.

Lang, L. H. P., and Stulz, R. M. 1994. "Tobin's Q, Corporate Diversification, and Firm Performance." *Journal of Political Economy*, 102 (6).

Lewis, M. 1990. "Banking as Insurance." In Edward P. M. Gardener (Ed.), *The Future of Financial Services and Systems*. New York: St. Martin's Press.

Linder, J., and Crane, D. 1992. "Bank Mergers: Integration and Profitability." *Journal of Financial Services Research*, 7.

Llewellyn, D. T. 1996. "Universal Banking and the Public Interest: A British Perspective." In Anthony Saunders and Ingo Walter (Eds.), *Universal Banking: Financial System Design Reconsidered*. Chicago: Irwin.

Lloyd, W. P., and Jahera, J. S. 1994. "Firm-Diversification Effects on Performance as Measured by Tobin's Q." *Managerial and Decision Economics*, 15.

Lown, C. S., Osler, C. L., Strahan, P. E., and Sufi, A. 2000. "The Changing Landscape of the Financial Services Industry: What Lies Ahead?" *Federal Reserve Bank of New York Economic Policy Review*, October.

Lubatkin, M. 1983. "Mergers and the Performance of the Acquiring Firm." *Academy of Management Review*, 8 (2).

Lubatkin, M. 1987. "Merger Strategies and Stockholder Value." *Strategic Management Journal*, 8.

Markides, C. C. 1992. "Consequence of Corporate Refocusing: Ex Ante Evidence." *Academy of Management Journal*, 35.

Markides, C. C. 1995. "Diversification, Restructuring and Economic Performance." *Strategic Management Journal*, 16 (2).

McLaughlin, R. 1990. "Investment-Banking Contracts in Tender Offers." *Journal of Financial Economics*, 28.

Mehra, A. 1996. "Resource and Market Based Determinants of Performance in the US Banking Industry." *Strategic Management Journal*, 17 (4).

Mitchell, K., and Onvural, N. 1995. "Economies of Scale and Scope at Large Commercial Banks: Evidence from the Fourier Flexible Functional Form." Working paper, North Carolina State University.

Molyneux, P., Altunbas, Y., and Gardener, E. P. M. 1996. *Efficiency in European Banking*. Chichester, West Sussex: John Wiley & Sons.

Montgomery, C. A. 1982. "The Measurement of Firm Diversification: Some New Empirical Evidence." *Academy of Management Journal*, 25.

Montgomery, C. A. 1994. "Corporate Diversification." *Journal of Economic Perspectives*, 8 (3).

Montgomery, C. A., and Wilson, V. A. "Research Note and Communication. Mergers that Last: A Predictable Pattern." *Strategic Management Journal*, 7.

Nayyar, P. R. 1992. "On the Measurement of Corporate Diversification Strategy." *Strategic Management Journal*, 13 (3).

Neely, Walter. 1987. "Banking Acquisitions: Acquirer and Target Shareholder Returns." *Financial Management*, 16.

Nonaka, I. 1994. "A Dynamic Theory of Organizational Knowledge Creation." *Organization Science,* (5).

O'Hara, M., and Shaw, W. 1990. "Deposit Insurance and Wealth Effects: The Value of Being 'Too Big to Fail.' " *Journal of Finance,* 45.

Palia, D. 1993. "The Managerial, Regulatory, and Financial Determinants of Bank Merger Premiums." *The Journal of Industrial Economics,* 41.

Palia, D. 1994. "Recent Evidence on Bank Mergers." *Financial Markets, Institution & Instruments,* 3 (5).

Palich, L. E., Cardinal, L. B., and Miller, C. C. 2000. "Curvilinearity in the Diversification-Performance Linkage: An Examination of Over Three Decades of Research." *Strategic Management Journal,* 21 (1).

Pekar, P. 1988. "A Strategic Approach to Diversification." *Journal of Business Strategy,* 5.

Penrose, E. 1959. *The Theory of the Growth of the Firm.* Oxford: Basil Blackwell.

Pilloff, S. 1996. "Performance Changes and Shareholder Wealth Creation Associated with Mergers of Publicly Traded Banking Institutions." *Journal of Money, Credit, and Banking,* 28.

Pitts, R. A. 1980. "Towards a Contingency Theory of Multibusiness Organization Design." *Academy of Management Review,* 5 (2).

Pitts, R. A., and D. H. Hopkins. 1982. "Firm Diversity: Conceptualization and Measurement." *Academy of Management Journal,* 25.

Porter, M. E. 1985. *Competitive Advantage: Creating and Sustaining Superior Performance.* New York: Free Press.

Porter, M. E. 1987. "From Competitive Advantage to Corporate Strategy." *Harvard Business Review,* 5.

Prager, R. A., and Hannan, T. H. 1999. "Do Substantial Horizontal Mergers Generate Significant Price Effects?" *Journal of Industrial Economics,* 4.

Prahalad, C. K., and Bettis, R. A. 1986. "The Dominant Logic: A New Linkage Between Diversity and Performance." *Strategic Management Journal,* 7 (6).

Puri, M. 1996. "Commercial Banks in Investment Banking: Conflict of Interest or Certification Role?" *Journal of Financial Economics,* 40.

Rajan, R. G. 1996. "The Entry of Commercial Banks into the Securities Business: A Selective Survey of Theories and Evidence." In Anthony Saunders and Ingo Walter (Eds.), *Universal Banking: Financial System Design Reconsidered.* Chicago: Irwin.

Ramanujam, V., and Varadarajan, P. 1989. "Research on Corporate Diversification: A Synthesis." *Strategic Management Journal,* 10 (6).

Rau, R. P. 2000. "Investment Bank Market Share, Contingent Fee Payments, and the Performance of Acquiring Firms." *Journal of Financial Economics,* 56.

Rhoades, S. A. 1987. "Determinants of Premiums Paid in Bank Acquisitions." *Atlantic Economic Journal,* 15 (1).

Rose, P. S. 1991. "Bidding Theory and Bank Mergers Premiums: The Impact of Structural and Regulatory Factors." *Review of Business & Economic Research,* 26 (2).

Rosenstein, S., and Wyatt, J. 1997. "Inside Directors, Board Effectiveness, and Shareholder Wealth." *Journal of Financial Economics,* 44.

Rosenstein, S., and Watt, J. 1990. "Outside Directors, Board Independence, and Shareholder Wealth." *Journal of Financial Economics,* 26.

Rumelt, R. P. 1974. *Strategy, Structure, and Economic Performance.* Boston: Harvard Business School Press.

Rumelt, R. P. 1982. "Diversification Strategy and Profitability." *Strategic Management Journal*, 3 (4).

Salter, M., and Weinhold, W. A. 1978. "Diversification Via Acquisition: Creating Value." *Harvard Business Review*, July–August.

Santomero, A. 1995. "Financial Risk Management: The Whys and Hows." *Financial Markets, Institutions, and Instruments*, 4.

Santomero, A., and Chung, E. J. 1992. "Evidence in Support of Broader Bank Powers." *Financial Markets, Institutions, and Instruments*, 1.

Santos, J. A. C. 1998. "Commercial Banks in the Securities Business: A Review." *Journal of Financial Services Research*, 14.

Saunders, A., and Cornett, M. M. 2002. *Financial Institutions Management.* Fourth Edition. New York: McGraw-Hill.

Saunders, A., and Wilson, B. 1999. "The Impact of Consolidation and Safety-net Support on Canadian, US and UK Banks, 1893–992." *Journal of Banking and Finance*, 23.

Saunders, A., and Walter, I. 1994. *Universal Banking in the United States.* New York: Oxford University Press.

Savage, D. T. 1993. "Interstate Banking: A Status Report." *Federal Reserve Bulletin*, 73.

Sayrs, L. W. 1989. *Pooled Time Series Analysis.* Sage Publications, Sage University Paper No. 70, Newbury Park.

Schipper, K., and Thompson, R.. 1983. "The Impact of Merger-Related Regulations on the Shareholders of Acquiring Firms." *Journal of Accounting Research*, 21.

Servaes, H. 1996. "The Value of Diversification During the Conglomerate Merger Wave." *Journal of Finance*, 51 (4).

Servaes, H., and Zenner, M. 1996. "The Role of Investment Banks in Acquisition." *The Review of Financial Studies*, 9 (3).

Seth, A. 1990. "Value Creation in Acquisitions: A Reexamination of Performance Issues." *Strategic Management Journal*, 11.

Shawky, H., Kilb, T., and Staas, C. 1996. "Determinants of Bank Merger Premiums." *Journal of Economics and Finance*, 20.

Shelton, L. M. 1988. "Strategic Business Fits and Corporate Acquisition: Empirical Evidence." *Strategic Management Journal*, 9.

Siems, T. F. 1996. "Bank Mergers and Shareholder Value: Evidence from 1995's Megamerger Deals." *Federal Reserve Bank of Dallas Financial Industry Studies*, August.

Simmonds, P. G. 1990. "The Combined Diversification Breadth and Mode Dimensions and the Performance of Large Diversified Firms." *Strategic Management Journal*, 11.

Singh, H., and Montgomery, C. A. 1987. "Corporate Acquisition Strategies and Economic Performance." *Strategic Management Journal*, 8 (4).

Smith, C., and Stultz, R. 1985. "The Determinants of Firms' Hedging Policies." *Journal of Financial and Quantitative Analysis*, 20.

Smith, R. C., and Walter, I. 2003. *Global Banking.* Second Edition. New York: Oxford University Press.

Smith, R. C., and Walter, I. 1997. *Street Smarts: Leadership and Shareholder Value in the Securities Industry.* Boston: Harvard Business School Press.

Srinivasan, A. 1999. "Investment Banking Relationships: Theory and Evidence from Merger Fees." Doctoral Dissertation, New York University Stern School of Business.

St. John, C. H., and Harrison, J. S. 1999. "Manufacturing-based Relatedness, Synergy, and Coordination." *Strategic Management Journal,* 20 (2).

Stefanadis, C. 2002. "Specialist Securities Firms in the Gramm-Leach-Bliley Era." Working paper, Federal Reserve Bank of New York.

Story, J., and Walter, I. 1997. *Political Economy of Financial Integration in Europe: The Battle of the Systems.* Manchester: Manchester University Press.

Stultz, R. M., Walking, R. A., and Song, M. H. 1990. "The Distribution of Target Ownership and the Division of Gains in Successful Takeovers." *Journal of Finance,* 45.

Subrahmanyam, V., Rangan, N., and Rosenstein, S. 1997. "The Role of Outside Directors in Bank Acquisitions." *Financial Management,* 26.

Sushka, M. E., and Bendeck, Y. 1988. "Bank Acquisitions and Stock Holders' Wealth."*Journal of Banking and Finance,* 12.

Travlos, N. 1987. "Corporate Takeover Bids, Methods of Payment and Bidding Firms' Stock Returns." *Journal of Finance,* 42.

Trifts, J. W., and Scanlon, K. P. 1998. "Interstate Bank Mergers: The Early Evidence." *The Journal of Financial Research,* 10.

U. S. General Accounting Office. 1991. "Deposit Insurance: Overview of Six Foreign Systems." Washington, D.C.: GAO/NSIAD-91-104.

Van den Berghe, L. A. A., and Verweire, K. 1988. *Creating the Future with All-Finance and Financial Conglomerates.* Dortrecht: Kluwer Academic Publishers.

Van den Brink, R. G. C. 1998. "Universal Banking: An Answer to the Challenges Facing the Financial Sector." *Mimeo,* ABN AMRO.

Vancil, R. F. 1979. *Decentralization: Managerial Ambiguity by Design.* New York: Dow Jones.

Vander Vennet, R. 1998. "Causes and Consequences of EU Bank Takeovers." In Sylvester Eijffinger, Kees Koedijk, Marco Pagano, and Richard Portes (Eds.), *The Changing European Landscape.* Brussels: Centre for Economic Policy Research.

Verweire, K., and Ven den Berghe, L. 2002. "The Performance Consequences of Diversification in the Financial Services Industry: The Case of Financial Conglomerates in Belguim and the Netherlands." Working paper, Vlerick Leuven Gent Management School.

Wall, S. 2001. "Making Mergers Work." *Financial Executive,* March-April.

Walter, I. 1988. *Global Competition in Financial Services.* Cambridge: Ballinger.

Walter, I. 1993. *The Battle of the Systems: Control of Enterprises in the Global Economy.* Kiel: Kieler Studien Nr. 122, Institut für Weltwirtschaft.

Walter, I. 1998. "Universal Banking: A Shareholder Value Perspective." Schriftenreihe des Instituts fuer Kapitalmarktforschung as der Johann Volfgang Goethe-Universitaet, Frankfurt am Main, Germany, 42.

Walter, I. 1999. "The Asset Management Industry in Europe: Competitive Structure and Performance Under EMU." In Jean Dermine and Pierre Hillion (Eds.). *European Capital Markets With a Single Currency.* Oxford: Oxford University Press.

Walter, I., and Smith, R. C. 2000. *High Finance in the Euro-zone.* London: Financial Times.

Yu, L. 2001. "On the Wealth and Risk Effects of the Glass-Steagall Overhaul: Evidence from the Stock Market." Working paper, New York University.

Zollo, M. 1996. "An Evolutionary Model of Post-Acquisition Integration and Performance." *Academy of Management Best Papers Proceedings.*

Zollo, M. 1998. *Knowledge Codification, Process Routinization and the Creaction of Organizational Capabilities: Post-Acquisition Management in the United States Banking Industry.* Doctoral Dissertation. The Wharton School, University of Pennsylvania.

Zollo, M. 2000. "Can Firms Learn to Acquire? Do Markets notice?" Working paper. The Wharton School, University of Pennsylvania.

Zollo, M., and Singh, H. 1997. "Learning to Acquire: Knowledge Codification, Process Routinization and Post-Acquisition Integration Strategies." Working paper, The Wharton Financial Institutions Center, presented at the Annual Meeting of the Academy of Management in Boston.

Index